LISTENING *to the* FUR TRADE

MCGILL-QUEEN'S STUDIES IN EARLY CANADA / AVANT LE CANADA
SERIES EDITORS / DIRECTEURS DE LA COLLECTION : ALLAN GREER
AND CAROLYN PODRUCHNY

This series features studies of the history of the northern half of North America – a vast expanse that would eventually be known as Canada – in the era before extensive European settlement and extending into the nineteenth century. Long neglected, Canada-before-Canada is a fascinating area of study experiencing an intellectual renaissance as researchers in a range of disciplines, including history, geography, archeology, anthropology, literary studies, and law, contribute to a new and enriched understanding of the distant past. The editors welcome manuscripts in English or French on all aspects of the period, including work on Indigenous history, the Atlantic fisheries, the fur trade, exploration, French or British imperial expansion, colonial life, culture, language, law, science, religion, and the environment.

Cette série de monographies est consacrée à l'histoire de la partie septentrionale du continent de l'Amérique du nord, autrement dit le grand espace qui deviendra le Canada, dans les siècles qui s'étendent jusqu'au début du 19ᵉ. Longtemps négligé par les chercheurs, ce Canada-avant-le-Canada suscite beaucoup d'intérêt de la part de spécialistes dans plusieurs disciplines, entre autres, l'histoire, la géographie, l'archéologie, l'anthropologie, les études littéraires et le droit. Nous assistons à une renaissance intellectuelle dans ce champ d'étude axé sur l'interaction de premières nations, d'empires européens et de colonies. Les directeurs de cette série sollicitent des manuscrits, en français ou en anglais, qui portent sur tout aspect de cette période, y compris l'histoire des autochtones, celle des pêcheries de l'atlantique, de la traite des fourrures, de l'exploration, de l'expansion de l'empire français ou britannique, de la vie coloniale (Nouvelle-France, l'Acadie, Terre-Neuve, les provinces maritimes, etc.), de la culture, la langue, le droit, les sciences, la religion ou l'environnement.

1 A Touch of Fire
  Marie-André Duplessis, the Hôtel-Dieu of Quebec, and the Writing of New France
  Thomas M. Carr, Jr

2 Entangling the Quebec Act
  Transnational Contexts, Meanings, and Legacies in North America and the British Empire
  Edited by Ollivier Hubert
  and François Furstenberg

3 Listening to the Fur Trade
  Soundways and Music in the British North American Fur Trade, 1760–1840
  Daniel Robert Laxer

LISTENING *to the* FUR TRADE

Soundways and Music in the British North American Fur Trade, 1760–1840

DANIEL ROBERT LAXER

McGill-Queen's University Press

Montreal & Kingston • London • Chicago

© McGill-Queen's University Press 2022

ISBN 978-0-2280-0859-0 (cloth)
ISBN 978-0-2280-0981-8 (ePDF)
ISBN 978-0-2280-0982-5 (ePUB)

Legal deposit first quarter 2022
Bibliothèque nationale du Québec

Printed in Canada on acid-free paper that is 100% ancient forest free (100% post-consumer recycled), processed chlorine free

This book has been published with the help of a grant from the Canadian Federation for the Humanities and Social Sciences, through the Awards to Scholarly Publications Program, using funds provided by the Social Sciences and Humanities Research Council of Canada.

Funded by the Government of Canada   Financé par le gouvernement du Canada   Canada   Canada Council for the Arts   Conseil des arts du Canada

We acknowledge the support of the Canada Council for the Arts.

Nous remercions le Conseil des arts du Canada de son soutien.

Library and Archives Canada Cataloguing in Publication

Title: Listening to the fur trade : soundways and music in the British North American fur trade, 1760–1840 / Daniel Robert Laxer.

Names: Laxer, Daniel Robert, author.

Series: McGill-Queen's studies in early Canada ; 3.

Description: Series statement: McGill-Queen's studies in early Canada ; 3 | Includes bibliographical references and index.

Identifiers: Canadiana (print) 2021032595x | Canadiana (ebook) 20210326174 | ISBN 9780228008590 (cloth) | ISBN 9780228009818 (ePDF) | ISBN 9780228009825 (ePUB)

Subjects: LCSH: Fur traders – Songs and music – History and criticism. | LCSH: Fur trade – Canada – History – 18th century. | LCSH: Fur trade – Canada – History – 19th century.

Classification: LCC ML3563.3 .L39 2021 | DDC 780.97109/033 – dc23

This book was designed and typeset by Peggy & Co. Design in 11/14 Adobe Garamond Pro.

Contents

Tables and Figures   vii

Preface   ix

Acknowledgments   xi

Special Terms   xiii

Introduction   3

1 With a Bang: Gunpowder and Firearms   24

2 Musical Encounters   50

3 Military Instruments and "Turned" Drums   62

4 Dances of Diplomacy   81

5 Soundways Montreal to La Cloche   107

6 Paddling Songs; *Chansons D'aviron*   130

7 Indigenous Hunting and Healing Songs   157

8 Music of the Trading Posts   191

Conclusion   230

Notes   237

Bibliography   269

Index   301

Tables and Figures

Tables

8.1 Jaw harps at North West Company trading posts, 1821 210

8.2 Violin strings at North West Company trading posts,
1820–21 210

Figures

0.1 Overview map of trading posts mentioned in this book xv

1.1 North West Gun, c. 1813–20. Royal Ontario
Museum. 969.75 33

3.1 Rudolf Steiger, *Deputation of Indians from the Chippewa Tribes to
the President of Upper Canada, Sir Frederic Ph. Robinson, K.C.B.,
Major General, etc. in 1815*, 1815. Watercolour, gouache, and gum
arabic on wove paper, mounted on wove paper, 25.5 × 35.8 cm.
Purchased 1989, National Gallery of Canada. Accession no. 30237.
Photo: NGC 72

4.1 Calumet Song transcribed by Jolliet and Marquette, *Early Narratives
of the Northwest*, edited by Louise Phelps Kellogg, (New York:
Charles Scribner's Sons, 1917), 247–8 88–89

5.1 Map, St Anne's and Lachine 113

5.2 Map, Petit Rocher to St Anne's 117

5.3 Map, La Cloche to St Anne's 127

5.4 "Sketch of Lake Huron, 1788 circumnavigated by Gother
Mann, Capt. commanding Royal Engineers in Canada."
Maps and cartographic material, Item ID 4169996, Library
and Archives Canada 128

5.5   "La Cloche," in a postcard from the 1920s.
       Private collection   129
6.1   From the collection of fur trader Edward Ermatinger,
       recorded ~1827–30, "Folk songs, French-Canada, ca. 1830."
       Library and Archives Canada, Series A2, Volume 4, Item 9
       (MG 19, R7712-0-7-E): 2   143
8.1   Painted panel ca 1800, York Factory Depot Building. Photo: Parks
       Canada / York Factory National Historic Site   196
8.2   Plan of Fort William, sketch drawn by Lord Selkirk, 1816 (Archives
       of Ontario, F 481, MU3279)   205
8.3   Excavated jaw harps. Left: Fort White Earth, "Historic HBCO +
       NWCO 1810–1813," Royal Alberta Museum (Borden #: GaPb-3,
       Catalogue #H69.3.1154). Right: Rossdale site near Fort Edmonton,
       Royal Alberta Museum (Borden #: F; Pi-63, Catalogue #2127).
       Photographs by the author   209
8.4   Red River jig, *Harper's New Monthly Magazine*, 1860,
       Volume 21, 585. Reproduction courtesy Michigan State
       University Libraries   226

Preface

If the historian's task is to cobble together an understanding of the past, however imperfect, based on fragmentary evidence, how on earth is it possible to reconstruct how it *sounded*? Time destroys all but the most resilient materials, under the most favourable conditions. By their nature, sound, music, and dance are ephemeral. No matter how much we wish otherwise, performances vanish when they finish, except in the minds of the performers and audience. After centuries, there are but tenuous connections with our sounded past. How can we trace intangible cultural phenomenon from the era before sound recording? If you look carefully, as I do in this book, it is actually remarkable how much of the fur trade's written record, oral history, and material culture describes and reveals its sounded and musical history. In the period from 1760 to 1840, the landscape over which the fur trade was conducted was punctuated by many human-made sounds. Generally, only the prominent and noteworthy made it onto the written page. They were produced by shouting, gunpowder, singing, dancing, rattles, jingles, drums, fiddles, and, very occasionally, bagpipes. Fur trade interactions were usually, in a word, noisy.

In the pages ahead, I explore how sound and music operated between peoples in the rapidly expanding fur trade network: between men and women; Indigenous and European; bourgeois and voyageur; master and servant. In the late eighteenth century the fur trade reached the furthest extents of North America and had global supply networks of personnel and materials. Logistical considerations were shaped by the seasons. Water routes that stretched thousands of kilometres and connected trading posts from the St Lawrence to Lake Athabasca and Hudson Bay to the west coast were reliant on the precious summer months when the northern rivers were ice-free. The human encounters that manifested along these routes during the eighty-year period of this study were remarkable for a number of reasons. The fur trade brought not the arrival of settler colonialism in these parts of the continent, but instead a pattern of human interaction based on trade and reciprocity. Trading posts were a complex polyglot of highly mobile people from different national, linguistic, religious, cultural, and class backgrounds. They found ways to interact every time they met, not only in exchanging goods but in forming the kinds of relationships that facilitated their interests and survival. Indigenous protocols of ceremony and treaty-making were adopted by fur traders who supplied materials and technologies, such as guns, which in turn sometimes changed how these sounded.

The period encompassing the height of the British North American fur trade, roughly from 1760 to 1840, presents a fundamentally different kind of cultural engagement than in the period that followed. Those dates, while arbitrary, correspond at the one end to the arrival of English-speaking fur traders in the Great Lakes, and at the other to the invention of syllabics, a written language system for the Cree and Anishinaabe languages developed by Methodist missionary James Evans at the Hudson's Bay Company's (HBC) Norway House and nearby Cree village of Rossville.[1] Between these two symbolic events was the rapid expansion of the fur trade from Hudson Bay and the St Lawrence. It produced a rich history of encounters and partnerships. While not without its negative consequences, the fur trade represents the best period of Indigenous–European relations to date. As Arthur Manuel writes in *The Reconciliation Manifesto,* it was during the fur trade when Europeans "had to make deals" to travel and hunt on Indigenous land: "This partnership lasted almost two hundred years and it is during this period that the possibility of living side by side and respecting one another seemed to be a real possibility." Many aspects of these partnerships become evident when exploring the cultural realms of soundways and music. Understanding how we got along successfully is important when considering how we might get along better in the future. If "listening" to our shared history is any guide, I suggest we start dancing together again.

Acknowledgments

I am grateful to the many scholars whose helpful suggestions and references guided me along this fifteen-year journey, including Allan Greer, Carolyn Podruchny, Heidi Bohaker, John Haines, Carl Benn, Laura Peers, Richard Cullen Rath, Gerhard Ens, Jennifer Brown, George Colpitts, Arthur Ray, Brenda Macdougall, Patricia McCormack, Shelley Pearen, Cory Willmott, and Maureen Mathews. I learned much from inspiring historians at the University of Alberta, York University, and the University of Toronto, in particular Leslie Cormack, David Johnson, Elizabeth Cohen, Colin Coates, Ian Radforth, Jan Noël, Abraham Rotstein, Steve Penfold, and David Wilson. I am grateful to Jonathan Dueck and Michael Frishkopf for sparking my interest in ethnomusicology as an undergraduate. I would also like to acknowledge fruitful conversations with Lynn Whidden, Beverley Diamond, David Gramit, Frances Wilkins, Mike Evans, Dylan Robinson, Stacy Nation-Knapper, Victoria Freeman, and Jesse Thistle. Your words influenced me more than you might realize.

Ruth McConell and Karen Giering at the Royal Alberta Museum, Benoît Thériault, Sam Cronk, Jonathan Wise, and Jean-François Lozier at the Canadian Museum of History (then CMC), and Trudy Nicks, Arnie Brownstone, and Carol Baum at the Royal Ontario Museum were all very helpful. Thank you to Diane Lamoureux at the Provincial Archives of Alberta as well as Nora Hague at the McCord Museum in Montreal. Special thanks to Anne Lederman, whom I took fiddle lessons from in 2008–13, and whose research, teaching, and zeal changed how I listen to the past. I am appreciative of the many students whom I've had the privilege of teaching at U of T, York University, and numerous institutions of lifelong learning around Toronto. Your support and enthusiasm for my topic often encouraged me onwards.

Special thanks to Alan Corbiere for his invitation to Manitoulin Island in 2012 and assistance on a translation from Anishinaabemowin for this book.

I look forward to continuing to learn from your scholarship and teachings. I would also like to thank Peter Ittinuar, whom I had the privilege of working with and who kindly provided a translation for this book from Inuktitut. Many thanks to the historians who encouraged me to prepare my manuscript for book publication, in particular Alison Norman, Jane Thomas, Jay Cassel, and James Cousins. Thank you to the anonymous peer-reviewers for their helpful critiques and suggestions, and Nathan Torrence for producing the maps.

I would not have written this book if I did not grow up as I did in Edmonton, Alberta. I played in the punk rock scene as a teenager and in my early twenties, witnessing music bringing strangers together at energetic shows across Canada. It instilled a deep wonder about the history of this land and its people. In 2005, the North Saskatchewan River drew me eastwards to begin my graduate studies. I rented a small room in a very old house near Markham and Ulster Streets in Toronto to complete my PhD and write this book. The dilapidated floorboards bore witness to years of research, discordant fiddle scrapings, struggles, setbacks, and eventual successes, allowing me to complete this study in an impossibly expensive city.

Special thank you to my brothers, Christopher and Damon, for introducing me to diverse music from a young age, to my dad, Gordon, for inspiring me with his love of history, and to my mom, Judith Beirs, for demonstrating indomitable determination and will. I love you all so much. I would also like to acknowledge my late uncle James Laxer, a prolific author and inspiration in my life. Finally, a heartfelt thank you to friends and partners along the way who were loving and supportive. I am eternally grateful to you all.

Though I was helped by many, I accept responsibility for any and all errors in this book.

Special Terms

Anishinaabe(g) – A term referring to Odawa, Ojibwe, and Potawatomi people. A *g* or *k* at the end makes the word plural.

Anishinaabemowin – The language of Anishinaabe people, part of the Algonquian language family.

bourgeois – After the Conquest of New France, this term properly referred to the fur trade companies' partners but was commonly used by voyageurs to refer to all fur trade masters.

bouts – The bowsman and steersman of voyageur canoes who typically started the paddling songs.

fiddle – Serving as a verb and noun, this is another term for the violin and usually refers to the non-literate folk tradition and repertoire.

Haudenosaunee – A term for the Iroquois Confederacy or Six Nations, or an individual from it.

HBC – Hudson's Bay Company.

Hudson Bay fur trade – The fur trade operating out of Hudson Bay.

jig – A type of song and dance somewhat popular in the fur trade with a 6/8-time signature.

jongleur – A term used by the French for shaman or medicine man.

medicine man – An Indigenous man who conducts healing ceremonies.

music – Humanly organized sound.

Ojibwe – Sometimes spelled Ojibwa or Ojibway; an Anishinaabe Nation.

NWC – North West Company.

partner dance – A generic term for any dance style that involves dancing with a partner.

pattern dance – Any dance that follows a pattern on the floor: circles, lines, squares, and figure eights are common examples.

pays d'en haut – Literally, "the land up there," the country upriver from the St Lawrence. It could refer to the Ottawa River, the Great Lakes, or further west.

reel – a fast-paced song and dance popular in the fur trade possessing a 2/4 time signature.

Saulteaux (or Sauteaux) – Ojibwe from near Sault Ste Marie named by the French in the seventeenth century. Some moved westwards in the eighteenth century.

servant – Many labouring employees of the fur trading companies signed contracts of three to five years and were known as "servants" to their masters and company.

shaman – An Indigenous person who interacts ritually with unseen forces or spirits.

St Lawrence fur trade – The fur trade that operated out of the St Lawrence valley. This flourished especially before the ascendancy of the HBC in 1821.

soundways – Practices of producing or engaging with specific sounds.

soundscape – The audible acoustic environment as perceived by humans, including both natural and humanly produced sounds.

step dance – A generic term for dance styles in which footwork is the most important element.

syncretic – Music that combines and blends different styles and practices.

vocable – A non-semantic utterance featured in Indigenous and European music. Sometimes called a "nonsense syllable": "fa," "la," "hey," "uh."

voyageurs – The men who paddled the canoes of the fur trade. Predominantly French Canadians associated with the St Lawrence fur trade.

war whoop – An Indigenous soundway consisting of a loud piercing yell or howl. It was used as a signal for attack, to intimidate enemies, and in various contexts and ceremonies.

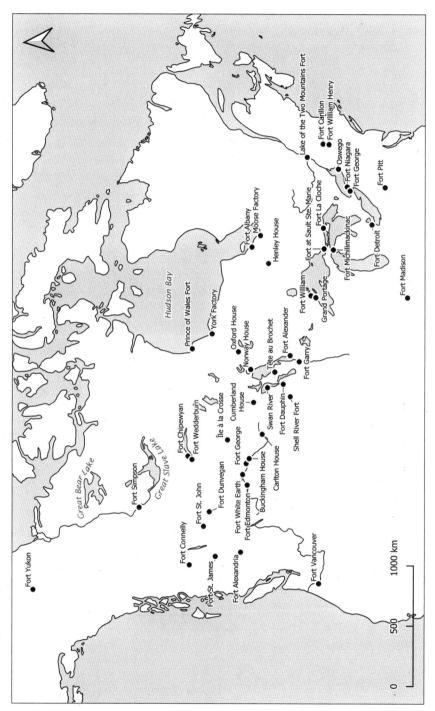

Fig. 0.1 Trading posts mentioned in this book

LISTENING *to the* FUR TRADE

Introduction

In the summer of 1814, the naval officer Lieutenant Edward Chappell piloted HMS *Rosamond* into Hudson Bay. Escorting two Hudson's Bay Company (HBC) ships, the convoy was to spend the season navigating various posts along the coast. On 31 July, Chappell was in his bed when he heard the "shouts and cries" from Inuit men who paddled up alongside the ship in kayaks. For Chappell then, this encounter began with sounds. In his memoir, he recalled how he raced to the deck, gawking and marvelling at the light-frame construction of the Inuit crafts. The oiled seal skins were expertly sewn "as tight as parchment upon the head of a drum."[1] Chappell remarked that it was difficult to convey the delight expressed by the Inuit once they had reached the ships, as "they jumped, shouted, danced, and sang, to express their joy."[2] The encounter that began with shouts on approach evolved into singing and dancing on board. At each stage, more trust was required. Together, the entire group made their way to shore at Cape Saddleback in Hudson Strait.

On landing, the Inuit reportedly said, "*Pillitay! Pillitay! Pillitay!*" Chappell and his men interpreted this to mean "gift." There is a word in Inuktitut, *pilauqta*, that means "give us something."[3] Gift-giving ensued. Then, an abrupt shift. A song was initiated by the HBC men. This was, according to Chappell, "absolutely necessary" as "a means of diverting their attention." He described how, "accordingly, one of our party, who was well acquainted with the manners of the *Indians of Hudson's Bay,* began a song in the language of the *Cree* tribe. The *Esquimaux* [Inuit] gaped with great astonishment and evident pleasure, preserving the most profound silence, until he gave a loud shout, as a finale; when they sat up an universal shouting and jumping, and it appeared as if they were half beside themselves with delight: yet we were certain that they understood nothing of the sense of the song."[4]

We do not know the perspective of the Inuit in this incident. It is evident that they appreciated, or at least politely received, the performance. Chappell's assumptions about their lack of understanding, however, are unsubstantiated. They may well have recognized that the fur traders from the big wooden boat were attempting to sing them a Cree song. The potential for bewilderment, amusement, and misunderstanding was great. The Inuit listened with rapt, silent attention and burst into hearty applause at the conclusion. They appear to have embraced this aspect of the encounter every bit as much as the English. They jumped at the opportunity to reciprocate with their own performance.

Chappell continued to describe the musical encounter: "We thought this a good opportunity to petition them for a similar favour: our signs were instantly comprehended, and a ring immediately formed, consisting entirely of women, with the exception of an old man, whom we recognised to have seen before, as steersman of one of the large women's boats." The Inuit were prepared to reciprocate musically with these strangers. The gestures of the HBC men produced a prompt response, with the Inuit women moving quickly into a ring or circle formation. The comment about the elderly man demonstrates Chappell's attention to the gender of the performers. This is a recurring pattern in fur trade descriptions where gender dynamics, as they were communicated through performance, were often carefully observed. In this case, the ensuing song is not further described. What began with shouts, songs, and dancing on the water, ended on the shore of Hudson Strait with more elaborate reciprocal musical exchanges. The musical aspect of the encounter may well have taken up more time and proven more memorable than the material exchanges.

Chappell witnessed a young Inuit woman dance aboard his ship, describing her sounds and movements, as well as gestures and facial expressions. He seemed to identify her throat singing by describing "a convulsive gurgling in the throat, and deep-drawn sighs."[5] This performance would have been lost to time had Chappell not written it down. It is the kind of detail that is unlikely to be preserved in oral histories of encounter two hundred years later. Yet it was immortalized, however imperfectly, by Chappell's pen. This is the challenge of attempting to "listen" to the past. The clues left behind that describe how it sounded are primarily in the form of the written word, hardly sufficient for capturing the full sense of an auditory experience, song, or dance. Yet such descriptions are sprinkled throughout the historical record. In Chappell's *Narrative*, musical descriptions take up more space than material exchanges. In investigating encounters under the banner of the "fur trade," historians have, with a few notable exceptions discussed ahead, largely bypassed intangible cultural exchanges. Music, dance, and aspects of performance played a central role in countless European-Indigenous encounters. At its height, the fur trade dramatically transformed the soundscape of North America in such an indelible way that we can still hear its echoes in folksong repertoires today. While sounds and music are ephemeral, they were central to the operation of the fur trade.

"Peak" Fur Trade

The period of this study from 1760 to 1840 encompasses the height of the North American fur trade. The first decades involved a rapid expansion of the St Lawrence and Hudson Bay fur trade networks across the northern continent as outfits and companies vied for inland supremacy. After 1821, the HBC assumed control and achieved a near-monopoly throughout northern North America. By 1840, restructuring and decreasing yields signalled decline. Yet, during the preceding eighty-years, the fur trade had been a leading industry. It was the main mechanism by which Europeans, Americans, and Canadians travelled great distances to encounter, live, travel, and trade with Indigenous peoples. For the hundreds of Indigenous Nations inhabiting the vast territory between the Great Lakes, the west coast, and the Arctic Circle, this timeframe usually represents when their communities encountered and established regular interactions with the newcomers. Trading posts were constructed across this landscape, yet this did not mark the arrival of settler colonialism. Unlike that system, the fur trade was predicated on ongoing exchanges based on reciprocal relationships. The fur traders and "servants" of the companies, while not insignificant in number, especially by 1800, were a small minority across this vast landscape compared with Indigenous peoples. This was obvious to officials in Montreal and London, who described the territory in which the British North American fur trade was conducted as "Indian country."

In 1670, Charles II named the entire Hudson Bay watershed Rupert's Land after his cousin Prince Rupert of the Rhine. A representative and audacious act; he did not have any idea how large it was or where its borders lay. He issued a royal charter to establish the HBC's rule over this vast new domain. It was of little concern to the king that Indigenous peoples lived on this land. He would not have known that the Cree had their own name for this territory, *Nituskeenan*, meaning "our land."[6] If he had known, it is unlikely that it would have deterred him. Aside from the voyages of Henry Kelsey and Anthony Henday, the HBC was reticent to depart from the bay's shores over the following hundred years. The French were much more prolific in exploring the interior of the continent, using the St Lawrence watershed to ascend to the Great Lakes region and beyond the height of land. French Canadian *coureurs du bois* and voyageurs employed the term *pays d'en haut*, meaning "country up there" or "upper countries" to refer to the enormous territory upriver from the St Lawrence.[7] After the conquest of Quebec, the fur trade that developed out of Montreal forked in two distinct directions beyond the western depot of Michilimackinac. The southwest trade extended beyond Lake Michigan into the Mississippi watershed. The northwest trade extended through Lake Superior into the Hudson Bay, Arctic, and Pacific watersheds. Fur trader Roderick Mackenzie reported that "the North West, as it is called, includes (as I understand it) all that extensive Country which lies between Lake Superior and the Frozen Ocean, between Hudson's Bay and the river of the West – Many parts of which are very little known except from Indian Reports."[8] Montreal fur traders adopted the Indigenous technologies of the moccasin, snowshoe, and canoe, and hired Indigenous guides and French Canadian voyageurs to make, guide, and power them. HBC fur traders stuck largely to the coastal forts or "factories" until the 1770s when competition drove them inland. They too adopted Indigenous technologies of travel, although they replaced canoes with York boats on many routes by the early nineteenth-century and hired servants, often from the British Isles, particularly the Orkney Islands north of Scotland.[9]

After the Seven Years' War (1756–63), European settlements were restricted to a relatively thin strip along the eastern seaboard of North America. The war's conclusion transferred European influence in the St Lawrence and Great Lakes from the French to the British Crown. Yet Anishinaabeg, Wendat, Shawnee, Seneca, and other Indigenous Nations firmly rejected the imposition of British control with "Pontiac's Rebellion" or "Pontiac's War" in 1763. In just a few weeks, every British fort west and north of the Allegheny Mountains, including the Great Lakes, was captured by Indigenous warriors except Fort Pitt, Detroit, and Niagara.[10] The Royal Proclamation of 1763 and the Treaty of Niagara of 1764 smoothed relations and opened the Great Lakes fur trade to British merchants operating out of Montreal. Many, such as Simon McTavish and Peter Pond, arrived from New York and New England. They began operating out of Montreal and hiring from the experienced French Canadian labour force of the St Lawrence. During the ensuing two decades, fur traders followed river arteries over the heights of land beyond the Great Lakes to the southwest and northwest. The most successful enterprises consisted of merchants who combined their capital and coordinated their efforts. In 1766, for instance, Alexander Henry combined with French *coureur* J.B. Cadotte on a very profitable expedition to Fond du Lac. In 1769, Isaac Todd, James McGill, and three Frobisher brothers sent an expedition to the northwest through Rainy Lake into the Lake Winnipeg area. The southwest trade was also pursued vigorously, as Todd, McGill, and Company as well as Forsyth, Richardson, and Company focused on that region with much success. In 1775, James McGill, Benjamin Frobisher, Maurice Blondeau, and Alexander Henry extended their trade northwest into the Saskatchewan Valley. Due to the desire to push further northwest, in 1776, they moved their supply base to Grand Portage on Lake Superior. The southwest trade remained profitable through the American Revolution until Jay's Treaty of 1794, while the northwest trade flourished after 1779. That year, Peter Pond returned to Montreal with over eighty thousand fine beaver skins from the Athabasca region. It became the "El Dorado of the fur trade" and was where the newly formed North West Company (NWC) focused its efforts.[11]

Competition between the trading outfits was often tense and sometimes vicious. In 1781, Peter Pond and Etienne Wadden both overwintered at Lac la Ronge. In the spring, the two men quarrelled and Wadden was killed. In 1787, in the Athabasca region, John Ross of Gregory, McLeod, and Company were murdered at the hands of Peter Pond with the NWC.[12] Competition was stiff. The HBC enjoyed shorter supply lines from Hudson Bay, and slowly began competing with the "Nor'Westers." Their initial efforts at constructing the inland post of Henley House in the 1740s and '50s were disastrous, yet they began successful inland operations after Cumberland House was sited on the Saskatchewan River by Samuel Hearne in 1774. Fierce competition with the Montreal traders ensued. In this atmosphere, Indigenous peoples had a great deal of agency. They traded at different trading posts and developed personal relationships with fur traders who sometimes lent them goods on credit. This period witnessed attempts by fur traders to win over Indigenous hunters, from providing them with the best goods and deals for their furs, to courting them with gifts of gunpowder, tobacco, and alcohol. There was inherent reciprocity in these trading relationships, yet there was also occasionally intimidation and deception.

Enormous quantities of liquor were traded by the companies. Kegs and cases were transported tremendous distances by canoe and York boat. The main forms of traded liquor were brandy, rum, and high wines.[13] Alcohol was introduced, and so was the social practice of binge drinking. This led to many tragic cases of documented violence in and around the trading posts.[14] Countless more were never recorded. This aspect of the trade had a truly detrimental effect on Indigenous communities. When some outfits abstained from the practice, out of principle or strategy, it was usually circumvented by a competitor. Brenda Child has called this the "darker element of the exchange," one that introduced alcohol and binge drinking: "While it may have been a social ritual or a coping mechanism during a period of cultural adaptation and tension, it sometimes had a destructive effect on family and community life."[15] Alexander Henry described the custom aboard the Montreal trade canoes departing for the west, whereby eight gallons of rum were distributed to each canoe, approximately one gallon per man, and customarily consumed immediately.[16] There were many alcohol-related accidents and tragedies. Alcohol was commonly traded with Indigenous peoples and served by the master at the trading post dances. The excessive alcoholism of the fur trade was problematic for all, yet its detrimental impact on Indigenous communities in particular must be acknowledged from the outset.

The speed of the expansion of the fur trade across the western and northern reaches of the continent in the late eighteenth century is remarkable. The Montreal traders under the NWC dominated the Athabasca trade with their large depot at Fort Chipewyan. This post was established on the west end of Lake Athabasca in 1788. From there Alexander Mackenzie launched his voyages to the Arctic Ocean via the Mackenzie River in 1789 and to the Pacific Ocean via the Bella Coola in 1793. The most intense fur trade competition took place during the period from 1798–1805, when Alexander Mackenzie broke away from the NWC with his own company, the XY Company.[17] After much expense, disruption, and loss, the Montreal companies largely consolidated under the NWC in 1805, mounting a concerted and successful opposition to the HBC's increasing competition. The focus was the northwest after the southwest trade had fallen to American outfits such as John Jacob Astor's American Fur Company, founded in 1808. The NWC's northwest trade overlapped into the HBC's Rupert's Land, and the NWC and HBC competed over thousands of kilometres for the trade of Indigenous peoples.

Tensions between the NWC and HBC reached a boiling point in the 1810s. The HBC's adoption of Lord Selkirk's plan to relocate displaced Scottish farmers to Red River met numerous difficulties and disasters. It greatly increased the struggle between the HBC and the Montreal traders. The junction of the Red and Assiniboine Rivers was a key location for canoe travel along the transcontinental east-west corridor. HBC governor Miles Macdonell issued the Pemmican Proclamation in 1814 forbidding the export of pemmican from the Red River area in a foolhardy attempt to secure food for the struggling settlement. It was met with immediate resistance by Indigenous peoples and the Montreal traders. The mixed-ancestry population of the Red River area had, for decades, pursued the bison hunt and traded the pemmican necessary for the long-distance canoe brigades central to the Montreal transportation network. The tensions culminated in the most violent encounter at the Battle of Seven Oaks in 1816. Twenty HBC men including Governor Semple and some Selkirk settlers were killed while confronting a NWC party led by Cuthbert Grant, son of a Scottish fur trader and a woman of French and Cree descent, with only one casualty on the NWC side.[18] This event is known to have sparked Métis national consciousness. Present was Pierre Falcon who wrote the "chanson de la grenouillère" to document the perspective of the largely mixed-ancestry NWC party. The lyrics assert that the "Bois Brûlés" were the original occupants of the land, and the HBC and Selkirk settlers arrived "pour piller notre pays." This song has served as the Métis national anthem ever since.[19]

London was galvanized to take action. In 1820, a deal was arranged whereby the HBC and NWC merged under the banner of the HBC. This dramatic shift initiated a period of reform in the fur trade. Under a unified company, traffic was largely re-routed out of Hudson Bay. Increasing reliance was placed on York boats – large, heavy wooden boats that were rowed and had a sail – over canoes. The remaining competition was with the American Fur Company to the south, and the border or "medicine line," at least hypothetically, served to delineate territories of jurisdiction. After 1821, the HBC held a virtual monopoly over the British North American fur trade, including the enormous territory of what would become central, western, and northern Canada. This study ends around 1840 because that is when the culture of soundways and music that had developed between British, French, and Indigenous peoples up until that point was directly challenged. Reform efforts were led by Anglican, Catholic Oblate, and Methodist missionaries who began using the trading post network in their proselytizing efforts of western Indigenous Nations. Governor George Simpson's efforts to streamline operations, reduce labour costs, and improve the HBC's reputation combined with this factor to fundamentally alter how the fur trade sounded. By 1840, Methodist missionary James Evans was printing bibles and hymnals in the syllabic writing system he had developed for the Cree language while working around the HBC's Norway House. It represents a fitting end to this study. The fur trade increasingly shed the soundways and musical traditions developed over the previous eighty years and became a springboard for the "civilizing project" and Christianization of Indigenous peoples.[20]

Trade, Treaties, and Music

To a large degree, the cultural background of those involved in the fur trade shaped the soundways and music they created. The Montreal merchants hired their labour in the St Lawrence valley, primarily French Canadians from around Montreal. Approximately 10 per cent of the crews consisted of Mohawk men hired from Kanesatake and Kahnawake.[21] In contrast, the HBC hired primarily from northern England, Ireland, Scotland, and the Shetland Islands. By the early nineteenth century, the largest portion of inland HBC employees were from the Orkney Islands north of Scotland.[22] If fur traders were themselves a diverse lot, the Indigenous peoples they encountered were even more diverse. Major language families encountered by the fur trade include Iroquoian, Algonquian, Siouan, Athapascan, and numerous others on the west coast. There were hundreds of Indigenous Nations and languages across this enormous landscape.[23] To enable this polyglot intersection of humanity to trade successfully, new rituals and ways of interacting developed alongside long-standing Indigenous ceremonies. Relationships and agreements were made, often accompanied by music and dancing.

By the mid-eighteenth century, dozens of Indigenous Nations in northeastern North America were drawn into the Seven Years' War, the cataclysmic confrontation between Britain and France. When the French "father" Onontio's armies were defeated and withdrawn from the St Lawrence and Great Lakes around 1760, British forces moved in. They occupied the former French forts at Michilimackinac and Niagara. Yet the British had not entered into peaceful relations or established treaties with the Anishinaabeg and other Algonquian-speaking nations of the Great Lakes region. In the previous decade, these Indigenous peoples had largely fought on the French side of the vicious conflict. In the ensuing Pontiac's War, eight British forts were captured by pan-Indigenous forces, including Michilimackinac.[24] Fort Detroit and Fort Pitt were besieged but did not fall. It was a dramatic defeat for the British on the heels of their victory over the French. It precipitated a major shift in British diplomatic strategy with Indigenous Nations.

During the Seven Years' War, Britain's northern Indian agent, William Johnson, had been crucial in securing alliances with the six nations of the Haudenosaunee Confederacy. He arranged the subsequent Treaty of Niagara in 1764, with representatives of over twenty Indigenous Nations consisting of around two thousand people.[25] Johnson used the well-tested metaphor of the "covenant chain" to symbolize the alliance, first utilized by the Dutch and Mohawk in the early 1600s and then adopted by the British by the 1670s. The meetings of English representatives and Haudenosaunee headmen became known as "brightenings," with rituals and feasting, exchanging wampum, gift-giving, and speeches.[26] Doing these things, metaphorically, was "polishing" the chain, renewing the commitments and obligations of the alliance. The wampum belt presented at the Treaty of Niagara depicts two figures holding hands linked with the covenant chain on either side. This treaty facilitated British travel and commerce in the Great Lakes. It demonstrated British officials engaging in treaty-making with dozens of Indigenous Nations over a large territory, and followed Indigenous protocols of pipe ceremonies, feasting, and exchanges of gifts and wampum belts. The fur trade that expanded rapidly in its wake was not only made possible by this treaty, it replicated many of these treaty-making customs on a smaller scale. An underappreciated aspect of these agreements were their various soundways, and frequent music and dance.

As Inga Clendinnen wrote in her pathbreaking *Dancing with Strangers*, "we don't readily think of dancing as a phase in the imperial process."[27] Yet in the first few years of encounter between Britons and Indigenous people in Botany Bay, Australia, intercultural dancing was common, as it was between fur traders and Indigenous peoples in North America over a much longer period. In Australia, dancing together was a key reinforcer of trust during the initial years of relative co-operation. This changed within a decade as demographics and power dynamics shifted and racial segregation hardened. In the North American fur trade, predominantly peaceful and reciprocal relations between fur traders and Indigenous peoples were the norm from the eighteenth to the mid-nineteenth centuries and were similarly characterized by frequent intercultural music and dance. They often played a big role in how relationships were initiated. Ceremonial pipe dances and "war dances" of various Indigenous Nations were described by fur traders who witnessed or were presented with them outside or inside the gates of the trading post. Fur traders brought their own music, and it too played an important role in diplomatic relations with First Nations. Inside the trading posts was where step dancing – solo or in lines, squares, or patterns – to violin or "fiddle" music was practised. Indigenous women from nearby communities were frequently invited to be dancing partners, functioning to introduce and intertwine fur traders with the local community. It was often on these occasions when fur traders courted Indigenous women, resulting in marriages *à la façon du pays* or according to the custom of the country. These were usually celebrated with dancing inside the trading post.[28] These marriages often proved to be crucial to fur traders' survival and success, solidifying kinship and trading relations between the community and trading post.

A key aspect of these encounters was that relationships were defined by reciprocity. This idea was fleshed out in *The Middle Ground,* a history describing the Great Lakes during this period as a kind of meeting place where accommodating the other was necessary and misunderstandings were common.[29] Fur traders were armed to the teeth but vastly outnumbered by Indigenous warriors. Yet by the late eighteenth century, many Indigenous peoples were largely dependent on the gunpowder and shot that the fur traders provided. In Cree and Anishinaabeg societies, the giving of objects to others signified much more than just material exchange. It embodied intentions and served as an entryway into fictive kinship relationships predicated on reciprocity.[30] These allowed fur traders access to the furs, meat, handicrafts, and labour of Indigenous kin-networks. Gift-giving was central to establishing and renewing relationships over the years. It reinforced the bonds of fictive kinship. With it came mutual obligations concerning the hunt and warfare. How trade, alliance, and warfare played out between European empires and Indigenous Nations in the Great Lakes region from the seventeenth to early nineteenth centuries has been examined by, among others, Daniel Richter, Alan Taylor, Gilles Havard, Michael Witgen, and Michael McDonnell.[31] In addition to gift-giving, their studies shed light on other protocols of diplomacy, including the use of wampum, feasting, speeches, and pipe ceremonies. Dancing is occasionally mentioned as part of the diplomatic proceedings.[32] As both sides of the encounter struggled to understand the other, this core set of diplomatic tools facilitated treaty-making and allowed the establishment of alliances and relationships that endured massive upheavals and change.

This study of music's role in the fur trade builds on histories that focus on culture, gender, relationships, and Indigenous peoples. The two mains schools of historiography in the twentieth century hardly considered these topics, much less music. The "national" school, epitomized by Harold Innis's *Fur Trade in Canada,* examined the global patterns that shaped the nascent Canadian economy. The "company" school, epitomized by E.E. Rich's *The Fur Trade and the Northwest to 1857,* examined the fur trading companies' manoeuvrings for mercantile supremacy. In the 1960s and '70s, crucial developments in gender studies, cultural studies, and ethnohistory transformed the field. The historical analysis of the fur trade shifted from material transactions to relationships; from an economic focus toward social and cultural considerations. Sylvia Van Kirk and Jennifer Brown investigated Indigenous women's contributions, including their partnerships and marriages with fur traders and their families that formed a distinct "fur trade society." The ceremonies of courtship and marriage often involved dancing and allowed fur traders access to Indigenous kinship networks.[33] Yet it was not only Indigenous women who interacted musically with fur traders. Scholarship focusing on the Indigenous experience of the fur trade, such as Arthur Ray's *Indians in the Fur Trade*, highlighted the Indigenous hunters and trappers who were autonomous yet integral to the fur trade.[34] These hunters engaged on their own terms, knowing that fur traders held the supply of guns, gunpowder, and shot. Many Indigenous peoples adopted practices of saluting with their guns upon approach to the trading posts, a custom examined in Chapter 1.

This work draws on and contributes to the historiography of European and Indigenous diplomatic relations. In the seventeenth century, both the French and the English learned that to have a trading relationship with an Indigenous community usually meant becoming their military ally. J.R. Miller identified the "commercial compacts" between fur traders and Indigenous Nations as the first phase of treaty-making: "trade was something that people in close relationships engaged in only after important social observances occurred in a formal and ritualistic manner."[35] A major part of these ceremonies involved gift-giving or "material diplomacy." But the element that is often overlooked could rightly be called "musical diplomacy." It is clear from the written record that the fur trade was about much more than material exchanges. The materialist lens has often bypassed evidence of how intangible acts, behaviours, and ceremonies were inherent and essential to the maintenance of relationships. This is something that Douglas Harvey has called "intercultural performed negotiations."[36] They could include gestures, gunshots, processions, ceremonies, rituals, speeches, silences, songs, and dances. These cultural scripts became expected components of fur trade interactions.

Just as evident are the trading company servants' and voyageurs' expectations of their masters. These included providing periodic "balls" or dances, offering alcohol, food, and space indoors. Scott Stephen has recently analyzed this "household" relationship, identifying it as vertical consciousness more than class consciousness. The interests of masters and servants were linked through reciprocal obligations and emotional bonds.[37] Fiddle music and step dancing were a major way in which these bonds developed and were strengthened. Rhythmic voyageur songs used for paddling canoes represented a mechanism for building and solidifying a unique work identity. While never truly adversarial, the voyageurs did poke fun at the *fils du roi* and mythologize themselves as knights feasting and romancing.[38] The contracts through which *engagés* and voyageurs were bound to the Montreal merchants had many similarities with the household relationships of the HBC, although voyageurs tended to have more autonomy than HBC servants. Soundways and music were integral to the obligations that masters had with their servants and voyageurs while travelling and working at the trading posts. These aspects of intercultural relationships and social history usually did not leave a trace. Yet they took considerable time, effort, and resources, and were described in fur trade records.

If we must define music (and some will insist) let us use John Blacking's "humanly organized sound."[39] It is the most defensible and culturally inclusive definition. It allows music to form a meaningful category of analysis in the fur trade era, even though European and Indigenous understandings of it were remarkably different. Various strategies have been adopted to get around imposing a Eurocentric definition of music on non-Western cultures. In his recent book about intertribal Native American music, John Perea adopts the term "soundings" to challenge the notion of music as a thing or object, instead stressing its collective origins and social activity.[40] This safeguards against the trappings of well-worn arguments about what is and what is not properly defined as "music." This approach resembles that of the musicologist Christopher Small, who stressed the importance of social behaviours and relationships that underpinned the notes and time signatures of music. He presented his own term "musicking" as a holistic concept for examining music from its social production to reception.[41]

While these terms have their place, what seems most remarkable from a historical perspective is how "music," or instances of humanly organized sound, served to organize groups of people in particular times and places. Songs moved people, emotionally and physically, and were intrinsically linked to elaborate dance traditions in both European and Indigenous societies. In the fur trade, dancing was a favourite physical exercise that provided entertainment and warmth. It reminded people of home while providing a venue for inter-acting with someone new. Performer and audience, dancer and spectator – all comprised each musical event and helped shape its significance. All participated according to ascribed and un-ascribed roles and behaviours. All interpreted and internalized meaning. While history occasionally hands us some fragment of lyrics or tunes, more often we get other information. Often, it is devoid of musical details but full of social details and historical context. For this study, what a piece of music was or is, with its precise notes and lyrics, is less significant than how it functioned. Sound and music are ephemeral and we cannot literally listen to the past. But we can develop understandings of how it sounded and what the sounds meant for people at the time.

Music and dance functioned as an integral platform of cultural interaction during fur traders' encounters with Indigenous hunters and their communities. Yet several factors have worked against this pattern being fully recognized by historians. Written descriptions of "encounter music" have sometimes been dismissed by scholars as too impressionistic to be of much value, and others have argued that they reveal more about the authors' biases than the music itself.[42] New France had strong Catholic institutions and missionaries that were deeply suspicious of both French folk traditions as well as Indigenous traditions. The Récollet missionary and historian Gabriel Sagard wrote that Indigenous peoples appreciated the ritual music of the Catholic Church but "expressed repugnance at the profane and dissolute songs of the French." He went so far as to wish that "Jesus may condemn the evil Christian singers of dissolute and mundane chansons."[43] To the chroniclers of New France, the folk culture of the *habitants* and *coureurs du bois* was perhaps as dangerous and problematic as that of Indigenous cultures. They helped establish the stereotype that there was no fertile arena of cross-cultural musical exchange between Euro-Canadians and Indigenous peoples outside of the religious realm, only the transfer of vice and sinful activities. This is long overdue for reconsideration. In a recent study of Nicolas Baudin's 1802 scientific expedition to Australia, Fornasiero and West-Sooby argue that "music was clearly the factor that enabled the most pleasant and mutually satisfying cross-cultural encounters, in contrast to the moments when other forms of exchange, notably of weapons, were the source of misunderstandings and tension."[44] Music was a key feature of positive cross-cultural encounters, and it constituted an exchange of intangible culture. It can easily be overlooked.

What did participating in musical interactions *mean*? If they were so prevalent, what social functions did they serve? These questions have been addressed only peripherally by historians of the fur trade. Over the twentieth century, there was increasing recognition of the fur trade's non-economic aspects and Indigenous diplomatic institutions. Gift-giving was recognized as central to trading relationships, producing debate over whether this and other non-material aspects of trade disrupted its economic analysis. Indigenous peoples had their logic for entering into trade, including political, kinship, and non-economic factors. These arguments were advanced by economist Abe Rotstein in the late 1960s and Arthur Ray and Donald Freeman in the 1970s. This represented the "substantivist" position that reoriented fur trade studies away from the "formalist" position of previous economic historians.[45] Gender studies and the cultural turn further led to a closer examination of non-material aspects of fur trade relationships. Sylvia Van Kirk described marriages *à la façon du pays* that were a combination of European and Indigenous traditions. Ceremonies established kinship and these unions were generally solemnized with two common features. The fur trader provided a gift to the woman's family, and he went through a pipe ceremony with her parents and/or close relations to "seal the alliance."[46] The accompanying soundways and music depended on the circumstances and Indigenous culture into which the fur trader was marrying. These symbolic actions announced the new social reality to the Indigenous community and trading post.

Gift-giving was often an important formal precursor to trade.[47] Trade was recognized as part of a broader socio-political context of treaty-making and military alliances. For the Anishinaabe, gift-giving and trade together were important functions of kinship.[48] Michael Witgen described "the culmination of social practices that drew from the hybrid cultural logic of the alliance," allowing Indigenous and non-Indigenous peoples to imagine themselves in a relationship "defined by their kinship to one another."[49] Gift-giving was the "core of the shared middle ground ceremonial culture" and a primary mechanism by which fur traders recognized or created Indigenous chiefs who could, in turn, redistribute the spoils to their community.[50] Gift-giving and trading meant much more than the obvious economic and material consequences. They were key activities in fulfilling expectations, securing alliances, and demonstrating reciprocity in an ongoing relationship. They signalled kinship, enacted through ceremonies, and often actualized through cohabitation and intermarriage. This created an important bond of trust between the fur trader and the Indigenous community, and fur traders frequently advanced goods such as firearms and gunpowder to hunters from the woman's community on credit. Beyond fostering these relationships and building trust, what did the exchange of music mean?

The presentation of songs, dances, or soundways could be a gift of knowledge or honour. Across Indigenous cultures, knowledge may come from a gift, including song knowledge from a dream or spirit, or a human source.[51] This kind of gift also has important implications for relationships, just as gift-giving with material objects. Mi'kmaq Chief and museum curator Stephen Augustine made the point that "songs and dances reflect the experiential relationships of humans and animals." Furthermore, he stressed that without "knowledge of the relationship, the gift (of song or dance) is less meaningful."[52] Reflecting the relationship, songs and soundways shared between fur traders and Indigenous peoples were often akin to temporally bound, intangible gifts.

This kind of gift demonstrated and promoted trust. This is also the case with firearm salutes. They were a kind of intangible gift and signal of honour that was not only heard but felt. Exchanges of songs, dances, and firearms salutes demonstrated and improved relationships and were generally sought and reinforced by all parties in the fur trade.

Ironically, one of the best ways to study intangible cultural exchanges is to examine material culture. Some useful concepts have been presented by anthropologists studying cross-cultural exchanges. Laurier Turgeon identified the "creative tension involved in identity formation" inherent in the adoption of new material goods such as kettles in the seventeenth century.[53] Archaeologists have begun using material objects to gain insights into social processes such as ethnogenesis.[54] Material objects played an important role in the creation, maintenance, and transformation of ethnic identity in the context of intense cultural interaction.[55] Today these objects serve as an important avenue for tracing change over time. Similarly, music was intertwined with identity formation and expression. As material objects, musical instruments were inherently positioned to bring people together both spatially and temporally. Roland Sawatzky has traced how a fiddle brought by Pierre Bruce to the Selkirk settlement around 1815 served multiple generations with music and meaning that evolved with the family's expanding connections and Métis identity.[56] At the height of its popularity around the turn of the nineteenth century in Europe and the St Lawrence, the violin or "fiddle" was particularly suited to the conditions of the fur trade. It was small and light enough for long-distance travel and had longevity with its four replaceable strings. Loud enough to project tunes to an entire room of dancers, it was frequently accompanied by the clapping of hands, stomping of feet, or percussion on a drum or pan. Its appreciation seems to only have been heightened at the remote outposts of the fur trade where the arrival of a fiddle invariably caused great excitement. This is what Archibald McLeod described in 1801 when his men's suffering condition was not enough to prevent a dance once an instrument arrived: "Cold &. blowing hard, the people are some cutting fire wood others hauling, some for Gum &. others working at the Batteau. Several of the people are ill with severe Colds. One of the Shell river men having brought his Violin with him the people danced all night."[57]

Within the household economies of the trading companies, music and dance played an important role in the fulfillment of expectations and obligations between masters and servants. Masters were expected to give their men dances periodically, at the very least on the major holidays. At the height of fur trade competition before 1821, it was more frequent, sometimes once per week or more. It usually meant providing the men with indoor space to dance in addition to drinks and food. Some fur traders were avid musicians who enjoyed performing for servants and guests alike. Such was the case with Willard-Ferdinand Wentzel, a fur trader violinist who had a long career in the far north. Yet, even if the fur trader was not musical, hosting dances was a key method for strengthening vertical bonds in the household economy while also extending them horizontally beyond the walls of the trading post. It brought the different classes, genders, and vocations of the trading post together, and often included women and sometimes men from the local Indigenous community. As Kate van Orden detailed in early modern France, "social bodies cohered" through the "action" of music.[58] Music brought people together, fulfilled obligations between masters and servants, provided a cultural bridge with the local Indigenous community, and characterized the intercultural soundscape of the fur trade.

Music served in many ways to maintain the social order. Yet it could also promote egalitarianism. There are accounts of voyageurs and servants passing the fiddle between themselves throughout the dance, sharing the duties of playing the tunes. For some this was a rare opportunity to play a fur trader's treasured violin. For Métis fiddler Peter Erasmus, playing the fiddle at fur trade dances was something of a social obligation or duty.[59] While there was some risk to the instrument, the owner benefitted from sharing the fiddle because it meant everyone could continue dancing uninterrupted. In providing for dances, the fur trader could curry favour with his employees and trading partners. He relied on them for his success and they could revolt or be poached by a rival trading company. While there were costs to hosting a dance, fur traders often found ways to benefit in terms of gathering information, re-engaging servants, and selling them alcohol at a hefty profit. For the servants, dances were a time for recreation and a break from the work routine. It was a cherished time for drinking, eating, socializing, and engaging in "play" with acquaintances and colleagues.

Drums were the primary musical instruments of Indigenous North America. They came in many varieties, from single- and double-sided, hand-held frame drums, to large drums on wooden stands in the ground, to water drums.[60] Drums symbolize for many Indigenous Nations the heartbeat of Mother Earth and her children.[61] They were a living presence in communities, able to communicate with its human and non-human (spirit) beings. Trading posts were usually built along travel routes or near sites where Indigenous peoples lived or gathered, and as such, fur traders overheard drumming from Indigenous peoples and communities. Fur traders did not apparently bring drums with them as personal items, although tambourines are listed in some trading post inventories. Drums from European military regiments were sometimes observed and retrieved by Indigenous peoples who fought in the Seven Years' War, the American War of Independence, and the War of 1812. Some military drums ended up repurposed or "turned" by Indigenous hands. At the HBC's Moose Factory at the south end of James Bay, before unloading the cargo ships at Charlton Island, a pipe and drum band would march out of the ship in full procession. Fiddle music was introduced by the fur traders, and the local Cree developed a double-headed *taawahekan* drum specifically to accompany the fiddle at community dances. Unlike other Cree drums used for spiritual purposes and hunting ceremonies, these were made specifically to accompany secular fiddle dances.[62] These traditions have been continued in the Moose Cree community until the present day, representing an enduring legacy of European and Indigenous influences that came together during the fur trade.[63]

Fur traders were relatively few compared to Indigenous peoples, yet they made their presence known. Their main power was gunpowder. By carrying, trading, and utilizing large amounts, they dramatically transformed the soundscape of North America. Cannons and muskets were often used explicitly for their sound-making function. They served as long-distance signalling devices, with booming reports that could be heard many kilometres away. In exchanging salutes with incoming and outgoing parties, whether they be on foot, or in a canoe, bateaux, boat, or ship, they audibly marked the annual cycles at the posts. Indigenous hunting groups adopted these practices in their interactions with fur traders, sometimes sending a party in advance to fetch gunpowder from the trading post so that on formal arrival proper gunfire salutes could be exchanged. Firing guns in celebration or salute was generally known as *feu de joie*.[64] This auditory custom was utilized widely including by French Canadian voyageurs in their travels and rites of passage. In terms of musical instruments brought by fur traders, the loudest were bugles and bagpipes. These were rare enough that their presence generated commentary in the written record. George Simpson used them on his 1828 voyage around the trading post network to make a grand impression on fur traders, servants, and Indigenous peoples.[65]

Long-distance canoe travel was characterized by distinct soundways and paddling songs. Singing served to set the pace and synchronize the stroke of the paddles. This was especially crucial on departure in large canoes, when many paddlers had to commence simultaneously. If the men's spirits were flagging, or if the paddling became irregular, a new song brought order. The Montreal-based outfits hired French Canadian voyageurs as their canoemen and labourers. There was continuity with the *ancien regime coureurs de bois,* as the voyageurs in the late eighteenth century continued the singing tradition that had arrived from northwestern France and had thrived in the St Lawrence during the previous century. The call-and-response structure and simple rhyme scheme used in folksongs and military marches had been adapted to the canoe and paddle. By the late eighteenth century, the voyageurs had a robust repertoire of paddling songs that shared distinct features. These appear to have been described in fragmentary form only before Edward Ermatinger's transcriptions from the late 1820s.[66] In Britain, a well-known romantic interpretation of their songs was Thomas Moore's "A Canadian Boat Song," spawning a genre of "Canadian Boat Songs" that were actually English glees set to the piano.[67] The real voyageur songs were recognized for their historical importance and explored in both Grace Lee Nute's classic *The Voyageur* and more recently in Carolyn Podruchny's *Making the Voyageur World.*[68] These studies effectively interpret the voyageurs' songs and lyrics as demonstrating aspects of their social and cultural attitudes and identities. The voyageurs as a vocational group clearly expressed their individual and collective identity through their work songs. They were usually non-literate, and their songs are one of the only ways in which their voices have been captured for posterity.

Yet determining which songs truly represent voyageur voices has been a challenge. There is a tendency to gravitate to the bountiful material collected around the St Lawrence by folklorists starting in the 1860s. We must be wary of their editorial hand and version selection, however, as well as armchair literary creations.[69] I have limited my focus to songs written down, collected, or referenced in the primary accounts of the fur trade from 1760–1840. These most clearly reveal insights about work culture at the height of the fur trade. A close examination reveals how traditional songs in the folk repertoire were extended and adapted with new material. The Ermatinger collection captures crude and spirited expressions of desire for women, food, and alcohol. It reflects the masculine work culture of the voyageurs, where groups of men travelled long distances together for months or years, leaving behind homes, loved ones, and a secure food supply. The voyageurs constructed overwhelmingly positive and idealistic scenarios in rhymed couplets at the end of standard folk songs, reflecting a distinct strategy for long-distance travel. Each hopeful syllable pushed the paddles onward. There are voyageur paddling songs with Indigenous influence and lyrics.[70] Pierre Falcon, "the bard of the prairies," worked in the fur trade canoes, a fact evident in his 1816 composition that became the Métis national anthem.[71]

Not only did the voyageurs frequently sing as they paddled, but they progressed along their routes with ritual soundways. Significant locations came to be defined by gunshots, prayers, songs, and oral stories. The most famous voyageur ballad from this period related to a long portage on the Ottawa River. The "Complaint de Jean Cadieux" tells the story of a voyageur left behind on Grant Calumet Island by his comrades to alone face hostile Iroquois. The song is from his perspective, describing a voyageur forced to dig his own grave with his paddle. He supposedly wrote this death song on birch bark and left it on the portage. Fears about abandonment and ambush were heightened on this long forest footpath on the Ottawa route. This song reflected and addressed these worries, instilling the values of solidarity and diligence. It supposedly presented real history, and it certainly taught real values to young voyageurs. On the "voyageur highway" from Montreal along the Ottawa, Mattawa, and French Rivers to Georgian Bay, and then along the north shore to Sault Ste Marie and Lake Superior to Grand Portage (Fort William after 1803), features were noted for their sound-making potential and often encountered with ritual soundways. There was a distinct progression on the westward journey from Montreal that reflected the deeper significance of moving individuals and groups away from European society and into Indigenous territory.

Fur traders working from 1760 to 1840 lived in close relations with Indigenous communities. They were observers and participants in Indigenous ceremonies, and they sometimes provided early ethnographic sketches. While Récollet and Jesuit missionaries in the Great Lakes region in the seventeenth century documented aspects of Indigenous musical cultures, they intended to leverage this knowledge for their missionary work. Their goal was to convert Indigenous peoples by transforming "pagan" culture. Fur traders ran no such interference. They listened to the songs of Indigenous warriors and medicine men, sometimes documenting their occurrence, effect, and reception. Some fur traders were curious, some were not; some were complimentary, some were disparaging; some wrote respectfully, others condemned "superstition"; some were culturally open, others were bigoted. Many of the ablest and most significant fur traders during this period were relatively culturally open-minded for their era, living for many years with Indigenous peoples, marrying into communities, and adopting many aspects of Indigenous culture into their work and travels. Fur traders had to be welcomed into local Indigenous communities to have much success. They received invitations to feasts and dances, exposing them to the social and spiritual practices of their hosts. Sometimes they described this as an unexpected imposition on their work duties, while other times they observed with keen interest. This was especially prevalent before 1821 when fur traders were competing for business. If a fur trader navigated the social interactions adeptly and did not offend the Indigenous community with whom he was trading, he was more likely to gain their trust and trade. He might be invited to their sacred ceremonies, such as the shaking tent, healing ceremonies, or Midéwiwin, spiritual practices that were significant to the community. Not only do fur trade accounts provide a sense of Indigenous cultures before substantial missionary activity and settler colonialism, but they also reveal that Indigenous ceremonies were meaningfully encountered, engaged with, and described by fur traders.

A note on sources and scope. While the musical encounters of oceanic voyages can be traced through the naval documentation of ships, the records from the fur trade are aggregated by company and individual. Many small outfits operated successfully over short periods of time and left few or no records. The prolific NWC left only fragmentary records, whereas the HBC produced and maintained a huge archive. Formal records were produced at HBC trading posts, but these rarely describe musical activities or soundways. Inventory lists are important sources and sometimes contain musical items. The letters, diaries, journals, and memoirs of fur traders in the St Lawrence and Hudson Bay fur trade constitute the main primary sources of this book. Published Indigenous oral history, such as that of Louis Bird and Peter Erasmus, is also referenced and incorporated into the analysis. Further research into oral history of the fur trade would deepen understandings of Indigenous perspectives and be a valuable future study. After years studying historical evidence from the fur trade, the chapters of this book took shape organically. I did not anticipate the outcomes of this research, or that gunpowder or Indigenous healing ceremonies, for instance, would become substantial topics. As an avenue of historical inquiry, "listening" to the past is inherently unpredictable and often does not align with contemporary expectations. I have attempted to contextualize the historical evidence without heavy-handed theoretical or interpretative frameworks, instead citing relevant studies and whenever possible letting the primary sources speak for themselves.

By listening, we can better understand the fur trade's social dynamics and cultural contours. As Mark Smith wrote in *Listening to Nineteenth-Century America*, "aurality was important enough to contribute meaningfully and significantly to the construction" of identities.[72] This was even more the case in the fur trade, whose participants were mostly non-literate and for whom the written word was not a primary medium of interaction. The spoken word stumbled on language barriers. In this context, music and dance played a particularly important role in relations and interactions. It helped define the activities and identities of masters, servants, hunters, voyageurs, and Indigenous peoples in the fur trade. Encounters had to be navigated, trust had to be built, and relationships had to be renewed. This frequently involved singing and dancing. Even with language barriers, the general idea or purpose of a song or dance was often believed to be understood. Music with the most cross-cultural resonance often had simple lyrics and vocables, while the most popular dance music at the trading posts, reels on the fiddle, was purely instrumental. By listening, we can hear the ways in which the fur trade went far beyond the mere exchange of material goods.

With a Bang:
Gunpowder and Firearms

"Like Thunder Over the Ice"

According to an Omushkego Cree oral tradition, their ancestors first *heard* Europeans arrive. Elder Louis Bird relates how, on the west coast of Hudson Bay, they first detected a "noise which resembled sound that comes when the ice pieces in the bay collide with each other." Yet it did not sound like ice churning, as "the sound was a booming sound like thunder at times."[1] Ice and thunder are frequently heard along the rocky shoreline of Hudson Bay. These sounds travelled tremendous distances. As the "booming" seemed familiar, the Omushkego initially paid it no particular attention. Yet, eventually, their familiarity with the auditory environment made them recognize something was amiss:

> These ancestors when they heard these things it never bother[ed] them – until one day – it was in the evening – they hear this thing. It was not the right conditions to hear an echo and the wind was not strong enough to make the ice pieces collide with each other. And they heard this thing in the evening, and they became to hear it coming over and over so rapidly – and then they looked. They went to the high ground and look at where the sound come from – and it was late in the evening – and they actually saw the lightning on the Water. But by this time they couldn't see no sails or anything – just the light on the water, a lightning sort of thing. And that's what scares them. And they now begin to think there is a thing there – there is something.[2]

Sounds had drawn the Cree to the water, but darkness had prevented them from seeing the ships that produced the "lightning." While the sounds resembled ice colliding, their distinct rhythm, "coming over and over so rapidly," distinguished them. According to the oral history, it was years before the Omushkego learned that "when they would hear that booming sound, it was the cannon." Overhearing voices, they discovered that the sailing vessels that made these sounds were controlled by people.[3] The origin of the new booming sounds that occurred at unusual times and with inexplicable rhythms had been determined. It was a history worth telling and re-telling.

Hudson Bay's topography gave the sounds of the cannon a special auditory quality. When Lieutenant Edward Chappell of the Royal Navy accompanied HBC ships and became enveloped in thick fog, they fired three shots to signal to the rest of the convoy. At the report, the crew was "astonished." "The explosion issued like thunder over the ice; then appeared to roll rumbling back towards the ship; bellowing forth again in tremendous peals. The echo died way in distant reverberation."[4] The sound was augmented by the environment, amplified into a remarkable sound that echoed with tremendous magnitude over the low terrain. This became a familiar sound in Hudson Bay after the HBC received its Royal Charter in 1670.

As the fur trade developed over the following two centuries, cannons and muskets regularly punctuated the soundscape. The sounds they produced came to possess a variety of meanings for European and Indigenous peoples. Gunpowder was used not only in hunting and warfare, but also for communication as a means of signalling and saluting. Firearms were, by nature of the business, a central part of every fur trader's cargo and played into virtually every interaction. Guns, shot, and gunpowder, heavy though they were, were essential items commonly transported to the distant reaches of the trading post networks. Indigenous communities encountered and gained access to them at different times. Muskets revolutionized hunting and warfare in North America, and so too did they transform travel and trade.

Guns broadcast information across the acoustic space surrounding and between trading posts. They signalled the presence of fur traders, with their retinues of trade goods. An Indigenous fur trade in North America existed long before the arrival of Europeans. But after the French and English established themselves in the St Lawrence and Hudson Bay, it never sounded the same. As we shall see in later chapters, fur traders adapted to Indigenous protocols such as gift-giving and pipe ceremonies. Indigenous peoples adopted muskets and aspects of the ceremonialism introduced into their communities by fur traders. In this era, European military tactics were predicated on the combination of musketry into coordinated volleys on the battlefield, known to have a powerful auditory effect that could turn the tide of battle. Gunpowder was no less potent along lakes and rivers, yet its functions and effects were much different.

In northeastern North America in the seventeenth century, Indigenous peoples were forced to adapt to repeated European incursions. Imperial competition between England and France produced numerous voyages of exploration, trade, and alliance-making. Both the St Lawrence and Hudson Bay witnessed sieges, skirmishes, and fortified establishments change hands. Samuel de Champlain built the fortifications at Quebec City on an imposing hill overlooking the St Lawrence during the 1620s. From there, the French commanded the river and restricted European access to the Great Lakes. Yet they also had to navigate a complicated diplomacy with Indigenous Nations.

Almost immediately, the French became involved in alliances and military entanglements. They made peace with the Montagnais, Algonquin, and Huron-Wendat, but this pulled them into conflict with the Haudenosaunee. In the battles Champlain fought alongside his allies, he described his muskets shattering the wooden armour that protected the Haudenosaunee chieftains. Yet his accounts also indicate that muskets had an auditory effect that went far beyond their physical efficacy. In one battle, on encountering fierce resistance, he wrote that "neantmoins nous leur montrasmes ce qu'ils n'auoeient iamais veu, ny oüy."[5] The sounds were intended to cause terror, "car aussi-tost qu'ils nous veirent, & entendirent les coups d'harquebuse, & les balles siffler à leurs oreilles, ils se retirerent promptement en leur fort, emportant leurs morts."[6] Champlain attributed the enemy retreat largely to the sounds of French firearms. He stated that his Huron-Wendat allies could attack far ahead when they had a few French arquebusiers. These gunmen were, apparently, "greatly feared and dreaded."[7] The psychological impact of firearms upon those unfamiliar is evident, rendering long guns that were fairly inaccurate and slow to reload into objects of great terror.

The Haudenosaunee soon became familiar with firearms and, to the chagrin of the French, masters of them. Their supply lay to the southeast with the Dutch who colonized the Hudson River and established trading posts. By the 1630s, the Dutch began supplying large numbers of flintlock muskets upriver into what is now northern New York State. The flintlock was much more dependable and easier to maintain than the guns used by Champlain. When the trigger was pulled, the flint struck steel and produced a spark that ignited the gunpowder in the small pan that led to the charge in the chamber. It became the firing mechanism and musket of choice in the fur trade for the next two hundred years. The bow and arrow remained a part of Haudenosaunee culture as reliable, accurate, silent, and deadly weapons, and an experienced archer could exceed the shooting speed of the fastest gunman using a single-shot, muzzle-loading firearm.[8] For these and other reasons some historians have questioned the degree to which muskets represented an improvement and replacement for bows and arrows in Indigenous cultures.[9] Yet, as David J. Silverman details in his book *Thundersticks: Firearms and the Violent Transformation of Native America*, firearms were key to the intertribal jockeying and violence that escalated in northeastern North America and the Great Plains from the 1600s to 1700s.[10] From the time of the Dutch trade in the 1630s, flintlock muskets proved devastating, particularly when used against other Indigenous Nations who did not have access, such as the Erie and Neutral. Flintlock muskets facilitated the Haudenosaunee becoming the dominant military power in northeastern North America, as they effectively utilized this technology to raid, attack, disperse, and adopt by force neighbouring Indigenous peoples.[11] The military imbalance these guns produced contributed to the near cataclysm of the Huron-Wendat when the Haudenosaunee invaded their territory in 1648–49.

European forts were inherently vulnerable to siege by ship. In the St Lawrence, despite Champlain's fortifications at Quebec, the river was blockaded in 1628 and Quebec City was captured in 1629 by the Kirke brothers. The great cannons and impregnable hilltop position proved no remedy for a sustained siege, as incoming supplies were halted. This same vulnerability existed in Hudson Bay, where lifelines to Britain were tenuous. The HBC was slow to gain a permanent foothold on the shores of Hudson Bay. In 1670–71, English ships passed the winter in the bay but did not establish a permanent presence. By 1675, the HBC overwintered two ships in the bay, including the guard ship *Rupert* armed with twelve guns.[12] The French *coureurs de bois* reached Hudson Bay and were trading in the hinterland of Fort Albany and Moose Factory from the late seventeenth century.[13] Ships could also reach the bay from France. The HBC prioritized building forts along the Hudson Bay coast at mouths of strategic rivers. The ships destined for the bay carried bricks and mortar as well as "great Gunns."[14]

Despite the HBC's enormous efforts and expenses in constructing and fortifying their posts during the first fifteen years, the French, led by Chevalier de Troyes, captured them all relatively easily in the summer of 1686. Although Moose Fort had strong bastions and ten cannons, it was captured in half an hour. Fort Charles and Albany were taken soon afterwards.[15] The English efforts to fortify their posts had been in vain, yet this did not prevent renewed efforts. When York Fort was refortified in 1723, stone-faced bastions were erected and more guns were sent out.[16] While the HBC was challenged by the French traders in the hinterlands upriver, their posts on Hudson Bay were rarely again confronted by rival trading companies or imperial foes. The forts' cannons would be used regularly over the following century, but not for the purposes of war.

Interacting with Thunderbirds

As we saw at the beginning of this chapter, the Omushkego Cree first interpreted the sounds of the cannons as ice colliding on Hudson Bay. This natural effect produced a "booming sound like thunder." However, they realized this was not the source and that something else on the water was creating the sounds. What was this "lightning sort of thing?" Before firing, the cannons would extend out of the hulls of the ships. Their dramatic ignition could be seen, with a bright flash and billowing smoke, and the report was heard over long distances. The mysterious appearance of this phenomenon on the water with unknown origin "scare[d]" the Omushkego for some time, until it was observed up close. Eventually, the ships and cannons became familiar.[17] The sounds were perceived by the Cree as "like thunder," which was a similar interpretation to Lieutenant Chappell's observations of cannons echoing "like thunder over the ice."[18] The English and Cree compared the sounds of cannons to thunder, yet their conceptions of how thunder was produced were very different.

In the 1600s, most European and Indigenous peoples attributed thunder to the activity of supernatural beings. The European mythology of the ancient world personified thunder as broadcasting the activities and emotions of the gods Donner, Thor, and Zeus. Only supernatural figures could produce sounds that were "well outside the human scale of soundmaking."[19] In Christendom, thunder symbolized God's activities and the tremendous gulf between God and man. In seventeenth-century New England, it was the sound rather than the flash that was interpreted as possessing the destructive force of lightning. It was thought by the Puritans to be commanded by God, or sometimes demons.[20] In the eighteenth century came the recognition that the potentially harmful effects of lightning came from the flash rather than the sound.[21]

To many Indigenous peoples in northern North America, thunder was created by powerful non-human beings. Louis Bird speaks about the centrality of thunder and lightning to Cree cosmology and the importance of thunderbirds. Omushkego oral traditions describe shamans who through their dreams attained powers beyond those of ordinary people and could connect with these beings. Shamans mastered a significant body of knowledge and techniques, but only the "highest level ... can control the thunderbird."[22] These traditions speak of powerful shamans controlling lightning to defeat enemies. Yet this was reserved for the few who had "acquired the knowledge of the thunderbird." Louis Bird describes thunderbirds as "very highly regarded as being part of the power of all First Nations people in Canada," a common thread that connected Indigenous cosmologies. "No matter where I have gone," he stated, "the thunderbird is always highly regarded and respected."[23]

The traditional worldviews of Anishinaabeg and Cree living from the Great Plains to the Subarctic were replete with symbols, beliefs, and practices alive with the presence of other-than-human people called *manitous* or *manitouk*.[24] These beings were encountered in dreams or visions, and they shaped how people operated in the world. In traditional stories, the thunderbirds that created thunder in the sky were thought to be in perpetual warfare with the underwater serpents and water-lynx. These beings were potentially helpful or malevolent and had to be treated with caution and respect.[25] Small sacrifices and offerings were left for these spirits at dangerous rapids and while passing along rivers and lakes.[26] Ultimately, in most Cree and Anishinaabe narrations the thunderers are represented as the allies and advocates of humans while the aquatic subterranean creatures such as giant lynxes and horned snakes are more often malevolent and dangerous.[27] Thunder spirits were dangerous and powerful spirit guardians closely associated with success in war and medicine. Thunderbirds played a role in how the Anishinaabeg and Cree conceptualized and understood their acoustic environment. The sounds of thunder signalled "the arrival of powerful people."[28] Tobacco was burned as an offering and to encourage them to move on. Thunderbirds are important to the Midéwiwin or Grand Medicine Society, a central component of traditional Anishinaabe religious life. Shared with other Indigenous Nations such as the Sioux and Cree is the notion that they caused thunderstorms and resembled very large eagle-like birds.[29] With the arrival of the fur trade, gunpowder became interwoven into relationships with these non-human beings.

This relationship would become documented in some of the written accounts of the fur trade. John Tanner was a Kentuckian who was captured as a child and grew up with Anishinaabeg peoples. He would become involved with various companies in the fur trade and provided the insights of someone who moved between Euro-American and Indigenous cultures.[30] He described early one spring when a severe thunderstorm roused him and those he was travelling with from their sleep. An Indigenous man named Pich-e-to, "becoming much alarmed at the violence of the storm, got up and offered some tobacco to the thunder, intreating it to stop." Tanner explains and describes thunderbirds: "The Ojibbeways and Ottawwaws believe that thunder is the voice of living beings, which they call An-nim-me-keeg. Some considered them to be like men, while others say they have more resemblance to birds."[31] Tobacco was burned as an offering to the non-human beings that controlled the thunder in an effort to stop or divert the storm by encouraging the thunderbirds to move on. Tobacco was likely a pre-contact method of interaction, while the fur trade's introduction of gunpowder augmented Indigenous methods of communication with these non-human beings.

Documented instances of Indigenous peoples using firearms to interact with thunderbirds suggest that this technology was incorporated broadly into Indigenous cosmologies based on its sound-making capacity. Based on oral interviews of Anishinaabe people, Theresa Smith documented that "when a thunderstorm appears especially violent, some people say that it is because the Thunderbirds are flying too low."[32] Informants indicated that when this would happen, some among the older generation would shoot into the sky. Was it the shot or the auditory report of gunpowder that was thought to influence the thunderbirds? That it was the sound is suggested by the following account: "I saw my dad do this one time. He got the muzzle loader and fired into the air to scare them up. Boy! It was lightning and raining. Coming down! Coming down! They were so low you could almost hear their wings flapping; they were too low. No! Nothing. It did not work. So he said, 'I'll try shooting up again a little later.' Then he loaded up his gun the second time and shot it into the air again. You know the storm died right away; it went off into the east."[33] The Anishinaabe elder used the gun to scare the thunderbirds and influence the thunderstorm.

Momentous Build-Up

While cannons produced the loudest reports, the soundscape was more significantly transformed by small arms. In many Indigenous communities, the arrival of muskets preceded the arrival of fur traders. Gunpowder made the largest impression on those with no prior exposure or experience to guns. When fur traders did arrive, the sound of gunpowder was almost invariably their most prominent auditory trademark. Firearms placed remarkable sound-making capacity in human hands that was extended to fur traders, voyageurs, servants, and Indigenous peoples. Muskets enabled individuals to easily create loud reports that could carry kilometres through forests, over plains, and along rivers. They developed signalling and ceremonial functions that would play an important role in the fur trade.

Some Indigenous peoples have maintained oral traditions about their initial encounters with firearms. The Blackfoot encountered both horses and guns before they met Europeans. An oral tradition attributes the first encounter with guns to an exchange with the Cree: "One time a party of Blackfeet were in the woods north of the Saskatchewan. They heard a frightening noise and began to run away. Some Crees, who had made the noise by shooting a gun, motioned to the Blackfeet and told them to come to them. The Crees then showed the Blackfeet how to load a gun from the muzzle and to fire it by pulling the trigger."[34] After obtaining muskets themselves, a Blackfoot war party attacking the Crows and Shoshonis employed firearms to tremendous effect. When the Crows and Shoshonis heard the noise of the guns, they were so frightened that they left their tipis, horses, and equipment behind, fleeing southward from their camp near present day Calgary. According to this tradition, the Blackfoot subsequently drove the Crows, Snakes, Flatheads, and Nez Percés from the Bow River southward beyond the Sweetgrass Hills, through the "noise of these guns alone."[35] Historian Arthur Ray suggests that initial demand for muskets was "quite high, since they had great shock value." Firearms exerted "pressures that were out of proportion to the actual effectiveness of the guns."[36] Indigenous hunters travelled long distances, for instance from the northern Plains to Hudson Bay, to trade for guns. Firearms were a highly valued commodity the fur traders provided whose sounds reverberated far beyond the surroundings of the trading posts.

Firearms and ammunition formed a significant portion of the fur trader's merchandise. In value and volume, it was usually second only to textiles and clothing. Supplies were quite variable during the French period in the Great Lakes and tied to supply networks that were prone to interruption during times of war.[37] Estimates of French cargoes departing for the Great Lakes in the 1670s indicate that between 320 and 440 guns were shipped annually, increasing to between 680 and 1040 by the 1690s.[38] Estimates for the HBC in the last three decades of the seventeenth century indicate between 10,000 and 16,000 guns were acquired for the trade with Indigenous peoples in North America.[39] These figures suggest the significance and scope of the firearms trade from an early date.

The development of the large *canots du maître* by the 1720s increased the size of cargoes. In 1732, as the French were leading up to war against the Fox, 509 livres worth, or 36 per cent, of the cargo sent to Detroit was comprised of arms and ammunition. The number fell to 68 livres, or only 8 per cent, of the cargo in 1736 when war with the Fox had died down. The 1740s saw an increase in the trade of firearms and ammunition to the western end of the Great Lakes. At Green Bay, arms and ammunition made up 2,549 livres worth or 30 per cent of cargo in 1740, and 3,049 livres or 15 per cent in 1747.[40] This was the lead-up to the Seven Years' War (1756–63), in which the French distributed and traded unprecedented amounts of munitions to their Indigenous allies and trading partners. The French militia officer Le Mercier informed his superiors in Paris that if the French were "unable to provide them [Indians] with guns, we would soon see them abandoning the French and throwing themselves on the side of the English. This article [firearms] and our gunpowder are what keeps them, to a greater extent, bound to us."[41] In 1759 alone, two thousand guns were sent to Canada; New France and Louisiana combined to give five hundred and trade four thousand muskets to Indigenous allies, while also distributing 1,400 tons of powder.[42] The Seven Years' War increased the supply of guns, gunpowder, and shot from the St Lawrence network, and yet a major de-escalation did not follow. The market for firearms was strong and the British fur trade became the primary conduit of supply.

Gun makers in France and England began designing and manufacturing guns specifically for Indigenous consumers. They produced relatively short, lightweight, smoothbore muskets with sturdy flintlocks, often called in the early period "fusils."[43] By the mid-late eighteenth century, this style of fur trade musket became largely standardized throughout British North America. It was known variously as the "North West gun," "Hudson's Bay fuke," "Mackinaw gun," or "Trading gun." Due to their smoothbore barrels, these muskets could fire makeshift projectiles when ammunition was low. They were commonly gauged from .58 calibre to .67 calibre, or large enough for a one-ounce ball. The trigger guard was designed extra-large to permit operation by a gloved or mittened hand, a feature introduced by the HBC in 1741.[44] This firearm profile was well-suited to the northern landscape, both for canoe travel and portage as well as horseback. While many western Indigenous communities continued traditional hunting techniques with bows and arrows and animal pounds, firearms became used in the hunt, including of bison.[45] That this gun evolved to fit the needs of Indigenous hunters and warriors and was standardized by the later 1700s is a testament to the long history of firearms as important objects in gift-giving and cross-cultural trade. Muskets were commonly provided by the NWC and HBC to Indigenous hunters in exchange for furs or on credit.[46] Getting guns into Indigenous hunters' hands encouraged the fur trade and in turn transformed the soundscape.

Fig. 1.1 North West gun, ca 1813–20. Converted from flintlock to percussion. Lockplate marked Wheeler & Son. Barrel top marked London with North West Company mark.

The most distinctive decorative feature of these North West guns is their sideplate, which is designed like a serpent. Dragon and serpentine motifs appear on European guns from the early seventeenth century along with other heraldry such as mascarons, leaves, and flowers. It is unclear how the serpent became the standardized motif for the Indigenous market in the eighteenth century. While the serpent motif had European precedents, like other aspects of the gun it likely attempted to cater to Indigenous tastes. Some have suggested that Indigenous customers viewed the mark as meaning that the article was genuine.[47] It has also been suggested that Indigenous peoples viewed firearms as manifestations of the thunderbird and the horned underwater serpent. This is reflected in northeastern North American Indigenous languages, where the word for gun translates as "Thundersticks" and "Thunderbolt" and "Metal-Lightning."[48] Like powerful non-human beings, guns could strike from afar. The metal of guns and bullets resembled the metallic scales of the horned underwater serpent. The serpent was traditionally depicted as having both metallic copper and flint scales, and the flint of the musket's firing mechanism evoked the substance the serpents used in defence against the thunderbirds.[49] Gun bags and ammunition pouches crafted by Indigenous peoples sometimes had images of horned underwater serpents and/or thunderbirds, reinforcing this connection. Silverman argues that these beliefs were sustained because muskets consistently produced lethal results.[50]

It may have been expected that the supply of guns would have dropped after the cessation of hostilities after the Seven Years' War. However, fur traders peddled large quantities via the St Lawrence to Great Lakes route. The records indicate that in 1769 Maurice Blondeau obtained a licence for three canoes to "Michilimackinac and La Mer de l'Ouest" including a cargo of 800 lb. of gunpowder and 14 ½ cwt. ball and shot, as well as twenty-four guns. Lawrence Ermatinger sent two canoes with 500 lb. gunpowder, 1,000 lb. ball and shot, and sixteen guns.[51] In 1770, Blondeau sent 1,100 lb. of gunpowder and 17 cwt. ball and shot, while Benjamin Frobisher sent 1,100 lb. of gunpowder and 24 cwt. ball and shot to Michilimackinac and Grand Portage. In 1772, Benjamin and Joseph Frobisher sent 1,400 lb. of gunpowder, 22 12 cwt. of ball and shot. By 1774, these numbers increased further, including cargoes of 1,500 lb. gunpowder for Maurice Blondeau and 1,700 lb. of gunpowder and 2,100 lb. ball and shot from Benjamin Frobisher.[52] In 1775, Lawrence Ermatinger sent 2,000 lb. of gunpowder and 3,600 lb. of ball and shot.[53] The need to replace broken guns and provide a continual supply of powder and shot meant that a considerable portion of the fur traders' cargo was inevitably devoted to these items. These numbers provide a sense of the degree to which the soundscape was affected by the fur trade's most potent sound-making material.

By the late eighteenth century, Indigenous peoples from the Great Lakes to the Pacific Ocean and the Subarctic were supplied with guns and ammunition through the fur trade. Guns had been adopted by the "Home Guard" Cree around Hudson Bay as well as the Assiniboine and Cree in the woodlands and northern Plains. Once the trading post networks had reached the western Plains, the Blackfoot were able to access guns directly. Yet they, along with the Siksika and Gros Ventres, periodically raided NWC and HBC trading posts on the western Plains from the 1790s to the 1820s because they also supplied the Cree with guns.[54] They were responding to frightful episodes such as a summer attack in 1793 in which a mixed Cree-Assiniboine force of more than one thousand men reportedly massacred 150 lodges of Gros Ventres.[55] Indigenous Nations on the western Plains had access to firearms by the height of fur trade competition in the late eighteenth and early nineteenth centuries. A result is that the sound of gunshots was a regular feature of fur traders' working environment. When travelling near the Rocky Mountains, fur trader Archibald McDonald reported that he "heard a shot in the afternoon." Its source was not identified, but it was nonetheless noteworthy.[56] The fur traders travelled and worked in an altered soundscape that they helped create.

By the end of the eighteenth century, guns had been familiar across the northern Plains for decades. Yet coastal Indigenous Nations were still relatively unacquainted. When Alexander Mackenzie made his historic voyages to the Pacific and Arctic Oceans in the final decades of the eighteenth century, he and his fellow NWC crew were heavily armed. He engaged in fur trade diplomacy with the Nuxalk people along the Bella Coola river in 1793. He reported that communication was "awkward and inconvenient," and "carried entirely by signs, as there was not a person with me who was qualified for the office as an interpreter."[57] On his first arrival at their village, "they requested us not to discharge our fire-arms, lest the report should frighten away the salmon."[58] This remarkable request demonstrates that the Nuxalk were already aware of firearms and their auditory effects, and were wary of them. Salmon was central to their existence and culture, vital to their physical and spiritual well-being. After spending considerable time with a Nuxalk man curious about his equipment, Mackenzie reported he "frequently repeated the unpleasant intelligence that he had been shot at by people of my colour."[59] How the man did this without spoken language is not recorded, but it may well have involved the use of sounds.

Continuing down the Bella Coola River to the Pacific Ocean, Mackenzie passed through this same village on his return. Canoes customarily stopped shortly before arrival to arrange appearances and prepare. "As it was uncertain what our reception might be at the village, I examined every man's arms and ammunition, and gave Mr Mackay, who had unfortunately lost his gun, one of my pistols."[60] Encountering the village "in a state of perfect tranquility," Mackenzie ordered his men to put down their guns and not fire a salute. Whether he heeded the Nuxalk's request in order not to frighten the salmon is unknown, but it is noteworthy that neither he nor his men fired their guns on arrival. Later during this visit, the Nuxalk "expressed a wish that I should explain the use and management of them [firearms]," and Mackenzie obliged. According to his account, he fired one of his pistols at a target, landing four out of five buckshot. The Nuxalk reacted with "extreme astonishment and admiration."[61] The suspicion and fear about the shocking auditory effects of gunfire were overridden for some Nuxalk by observing their accuracy and power. This indicated a relatively quick reversal on the issue of firearms from a community initially opposed. There may have been Nuxalk who continued to object, but the return of the fur traders convinced some in the community of the utility of this powerful new technology.

Feu de Joie

When a group of people shot into the air as a salute or celebration it was known as *feu de joie*. This term was employed by both the French and English from at least the seventeenth century, with the French associating it more with celebratory fire. The English sometimes called it "joy sound" and used it to refer to rippled or sequential firing more generally.[62] A nineteenth-century *Dictionary of Nautical Terms* defines it simply as "to return a salute."[63] Hudson Bay and the St Lawrence served as the major conduits through which firearms, and the cultural practices associated with them, spread throughout northern North America. Firearm salutes date to the fourteenth and fifteenth centuries in Europe, when firing at a distance and slow reload times meant guns would be empty when entering firing range. This served to ease tensions, lessening the potential for accidental or premeditated discharge. The custom became institutionalized in Europe, and systems of honours evolved that granted high military and civil officials specific numbers of gun salutes. In the British military tradition, the number increased with rank by odd numbers up to twenty-one.[64] In the fur trade, the *feu de joie* was less formal and referred to the act of firing guns in celebration or salute at the arrival or departure of a ship, boat, canoe brigade, or Indigenous trading party.

The fleets and forts of the HBC and NWC employed gunpowder to signal and commemorate arrivals and departures of ships and canoes. For Euro-Canadians in the distant reaches of fur trade country, communications and lifelines were tenuous, and ceremonies of arrival and departure took on heightened importance. Arrivals sometimes had life or death significance, bringing crucial food, supplies, trading goods, and gunpowder. For fur traders and Indigenous peoples living near trading posts, gunshots signalled the arrival of new supplies and people. They marked moments of great significance and celebration, beyond mere pomp and ceremony. Successful transatlantic voyages by ship and transcontinental voyages by canoe represented significant victories over inherent dangers. Arrivals and departures were key events for those in and around the trading posts, and they were emphasized in the soundscape with gunpowder. In the 1760s, when Peter Pond's fleet of the "Largest" canoes in the country was spotted over a mile and a half (2.41 kilometres) away from Mackinac, he described how "ye Cannon of the Garreson Began to Play Smartley," and continued until they "Reacht ye Shore."[65] Pond does not mention if he returned the salute, but this auditory reception broadcast his approach and would have allowed for those at the fort to prepare for his arrival.

Fur traders travelling through Indigenous territory in the 1760s were in a different world than the *coureurs de bois* of the previous century. Now Indigenous peoples might salute fur traders with firearms. Arriving at an Odawa town on the island of Grand Traverse near Michilimackinac in 1766, Jonathan Carver was received in a manner altogether bewildering and shocking to his senses. "But what appears extremely singular to me at the time, and must do so to every person unacquainted with the customs of the Indians, was the reception I met with on landing. As our canoes approached the shore, and had reached within about three score rods of it, the Indians began a feu-de-joy; in which they fired their pieces loaded with balls; but at the same time they took care to discharge them in such a manner as to fly a few yards above our heads; during this they ran from one tree or stump to another, shouting and behaving as if they were in the heat of battle."[66] Carver was taken aback and "on the point of ordering my attendants to return their fire, concluding that their intentions were hostile." Luckily, the intervention of some fur traders prevented bloodshed. They relayed that "this was their usual method of receiving the chiefs of other nations." Carver realized this was a gesture of respect, although it still proved intimidating. The notion that firearms could be used in unfamiliar ways and this custom of saluting in particular seems to have surprised Carver in his early career. Nothing in his military experience had trained him for this reception at the Odawa village on Grand Traverse Island.

Fur trader George Nelson recalls a reception at Fort Dauphin on Lake Winnipeg that thoroughly shocked his senses. The Cree waiting at the fort had carefully prepared their appearances for his arrival. He described their painted faces and ornamented bodies as "hideous" and "barbarous indeed," but stated that it "became them well" and conveyed a "wild yet pleasing effect." The visual depiction was accompanied by a description of a remarkable auditory salute. He writes that when he "entered the river they greeted us with cries de joie, + when we reached the beach they came running down with their guns in their hands, load + firing over our heads, between us + under our Canoes sending the water flying in sprays over our heads. It was certainly a 'wild delight,' but not without a little danger, lest the guns might burst."[67] While a musket salute was expected on arrival, the way it was delivered surprised and alarmed Nelson. It was an intense sensory experience.

This soundway may have been linked to a more widespread Indigenous custom of gathering war parties. John Tanner, while on an expedition from Red River, observed a cross-cultural encounter between Cree, Assiniboine, and Anishinaabeg war parties that he estimated to number around one thousand people. How firearm salutes would be conducted was of utmost importance and something of a delicate matter. There was a consultation among the chiefs as to the appropriate "ceremony of salutation to be used." The difficulty was that a very large number of warriors were involved.[68] Tanner wrote that "it is customary for war parties engaged in the same cause, or friendly to each other, when they meet, to exchange a few shots by way of a sham battle, in which they use all the jumping, the whooping, and yelling of a real fight."[69] In this case, the chiefs decided to override this custom because the group was so large that there was potential for real violence. Although Tanner does not specify exactly what happened, the assembled chiefs proposed "to use a different method of exchanging compliments in meeting" on that occasion.[70] This example demonstrates that firearms were employed in Indigenous military and diplomatic ceremonies and that the protocols were adaptable and negotiated by chiefs. Yet the style of "mock warfare" described here may have been related to the Indigenous style of *feu de joie* recorded by fur traders.

By the end of the eighteenth century, gunfire salutes appear to have been standardized into fur traders' ceremonial relations with most Indigenous Nations. Andrew Graham was a fur trader who worked for twenty-four years at York Factory. He described the arrival of an Indigenous canoe flotilla from the interior: "This being settled they re-embark and soon after appear in sight of the Fort, to the number of between ten and twenty in a line abreast of each other. If there is but one captain his station is in the centre, but if more they are in the wings also; and their canoes are distinguished from the rest by a small St George or Union Jack, hoisted on a stick placed in the stern of the vessel. At the distance of four or five hundred yards is another fleet marshalled in the same manner; others behind them and so on until they are all come. Several fowling-pieces are discharged from the canoes to salute the Fort, and the compliment is returned by a round of twelve pounders, less or more for each division, and the Great Flag flying from the Fort, as it continues to do every day they stay."[71] This momentous arrival at the end of a long voyage of hundreds of kilometres was broadcast across the landscape. It is noteworthy that the first signals came from the canoes themselves. These musket shots were considered a "compliment," and the cannons of the fort returned the salute. The flotillas prepared to depart after spending a few days at the post, and they were treated in a similar ceremonial way. The captains were given gifts that included a new gun, half a pound of powder and shot conform, tools, hawks bells, and other items. These items signalled the honour of gift-giving and reinforced the Indigenous captain's status. On their departure, the cannons of the fort were fired "as a final gesture of respect."[72] Here the fur trader identified the sentiment intended by the parting salute. These honours would have been heard and felt by all parties in vicinity of the fort.

In 1794–95 Duncan M'Gillivray of the NWC described Indigenous hunters approaching Fort George on the Saskatchewan River. They announced their arrival with gunshots. "At a few yards distance from the gate they salute us with several discharges of their guns, which is answered by hoisting a flag and firing a few guns. On entering the house they are disarmed, treated with a few drams and a bit of tobacco."[73] The exchange of firearm salutes on approach was followed by gift-giving on arrival, another activity that fostered reciprocity and trust. Indigenous trading parties arriving at posts sometimes sent advance messengers to obtain gunpowder to enable a proper salute. This was described by one fur trader as a "practice introduced by the Canadian traders." Yet it clearly took on an Indigenous form, as the "few small gifts" retrieved included tobacco, paint, and gunpowder. When the larger group was "within a few yards of the gate, the Indians salute the traders with several discharges of their guns. This is answered by hoisting a flag and firing a few guns."[74] On Slave Lake in what is now the Northwest Territories, James Porter, an overwintering fur trader, wrote in his journal for the year 1800–01 that when sixteen Red Knives (Dene) arrived at the fort, he "Gave them the usual honours. Hoisted our flag and fired a few shots."[75] This suggests the extension of the custom of firearm salutes to Indigenous Nations far removed from Hudson Bay and the St Lawrence.

Sometimes fur traders denied advance requests for gunpowder. This indicated a problem with the relationship. The journal of an unnamed NWC fur trader in the Pine River district includes the following entry: "This morning 2 Young men arrived from L'Homme Seul's band; they informed me that the Gauché's band have joined the others; and L'H. Seul sent them for some powder to fire on his arrival here." An advance party arriving and expecting small gifts of gunpowder before the arrival of the group would hardly be worthy of note. Yet the anonymous fur trader reported sternly, "but I did not think it proper to send him any," explaining his rationale for breaking with convention. He "harangued" the group upon their arrival, saying they should be "ashamed of the scandalous hunt they have made since they were here last."[76] This denial of gunpowder and the ensuing silent and unceremonious arrival of the group at the post signalled that something was amiss. Mutual honours had not been exchanged. While we do not know enough about this occasion to assess it properly, clearly the fur trader felt he was validated in withholding the gunpowder due to what he deemed were poor returns from the hunt. Yet the Indigenous trading party may have felt that they were betrayed by their supposed ally and trading partner. Withholding gunpowder demonstrated the fur trader's power and control over firearm materials. Yet it also breached protocol and expectations for the Indigenous group, who may have decided to trade their furs elsewhere in the future.

Important fur traders of the NWC were honoured in their comings and goings with *feu de joie*. Alexander Mackenzie provided a description of his departures and receptions at trading posts, which were noisy affairs involving gunpowder. He reported departing from Mr Finlay "under several vollies of musketry."[77] He described his reception back at Fort Chipewyan after his historic traverse of the Rocky Mountains to the Pacific Ocean in the summer of 1793. "At length, as we rounded a point, and came in view of the Fort, we threw out our flag, and accompanied it with a general discharge of our fire-arms; while the men were in such spirits, and made such an active use of their paddles, that we arrived before the two men whom we left here in the spring, could recover their senses to answer us." Mackenzie's appearance and rapid advance outpaced the time it took to prepare the return salute. He does not specify whether the flag was the Union Jack or the NWC's colours. That his salute went unanswered foreshadows his later experience of receiving a muted public response to his historic voyages.[78]

The use of firearms in the travel culture of fur traders could have negative consequences in their relationships with Indigenous peoples. A loud musket report could be interpreted variously. Alexander Mackenzie described some NWC employees discharging their firearms as his canoe was pushing off up the Mackenzie River, a familiar gesture to commemorate a significant departure. Yet this terrified his newly acquired Indigenous guide: "As we were pushing off some of My Men fired a Couple of Guns load[ed] with Powder at the Report of which the Indians were startled, having never heard or seen any thing of the kind before." If this was all, it may have been a minor episode, but Mackenzie described how it almost made the man reconsider his participation in his expedition: "This had like to have prevented our Indian to fulfil his promise, but our Indians made him understand that what we had done was as a Sign of Friendship & prevail'd on him to embark."[79] Gunshots as honours or salutes were not obviously friendly signals to the unacquainted. They could be regarded as startling and ominous signs of aggression. Thus, their true significance and intention had to be communicated across cultures, something that historically played out in a myriad of ways.

On the Pacific coast, ship captains used their cannons for various auditory functions related to the fur trade. Writing in 1799, William Sturgis reported using cannons to draw the attention of Indigenous peoples: "We shall inform them of our arrival by our great Guns."[80] Where there was competition between ships, Sturgis was explicit that they were using their guns to signal their presence to Indigenous peoples. This method was also used by the HBC. James Douglas described sounding "guns of invitation" and offering "friendly salute[s]" in an attempt to alert Indigenous people to his presence and trade.[81] The continuity of this custom is noteworthy and suggests it must have had some efficacy. Certainly, it would have prompted investigation by Indigenous people who heard the auditory reports. It may have served to invite trade, but it also undoubtedly scared some away, people who likely were not noticed and did not make it into the written record. Cannon shots carried the inherent implication – and potential reality – of force. They were used as a warning to other rival European traders, simultaneously broadcasting and delineating a ship's trading territory.[82] By utilizing the auditory power of gunpowder to invite Indigenous people to trade while warding off other Europeans, ships on the west coast made prominent use of the sound-making capacity of their cannons. The potential for ambiguity and misinterpretation was great.

Salutes became so institutionalized in the fur trade's operations that their failure to proceed according to custom was noteworthy. In the fur traders' accounts, this kind of event would be subject to commentary and explanation. Francis Ermatinger made note of an abnormal departure from Fort Vancouver, commenting that "in passing the Fort the Men discharged their pieces and a salute of Canon was returned upon our embarking, but the Captain of the Eagle being either taken upon short notice, or what is more probable being out of powder, instead of one round of Guns gave us three of cheers."[83] Either short notice or a lack of powder were given as explanations for the substitution of the cheers for the customary departing salute. The salute had to be acknowledged and sound had to be returned, so cheers were sufficient.

HBC governor George Simpson referred to salutes as "honours." He described interacting with Indigenous peoples such as "Poucecoupee & Lezett's bands," who left to go to their winter hunting grounds: "When putting off from the shore, they honoured us by hoisting their colours and discharging some vollies of fire arms, which we returned." Here the gunshots seem to have been interpreted cross-culturally as honouring gestures. Simpson returned the salute. He was eager to impress and maintain allegiance with these nine or ten skilled hunters, who he thought would "do great things this Winter."[84] Robert Longmoor of the HBC instructed his men on one occasion to "salute them in the usual form."[85] These examples support the notion that firearm salutes between fur traders and Indigenous hunters were well-established honouring systems.

The custom of the *feu de joie* unified the soundways of the Hudson Bay and St Lawrence fur trade. In the 1820s, Archibald McDonald described York Factory's cannons as producing loud signals that had symbolic meaning. He described the fort's mounted artillery as consisting of "four handsome eighteen or twenty-four pounders," positioned on a high bank near the storehouses. "Gun firing is, (or was during my time there)," McDonald wrote, the customary "mode of salute throughout the whole North."[86] At Fort William in the early 1820s, the new deputy governor of the HBC Nicholas Garry described his arrival: "We were received with the firing of Guns, and the Shouts of the Indians, Canadians, &c. !!"[87] The effect was "heart-quickening" as the sound "crackled across the water."[88] Although it is not clear whether the fort's cannons were fired in this instance, it is nonetheless descriptive. This was a shared soundway, as Indigenous peoples and Canadians alike participated by lending their voices to the occasion. It was mostly characterized by the firing of guns. Scots-Anglo merchants, French Canadian voyageurs, and Indigenous peoples all participated in the custom on arrival.

Archibald McDonald explained his understanding on an 1828 voyage. It is clear from his diary that "parting cannon shots" were an integral part of the operational and social fabric of the trading posts. Rather than an off-hand reference, he reported their specific purpose. They were "for good luck."[89] This interpretation acknowledged the vulnerability and courage of travellers in the fur trade. Voyages by watercraft, whether canoe, York boat, or sailing ship, were inherently fraught with danger. The distances between the trading posts in northern North America were extensive, and the travel season was short. Accidents or unforeseen disasters were often deadly. Firing parting shots for good luck may have been a way of expressing agency, changing the soundscape, modifying something within human grasp. This may have psychologically mitigated the vulnerabilities and anxieties of fur traders.

Signals

On a macro level, the effects of gun blasts can be interpreted in terms of geo-political significances. On an individual level they could be associated with an array of direct experiences. Few fur traders lived to tell the kind of tale that John Tanner did of getting shot while paddling a canoe. He recounted the "discharge of a gun at my side … I heard a bullet whistle past my head, and felt my side touched, at the same instant that the paddle fell from my right hand, and the hand itself dropped powerless to my side." This recollection focuses on the sound of the shot in the most extreme example of the sensory effects of firearms. Tanner heard the shot pass by his head, recounting his harrowing narrative where he barely escaped with his life.[90] He described the terrifying effect firearms had on his Anishinaabe family when he had been away for some time. "My family had been so long unaccustomed to hear guns," he wrote, "that at the sound of mine they left the lodge and fled to the woods, believing the Sioux had fired upon me."[91] Indeed Tanner was hunting in contested territory and related how his gun was constantly present: "If I had occasion to do any thing, I held my gun in one hand and labored with the other." One time, after hunting a moose, he put down his gun while butchering the animal and heard a shot "not more than two hundred yards from me." Alarmed and thinking it was the Sioux, Tanner "immediately called out." He supposed his firing had been heard, "but no answer was returned." Finally, he returned home as quietly as he could and avoided an encounter in this tense situation. His account reveals the sonic impact of firearms and the ability of gunshots to transmit location through a forest environment, with potentially varied and ambiguous interpretations.

Fur traders sought the collective security provided by muskets, even when commercial rivalries divided them. Being within earshot was the distance in which two parties could quickly signal danger, even without line of sight. In the 1790s, the HBC and NWC established competing forts along numerous waterways including the North Saskatchewan River. There, Buckingham House and Fort George were established within firing distance or "a gunshot away."[92] Similarly, John McDonald of Garth described his competitors' proximity to Fort Augustus: "We had here, (beside the Hudson's Bay Company, whose fort was within a musket shot of ours) the opposition, on the other side of us, of the new concern [XY Company]."[93] This pattern of arranging the forts ensured that guns fired at one would be heard by the other.

These tight arrangements were not due to the lack of alternate locations. In deciding where to establish forts near Île-à-la-Crosse on Lac des Serpents, the competitors Mackenzie and McGillivray consulted each other on where to build. Mackenzie's first location was rejected by McGillivray, who expressed an awareness of "a much better one not far distant." While the two would be competing for the allegiances of Indigenous hunters and their furs in that region, McGillivray "suggested it would be for our mutual good" that they travel together, and they pitched their tents "within a gun shot of one another."[94] The logic for these close quarters between competitors appears to have been as a way to mitigate anxieties about attack and as a method of protection against Indigenous peoples. It allowed and practically ensured that each side would spy and eavesdrop on the other. When François Victor Malhiot worked for the NWC, he described what he overheard from the XY Company fort. On hearing gunshots, he inferred the arrival of a significant person due to the sound of guns: "We have just heard several gun-shots in the direction of Chorette's fort which leads us to presume that His Lordship had just landed."[95] Tracking movements at competitors' forts was facilitated by the customs of collective security and of saluting arrivals and departures with firearms.

Signalling protocol was created to suit different needs. Alexander Mackenzie described instructing his men how to signal while working at a distance. "They should fire two guns," he declared, "if they met with any accident, or found my return necessary." If Mackenzie needed to make contact, he would use the same signal, and told them that "they were to answer, and wait for me, if I were behind them."[96] Two gunshots in quick succession were distinct enough to serve as an effective signal. It would not be confused with an errant gunshot. The formidable noise-making capabilities of muskets allowed fur traders to establish signalling systems such as this. This provided a degree of safety in unfamiliar environments and group coordination when working at a distance.

Gun signals were a common method of attracting attention on the river. While passing an Indigenous encampment on the Ottawa River, Nicholas Garry identified the war whoop in combination with a gunshot as being "the customary Sign" to halt a canoe brigade.[97] He interpreted the signal to mean that the Indigenous man who created it "wished to speak to us." This is an important comment, as the voyageur canoes of the Montreal fur trade were notorious for their furious pace. They were often enlivened by the call-and-response voyageur songs "rising and falling" on the water. The dramatic report of the musket and war whoop was able to break through the din of paddles and voices. In Garry's case, the canoe brigade diverted from their route and landed on shore. Their reception was not what they expected: "We accordingly went to him when he laughed and said he had nothing to say."[98] Yet the sound signal had worked, resonating with Indigenous and non-Indigenous understandings of soundways on the river.

There are other examples of fur traders encountering Indigenous peoples who deliberately used the sonic capacity of firearms to get their attention. Thomas Connor of the NWC reported from the intersection of the Yellow and St Croix Rivers in 1804 that "several Volleys of Small Arms" from an Indigenous village were fired to signal to his brigade to stop and trade.[99] This is interesting because it suggests a "volley" style of firing, discharging multiple muskets simultaneously, rather than the "Indian style" commonly described as staggered shots fired sporadically and sequentially. Perhaps the objective, in this case, was to increase the amplitude and call the attention of the canoes by combining into a volley. Or perhaps the idea was that to get the attention of Europeans, their own style of firing should be imitated. Either way, it worked.

Ceremonies of travel and holidays

The fur trade developed other ceremonial uses of gunpowder. It was central to the progression of voyageurs from the St Lawrence to the Great Lakes and beyond. Voyageurs oversaw rituals they called "baptisms" at specific locations along the journey. These milestones marked the progression into new landscapes or watersheds and simultaneously symbolized advancing through the voyageurs' vocational ranking, from novice *mangeurs de lard* (porkeaters) to experienced *hivernants* (overwinterers) and *hommes du nord* (men of the north). To the west of Lake Superior at the height of land, fur trader John McDonell reported one such ceremony that involved sprinkling water on the heads of crew members and making pledges. Its most prominent soundway occurred when a dozen "gun shots fired one after another in an Indian manner."[100] This manner, in succession rather than as a volley, has been mentioned elsewhere.[101] This ceremony changed *mangeurs de lard* into the higher status *hommes du nord*, who relied more on Indigenous technologies, lifestyle, and diet. Firing guns in an "Indian manner," then, was an appropriate sound-symbol to commemorate such a transition.

Fur traders operating out of Hudson Bay and the St Lawrence adopted travelling rituals that drew, to some degree, on Indigenous customs. Yet relatively few had experience travelling with large groups of Indigenous peoples. James Smith was a Pennsylvanian man taken captive during the Seven Years' War by Algonquian and Iroquoian warriors. He described a war party departing with the "commander" singing the travelling song "hoo caughtainte heegana." As they made it to the edge of a town, "they began to fire in their slow manner, from the front of the rear, which was accompanied with shouts and yells from all quarters."[102] This account describes not a volley but succession of gunshots on leaving the village, which Smith designated as their characteristic style.

The fur trade custom of baptizing novices included this Indigenous style of firing in succession. It was an Indigenous sound-symbol repurposed by fur traders. This would have introduced and familiarized new employees of the trading companies with Indigenous customs and auditory features they could expect to encounter. Perhaps they were, as Carolyn Podruchny has suggested, trying to "indigenize themselves and their ceremonies to help them assume a new sense of belonging in a foreign land."[103] These soundways with muskets served as an auditory reinforcement of the rite of passage into a world with different rules and expectations. They changed voyageurs' identity as they made it further into Indigenous territory and fur trade country. There is circularity here, as the fur traders were responsible for supplying arms and ammunition to the Indigenous peoples from whom they adopted these practices.

Muskets were employed in servant-led ceremonialism every New Year's Day. Before dawn, the servants of the companies customarily awoke the master by discharging firearms outside his window. In exchange for this "honour," the master provided gifts of alcohol and food. This widely practised and fiercely enforced custom pressed superiors into providing for and fulfilling ceremonial obligations to their servants. Beyond the food and drink, respite from work was granted. This was known as a "*levée*."[104] The collective imposition of traditional customs on masters in this regard was similar to the temporary inversions of authority that occurred at points of ritual baptism, whereby they were pressured to give the men a dram of liquor or else get dunked in the river.

Alexander Mackenzie reported this custom extending to the distant reaches of the northwest. In 1793, "on the first day of January, my people, in conformity to the usual custom, awoke me at the break of day with a discharge of firearms, with which they congratulated the appearance of the new year."[105] This description of the ceremony congratulating the appearance of the New Year perhaps echoed language employed by the men. Yet this custom also seems to play into the pattern of passive resistance and thinly veiled threats that asserted servants' rights in the rigid paternalism of the trading company households. In return, they were treated with plenty of spirits, and when there was flour, cakes were added to their regales.[106] The servants and voyageurs demanded work stoppages and material gifts from their superiors through behaviours that had elements of *charivari* and carnival.[107] Gunshots were assertions of symbolic and real power, demanding not only reprieve from work but a fulfillment of the holiday customs associated with merry-making.

The historical record reveals how this custom was ceremonially pushed on fur traders. Alexander Henry (the younger) described how, near Red River on 1 January 1802, "the usual ceremony of firing &c, was performed." Though he does not provide with the details of his feelings on the proceedings, he does leave us with a record of his participation in the day's ceremonialism. Henry described presenting food and drink to the employees, with unspecified "neighbours" also arriving to partake of the feast. According to Henry, all the men were intoxicated "before sunrise." "I treated my people with 2 Gallons of High Wines, Five fms of Tobacco, and some Flour and Sugar. My neighbours' men came visiting and before sunrise both sexes of all parties were completely intoxicated." He commented that his intoxicated employees were "more troublesome than double their number of Saulteaux."[108] This suggests that fur traders had little choice but to perpetuate the alcoholism inherent in this holiday tradition.

Fur trader Willard-Ferdinand Wentzel of the NWC described this custom on 1 January 1805: "After having received the Customary Honors from the Men I invited them to Glass of Liquor – which was <u>graciously</u> received per them."[109] The following year he described the ceremonies in more cynical terms as the "<u>Drunken Day</u> of the North." He reported that he was awoken by "the report of several Guns" fired "at the Window of my room." After this "Salute," Wetzel writes that he had the "honour of receiving the good wishes of the bonne Ann[ée]." He gave the men spirits and high wines. With notable sarcasm, he described how "no one got out of order everything was lead [led] with great delicacy through the numerous ceremonies necessary [on] such a solemn occasion."[110] His resentment toward these customs of the servants is palpable, yet their demands were accommodated. John McDonald of Garth expressed his outrage when "during the customary firing of musketry," one of his "opponent's bullies purposely fired his powder" through his window. McDonald took the action as an affront and challenged the man to "single combat with our guns," which was not accepted but effectively deterred future provocations.[111] This demonstrates the potential for misunderstandings and violence. The shocking way these rituals started, with muskets fired outside the fur trader's window, must have reminded him of the servants' power and encouraged his cooperation in their holiday celebrations.

George Simpson described his first New Year's in the interior. He wrote that "the Festivities of the New Year commenced at four O'Clock this morning when the people honoured me with a salute of Fire arms." This commenced a long day of celebration, music, and revelry: "In half an hour afterwards the whole Inmates of our Garrison assembled in the hall dressed out in their best clothes, and were regaled in a suitable manner with a few flaggon's Rum and some Cakes; a full allowance of Buffaloe meat was served out to them and pint of Spirits for each man; the Women were also entertained to the utmost of our ability."[112] Fulfilling ritual obligations to their "servants" was something that fur traders accommodated with varying degrees of willingness and grace. Simpson was quite accommodating during his first season with the HBC. Yet once he became governor of an amalgamated Hudson's Bay and NWC in 1821, he implemented changes that reduced the distribution of goods and regales to servants and their families. He began restricting holidays and dances customarily held throughout the year. Yet certain occasions such as Christmas and New Year's were still celebrated.[113] The tradition of a New Year's *levée* persisted through the nineteenth century and has been continued by Canadian governor generals and lieutenant governors until the present day, although the tradition of ceremonial gunfire before dawn has not survived.[114]

The sound-making potential of gunpowder transformed North America through the conduits of the fur trade. It shaped the encounters and interactions of Europeans and Indigenous peoples. Materials and soundways were developed and exchanged. They over time produced new soundways. Before the seventeenth century, loud booms like thunder were associated with deities rather than human beings. Yet the arrival of guns and gunpowder augmented these auditory associations. As potent sound-making devices, cannons and muskets were useful as long-distance signalling mechanisms. They were institutionalized into the arrivals and departures of the ships and canoes of Euro-Canadians and Indigenous peoples. The conduits of the fur trade served as the mechanism by which arms and ammunition were carried throughout the northern reaches of the continent, and the ensuing firearm culture was shaped by both European and Indigenous influences. Indigenous styles of saluting developed and were occasionally adopted by fur traders. Auditory reports from guns travelled long distances and served as useful tools in travel and trade. They were ritually employed by the voyageurs and servants of the companies to exercise and demonstrate agency. Their influence transformed the soundscape dramatically, more so than any other material supplied by the fur trade.

2

Musical Encounters

Between 1760 and 1840, fur traders came into contact with a tremendous diversity of Indigenous peoples living in central, western, and northern North America. For the most part, the interactions were peaceful and gifts and honours were mutually extended. Unlike encounters between European ships and Indigenous coastal groups, those in the British North American fur trade usually involved Europeans travelling with Indigenous technology, the canoe, and meeting with Indigenous peoples on the banks of rivers or lakes. When people from such different cultural backgrounds first met in this context, how did they manage to communicate without a common language? How could they engage in sustained interactions and cooperate successfully? At every juncture, it involved trust. Trust at reception, gift giving, and trade. That music was included and facilitated this process should not be surprising. Music making and dancing have been shown to produce oxytocin, endorphins, and serotonin in people.[1] They were central to how the French encountered and allied with Indigenous peoples in the St Lawrence in the early 1600s.[2] These activities were encouraged by mutual curiosity and they facilitated social bonding and trust-building in potentially tense cross-cultural interactions.

After the Seven Years' War, European travel networks and trading post infrastructure expanded from the St Lawrence and Hudson Bay watersheds to the Pacific and Arctic Oceans. Fur traders encountered the Plains, western Subarctic, northwest coast, and Plateau-Basin regions and the diverse Indigenous peoples who lived there. Many kinds of encounters occurred. Some were with small groups; others were with large. The characteristics of Indigenous peoples across this landscape were varied and complex. This is reflected to some degree in fur traders' writings, where they make special note of the novelty of the cultures they were encountering and differences with other Indigenous cultures. Prominent fur traders who ventured in this capacity include Alexander Henry (the elder) on the Plains, Alexander Mackenzie in the western Subarctic, Simon

Fraser on the northwest coast, and David Thompson in the Plateau-Basin region. They all recorded remarkable and noteworthy musical encounters with Indigenous peoples on their voyages. These accounts are surprisingly detailed, especially considering the generally sparse style of fur traders' writings. Musical exchanges appear repeatedly in descriptions of encounters, indicating music's primary role during the initial phase of intercultural interactions. While the details of the musical encounters are idiosyncratic, in general, they included one or both sides performing songs and/or dances for the other.

Alexander Henry (the elder) was an influential fur trader who travelled northwest of the Great Lakes after the fall of New France. From 1761 until the mid-1770s, he traded and overwintered with numerous Indigenous communities, spending time on the northern Plains in particular. This area was encountered by Europeans in the 1730s and '40s under Sieur de la Vérendrye and his family, who had extended the French trading post network northwest from Grand Portage at the west end of Lake Superior to the Red and North Saskatchewan Rivers. Henry encountered Cree and Assiniboine peoples who had already adopted aspects of European material culture. They had adapted their culture to the new technology as well as adapted the new technology to suit their own culture. One such encounter was described by Alexander Henry in 1776.

Henry and his men had established a fort on the "Pasquayah," or the North Saskatchewan River and had drawn the attention of Cree and Assiniboine peoples. On a visit to an Assiniboine village, he was welcomed, and after trading and feasting for a few days, he found the opportunity to accompany a buffalo hunt. Henry related how all the dogs were muzzled so as not to scare off the herd with their barking. Then, "decoyers" disguised as bison approached within earshot of the herd and began "bellowing." On hearing the noise, Henry reported that the bison, from "curiosity or sympathy" advanced to meet those who were issuing the call. The bellowing was repeated, drawing the herd forward. The leaders of the pack followed the decoy into a pound, which was constructed wide at the entrance. Once the herd had been lured in, the slaughter began, creating a tremendous "uproar."[3]

Henry next described that evening, where there was feasting, music, and dancing in "all quarters" of the village. It was inescapable. Henry and his men retired to their tent where the music was still perceptible. They were soon visited by their hosts, when "the chief came to our tent, bringing with him about twenty men, and as many women, who separately seated themselves as before; but, they now brought musical instruments, and, soon after their arrival, began to play. The instruments consisted principally in a sort of tambourine, and a gourd filled with stones, which several persons accompanied by shaking two bones together; and others with bunches of deer-hoofs, fastened to the end of a stick. Another instrument was one that was no more than a piece of wood, of three feet, with notches cut on its edge. The performer drew a stick backward and forward, along the notches, keeping time. The women sung; and the sweetness of their voices exceeded whatever I had heard before."[4] This performance was described in detail. Drums, rattles, and rasps accompanied the women's singing. Henry reported that it lasted over an hour before the dance commenced. Divided by gender, the men and women lined up on either side of the room. Each moved sideways, first in one direction, and then the other. Henry mentioned how the clothing of the women enabled them to keep rhythm, suggesting that their garments made sounds and that their movements were rhythmically synchronized with the musicians. That this occurred in Henry's tent ensured that it was engrained in his memories and journal.

Deer-hoof clackers or "dew-claws" were used on traditional Indigenous garments to produce audible rhythms. Yet in this case, "bells and other jingling materials" were described.[5] The Assiniboine had acquired bells and incorporated them onto their garments. While not many Europeans had passed through this area by the 1770s, the Assiniboine's material culture had already been influenced by the fur trade in such a way that it had influenced their garments and transformed the sound of their dances. The bells were integrated purposefully to complement and amplify the dancers' movements. There is no evidence that European technology had, at this point, fundamentally changed Assiniboine music or dancing traditions. Rather, the Assiniboine strategically integrated new technologies and materials into their own cultural traditions in their own way. The "other jingling materials" reported may have included re-fashioned trade metals, which typically were flattened into uniform pieces or rolled into cones that became known as "tinkle cones."[6] The bells and potentially other trade materials suggest a discernable external influence on the Assiniboine dance and musical performance. Henry was struck by the sound of the women's voices, describing them in complimentary terms.

It was in the following decade that Alexander Mackenzie established the NWC's hub, Fort Chipewyan, on Lake Athabasca. He launched an expedition westward in 1789, but it soon turned north as it became clear that the large river that now bears his name flowed into the Arctic Ocean. Mackenzie travelled in a *canot du nord* with a small party of voyageurs and a Chipewyan guide named Nestabeck, also known as "English Chief." This area was beyond any territory traversed by Europeans until that point, and Mackenzie was wholly reliant on his crew for their labour and abilities. Mackenzie's journal described encountering the Yellowknife people, whom he described as speaking Chipewyan but being politically distinct from those with whom he was familiar. Nestabeck presumably assisted Mackenzie navigate these encounters. At the confluence of the Great Bear River and what would become the Mackenzie River, he encountered two families of Athapascan Dene, Slave (Slavey), and Dogrib (Tlicho). These people were shocked and terrified by his arrival. Mackenzie reported they were not familiar with the use of liquor or tobacco. They warned Mackenzie against attempting to follow the river northwards, claiming that it would be several winters before he arrived and that he would be plagued by monsters. Mackenzie had difficulty convincing his men to continue, with miniscule food resources, ominous reports, and scarce game reported further north. He struggled to procure a new guide among this group.[7] During much of the encounter, according to Mackenzie, the Dene were singing and dancing. He wrote that during their "short stay with those People they amused us with Dancing to their own Vocal Music, in either of which there is no great variety, at least as far as we cou'd perceive. They form a Ring Men and Women promiscuously, the former have a Bone Dagger or piece of Stick between the fingers of the Right Hand which they keep extended above the head & in continual Motion, the left they seldom raise so high but keep working backward & forward in a horizontal direction keeping time to their Music. They jump & put themselves into different Antic Shapes, keeping their Heels, close together. At every pause they make the Men give a howl of Imitation of the Wolf, or some other Animal & those that hold out the longest at this strong exercise seem to pass for the best Performers; the Women hang their Arms as if without the Power of Motion."[8]

This remarkable description combines both detailed observations as well as subjective opinion. Mackenzie's statement about their music as having "no great variety, at least as far as we cou'd perceive" is judgmental but self-aware. His description of the circle dance with the bone dagger and its movements is detailed, even describing dancers' leg positions, with heels close together and assuming a variety of "Antic Shapes." We can only imagine what these may have been, but the language is evocative. It clearly made an impression on Mackenzie. Was the purpose of this dance merely, as Mackenzie indicated, to amuse himself and his men? Or was there a deeper purpose – perhaps a spiritual dimension? The wolf howls may indeed have been a dramatic part of the performance, yet the sounds of other animals were also featured. In contrast to European dances with clearly delineated gender roles, here were men and women standing intermixed in a circle "promiscuously." Mackenzie focused on the features of the dance that diverged from his expectations. Though certainly shaded by his prejudices, Mackenzie's description captures many details of the performance. By publishing these he could not only provide fascinating material for his readers but more convincingly assert his "discovery" of new lands and peoples.

Another musical encounter followed. Once Mackenzie had gone a short distance, he met with another group of Dene. He managed to acquire a new guide from among them. This man and his brothers desired to demonstrate their abilities and knowledge to Mackenzie and his men. Yet, there was a language barrier. The men proclaimed their knowledge of the Inuit who lived downriver. Mackenzie described how they "amused us with Songs of their own & some in Imitation of the Eskmeaux, which seemed to enliven our new Guide, so much that he began to dance upon his Breech in his small Canoe & we expected every Moment to see him upset but he was not satisfied with his confined Situation. He paddled up along Side of our Canoe & asked us to embark him (which a little before he had refused) we allow'd him & immediately he began to perform an Eskmeaux Dance upon our Canoe when every Person in the Canoe called out to him to be quiet which he complied with & before he sat down pull'd his *Penis* out of his Breeches laying it on his hand & telling us the Eskmeaux name of it. In short he took much Pains to shew us that he knew the Eskmeaux & their Customs."[9]

The Dene guides found a way to demonstrate their abilities and knowledge, performing their own songs as well as those of the Inuit. How better to demonstrate familiarity with another culture than to sing their songs and speak their language? The overt reference to a penis is remarkable and unheard of in the records and journals of fur traders. Yet beyond the shock value, the guide was communicating that he knew Inuit vocabulary related to body knowledge. What Mackenzie describes in detail, along with singing and dancing in the canoes, was not just a distraction on his voyage. It was an essential part of the demonstration of knowledge and experience. The Dene guides danced in the canoes almost to the point of tipping, behaviour with serious consequences in the frigid northern waters. Yet executed successfully, this remarkable demonstration of agility and musicianship may have achieved its purpose of convincing Mackenzie of the guides' experience and abilities. While entirely reliant on Indigenous peoples along the way, Mackenzie successfully made it to the Arctic Ocean on 14 July 1789.

In 1793, Mackenzie embarked on another long-distance canoe trip, this time travelling down the Bella Coola River to the Pacific Ocean. On this voyage, he encountered the Heiltsuk who he referred to as the "Bella Bellas." Mackenzie described the singing he heard, which was "in a manner very different from what I had been accustomed to hear among savages." Not only was the sound different, but it was produced in an unfamiliar context. "It was not accompanied either with dancing, drum, or rattle," he wrote, "but consisted of soft, plaintive tones, and a modulation that was rather agreeable: it had somewhat the air of church music."[10] This observation reflects Mackenzie's perception of the difference between Indigenous singing on the northwest coast compared to central and northeastern North America. This may have evoked curiosity in readers about the diversity of Indigenous cultures. It seems clear that this description required a considerable degree of perception and musical attentiveness. George Vancouver had recently visited the mouth of this river and had no such musical encounter with the Heiltsuk. While Mackenzie acknowledged that he was encountering a significantly different musical culture, he had trouble describing it with his musical vocabulary. In emphasizing how different it was, he related it to something familiar. It reminded him of European church music, something that he and his readers could conceptualize and reference. Regardless of his intentions and limitations, Mackenzie's account acknowledged that he was encountering significantly different Indigenous cultures and musical styles on reaching the northwest coast.

When Simon Fraser made his voyage to the Pacific in 1808, he encountered numerous Indigenous communities. He was often greeted with singing. He described how on 27 June, the Nlaka'pamuk or "Thompson Natives" entertained his men with "a specimen of their singing and dancing."[11] He later described encountering various coastal Salish groups, some of whom presented him with feasts and dances. As fur traders often did, Fraser described the dance to communicate insights about the Indigenous culture. Yet it simultaneously revealed much about his own prejudices. As Sylvia Van Kirk has written, fur traders were both fascinated and concerned with gender roles in Indigenous societies.[12] That recurring interest manifested in episodes of musical encounter. Fraser evaluated Nlaka'pamuk gender dynamics, concluding that the Salish women were slaves to men: "Both sexes are stoutly made, and some of the men are handsome; but I cannot say so much for the women, who seem to be slaves, for in course of their dances, I remarked that the men were pillaging them from one another."[13] Fraser seemed to be referencing the fact that people were exchanging dancing partners. Yet women dancing with more than one partner was also a common feature of European line and pattern dances at the time. There is an associated event that offended his sensibilities. It was at this dance, according to his account, where his guide "was presented with another man's wife for a bed fellow."[14] This event confirmed Fraser's suspicions of promiscuity and dominated his evaluation of the musical encounter. Yet it does signal the role that dance played as a cross-cultural arena in forming partnerships and sexual relations.

Music and dance played an even more significant role in Fraser's interactions with the coastal Salish. His account indicates just how much song and dance played into diplomatic manoeuvrings. On arriving at a large village, the Salish "entertained us with songs and dances of various descriptions. The chief stood in the centre of the dance or ring giving direction, while others were beating the drum against the walls of the house."[15] On this occasion, Fraser noted both the variety of the performances and hierarchical structure of Salish society, with the chief orchestrating different bodies circling him in the middle. The drumming against the sides of the walls of the house had the effect of amplifying the encounter dramatically. The "terrible racket" alarmed his men who were at a distance and who rushed back ready to defend their colleagues. Here Indigenous singing and drumming functioned to alarm fur traders, while those directly present appear to have been engrossed in the powerful performance. Their interpretation of this Salish music was influenced by their sense that they might be unwelcome visitors. This may have been part of what was communicated cross-culturally through the musical performance.

This certainly was the case as Fraser continued downriver. Where the river divides at New Westminster, Fraser was greeted by canoes that had launched from a Salish village. Armed with bows, arrows, clubs, and spears, those aboard the canoes were "singing a war song, beating time with their paddles upon the sides of the canoes, and making signs and gestures highly inimicable." Fraser's guide responded in kind by becoming "very unruly singing and dancing, and kicking up the dust." Fraser tried to stop him.[16] He described how a chief with a "number" of canoes "well armed" overtook them and "kept in company, singing with unfriendly gestures all the while."[17] After attempting to seize Fraser's canoe, the chief resorted to threats and exhortations, and bloodshed was only narrowly avoided. The songs Fraser encountered from the Salish were not welcoming. They were intimidating and their message was interpreted clearly across the linguistic and cultural divide. What Simon Fraser did not and could not understand, however, is how he may have been interpreted by the Salish spiritually as a returning Xexá:ls, or Transformer.[18]

David Thompson was the most prolific of all the fur trader explorers of this era. He was born in London in 1770 and was hired by the HBC at the age of fourteen. By 1786, he was overwintering with Indigenous communities in the interior. He learned many useful abilities, from speaking the Cree language to techniques of survival, travel, and trade. He then apprenticed under the HBC's Philip Turnor, studying practical astronomy, surveying, and map-making.[19] Although he was valued as a fur trader, he preferred exploring. He switched allegiances in 1797 to the more dynamic NWC, where he spent the next fifteen years travelling and mapping. It was under this employment that he mapped large swaths of the western Plains and Subarctic. In 1807, he crossed the "Great Divide," making his historic descent down the Columbia River. His journals from the following years represent an important early record of the Indigenous peoples that inhabited this fertile valley before being disrupted.

Thompson recorded his reception with the Salish Simpoils (San Poils) people. He referred to some of his men – Thomas, La Fontaine, Bercier – French Canadian voyageurs who figured prominently in the musical exchanges that followed. After meeting on 3 July 1811 and smoking a "few pipes," the visit was coming to a close. "As the chief was going," Thompson recounted, "my Men wished to see them dance – I told the chief, who was highly pleased with the request."[20] Thompson acted as the intermediary between the chief and his men, and yet he does not explain how he communicated this particular sentiment. Thompson's subsequent description is rich in detail. He described three dances that were performed on the spot without instruments. He described "a mild simple Music," with "cadence measured." Yet the movements of the dancers were "wild and irregular." He described how on "the one side stood all the old People of both sexes – these formed groups of 4 to 10 who danced in time, hardly stirring out of the same spot; all the young & active formed a large group on the other Side, men women & children mixed, dancing first up as far as the line of old People extended, then turning round & dancing down the same extent, each of this large group touching each other with closeness – this continued abt 8 Minutes, when the Song being finished, each Person sat directly down on the Ground, where on the Spot he happened to be when the Song was done."

The moral judgments sometimes evident in Mackenzie and Fraser's accounts are absent here, although the phrase "touching each other with closeness" is suggestive. Indeed, like Mackenzie and Fraser's accounts, gender relations constituted one of Thompson's primary observations. After a speech that lasted a minute or two, the song began as it had before, with no fixed positions for the dancers. Instead, it seemed that they "mingled as chance brought them together." Thompson then focused his description on a woman who stood out from the others. He described a "young active woman, who always danced out of the Crowd & kept a line close along us, & always left the others far behind." This behaviour, which brought the woman close to the fur traders, was obvious subject matter for comment. It was "noticed by the Chief, who at length called her to order, & either to dance with the others or to take a Partner." Thompson read cultural power dynamics into the events of the dance: the chief seemed all-controlling, as the dancers apparently obeyed his wishes. Yet the commentary also seems to suggest that the woman had a degree of independence and agency. The chief's insistence that she either dance with the rest of the group or take a partner is difficult to interpret without further context.

The final dance was very different in both form and apparent purpose from the others. It was again ordered by the chief, who "told them to dance a third time, that we might be preserved and in the strong Rapids we had to run down on our way to the Sea. This they seemingly performed with a great good will. Having danced abt an Hour, they finished – we retired much sooner as the dust of their feet often fairly obscured the Dancers, tho' we stood only abt 4 feet from them, as they danced on a piece of dusty ground, in the Open Air."[21] This dance constituted a prayer for the safe travels of Thompson and his men. It is remarkable for a few reasons. The first is its duration. During the summer season, time was of the essence to fur traders. It is remarkable that Thompson devoted over an hour to this performance and described it in such detail. The second is the "great good will" that was communicated. We do not know what the dance looked like, but we have Thompson's interpretation that it was for their safe passage through dangerous waterways. The proximity of the dancers a mere four feet away must have produced a close kind of intimacy that etched itself into the memories of both parties. The dance's meaning seems to have been conveyed cross-culturally, even if its movements were foreign.

After leaving the Simpoils, Thompson met and traded with a group identified as speaking a Salish dialect. They approached "singing us a Song of a mild Air." This seems to have earned the trust of Thompson and his men, and the rest of the encounter was positive. After discussing the river and the Indigenous groups below, they "offered to dance for our good voyage & preservation to the Sea & back again." Men, women, and children danced together in an ellipsis. To Thompson, their movements resembled running on the spot while keeping time with their arms, which were close by their sides. Some older women were noted as dancing apart from the rest of the group, and their steps were judged "much better than the others." Here they were dancing separately from the main formation and their dance steps were recognized and admired. It is interesting to note the difference with the previous example of the young woman being reprimanded for dancing outside the circle. This likely held symbolic resonances far deeper than Thompson realized. This Salish group danced three dances for Thompson and his men. Each began with a speech from the chief and ended "with a kind of prayer for our safety, all turning their faces up the River & quickly lifting their hands high & striking the Palms together then letting them fall quickly." Why these movements were all interpreted by Thompson as prayers for their safety is uncertain. Could these actions not have symbolized something else or been for some other purpose? There is not enough description of the encounter to adequately consider other interpretations. Thompson reported that these actions were repeated "'till the kind of Prayer was done," which lasted between one and a half and two minutes.[22] Thompson does not provide the duration of the three dances, but they clearly took up a considerable amount of time.

Thompson followed these descriptions in his journal with a note about Salish music and dance more generally. Though this might seem remarkable for a fur trader, in the context of Thompson's encounters, it was obvious. The Indigenous peoples of the Columbia River had consistently greeted him and his crew with song and dance. Within these performances, there was much variety, as his descriptions testify. Yet Thompson identified a common thread: "I may here remark that all their Dances are a kind of religious Prayer for some end." He felt this was a distinguishing feature between European and Indigenous dances, and that this was something worthy of clarification. He continued to describe features of the Salish communities of the Columbia River by saying that "they in their Dances never assume the gay joyous countenance, but always a serious turn with often a trait of enthusiasm."[23] After witnessing a number of dances, Thompson made the comparison with European varieties, describing the gravity of the performances by which he and his men were received.

Each day from 5 to 9 July 1811, as they descended the Columbia River, Thompson's party encountered more people, receiving feasts and dances and participating in ceremonies of peace-making. On 6 July, after exchanging gifts, the women danced "in a body to the tune of a mild Song which they sang." Here synchronicity is emphasized by identifying the individuals as moving in a singular body. On 7 July, Thompson's group encountered a village whose inhabitants "received us all dancing in their Huts."[24] The following encounter with a group of "Shawpatin" (Sahaptin) interior Salish people was granted more description. The women "advanced singing & dancing in their best dress, with all of their Shells in their Noses – two of them naked, but no way abashed." Here Thompson again described Salish people dancing while advancing to receive his party. The distinguishing shell jewellery worn in the nose was subject to comment. As in previous encounters, the women danced while the men smoked, and were "like the rest something of a religious nature."[25] Thompson demonstrated his increasing familiarity with Salish music, as during his next encounter he described how, after smoking, "they gave us a Dance after the fashion of the others." At the subsequent village, the chief "ordered" the women to perform a dance.[26] Thompson elaborated on this dance and was effusive with praise: "They danced in a regular manner & by much the best I have seen: all the young of both Sexes in two curve[d] Lines, backwards & forwards – the old formed the rank behind; they made much use of their Arms & Hands. The Dance, Song & Step were measured by an old Chief. Sometimes they sat down at the end of 3' sometimes at the end of 10', but never reposed more than 1/2'."[27] The complexity of this multi-generational dance was admired and described in detail.

There is quite a bit of information relayed in this description. The division of the group by young and old, boys and girls: each had their place. Thompson noted details such as the curved rows of youthful dancers moving backward and forward while the older dancers danced behind them with dramatic hand gestures. Thompson was so curious that he counted the steps and intervals that the dancers employed in their movements. As Thompson encountered larger and larger communities approaching the coast, he recognized their good fortune in being received so amicably. On 5 August 1811, Thompson's party encamped among at least two hundred men who gave them a dance, after which Thompson wrote "thank Heaven for the favour we find among these numerous people."[28] This welcoming reception was expressed most clearly, and consistently, through songs and dances.

Dance figured prominently in fur traders' encounters with Indigenous peoples. They consisted of visual and auditory components. Indigenous peoples danced and sung to communicate with these newcomers. Mostly serving to welcome, entertain, and build trust, they could also convey hostility and intimidation. Musical traditions were presented to fur traders as a central part of the intercultural dynamic of encounter and they devoted a considerable amount of energy observing and describing these dances. This seems to have occurred for a few reasons. They were certainly fuelled by curiosity, as demonstrated by the surprise, awe, or compliments expressed in their descriptions. This seems to particularly be the case when it came to observing gender dynamics. David Thompson's men requested a musical performance when one was not presented by the community. This reflected an interest on their behalf and pattern of musical curiosity. It was a reasonable expectation when encountering a new group. There was also undoubtedly a strong element of pragmatism. Thompson realized that music and dance were an important part of the intercultural ceremonialism associated with peace-making, trade, and successful passage through Salish territories and villages.

Performances of music and dance were interpreted as significant events that could be extrapolated. Alexander Henry recognized that the performances in his tent after the bison hunt, while utilizing strictly Indigenous musical instruments, were nonetheless touched by European influence because of the addition of bells to the women's garments. The music of Indigenous Nations who had not encountered Europeans, both the Dene and the coastal Salish, was described by Alexander Mackenzie as novel and different in memorable passages in his journals. While this served to convey the great distance Mackenzie travelled, it also emphasized the cultural diversity of Indigenous peoples. Fur traders analyzed dances for insights into social structure and gender dynamics. Their commentary reflects aspects of Indigenous societies as well as the fur traders' attitudes and prejudices. The mixing of men and women on the dance floor may not have signalled "promiscuous" behaviour as they suggested, and yet fur traders were careful to note gender dynamics, especially when they departed from European norms.

While the details in every case were remarkably different, the common thread of these events is the musical encounter. For Indigenous peoples, music and dance were an important part of how outsiders were received. Fur traders recognized they were part of safe passage and expressed goodwill and trust, even offering insights into the culture of newly encountered peoples. While fur traders were ignorant of the deeper spiritual significances, some, like David Thompson, interpreted Salish music and dance to be forms of prayer. These accounts suggest how prominently cultural encounters were shaped by music and dance and manifested into a multiplicity of experiences. The fur traders could not anticipate what they would encounter, nor when. Whether after the hunt, at first meeting, with a guide, as an offering or prayer for safe passage, or as a threatening war song, song and dance were primary vectors of intercultural contact and communication. The details are as diverse as the people and contexts of creation. Formal relations and treaties had not been established with Indigenous peoples in regions newly accessed by fur traders. As they travelled into uncharted territories, the fur traders' material gifts were reciprocated with furs and the intangible gifts of song and dance. These features, along with feasting and smoking, provided a peaceful platform of interaction. While they were expected, novel performances provided significant experiential realizations of place.

Military Instruments
and "Turned" Drums

It has been proposed by ethnomusicologists that musical exchanges occur most readily between cultures with pre-existing common features. Many of the instruments that arrived with Euro-Canadians in the Great Lakes region and the west in the mid-late eighteenth century were military instruments: drums, bugles, fifes, and bagpipes. Of these, only drums were shared between European and Indigenous cultures. The historical evidence, as we shall see, suggests that musical interactions, exchanges, and adaptations indeed occurred with drums in ways that they did not with the others. Yet all these musical instruments proved to be objects of cross-cultural interest and played a role in the musical interactions of the fur trade.

Drums were, and still are, a central feature of Indigenous traditional music and ceremonial culture. Indigenous drums were designed in various shapes and sizes, from lightweight hand drums to standing frame drums and water drums. Their purpose or function was often expressed by their ornamentation and specific protocols of handling. They were usually revered as sacred, animate, beings.[1] Drumming played a central role in many of the traditional ceremonies and activities of communities. The Ojibwe addressed drums as *gimishoomisinaan,* or "our grandfathers."[2] A comprehensive examination of traditional Indigenous drumming is beyond the scope of this book. Yet it is important to recognize the centrality of the drum in Indigenous cultures if the exchanges and interactions with European drums in the fur trade era are to be understood.

The military was the primary vehicle for the dissemination of European drums in the eighteenth century. Drums were integral to the functioning of European armies, facilitating manoeuvres and the coordination of large numbers of soldiers. Commanding officers relied on drummers to broadcast orders to their regiments. It was largely from military uses that European drums made their way into the Great Lakes fur trade, sometimes manifesting a fertile arena of cultural contact, communication, and exchange. The military instruments of the drum, bugle, horn, and bagpipe all made their way to trading posts during this period, though the historical evidence suggests that they were relatively limited in number. They shed their disciplinary functions and were employed for ceremonial arrivals, recreation at dances, and as objects of curiosity during trading encounters.

The height of colonial warfare in the mid-late eighteenth century coincided with the aggressive pursuit of the fur trade by merchants in Montreal. The recurring conflicts in eastern North America and the Great Lakes region from the Seven Years' War (1756–63) until 1814 have been dubbed a "Sixty Years' War."[3] While not continuous, the recurring conflicts affected the fur trade. Trading routes and supply lines sometimes intersected contested territory and trade was at times interrupted or halted.[4] While the northwest fur trade was geographically removed from the epicentre of military conflicts in northeastern North America, the Great Lakes were significantly affected. The heightened tensions and skirmishes that spilled over into North America during the war of the Austrian Succession intensified into the Seven Years' War, the cataclysmic conflict that ultimately transferred the St Lawrence and Great Lakes fur trade from the French to the British. Newly arrived merchants entered the fur trading hub of Montreal, with its favourable location and experienced French Canadian labour supply. This was an uneasy process, with Pontiac's War (1763–64) comprising a broad confederacy of Indigenous Nations forcefully rejecting British takeover. Yet most former allies of the French made peace with the British at Niagara in 1764. They remained military allies through the following decades, entering into successive treaties with the British Crown in Upper Canada.[5] Most Algonquian and Iroquoian peoples came to fight with the British against expansionist America during the Revolutionary War and the War of 1812. The fur trade continued to expand during this era despite the disruptions, especially in the northwest.

The trading posts and forts around the Great Lakes served military and commercial functions. They extended economic and political influence. They were also nodes of intense intercultural contact and exchange with Indigenous peoples. The fur traders who pushed westwards shortly after the Seven Years' War such as Alexander Henry (the elder), Peter Pond, and Jonathan Carver mentioned military instruments in their journals and memoirs. George Simpson's governorship of a united company in 1821 brought another wave, as a martial tone was established entering the era of consolidation and monopoly. Indigenous peoples were notified of the fur traders' presence not only from the sounds of firearms but from the novel timbres of military musical instruments.

Music and Discipline

Late eighteenth- and early nineteenth-century military music served quite distinct functions for civilians and soldiers. For the public, martial displays of colour, movement, melody, and rhythm combined to showcase the power and coordination of infantry units. It turned soldiers into a moving spectacle accompanied by loud, attention-grabbing music. Armies paraded through population centres as displays of force to impress and inspire support and enlistment. In battle, musicians wore bright attire that enabled them to be seen through the smoke and confusion. The military band was by the seventeenth and eighteenth centuries seen as fundamentally important to the European model of warfare. According to Carl Benn, military music functioned to "add spirit to military events, boost morale, inspire people to enlist, maintain good relations with civilian society, and affirm traditions and values."[6] These functions were often fulfilled simultaneously when parading.

In the eighteenth century, military bands attracted enrollment for service. This is how Peter Pond began his career as a soldier. He later became the fur trader to locate Methye Portage with the help of French Canadian voyageurs and Cree guides. This served as the entryway into the vast Athabasca region after the 1770s. His remarkable career began at the outset of the Seven Years' War when one of General Braddock's contingents arrived in Milford, Connecticut. In his memoirs, he relates that he enlisted for the army after being moved by the music: "One Eaveing in April the drums an instraments of Musick were all imployed to that degrea that they charmed me," he wrote, joining others inspired to sign up with the recruiting officer Captain Baldwin.[7] This marked Peter Pond's introduction to the soldier's life and travelling throughout the Great Lakes, which led him eventually into the fur trade. The military drums and music that inspired him are the sole reference to music in Pond's memoirs, a testament to their lasting impression.

What Peter Pond witnessed was the military ceremonialism of parading or "trooping of the colours." This meticulous display involved presenting the colours, flags, and symbols of the regiment with "full ritual and solemnity" while marching to the music of the military band.[8] In the seventeenth and early eighteenth centuries there was an enormous expansion of military colours, with regiments having one for each of the colonels, majors, and captains, in addition to the king's standard. Most were painted or embroidered with heraldic designs such as dolphins, cannons, flags, or rising suns. These "colours" were treated with respect, honour, and ceremonialism.[9] Drummers were subject to strict protocols. A military manual from 1794 indicated that drummers were to keep six paces behind their respective companies while on the march.[10] Military marches were "functional pieces composed by bandmasters when required," borrowing not only popular tunes but also opera and oratorios from composers such as Thomas Busby, John Callcott, William Crotch, James Hook, John Mahon, and Alexander Reinagle, in addition to more popular pieces by Handel and Haydn. Music was provided to the troops from the personal funds of British regimental commanders, whose tastes largely determined the tunes of the march.[11] Popular songs were often adapted for military use. Certain marches became potent symbols of patriotism, especially the English "Grenadiers March" or "British Grenadiers," the French "Malbrook" and "Marseillaise," and the American "Yanky Doodle."[12]

This highlights the entertainment function provided by military music. Many soldiers enjoyed the music provided by their bands, and civilians enjoyed it too. Marches and parades were the most common way to display the precision of the regiment and the talents of its musicians. The interconnections between military and civilian life went even deeper. In the mid-1790s in the British garrison town of Niagara, for instance, there were frequent dances that brought together military officers with the local officials and upper classes. Regimental military bands were supported and enjoyed by military personnel and townspeople alike.[13] Musicians from military bands played in town at popular events such as country dances.[14] One can distinguish broadly between two sets of musicians in the army, the corps of drums and the bands of music that many regimental officers paid for and whose musicians played a wider range of instruments. Martial music was intertwined into daily life in garrison towns due to proximity, constantly reminding civilians of the military's presence. Civilians even structured their lives around the "military musical timetable."[15] Standardized drumbeats instructed soldiers when to rise, eat, work, and sleep, alerting those not only within but also outside the walls. A similar phenomenon occurred where military forts and trading posts were shared or close in proximity, such as Michilimackinac.

Within the regiment, military music functioned as an overt method of social control. It provided a mechanism for coordination and reinforced the hierarchy of command by allowing the officers to set the men's movements and marching speed. On the final page of the 1757 *Exercise of the Foot* appears an excerpt from Windham's *Plan of Discipline,* where it is explained that marching to the sound of drums presents "the greatest order and regularity," allowing soldiers to keep "the most exact time and cadence." Even militia could be trained relatively quickly, it was touted, with the music helping them "move all together," and "regulating the step" of each soldier. Music was written about by military strategists as "the best and indeed the only method of teaching troops to march well." This mid-eighteenth-century military treatise described in enthusiastic terms how "the effect of the music in regulating the step and making the men keep their order, is really very extraordinary."[16]

To understand the functions of military music, it is helpful to first recognize the disciplinary regime of regular and militia soldiers. Eighteenth-century military strategy was influenced by attempts to rationalize social systems, with authoritarian and utilitarian impulses combining to demand silent and obedient subjects. The 1757 publication from the Duke of Cumberland emphasized that "every Soldier will give the greatest attention to the words of command, remaining perfectly silent and steady." Silence ensured "attention and obedience," and ultimately "ensure[d] success to his Majesties arms."[17] Integral to the strict disciplinary order of the military, silence ensured nothing compromised or interrupted the command structure of the unit or regiment. The soldiers stood ready to obey their orders. In this idealized and ordered world, the drumroll and voice were the essential communication tools. As Michel Foucault discussed in the context of various models of eighteenth- and early nineteenth-century justice, the drum effectively commanded authority over silent subjects in a variety of contexts including prisons.[18] The relationship between the disciplinary techniques of armies and society as a whole was complex, and scholars have recently extended this analysis. Kate van Orden's study of early modern music explores these ideas in conjunction with military music and dance, exploring the influence of military themes on the cultures of the upper classes. She highlights how soldiers were managed through rhythmic commands, and drummers were the crucial conduit between them and the officers.[19]

The progression of the soldiers' day began and ended in camp with the sound of drums. In the morning, the "reveille" roused the soldiers, and in the evening, the final inspection of watch posts was announced with the "last post" or "tattoo."[20] On campaign, after the "last post" or "tattoo" was beat, the camp was expected to remain quiet, although commanders often struggled to enforce compliance. On the Ticonderoga campaign of 1759–60, Major John Hawks, serving under General Jeffrey Amherst, condemned the "very rietous noise in the camp till one o'clock," which took place "contrary to the orders of this camp & the rules in the army." Issuing a forceful statement to the officers of the guards ensured that after the "tattoe is beat," there would be no noises in the camp. Patrols were arranged and anyone found making a noise or disturbance was ordered to be "still and silent." If, after that point, any auditory transgressions were detected, the guilty party would be confined and punished according to "Marshel law."[21] Silence, then, was enforced with violence.

While on the battlefield, silent soldiers provided the essential backdrop against which the chain of command operated. The commanding officers' shouted orders were signalled to the group with military instruments. Seventeenth-century military theorists promoted the use of drums and fifes. Montgommery recommended two drummers for each company, one ordinary player who worked with the fife player and the second a *tambour colonel* as their captain.[22] By the mid-eighteenth century, each company of infantry had at least one large field drum to beat out the "calls of warre," with a corps of drums led by a drum major. The English army created the rank of drum-major-general, which existed from 1690 until the late 1700s.[23] During the Seven Years' War, drummers made four pence more per day than private soldiers and were classified as non-commissioned officers, underscoring their importance and standing.[24] From the late 1700s to early 1800s, there was an evolution of band music from favouring woodwinds to brass instruments. The nuanced history of this transition is beyond the scope of this work, but we should acknowledge that various types of instruments, including the flute, oboe, clarinet, and bassoon were used in the late eighteenth century by the British military and may have appeared in the St Lawrence and Great Lakes theatres of war.[25]

On the battlefield, the musicians played the vital role of rebroadcasting orders to the soldiers. The military literature of the era emphasizes that from a tactical perspective, it was essential to amplify the spoken orders of the commanding officer. In the Duke of Cumberland's 1757 *Exercise of the Foot,* each procedure is categorized by its "word of command" and corresponding drumbeat.[26] T.H. Cooper's 1806 *A Practical Guide for the Light Infantry Officer* asserts that "words of command are on all occasions to be used." Cooper insisted that "signals are only to be resorted to in aid of the voice."[27] Each command had a corresponding distinctive rhythm. These could be adapted to suit the commander's wishes, as they were for the American army and militia in September of 1813 when signals for only two basic manoeuvres were employed.[28] In warfare, the auditory realm was often as important as the visual, and battlefields could become overtaken with smoke from the volleys of musketry. Yet the drums could penetrate the chaos, bringing order to the unit and instructions to the soldiers.

Alexander Henry (the elder) was an English merchant who transported a canoe of goods from Montreal into the Great Lakes in 1761 before the Seven

Years' War was resolved. He provided a remarkable first-hand account of the massacre at Fort Michilimackinac during Pontiac's War. Henry heard a series of sounds and silences that signalled British authority had evaporated. Henry had been writing letters in his private quarters, when he "heard an Indian war-cry, and a noise of general confusion," and perceived from his window that Indigenous warriors had stormed the fort and a massacre was unfolding. Grabbing his gun, he "held it for a few minutes, waiting to hear the drum beat to arms." This drumbeat would have signalled the rallying of the British troops. No such drumbeat came. The surprise attack was too effective. Henry described this "dreadful interval" when he waited for the sound-symbols of British authority to return, but to no avail. The British had lost control of the soundscape and the fort.[29]

At military camps and forts, the progression of the daily regimen and various orders were broadcast for those inside and outside to hear, Indigenous warriors sometimes became familiar with these signals. In the Sauk chief Black Hawk's memoirs, he recounted digging a hole to hide in ambush outside of Fort Madison. He was so close to the fort that he "could hear the sentinel walking," and prepared his gun when he heard "the drum beat" from within the fort, signalling the impending emergence of soldiers.[30] These examples describe how auditory perceptibility had evident military implications. Yet only certain trading posts around the Great Lakes had nearby military garrisons, and their size fluctuated dramatically from the 1760s to the 1820s.[31]

Military drummers directly enforced regiment discipline. It was part of their duties to beat their comrades' backs by administering floggings. The public spectacles of discipline that fell into disuse in civilian society during the eighteenth century persisted much longer in the military.[32] The drummer's roles of signalling commands and administering punishment constituted a continuum within the disciplinary order. To the marching soldiers, the signals conveyed through the pounding drum skins were the orders of the officers. Perhaps these sounds also reminded them of their fate if they transgressed the rules. One chapter of a recent social history about the British military entitled "Following the Drum" details discipline in the British army. Older forms of military punishment such as "running the gauntlet" were replaced in the eighteenth and early nineteenth centuries almost exclusively by flogging, also known as the "lash," shifting the burden of corporal punishment from the entire group to the specialized role of drummers.[33] The custom of the lash earned British soldiers the nickname "bloody backs."

A severe form of punishment was a "drum head court martial." This was an elaborate disciplinary spectacle, whereby offenders were "drummed out" of the regiment. A young drummer in General Jeffrey Amherst's army moving through New York in 1758–59 was accused of stealing a glass of milk from a local farmer. Colonel Fraser took the severe measure of subjecting him to a "drumhead court-martial" on the side of the road. This name reflected the tradition of drafting the court-martial on the flat surface provided by the skin of a drum. This account described the drummer being "tied-up and punished with two hundred lashes on his bare back, and then drum'd out of the Regiment."[34] "Drumming out" contributed musical emphasis to what was meant to be a disgraceful and pitiful ceremony. It was a display of military punishment heightened by the musicians, both by administering direct force and in setting the emotional tone with their music.

Military executions were the most severe disciplinary action. The band set a somber tone. A composition known as the "Rogue's March" became a common tune in British and American armies to accompany this grisly procedure.[35] When the fifteen-year-old Pequot William Apess joined the army in New York City during the early years of the War of 1812, he recorded a significant experience with a military execution. He first "enlisted for a musician," and was instructed on Governors Island "in beating a drum."[36] He reminisced glowingly on his initial experiences as a drummer. Yet an incident changed his view of European drumming and the military more generally: "It is impossible for me to describe the feelings of my heart when I saw the soldiers parade, and the condemned, clothed in white with Bibles in their hands, come forward. The band then struck up the dead march, and the procession moved with a mournful and measured tread to the place of execution, where the poor creatures were compelled to kneel on the coffins, which were alongside two newly dug graves."[37] These spectacles were designed to produce an emotional effect, and Apess described how his "heart seemed to leap" into his throat. The death march set the mood, heightening the feelings that Apess described as "impossible ... to describe." "Death never appeared so awful ... This spectacle made me serious."[38] The evocative potential of music, then, was used in conjunction with the execution ceremony to accentuate its impact, presumably to increase dread in observers and contribute to the deterrent effect. The role of the soundscape and music in contributing to spectacles of discipline seems to have been largely overlooked by historians.[39]

Military Imprint

Drummers served several essential functions – transmitting the commanding officers' orders, providing entertainment, conducting marches, and enforcing discipline. Military drummers were essential to the command structure of the British army. The primary sources indicate that although musicians formed only a small portion of colonial armies, maintained at just over 2 per cent of total army numbers, they were a top priority to recruit and resupply.[40] On the New York frontier in 1755, drummers were in demand as replacements for those lost in battle. Colonel Johnathan Bagley wrote on 27 November 1755 about his request for William Johnson to "Send Up [a] Good Drum[m]er" to fill the position of drum major and two more drummers, "if to be had."[41] Johnson's correspondence indicated the numbers of British casualties in battle, including "missing" drummers who had to be replaced along with their equipment.[42] Some drums are known to have been captured by Indigenous peoples. Nathan Whiting reported to Johnson on 28 October 1755 that his regiment lost seven guns, four swords, four horns, and one drum in Lake Champlain engagements with the French and their Indigenous allies.[43] The material exchanges resulting from warfare may have influenced Indigenous cultures around the Great Lakes.

Certain Indigenous peoples were recorded with drums of Euro-American regiments. A group of Anishinaabeg travelling through Upper Canada in 1815 are depicted in Rudolf Steiger's watercolour showing a dance around what appears to be an American military drum.[44] There is evidence European military drums were repurposed and incorporated into Indigenous cultures. One particularly interesting example is an old drum that was likely collected on Manitoulin Island in the 1850s. It is particularly fascinating due to its layered history. It originally served as a military snare drum but at some point was repurposed and redecorated by an Anishinaabe owner.[45] Alan Corbiere and Ruth B. Philips suggest that the drum, or *dehe'igan,* was probably a trophy of war. The images on the drum represent dream symbols, symbols of war, and thunderbirds. These suggest spiritually significant usages of the drum, and a trajectory from being a European military drum to a ceremonial Indigenous drum. In the twentieth century, European bass drums from marching bands were sometimes "turned" to become powwow drums. This not only referred to their transformation from vertical to horizontal but represented "a concept that is often used to describe how the energy or power of an object might be changed – in order to change its meaning from war to peace."[46] While the snare

Fig. 3.1 Rudolf Steiger, *Deputation of Indians from the Chippewa Tribes to the President of Upper Canada, Sir Frederic Ph. Robinson, K.C.B., Major General, etc. in 1815*, 1815. Watercolour, gouache, and gum arabic on wove paper, mounted on wove paper, 25.5 × 35.8 cm. National Gallery of Canada.

drum remained physically horizontal with subsequent owners, it appears to have been symbolically turned.

Military instruments left their biggest imprint at trading posts in the Great Lakes region. This makes sense as this was a major theatre of war in both the Seven Years' War and War of 1812. Military instruments either remained with their regiments or were lost in action. These are certainly the primary source of European drums in the region at the time. There is some evidence of percussion instruments on the trading company's inventory lists and shelves for purchase. On the NWC's lists for 1820–21, two "tambourines" are listed at the Lake of the Two Mountains for two shillings apiece.[47] Yet their relative infrequency in the post inventories indicates that they did not represent a common trading item. Tambourines are not military drums, yet they appear to have been the closest thing that was occasionally traded by the NWC. It may be revealing that they were listed at the Lake of Two Mountains trading post close to Lachine and Montreal, while not in inventories of the inland posts. Perhaps they were not enough in demand to transport long distances, in addition to their fragility, size, and weight.

The encounters of Indigenous peoples with European military drums occurred not only around the Great Lakes, but also along the shores of Hudson Bay. On board HMS *Rosamond* in 1817, Lieutenant Edward Chappell remarked on numerous musical activities and cross-cultural interactions between his English crew, Cree, and Inuit peoples. On one occasion, a Cree man was invited on board. He closely examined the musical instruments, including two sets of bagpipes and bugle or horn. Chappell reported that the man was "not particularly pleased with any of our musical instruments, except the drum."[48] It could be that the military drums most resembled the Cree's *taawahekan* frame drums and the cultural proximity inspired the favourable sentiment. It would align with the theory that musical influences and exchanges were more likely to occur between musical cultures that shared characteristics.[49] While different in many ways, European and Indigenous musical cultures converged around the drum.

Drums were brought by the HBC and influenced Cree peoples living around Hudson Bay. As Cree oral traditions from Moose Factory indicate, when the annual ships used to arrive in Hudson Bay, the first thing that happened after landing was that a marching band emerged and paraded up and down the gangplank. Only then were the cargoes unloaded. This ceremony made a considerable impression, and Moose Factory residents told stories into the later twentieth century about the arrival of the HBC's ships, known in Cree as *Shay Chee Man* or "great canoes." James Cheechoo described an oral history from his father, Noah Cheechoo who worked on Charlton Island in the early twentieth century unloading cargoes. He described how at that time, the ships "disembarked in the form of a pipe band wearing kilts, and paraded along the quayside for some time before unloading the supplies with the help of the local Cree."[50] Ethnomusicologist Frances Wilkins recently researched the musical traditions of this community and was informed by elders such as James Cheechoo that the HBC's military drums had inspired the invention of a new kind of Cree drum to accompany the dance music of the fiddle. The resulting double-headed *taawahekan* drum resembled a combination of European snare and bass drums. According to Cheechoo, these are only used on "secular occasions within the context of fiddle dance music" and are fundamentally different from the Cree hunters' drums.[51] Traditional *taawahekan* drums are made from birch or larch and covered by caribou skins, crafted with one or two heads.[52] These drums were constructed for hunting and were used by Cree hunters, trappers, and fishermen to aid in their endeavours and communicate with non-human beings. The new instrument, a modification of existing drum technology, was produced because of fur trade encounters and ongoing relationships with the fiddle music brought by the fur trade. The parading ceremonies and social dances introduced by the fur traders were potent cultural influences.

Military instruments made their way to the trading posts of the Plains region by at least the early 1800s. On a voyage from Portage la Prairie to the forks of the Red and Assiniboine Rivers, Alexander Henry (the younger) mentioned that he was "plagued with J. McKenzy, HBCo Drum fife &c."[53] This suggests a drum and fife band played at the forks in 1805, comprised of fur traders from the HBC. Similarly, R. Miles wrote to Edward Ermatinger from York Factory in 1833 about the band he had formed with John Tod, which continued after Ermatinger departed from the trade: "We have had a Complete band of fiddle fife & drum not forgetting your old triangle which our worthy friend Ballenden beats upon most admirably, we however regret your absence in the Pandean Reeds."[54] This example of a "Complete band" in the northwest is perhaps the earliest on record, and had a distinct fur trade quality. The fiddle was combined with fifes, drums, and triangles. In combining the fiddle with these military instruments, they were repurposed for recreation. These examples suggest military instruments had alternate functions and would have been played and received differently in the fur trade.

Brass instruments were rare but not unheard of at trading posts. Bugles or trumpets were widely assigned to cavalry and light infantry units in the army. A distant relative of the medieval herald, buglers were used in the late eighteenth century for transmitting messages. They acted with a courtly demeanor and served "as special orderlies to the Generals, who usually had several on their Staff."[55] Their calls pierced the din of battle, signalling various manoeuvres to the cavalry such as advance, retreat, halt, commence and cease firing, and assemble.[56] The special capacity of the bugle's sound to travel long distances gave them the power to communicate across the camp or field to a large number of soldiers, as well as across enemy lines. Cooper's *Light Infantry Officer* from 1806 suggested that a "good bugle" could be heard at the distance of three miles or almost five kilometres.[57] During the military engagements of the Seven Years' War, large forces amassed in various locations for sieges and bombardments. The visual symbol for capitulation was raising the white flag for the British, while for the French it was the red flag. For both, the bugle was the critical signal, the device that most effectively communicated across the battlefield. It traversed walls, gates, trenches, and earthworks. A sieging party could sound the bugle to request a parley. This is what happened after nineteen days of siege and bombardment of the French Fort Niagara in July of 1759, when "after a furious cannonade on both sides, a trumpet sounded from the trenches, and an officer approached the fort with a summons to surrender."[58] The bugle or trumpet served as an auditory punctuation mark to this battle, signalling a cessation of hostilities.

There is evidence of at least one bugle making it into the conduits of the fur trade. Fur trader John Tod wrote in a letter to retired trader Edward Ermatinger about how he had found an old bugle he had used decades before: "During my late abode at Kamloops amongst the musty records of the Fort I fell in with Your old Bugle, the sight did not fail most forcibly to recall the days of our Youth at Island Lake."[59] This passage reflects how musical instruments sometimes circulated between trading posts and remained in their inventories for decades. Encountering this material object triggered Jon Tod's memories of his younger years with Edward Ermatinger when they had played music together. It was an object of special significance, recalling meaningful social bonds that Tod and Ermatinger maintained until their old age. This reflected the sentimental power of a discarded musical instrument.

The Scottish regiments and their attendant bagpipers had a considerable influence on colonial warfare during this period. Shortly after the defeat at Culloden in 1745, Scottish Highland and Black Watch regiments were integrated into the British army under William Pitt's directives. Highland regiments with pipers were sent to North America, seeing action with Wolfe at Louisbourg in 1757 and again with Abercromby in 1758 during the ill-fated attack on Fort Carillon. The highest rank of pipe major was comparable to drum major, the equivalent of sergeant.[60] Pipers, like fifers, were often concealed in the rolls simply as "drummers" to circumvent the scrutiny of headquarters, making the quantification of those sent to the St Lawrence impossible.[61] Personal accounts, such as James Thompson's anecdotal description of three pipers crossing with Simon Fraser's Highland Regiment in 1757, provide some evidence of their presence.[62] In Highland units, bagpipers assisted the drummers in regulating the soldier's day, with specific songs to signal various duties and events. Though these varied from regiment to regiment, "Hey Johnnie Cope" was known to sometimes replace the "Reveille" in the morning, while "Bannocks o' Barley" or "Brose and Butter" called to lunch or dinner, "Bundle and Go" was used for tea, while "Sleep, Dearie, Sleep" was played for "Last Post," concluding the soldier's day.[63]

The accounts from the Seven Years' War suggest that it was on the battlefield where the bagpipes played their most important role. As military historian R.M. Barnes writes, warfare in this era resembled a highly controlled military exercise, and the soldier's challenge was maintaining the formation and drill no matter the intensity of the conditions. Soldiers were not allowed to take cover when under fire but rather had to "stand still in close order," performing manoeuvres as correctly as possible.[64] The bagpipes assisted by boosting morale and providing reassurance to those in the front lines. They could also serve to rally soldiers when their nerves broke. At the Battle of the Plains of Abraham, for instance, when the Highlander line "advanced to the charge," General Murray sought the services of his bagpiper, "knowing well the value of one on such occasions." Murray reportedly shouted: "Where's the highland Piper! … Five pounds for a piper!" Yet the piper was nowhere to be found. The charge proceeded without his assistance. For this absence at the crucial moment, the piper was shamed: "Disgraced by the whole of the Regiment, and the men would not speak to him, neither would they suffer his rations to be drawn with theirs."[65]

In the subsequent battle of Sillery on 28 April 1760, the bagpiper succeeded in rallying the troops once their line broke. Thompson's 78th foot regiment bore the brunt of cannon and musket fire from the *Troupes de la Marine* before breaking formation and routing. However, once "rallied by their piper," they provided crucial assistance to the 58th and 15th foot, providing cover for the retreating army.[66] The following April when the French tried to retake Quebec, the Highland regiment was again scattered until the piper played his bagpipes at the opportune moment: "A blast of his pipes … had the effect of stopping them short, and they soon allow'd themselves to be form'd into some sort of order."[67] Here the bagpiper intervened when the regiment was in disarray, tangibly altering the outcome of the battle. Highland regiments and bagpipes proved successful on the battlefield and they saw increased use in the British army after the Seven Years' War.

The Scottish merchants and clerks in the post-conquest Montreal fur trade occasionally brought bagpipes into the northwest. Military connections may also have played a role in bringing these instruments to the trading posts of the Great Lakes. Descriptions of these instruments are scarce but do exist. One example is provided by fur trader Daniel Harmon, who recorded that bagpipes were part of the music provided at a dance at Grand Portage on Lake Superior in July of 1800. During the day, an Indigenous group was "permitted to dance in the fort," while in the evening at the fur traders' dance, the bagpipe was played in combination with the violin and flute. This unusual combination of instrumental music was appreciated by Harmon who felt it "added much to the interest of the occasion."[68] That a bagpipe was present and employed on this occasion testifies not only to the Scottish influence on the fur trade but the unusual ways and contexts in which it was played at the trading posts.

Displays of Power and Play

George Simpson sought to broadcast his power and authority soon after arriving in North America in 1820. He spent his first winter at the HBC's Fort Wedderburn on Lake Athabasca, adjacent to the NWC's Fort Chipewyan and the hostile Simon McGillivray. That season he witnessed first-hand the tensions that had dominated the fur trade for decades. One year later, he became the new governor of an amalgamated HBC and NWC. His obsession with efficiency led to aggressive changes that curtailed the prevailing fur trade culture. He drastically reduced the formal workforce by 1,223 men, or about 65 per cent of the total, between 1821 and 1826.[69] He moved toward increased use of seasonal labour while also imposing a significant reduction on lifestyle expenses at the trading posts. Simpson would become notorious for making rapid and extensive canoe voyages across the continent in the summer months, sometimes travelling so quickly that he arrived unexpectedly.[70] In what seems to have been an attempt to amplify his grandeur and authority and invoke awe and fear, Simpson adopted customs of military pomp and ceremony. In the 1820s, the Columbia District had a reputation as a lawless backwater that had largely escaped his scrutiny. When he finally made a tour in 1828, the bugle and bagpipes were employed regularly to emphasize the governor's arrival.

On this voyage, George Simpson was accompanied by Archibald McDonald. In his published account, he described the bagpiper Colin Fraser playing frequently along the journey from Hudson Bay to the Peace River. As for its suitability as an accompaniment to travel, McDonald clarified at the outset that bagpipes make "but a poor accordance with either the pole or the paddle." As a drone instrument, the bagpipes' rhythmic articulations were not suitable to coordinate the paddling the way the voyageurs' *chansons d'aviron* did. This was a point worth making at the outset of a journey of thousands of kilometres.[71] Yet the bagpipes still played a prominent role on this voyage in entertaining Simpson's crew along the way and in impressing servants, fur traders, and Indigenous peoples at and around the trading posts.

On the river, travel days were strenuously long, often lasting sixteen or eighteen hours. A brief window for leisure presented itself around dinner. Social historian Hugh Cunningham has emphasized that leisure activities during the Industrial Revolution served both as expressions of class and forms of social control. Recreational social activities could bridge class divisions as well as serve to reinforce them.[72] McDonald recounted a difficult day traversing mountain portages, at the end of which the piper "gave us a few marches before supper." This is followed by the revealing statement that "this is admitted to have been a hard day's work,"[73] suggesting that the piper played for the men to cheer their spirits on what was acknowledged to be a difficult day. In the open air, the instrumental music bridged class divisions by bringing together both master and servant. Marches are favoured in both French Canadian and Scottish traditions as a dance music form, yet on this occasion, the strenuous activities of the day ensured that it was appreciated not with dancing but in the context of relaxation and leisure. The men asked Colin Fraser to "give" "a few of his favorite strathspeys on the bagpipes." These, in turn, are reported to have "went off very well to the ear of a Highlander."[74] How the rest of the crew reacted was unstated.

The subsequent examples in McDonald's diary indicate the instrument was used to create a more spectacular arrival. This was intended to impress local Indigenous peoples as well as the employees and families at the trading posts. Before arriving at Norway House, after the customary final stop for a meal and change of clothes, McDonald noted that "the Highland bagpipes" in Simpson's canoe were "echoed by the bugle" in McDonald's. This suggests that these instruments were combined for amplified effect to inspire their men and perhaps reach the fort ahead. In combination, they would have transmitted sound over a long distance, perhaps five kilometers, and functioned as an early signal of their arrival. "On nearer approach to port," these instruments were laid aside to allow the voyageurs an opportunity to sing their paddling songs. Moving from the bugles and bagpipes to the voyageurs' songs represented an intercultural performance with the canoes acting as a floating stage. Music bridged class and ethnic divisions; McDonald characterized the voyageur songs as "peculiar to them, and always so perfectly rendered."[75] Undoubtedly, the voyageur singing after the bagpipes and bugle provided a long and dramatic approach to the fort.

Simpson's grandiose entrance continued upon landing: "His Excellency" proceeded to the fort in a procession behind the piper, arriving like a small company of a Scottish regiment. At the fort, he was met by three gentlemen and "a whole host of ladies." This spectacle was meant to impress those in and around the fort. Yet McDonald's statement that their arrival was "certainly more imposing than anything hitherto seen in this part of the Indian country" suggests that it was also intended to be imposing for Indigenous peoples.[76] The women at the fort would have been Indigenous and they seem to have made up the bulk of the audience. Servants of the company and Indigenous hunters also likely would have been within earshot. The custom of a "Grand Entry" with singing on arrival at councils has a long precedent among Indigenous peoples in the Great Lakes region.[77] Simpson's use of martial instruments made his entrance decidedly militaristic. The voyageur songs were a deviation from this tone, and it was a significant deviation. Whether Simpson's arrival was interpreted as a hostile imposition or as conforming to fur trade customs is difficult to ascertain. Perceptions may have varied. The "imposing" intent reflected Simpson's style of governance whereby he ruthlessly reformed business practices, often to the detriment of employees and their families.

Simpson attempted a variety of techniques to amplify the grandeur of his arrivals. Approaching Fort St James by foot and horse, McDonald described an elaborate procession: "The day, as yet, being fine, the flag was put up; the piper in full Highland costume; and every arrangement was made to arrive at Fort St. James in the most imposing manner we could, for the sake of the Indians. Accordingly, when within about a thousand yards of the establishment, descending a gentle hill, a gun was fired, the bugle sounded, and soon after, the piper commenced the celebrated march of the clans – 'Si coma leum cogadh na shea,' (Peace: or War, if you will it otherwise.) The guide, with the British ensign, led the van, followed by the band; then the Governor, on horseback, supported behind by Doctor Hamlyn and myself on our chargers, two deep; twenty men, with their burdens, next formed the line."[78]

This procession with bagpipes and mounted riders struck a different tone. First came the gunshot. Then the bugle. Then the bagpipes. The tune was selected specifically from the context of Scottish clan warfare. Simpson and his men had council with the local Indigenous peoples: "At the close of the harangue, the chief had a glass of rum, a little tobacco, and a shake of the hand from the Great Chief, after which the piper played them the *song of peace*."[79] This time, McDonald did not provide the Gaelic name, yet the symbolism of the chosen tunes is apparent. They were selected as if the specific cultural meanings – whether of peace or war – were comprehended across linguistic and cultural divides. They may well have been.

Ultimately, it is impossible to know how Indigenous peoples responded to the bagpipes. They would likely produce a dramatic effect in their power and novelty. There is only one account discovered to date of Indigenous perceptions, yet it may well be apocryphal. A Cree man who heard Colin Fraser play the bagpipes at Norway House described it to his chief thusly: "One white man was dressed like a woman, in a skirt of funny color. He had whiskers growing from his belt and fancy leggings. He carried a black swan which had many legs with ribbons tied to them. The swan's body he put under his arm upside down, then he put its head in his mouth and bit it. At the same time he pinched its neck with his fingers and squeezed the body under his arm until it made a terrible noise."[80]

Whatever the origins of this account, it suggests the potential understandings and misunderstandings involved in encountering novel instruments. Indigenous peoples at the trading posts were entertained and provided with musical curiosities. McDonald commented on an encounter with three Dene, who were "amused at everything they saw," especially the "various musical instruments."[81] What may have been interpreted as intimidating became a point of interest and interaction, likely involving both listening and touching the musical instruments. At Fort Dunvegan, where violence in previous years had been attributed to alcohol, Simpson met with seven or eight local Indigenous men and through his interpreter La Fleur discussed the disturbances. The Indigenous men "appeared much pleased with what is said to them." Simpson then distributed "a little tobacco, and a very weak drop of rum and water with sugar." McDonald was convinced that the sonic displays and musical instruments made a big impact based on their reaction to the encounter. It was "the *sound* [my emphasis] of the bugle, the bagpipes, Highland Piper in full dress, the musical suuff [snuff] box, &c., [that] excited in them emotions of admiration and wonder."[82] On another occasion, Simpson stopped to meet the "principal Indians of the place," and McDonald reports "exhibiting before them our various musical performances, &c., to their utter 'amusement.'"[83] After the music ended, an address was made through the interpreter and council began. Musical instruments were intertwined in the diplomatic dealings with Indigenous leaders.

Military instruments played a limited though noteworthy role in the fur trade. Music was central to the diplomatic commercial dealings between the trading companies and Indigenous peoples. At certain places at certain times, drums, bugles, and bagpipes featured prominently in encounters. Military instruments contributed to the spectacle of Simpson's arrival at trading posts along his travel routes, bolstering the impression of his power. Yet these instruments also provided music for recreation and dance, and served as objects of novelty in cross-cultural interactions. Instruments of warfare were repurposed to serve the needs of those involved in the fur trade. They were imported into northeastern North America in the greatest numbers during the period of intensive warfare from the Seven Years' War until the War of 1812, yet they also had at least some influence in the 1820s and beyond. While during wartime they issued signals and served to rally troops, they were repurposed in processions to impress and in recreation to amuse. Simpson may have thought it wise to employ the bagpipes to foster unity between previously rival employees of the NWC and HBC, whose traders consisted of many Highland Scots who now had to work together. Of all the European military instruments, drums most bridged the cultural divide with Indigenous peoples. They served as a potent conduit of interaction, and in some cases, as among the Anishinaabeg of Manitoulin Island or the Cree of James Bay, were adopted and adapted into Indigenous musical cultures.

Dances of Diplomacy

In the tumultuous half-century from the 1760s to the 1810s, dancing constituted more than simple recreation. For non-Indigenous people travelling and trading in "Indian country," designated by the Royal Proclamation of 1763 as everything west of the Appalachians including the Great Lakes and northwest, dances were often encountered as part of diplomatic relations. Indigenous cultural protocol was unknown to many fur traders, and that mattered. The British officials and merchants who hoped for an uncontested welcome in the Great Lakes after the conquest of the St Lawrence were stunningly rebuked by a pan-tribal alliance of Indigenous Nations in Pontiac's War of 1763. These events powerfully sent the message that trade would not occur unless peaceful relations, alliances, and proper conduct was first established.[1] English-speaking fur traders began following the same diplomatic avenues that the French had before them. This included participating in ceremonial pipe rituals that the French called "calumet" and the English called "peace-pipe" with their Indigenous military allies and trading partners. It also included watching "war dances."[2] Indigenous peoples had different varieties, names, and understandings of pipe ceremonies and the dances associated with war. For fur traders, these diverse traditions were categorized together as components of being trading partners and military allies with Indigenous peoples. Being trading partners involved regularly renewing the relationship, meeting in ceremony, and exchanging materials that would help in the event of war. Pipe ceremonies helped solidify the bonds of peace and alliance. War dances demonstrated alliance, prowess, and military commitment. Even outside of wartime, these practices appeared in the fur trade. It was against the broader backdrop of colonial political alliances and diplomacy that fur traders often found themselves engaging with Indigenous dances.

Music and dance played a central role in the diplomatic encounters of fur traders. They were frequently important components of pipe ceremonies, which helped establish proper relationships. Generally speaking, the Indigenous peoples of the Plains and west coast would not trade with enemies. Gift-giving and smoking ceremonies were pursued because they established, as Cole Harris put it, "a favourable political climate for trade."[3] Forming good trading relationships with Indigenous communities usually involved ceremony, sharing food, and gift-giving. Part of successful adaptation to Indigenous cultural diplomacy was to participate in pipe ceremonies and sit audience to war dances. They were rarely fully understood or adequately described, and a variety of Indigenous dances were oversimplified into these categories. Still, these diverse cultural forms played a meaningful role in the fur trade, especially during the half-century following Pontiac's War. While pipe ceremonies signified peace and war dances ostensibly the opposite, in the fur trade context they both served to strengthen alliances and bolster social relations between Indigenous peoples and fur traders.

By listening to the fur trade, the dances of diplomacy observed by fur traders in the late eighteenth and early nineteenth centuries become apparent. The dances associated with the ceremonial pipe loom large in the seventeenth-century accounts and continue throughout the eighteenth century. Descriptions of war dances become prominent during the mid-eighteenth century and the Seven Years' War. In many ways, this reflects the fact that fur traders were often involved in two kinds of treaty-making – commercial compacts and peace and alliance treaties – and that generally one could not be had without the other.[4] War dances were performed by Indigenous peoples at trading posts from the mid-eighteenth century through until at least the 1820s. Fur traders, especially effective ones, received these performances with solemnity and respect, similar to the gift-giving that often preceded trade. Both the ceremonial pipe and war dances were part of the relationship building or renewing that occurred before trade. It is only after the War of 1812 and the establishment of the HBC's monopoly in British North America that the fur trade shifted away from these time-honoured avenues of diplomacy.

Seventeenth-Century Passage and Trade: The Ceremonial Pipe

In the mid-seventeenth century, French explorers and fur traders described pipe ceremonies because of their diplomatic centrality to Indigenous Nations around the Great Lakes. They played an important role for Nicholas Perrot who explored Lake Michigan and the Upper Mississippi valley for France. He described how the ceremonial pipe was "sung" to honour important individuals such as visiting chiefs and diplomatic convoys. Indeed, this is how he was received at villages of Miamis and Mascoutens at the west end of Lake Michigan in the late 1660s. In one instance, he stopped a distance from a village, sending someone to notify them of his arrival. At this, all "the youths came at once to meet him, bearing their weapons and their warlike adornments, all marching in file, with frightful contortions and yells; this was the most honorable reception that they thought it possible to give him." We are told that Perrot "was not uneasy, but fired a gun in the air as far away as he could see them; this noise, which seemed to them so extraordinary, caused them to halt suddenly, gazing at the sun in most ludicrous attitudes. After he had made them understand that he had come not to disturb their repose, but to form an alliance with them, they approach him with many gesticulations. The calumet was presented to him." This passage indicates that Perrot discharged his firearm in response to the advancing procession. As soon as he made it clear that he wanted an alliance, the ceremonial pipe was presented and he was led to the cabin of a prominent warrior. There, all the men "danced the calumet to the sound of the drum."[5]

The ceremonial pipe continued to be the ticket to Perrot's safe passage. At the next village, he was presented with a remarkable calumet "of red stone, with a long stick at the end; this was ornamented in its whole length with the heads of birds, flame-colored, and had in the middle a bunch of feathers colored a bright red, which resembled a great fan." When this was presented, words were uttered that were "apparently addressed to all the spirits whom those peoples adore. The old man held it sometimes toward the east, and sometimes toward the west; then toward the sun; now he would stick the end in the ground and then he would turn the calumet around him, looking at it as if he were trying to point out the whole earth, with expressions which gave the Frenchman to understand that he had compassion on all men." Bacqueville de la Potherie, chronicler of New France, interpreted this ceremony and subsequent speech and prayer as favourable to Perrot and the French cause, assuming it was "to assure the Frenchman of the joy which all in the village felt at his arrival."[6] Perrot recognized that the ceremony was sacred and addressed to the spirits, while also conveying abstract concepts such as compassion toward other human beings. It is in this spirit of compassion that Perrot seems to have been received at the west end of Lake Michigan. La Potherie described how the distinguished men from the Miami villages appeared with their ceremonial pipes: "they sang, as they approached, the calumet song, which they uttered in cadence. When they reached the Frenchmen, they continued their songs, meanwhile bending their knees, in turn, almost to the ground. They presented the calumet to the sun, with the same genuflexions, and then they came back to the principal Frenchman, with many gesticulations. Some played upon instruments the calumet songs, and others sang them, holding the calumet in the mouth without lighting it. A war chief raised Perot upon his shoulders, and, accompanied by all the musicians, conducted him to the village."[7] This grand reception was interpreted as expressing welcome and honour. The next day, the French delegation gave the Miamis a gun and a kettle as a sign of their gratitude. In the Great Lakes, ceremonial pipe rituals constituted much of what initially brought Indigenous and non-Indigenous peoples together in a good way.

Contemporary scholarship emphasizes both social and spiritual considerations in explaining the significance of Indigenous pipe ceremonies. The rituals associated with the ceremonial pipe mediate simultaneously between people and the spirit world.[8] Their materials and procedures are highly symbolic and sacred within Indigenous cosmologies. The bowl of the pipe is often interpreted as "a sacrificial vessel that itself is a miniature cosmos," with pinches of tobacco constituting the sacrifice. The smoke is an offering, with the stem directing it toward points of symbolic significance. The ritual embodied a kind of "cosmos of social relationships," radiating outward from the self to family, clan, nation, animal relations, and the outermost powerful spirits represented by the four directions, and the winds, sky, earth, and sea.[9] The pipe bowl is generally interpreted as feminine, and usually made of stone or clay, the substance of female Earth. The stem is made from trees that point up toward the sky and is considered masculine. Only when the stem is inserted into the bowl is the pipe deemed potent and active. It is then "in their conjoining, plants and living creatures are created."[10] As the pipe is lit, the smoke rises to connect with the spirit-world.

Indigenous ceremonies were employed to form alliances and trading compacts with fur traders. Gift-giving, feasting, and calumet ceremonies rank centrally in this process. These traditions of alliance-making were not merely adopted because fur traders were reliant on Indigenous peoples for safe passage and the products of their hunt. Indigenous peoples used ceremonies to symbolically transform fur traders from strangers into relatives.[11] Some scholars have described this phenomenon as establishing "fictive kinship."[12] While the spiritual significance and symbolism of these ceremonies were often misunderstood by the French, heavily influenced as they were by their Catholic worldview, on a functional level they were correctly interpreted as a diplomatic avenue that represented and solidified goodwill.

On their voyage down the Mississippi in 1673, Joliet and Marquette participated in calumet ceremonies with a succession of Indigenous communities. The section of their memoirs entitled "Of the Character of the Illinois; of their Habits and Customs; and of the Esteem that they have for the Calumet, or Tobacco-pipe, and of the Dance they perform in its Honor"[13] is seemingly the most comprehensive description produced in the seventeenth century. It speaks of the dances as honouring the ceremonial pipe, which was treated as a form of deity. Welcoming a visitor was one, but not the only, occasion for its performance: "The calumet dance, which is very famous among these peoples, is performed solely for important reasons; sometimes to strengthen peace, or to unite themselves for some great war; at other times, for public rejoicing. Sometimes they thus do honor to a nation who are invited to be present; sometimes it is danced at the reception of some important personage as if they wished to give him the diversion of a ball or a comedy. In winter, the ceremony takes place in a cabin; in summer, in the open fields."[14] The setting for the ceremony was carefully chosen in the shade of a tree, where a large painted mat of rushes was spread, serving as a platform for the warriors to place their weapons and medicine bundles in reverence.[15] As the warriors filed into the circle to sit, they "salute the Manitou" by inhaling smoke and blowing on it as if "offering to it incense."[16] No less than a three-stage ceremony followed, beginning with each individual taking hold of the ceremonial pipe and dancing to the rhythm of the drumming and singing: "Every one, at the outset, takes the calumet in a respectful manner, and, supporting it with both hands, causes it to dance in cadence, keeping good time with the air of the songs. He makes it execute many differing figures; sometimes he shows it to the whole assembly, turning himself from one side to the other. After that, he who is to begin the dance appears in the middle of the assembly, and at once continues this. Sometimes he offers it to the sun, as if he wished the latter to smoke it; sometimes he inclines it toward the earth; again, he makes it spread its wings, as if about to fly; at other times, he puts it near the mouths of those present, that they may smoke. The whole is done in cadence."

The second part consisted of a mock-combat dance carried out to the sound of the drum. The man with the ceremonial pipe invited a warrior to equip himself with bows, arrows, and war-hatchets while he symbolically defended himself with the calumet. Joliet and Marquette found this aspect of the dance "very pleasing," as it was performed "so well, with slow and measured steps, and to the rhythmic sound of the voices and drums." The third and final part of the ceremony involved the ceremonial pipe holder making a speech about

Fig. 4.1 Calumet song transcribed by Jolliet and Marquette. *Early Narratives of the Northwest*, edited by Louise Phelps Kellogg (New York: Charles Scribner's Sons, 1917), 247–8.

achievements in war, victories, and captives taken, before passing it around once more. He received a gift from the host nation, in this case, a "fine robe of beaver-skin," as a "token of the everlasting peace that is to exist between the two peoples."[17] Joliet and Marquette deemed this ceremony with its attendant music so significant that they devoted to it an entire section of their account and notated its music. It survives as among the earliest and fullest European transcriptions of North American Indigenous music. Unlike the transcriptions of Jesuits and other missionaries, the motivation here for taking such careful account was primarily diplomatic with an eye (or ear) toward alliance and trade. The notation itself is presented with an earnest appraisal of its shortcomings, as the music on which it is based possessed "a certain turn which cannot be sufficiently expressed by note, but which nevertheless constitutes all its grace."

French explorer fur traders described ceremonial pipe dances not solely out of ethnographic interest. They recognized they were a crucial aspect of peace-making and diplomacy. Richard White characterized the calumet ceremonies of the western Great Lakes as a "conscious framework for peace, alliance, exchange, and free movement."[18] This is part of his analysis of a cultural "middle ground" whereby intercultural dynamics were navigated imperfectly but engaged with out of necessity. Colin Calloway described how dancing and smoking ceremonially was deemed "a prerequisite for negotiation and an essential foundation for good relations."[19] Pipe ceremonies symbolically transformed enemies into allies and outsiders into kin. They were an essential component of the 1701 Great Peace of Montreal, in which calumets and smoking ceremonies were integrated into councils and exchanges.[20] Various forms of diplomacy were enacted: "in an atmosphere of exuberance and reconciliation, Native people and Frenchmen exchanged goods and gifts, displayed wampum belts, smoked the peace pipe, and danced and feasted to establish a lasting alliance."[21] The chroniclers of New France suggested that the calumet originated on the Plains in the early seventeenth century, from there disseminating to the eastern woodlands and Great Lakes.[22] By the late seventeenth century, pipe ceremonies were commonly practised by Indigenous peoples from the St Lawrence to the Mississippi and Great Plains.[23] The French may have contributed to its dissemination, but it was undoubtedly an Indigenous cultural form.

The diplomatic usage of the ceremonial pipe persisted through the eighteenth century, and various European officials and traders adopted it in councils with Indigenous Nations. Seven Years' War veteran Robert Rogers described how the "calumet or pipe of peace" was revered "in many transactions, relative both to war and peace." He described how pipe stems were decorated so that on presentation to another nation, intentions of either war or peace were evident from the feathers alone.[24] The bowls were typically made of carved soft red stone and the stems made of "cane, elder, or some kind of light wood." The pipes were activated symbolically when connected. Due to their sacred esteem they were employed in religious ceremonies and treaties, and considered "as a witness between the parties; or rather as an instrument by which they invoke the sun and moon to witness their sincerity, and to be, as it were, guarantees of the treaty between them."[25] In council negotiations, the ceremonial pipe was understood to enhance the veracity of words spoken, and serve as a sacred witness. It figured not only in meetings between Crown officials and Indigenous peoples, but also with fur traders. The politics of peace and war were inextricably interwoven into trading relationships.

Dancing for Peace and War and Trade

By the early to mid-eighteenth century, colonial relationships with Indigenous peoples had developed and protocols had somewhat standard-ized. Indigenous diplomatic forms of gift-giving, feasting, ceremonies, and exchanging wampum were engaged in by the British and Haudenosaunee and the French with numerous Great Lakes and Mississippi Indigenous Nations. This physical territory and historical dynamic of accommodation have been referred to as a "middle ground."[26] No one Indigenous Nation had supremacy, and inhabitants and newcomers alike had to find creative ways to cooperate. There was an incredible plurality of Indigenous peoples around the Great Lakes with long political histories who continued living their lives and navigating through changing circumstances.[27] Intercultural meetings often included both a calumet ceremony and war dance to reaffirm alliance and enable trade. Trading relationships had always possessed connotations of military alliance. For Indigenous peoples, these two concepts were connected as mutual obligations of kinship. In other words, the alliance entailed both commercial and military obligations.[28] Dances associated with war existed in various forms and names among Indigenous peoples, and served various functions within the community. Indigenous scholar Taiaiake Alfred describes the ancient *Rotinoshonni* war ritual *Wasáse* as "a ceremony of unity, strength, and commitment to action."[29] In the atmosphere of heightened military tensions between France and Britain for North America, this was precisely the symbol that impressed allies who responded with gifts and trading goods.

This is perhaps nowhere as apparent as in the example of William Johnson, the Irish settler in the Mohawk Valley who became the towering figure of eighteenth century British – Indigenous relations. He exerted a "pivotal influence" on British "Indian policy."[30] It was from the Albany conference of 1754 that Johnson received a royal commission as "Sole Agent and Superintendant" of Indigenous peoples in northern North America.[31] Biographers have made the case that Johnson uniquely grasped the "ritual dimension of exchange in Indian cultures."[32] Under his purview, the British renewed the "covenant chain" treaty relationship that the Dutch had started with the Haudenosaunee in the seventeenth century, eventually extending it to other nations. Gift-giving, feasting, trading, and exchanging wampum belts were the tangible components of renewing the treaty relationship. Yet "polishing the chain" of friendship went beyond material exchanges to ceremonies and presenting intangible cultural heritage such as war dances.

Operating from his estate on the Mohawk River, Johnson described visits by various Indigenous peoples. He described one instance in 1757, when trading occurred "after an Entertainment which was made for them, at which they danced the War Dance, they were supplied with Provisions &c. for their Journey & then marcht."[33] This language suggests that something was provided by Johnson and his coterie before receiving the war dance. This exchange likely signified more than mere entertainment for the Indigenous party, tapping into deeper notions of honour and pride that served to strengthen the military alliance. A more detailed description from Johnson's estate appeared two years later on 17 September 1759. A war party of Mohawk from Caghnawaga arrived singing a slow march: "10 of their Warriors being naked, painted & feather'd, (one of whom had a Drum on his back made of a Cag covered with Skin) marched in Slow order in two Ranks, Singing their Song accordg. to the *Ottawa Custom*, Tom Wildman in the Rere Tank beating the Drum with one Stick, and the rest accompanying it with Notched Sticks which they Struck to good time on their Axes."[34] With the coordinated rhythm of drums and notched sticks, the procession slowly approached Johnson's house. The only named member of the war party, "advanced before the rest, & Sung his War Song, which he twice repeated, after which Sir Wm. gave them some Liquor, Pipes, Tobacco and Paint whereupon they returned back in the same order."[35] This account indicates that the gift-giving occurred after the war song was performed. By marching for Johnson with deliberate and well-timed movements and music, the war party demonstrated its intimidating potential, coordination, and military prowess. While it may have had spiritual significances and served other functions, to Johnson it demonstrated the military alliance. This detailed description suggests the Mohawk war song made a considerable impression on Johnson and was reciprocated with provisions.

Throughout the Seven Years' War, Johnson became ever more involved in treaty-making and diplomacy. He participated in gift exchanges, councils, and feasting. On one occasion, he arranged for "an Ox to be dressed for their War Dance."[36] On another, he was the subject of honour when he was given a feast of venison by 150 Oneidas. In this encounter they treated him, he felt, "as being one of their Tribe." This was accompanied by "a great War Dance."[37] Johnson was comfortable playing the role of host and providing space and provisions for dances. Yet he went further. On 20 March 1757, Johnson entered "the large Room where the Six Nations were dancing the War Dance & sung his War Song."[38] Johnson was so familiar with Haudenosaunee diplomatic forms and protocols that he sang his war song, perhaps lauding his own military experience. We lack details but know this was followed by a speech extolling the Six Nations in their preparedness and commitment to go to war. This reveals the political motivations underpinning Johnson's cross-cultural performances.

The following year, on 27 June 1758, Johnson again performed for a group of Onondagas, Oneidas, and Tuscarora warriors, as well as some French prisoners. He encouraged those who wished "to be thought Friends & Bretheren to the English," to be equipped immediately for war and join the military expedition that was departing for Fort Carillon (Ticonderoga). Johnson finished his speech and "threw down the War Belt & danced the War Dance, after which a principal Man of each Nation also Danced."[39] Johnson's diplomatic approach seemed to have been affirmed by the reaction of the chiefs in council. Yet these allies for the most part wisely resisted joining Abercromby's ill-fated attack on Fort Carillon.[40] Indeed, Johnson's unceasing efforts through gifts and cultural protocols such as war dances might be interpreted as British desperation for Indigenous allies during the Seven Years' War, particularly after the loss of Oswego and Fort William Henry. Johnson clearly grasped the significance of dances and songs in diplomatic negotiations. This was an aspect of engagement he participated in that continued with officials and fur traders over the following decades.[41]

War songs became part of the metaphorical language of diplomacy. Figures of speech were essential tools in intercultural diplomatic discourse. Orators employed metaphors and symbols that promoted cross-cultural understandings, yet sometimes led to misunderstandings.[42] To "sing the war song" was adopted into British parlance as signifying a commitment to go to war. The soldier

Jelles Fonda described in 1760 how the Onondagas initially declined to sing the war song but promised to sing it later at Oswego, signifying that they would then be ready for military engagement.[43] Similar to an oath, this was a public pronouncement that asserted military commitment. In the journal of Robert Rogers, on 8 August 1763, at Detroit, he described how after a long council the Wyandots were prevailed "on to sing the War Song."[44] From the British diplomatic lens, the war song was a confirmation and demonstration of the military alliance. The Wyandots may have been reluctant because of the implications, yet they eventually did sing. War songs and dances fulfilled important intercultural requirements of diplomacy, potentially galvanizing and reinforcing commitment during times of war. These interactions were significant because they occurred at the same time the fur trade was expanding into the northwest from the St Lawrence and Great Lakes corridor. British-Indigenous relations influenced the expectations and methods of fur traders, as well as Indigenous peoples in the Great Lakes region. As fur traders pushed into the Great Plains, Subarctic, and the Rocky Mountains in the late eighteenth century, they often brought with them understandings they had developed about intercultural interactions in the northeast.

Alexander Henry (the elder) was aware of the calumet's significance on his journey westwards in the 1760s. It became a key component of his success. He mentioned in his journal where pipe stone was quarried on the Ottawa River. During his tense reception with Indigenous peoples in the Great Lakes who had previously been allied with the French, Henry sat quietly "in ceremony." "Mina'va'va'na," an Anishinaabe chief loyal to the French, entered into the solemn environment.[45] In this delicate situation, the pipe ceremony provided a safe space for Henry to engage in diplomatic relations with someone otherwise hostile. He was shielded by the sacred ceremonialism of the pipe. Jonathan Carver was expecting pipe ceremonies as he travelled from Lake Michigan toward the Mississippi River in 1766, carrying as he did a copy of the Jesuit Father Hennepin's journal. While navigating the St Pierre [Minnesota] River, Carver encountered Indigenous peoples in canoes who fled at his approach. Nervous about a subsequent ambush, he travelled up the river with the "pipe of peace ... fixed at the head of [his] canoe."[46] He seems to have made this gesture as a flag of truce, and it seems to have worked. When Carver reached a village of over one thousand Dakota, he was taken by the hand and "according to the custom that universally prevails among every Indian nation, began to smoke the pipe of peace."[47] It was not actually universal, but this reveals the perspective Carver had gathered from his experiences among northeastern Indigenous Nations in the mid-late eighteenth century. His writing has ethnographic value, as he describes his overwintering experiences and participating in hunting and warfare while learning the Dakota's language and customs.[48] Calumet ceremonies were usually the first in a long series of diplomatic ceremonies Carver navigated when travelling and trading with Indigenous peoples west of Lake Michigan.

An entire chapter of Carver's publication relates to the subject of dancing. Indigenous peoples, from his observation, "never meet on any public occasion" without dancing. He claimed that when not at war or hunting, the youth of both sexes amused themselves by dancing every night.[49] He identified four categories of dance: "the Pipe or Calumate Dance, the War Dance, the Marriage Dance, and the Dance of the Sacrifice." Deciding to arrange the dances by function, Carver provided only a brief description of each, stating that while "the movements in every one of these are dissimilar … it is almost impossible to convey any idea of the points in which they are unlike."[50] He described how "The Pipe Dance is the principal, and the most pleasing to a spectator of any of them," owing to it "being the least frantic, and the movement of it the most graceful. It is but on particular occasions that it is used; as when ambassadors from an enemy arrive to treat of peace, or when strangers of eminence pass through their territories."[51] It is apparent from these descriptions that the honorary ceremonialism was intriguing and appreciated by Carver. He employs language commonly used to describe the courtly manner of the eighteenth-century aristocracy, obsessed as they were with maintaining proper "body carriage."[52] Being the most "graceful," the calumet dance was deemed by Carver to be the most pleasing. In another observation, he notes that "the women, particularly of the western nations, dance very gracefully. They carry themselves erect, and with their arms hanging down close to their sides."[53] Other fur traders may or may not have shared his opinion. Carver, like others, stated his preferences in his descriptions, yet still produced valuable ethnographic records.

War dances are described as being employed both before setting out and upon returning from war. In contrast to Carver's description of the calumet dance, war dances were said to strike "terror into strangers."[54] They were performed by a circle of warriors and begun by a chief who sings about his military exploits and those of his ancestors. On recounting each memorable action, a post sticking from the ground is struck with the war club. "Every one dances in his turn, and recapitulates the wondrous deeds of his family, till they all at last join the dance. Then it becomes truly alarming to any stranger that happens to be among them, as they throw themselves into every horrible and terrifying posture that can be imagined, rehearsing at the same time the parts they expect to act against their enemies."[55] Carver then described how they dance and whirl their weapons, imitating battle while yelling and war whooping. Crucially, he admits that he "frequently joined in this dance with them, but it soon ceased to be an amusement to me, as I could not lay aside my apprehensions of receiving some dreadful wound, that from the violence of their gestures must have proved mortal."[56] Dancing with the warriors was part of Carver's interactions with the Dakota. It influenced the relationship he had with them, and how they viewed him, being not only a supplier of European materials but also a military ally who engaged in the war dance.

Other fur traders were intrigued by the nuances of war dances. One early English-speaking fur trader in the Ohio valley, Christopher Gist, provided an account of a Twigtwee or Miami "Warriors Feather Dance," a variation of the Eagle dance. Gist and his companions were invited to the longhouse to watch three painted "Dancing Masters." According to this description, holding "long Sticks in their Hands, upon the Ends of which were fastened long Feathers of Swans, and other Birds, neatly woven in the Shape of a Fowls Wing: in this Disguise they performed many antick Tricks, waving their Sticks and Feathers about with great Skill to imitate the flying and fluttering of Birds, keeping exact Time with their Musick."[57] Then familiar features emerge: "while they are dancing some of the Warriors strike a Post, upon which the Musick and Dancers cease, and the Warrior gives an Account of his Achievements in War, and when he has done, throws down some Goods as a Recompence to the Performers and Musicians."[58] Striking the post in this case signalled a transition between group and individual performance. This passage also suggests that the warriors cycling through the middle of the circle gave gifts to the musicians for their services, an aspect often omitted from later descriptions.

The notoriety of William Johnson extended among the Indigenous peoples of the Great Lakes. The Treaty of Niagara in 1764 between the British and over twenty Indigenous Nations around the Great Lakes opened the door for English-speaking traders. Fur traders were often cognizant of Johnson's methods, as is sometimes revealed in their accounts. One of the early English traders working among the Anishinaabeg north of Lake Superior was John B. Long. He reported departing Montreal with two *maître* canoes manned by ten voyageurs each for the north shore of Lake Superior, arriving at Pays Plat on 4 July 1777.[59] Here they unloaded their cargo and packed it into smaller bales for easier transportation over the many difficult portages (his guide estimated 180 remained) before arriving at their overwintering grounds. A group of local Anishinaabe, who Long estimated to number 150, provided fish, dried meat, and skins in exchange for a few "trifling presents." According to his account, the Chief Matchee Quewish held a council proposing to adopt Long as a "brother warrior," something recommended by the experienced fur traders because it would result in being "favoured exceedingly." In the description of Long's adoption ceremony, he invoked William Johnson, "of immortal Indian memory," and his diplomatic practices. In particular, he described the symbolic use of wampum "when Sir William Johnson held a treaty," describing how he would hold one end of the wampum belt while the Indigenous chief took the other, touching it in relevant places when it was their turn to speak.[60] This invocation of the Treaty of Niagara is noteworthy and demonstrates the connection between diplomacy and the fur trade. This diplomacy involved the exchange of both material and immaterial culture.

Long depicts himself as participating in Anishinaabe adoption or initiation ceremonies. These featured war songs and dances. A feast was first made consisting of dog's flesh boiled in bear grease and huckleberries. After the meal, a war song was sung, according to Long with the following words: "Master of Life, view us well; we receive a brother warrior who appears to have sense, shews strength in his arm, and does not refuse his body to the enemy." "After the war song, if the person does not discover any signs of fear, he is regarded with reverence and esteem; courage … being considered not only as indispensible, but as the greatest recommendation. He is then seated on the beaver robe, and presented with a pipe of war to smoke, which is put round to every warrior, and a wampum belt is thrown over his neck."[61] This ceremony combined a war song with the ceremonial pipe and wampum belt.

Long wrote of the importance of the calumet as a "symbol of peace." He described its material composition and symbolic significance in detail. "The calumet, or Indian pipe, which is much larger than that the Indians usually smoke, is made of marble, stone, or clay, either red, white, or black, according to the custom of the nation, but the red is mostly esteemed; the length of the handle is about four feet and a half, and made of strong cane or wood, decorated with feathers of various colours, with a number of twists of female hair interwoven in different forms; the head is finely polished; two wings are fixed to it, which make it in appearance not unlike to Mercury's wand." It was held in such high estimation, according to Long, particularly when making agreements, "that a violation of any treaty where it has been introduced, would in their opinion be attended with the greatest misfortunes."[62] Long recognized its significance as a venerated and sacred entity that functioned as a powerful diplomatic tool.

Fur traders navigated delicate intercultural pipe ceremonies. In 1786–87 near Prairie du Chien, NWC voyageur Jean-Baptiste Perrault witnessed a calumet ceremony that was interrupted when a young Sioux warrior "refusa d'accepter le calumet."[63] He was reprimanded by a chief that "que ce lieu est sacré" and "tu devois faire tes réflexions avant de partir." The ceremony continued and peace was secured between the diverse group of Anishinaabe, Sauk, Fox, and Sioux.[64] In 1788, Perrault was witness to a tense meeting between groups of Sauteaux (Anishinaabe) and Siouan-speakers at Mackinac. Animosity was evident from the outset and violence threatened to break out. Yet the pipe ceremony and protection it offered allowed for constructive interaction. Perrault related how speeches and harangues were exchanged before the calumet dances began. At this point, "La Bécasse prit le tambour, le mit en ordre et il arrangea un calumet. Les Scioux commencèrent à danser le calumet et ensuite ils dansèrent des découvertes après quoi ils présentèrent le tambour et le calumet aux Sauteux qui en firent autant, mais avec beaucoup plus de gâces [sic]." After some time, a French man named Desnoyer observed that the Sioux watching the Sauteaux were starting to become hostile. They were making threatening facial expressions and muttering "quelques paroles mal placées." Concerned that the performance had transformed from peaceful to antagonistic, Desnoyer took action. He "prit le tambour" and the dance stopped.[65] It is not indicated what aspect of the dance was not well received, and Perrault related only that a sullen silence reigned for the remainder of the night. The calumet dance could serve as a framework for peaceful interaction between hostile adversaries. Yet even in ceremony, the potential for hostility and violence remained.

Jean-Baptiste Perrault also described a large intertribal war dance at Prairie du Chien in 1786–87. In his description, he stressed that there was a "chef de guerre" (chief of war) who led the expedition and the "chante la guerre" (song of war).[66] David Thompson witnessed a somewhat uneasy encounter between Iroquois employees of the NWC and the "Nahathaways" (Cree). It began with a feast of bison and deer, and after dinner the Iroquois performed "a few common dances." Then they "commenced their favorite dance the grand Calumet." This was "much admired and praised"; yet when the Iroquois finished and "requested the Nahathaways to dance their grand Calumet," they replied that they "had no smoking dance."[67] The response indicated something of the symbolic and diplomatic potency of these dances. This "elated the Iroquois, and they began their War dance from the discovery of the enemy, to the attack and scalping of the dead, and the war whoop of victory. The Nahathaways praised them. The Iroquois being now proud of their national dances, requested of the

Nahathaways to see their War dance, and intimating they thought they had none, which was in a manner saying they were not warriors."

Performing came with expectations of reciprocity. The challenge was clear across linguistic and cultural lines: if the Cree had no war dance, they could not possibly be warriors. At this point, according to the account, Thompson intervened. He noticed a "smile of contempt" on the lips of Spik a nog gan (The Gun Case), an experienced Cree warrior fifty years old who Thompson knew "excelled in the dance." Thompson claims he helped goad him into performing. "Somewhat nettled, he arose, put on a light war dress, and with his large dagger in his right hand, he began the War dance, by the Scout, the Spy, the Discovery, the return to camp, the Council, the silent march to the ambuscade, the war whoop of attack the tumult of the battle, the Yells of doubtful contest and the War whoop of victory; the pursuit, his breath short and quick the perspiration pouring down on him his dagger in the fugitive, and the closing War whoop of the death of his enemy rung through our ears. The varying passions were strongly marked in his face, and the whole was performed with enthusiasm. The perfect silence, and all eyes rivetted on him, showed the admiration of every one, and for which I rewarded him."

This performance had an effect on the audience and on Thompson. Spik a nog gan was rewarded with unspecified gifts. The Iroquois "seemed lost in surprise, and after a few minutes said, our dances please ourselves, and also the white people and Indians where ever we go, but your dance is war itself to victory and to death."[68] The appreciation of the Cree war dance underscored a degree of mutual comprehension and respect between these diverse peoples. For Thompson, he was "much pleased with the effect this dance had on the Iroquois," as it seemed to "bring them to their senses, and showed them, that the Indians of the interior countries were fully as good Warriors, Hunters and Dancers, as themselves." After this performance, the Iroquois dropped the antagonism and "turned to hunting." War dances seem to have served as an important marker of masculinity. These performances, according to Thompson, convinced the Iroquois of the strength and bravery of the Indigenous peoples in the "interior countries." To the south of Lake Superior in 1804–05, François Victor Malhiot described his apprehensions when at the fort with only one other employee a war party of seventeen Anishinaabe arrived. They were going to hold a feast. "After making me eat some, they left us, to my great satisfaction, for my provisions are diminishing rapidly."[69] This passage suggests expectations of a reciprocal exchange with the fur trader gifting provisions in return for food. Malhiot had recently learned of a "row" at the neighbouring XY Company fort. The trading post-master Chorette was roughed up and his stores pillaged when he ran out of rum during a visit. Malhiot expected another war party would arrive at his post any day, and was worried about meeting diplomatic expectations while facing a supply shortage.[70] In the fur trade, visitors brought gifts and expectations.

Beginning as a clerk into the NWC in 1784, Peter Grant served in the Rainy Lake and Red River departments. His description of the Sauteaux is ethnographically detailed. He categorized the "grand calumet dance" as one of their three main types of dance. He understood that the calumet dance was only performed on special occasions. He noted that the "stem is curiously ornamented with feathers of different colours." He described the dancers' movements and the cycle of the ceremony: "The dancer is provided with a rattle in his right hand and a war pipe stem in his left ... He holds the stem in a horizontal position, keeping exact time with the song and drum, shaking his rattle in every direction, and working himself up by degrees into many strange and uncommon posture, stamping furiously along, with his body sometimes parallel to the ground, twisting himself and turning in an astonishing manner, and, yet, always keeping time with the music. At intervals, he brandishes his stem or rattle toward some spectators in such quick and masterly a manner as would make a mere stranger imagine that he actually wished to devour or swallow him up. The performer finishes by presenting his implements to another person, which is always considered a compliment, and in this manner the dance continues so long as there are parties willing to join."[71] This remark-ably detailed description was produced by careful and repeated observation, evident by his use of the word "always." He struggled to describe the unfamiliar movements. He reverted to adjectives such as "strange," "uncommon," and "astonishing," while admiring how these movements were always made in time with the music. That a fur trader made such detailed observations about this form of Indigenous diplomatic ritual suggests its importance as an adjunct to trade. Appraisals of both functionality and aesthetics came from fur traders such as Grant who were outsiders yet welcomed into communities with pipe dances and who kept observing them sometimes for years. He noted that "the northern tribes, especially the *Maskegons* [Swampy Cree] and those about *Lac Lapluie* and River Ouinipic seem to have entirely neglected it, but the *Pilleurs* [Chippewa – Anishinaabe] and their southerly neighbours take great merit in their superior knowledge of this dance."[72] Grant's statement was more than amateur ethnography, it reflected the practical observations of a fur trader for whom calumet ceremonies mattered.

Grant described the "war dance" as one of the three common kinds of Anishinaabe dances that he witnessed, besides the "grand calumet" and "common dance."[73] His description of the war dance included warriors going through the motions of loading and shooting a gun, as well as using traditional weapons:

> The "war dance" is a representation of the different manoeuvres of discovering, attacking and scalping an enemy. The performer begins with a hanger, *cassetéte,* or some other offensive weapon, which he flourhishes in a variety of threatening attitudes, while dancing; he then hops along for some time, apparently with the greatest caution, and squats down suddenly on his hams behind his weapon. After having feigned the different motions of loading a gun, he levels his piece at his supposed enemy, runs forward and, supposing his victim yet alive, pretends to fall upon him, striking several blows of the *cassetéte* on his head and finally dispatches him by a mortal stab near the heart with his dagger. He then instantly pretends to make a circular incision with his knife around the head to raise the scalp, which he attempts to take with his teeth, after which he gives the whoop and dances around the circle.[74]

Integrating the gun into the traditional war dance, the only vocal contribution made by the performer was the whoop at the end. Grant stated how these performances were appraised, with merit accorded depending "on the dexterity and rapidity of the different movements." Yet there too was an artistic aspect, one largely defined by rhythmic parameters. The performers paid attention to the "measure and cadence of the music."[75] Thus, it was not only the movements but their execution in accordance with the rhythm that was seen as important. These performances displayed warriors' experiences and courage, preparing them psychologically and physically for future battles, and potentially forging community sympathy and support.

In the late eighteenth century, expansion of the fur trade across the northern Plains and Subarctic, fur traders brought pre-existing expectations of diplomacy and trade in the northeast that prominently included pipe ceremonies. It came as quite a surprise to fur traders that some Indigenous communities practised pipe ceremonies without an accompanying song and dance. Alexander Henry (the elder) noted the location where pipe stone was found while travelling north through Lake Winnipeg.[76] Establishing trading relations with Cree peoples along the North Saskatchewan River in the 1770s, he described numerous calumet ceremonies that were conducted in silence. These meetings were sometimes ended with the "Indian cry" as the departing salute.[77] The Assiniboine, Blackfoot, and Cree appear to have had pipe ceremonies when fur traders arrived, while the Dene did not. On 5 July 1789, Alexander Mackenzie encountered five families of perhaps thirty people from two different Dene nations, Slave and Dog Rib. He reported that his party enticed them to smoke, "tho' it was evident they did not know the use of Tobacco. We likewise gave them some grog to drink, but I believe they accepted of those Civilities more through Fear than Inclination."[78] Yet in his explorations to the northwest of Lake Athabasca, Mackenzie encountered a chief who was described as ceremonially opening his medicine bag and smoking from his sacred stem.[79] The pipe dances frequently described around the western Great Lakes and northern Great Plains, however, are not found in the fur trade accounts from these more northerly latitudes.

On the northern Plains, fur traders encountered ceremonial pipe songs and dances, yet they were often different from those with which they were familiar. In 1802, Charles McKenzie joined the Montreal fur trade as an apprentice clerk for McTavish, Frobisher, and Company. While serving under Charles Chaboillez in the Fort Dauphin department, he was sent with clerk François-Antoine Larocque to the Mandan and Gros Ventre (A'ani) on the upper Missouri River. McKenzie's account is valuable because it includes his preliminary discussions with fur trader Mr Gissom about the ceremonial pipe as a method of extending and securing trading relationships, followed by an account of the engagements that unfolded. The language used by the fur traders to describe their understandings of the ceremonies is revealing. McKenzie related how Mr Gissom "informed me that he was going to the Shawyens en Pipe." This meant that he was going to try to extend the ceremonial pipe and forge new trading relationships. In so doing he figured he would get increased returns compared to trading with more familiar and readily accessed Indigenous communities. Mr Gissom asked McKenzie if he intended to "push them a Pipe." McKenzie replied that he knew "nothing concerning pipes … but if they are not accustomed to trade, I can get a better bargain." Mr Gissom was warier about the unknown expectations of ceremonial protocol. "On the contrary," he replied, "they'll laugh at you."[80] The two continued their back and forth with revealing language. McKenzie asked Mr Gissom which "goods he intended to put upon the pipe," to which he responded a gun, horse, axe, fathom of cloth, one hundred balls, and powder. The metaphors of trading "en pipe" and of putting goods "upon the pipe" are here employed in the parlance of fur traders, who operated with a set of notions about protocols and the use of the ceremonial pipe to secure trading arrangements with new Indigenous Nations.

Charles McKenzie documented not only the activities of Mr Gissom but also an Indigenous man working closely with the fur traders named Rattle Snake. Upon approaching the Shawyen's (Cheyennes) camp, McKenzie's group stopped to prepare their pipes. They cut branches of a chokecherry tree and skewered pieces of dried meat, planting these in the ground alongside each pipe. "This being done, a deep silence reigned for some minutes, when the Rattle Snake burst out in a kind of a lamentation or a lamentable song, which lasted for a quarter of an hour, thus sung, a heavy murmur was heard at every fire, as a thanksgiving. Then the R't Snake gave his pipe to a lad who sat along side of him, and who after seeming to make the four elements smoke without lighting the pipe made a very hearty harrangue in which he mentioned all the feetes the Rattle Snake had ever accomplished, and implored the pity and the assistance of all the living animals, owls, and insects."[81] This passage suggests Rattle Snake was forwarding the interests of the fur traders by leading the diplomacy. His behaviour prominently included song, which was responded to positively by the Cheyennes. He was able to navigate these cultural forms adequately, contrasting silence and spoken word. There was occasion for mourning, and the Rattle Snake's public lamentation produced an obvious effect on the community. What follows is a remarkable description of what happened when a fur trader declined to participate in the pipe ceremonies and accompanying songs: "All these ceremonies being over and the pipe and green branch carefully put by, Mr Gissom was desired to go through the same ceremony, but Monsieur declined making a lamentation ... After making a grim face he hung down his head in deep meditation, and here I was obliged to leave the fire side for shame and laughter."[82] McKenzie described in detail the community's expectation of the fur traders' participation in the ceremonies associated with the ceremonial pipe.

Mr Gissom had seated himself alongside the Rattle Snake but could not proceed with the necessary rituals, harangues, or songs associated with the ceremony. He suggested instead that he should be exempted. He desired to "act like the Father of all the white people (meaning the King) when he made peace with his Children." This language of a fur trader suggesting he was representing the king was more common in the chartered company, the HBC, than among traders from Montreal such as McKenzie and Mr Gissom. Yet this example indicates that they too could adopt this rhetorical paternalism, which in this instance led Mr Gissom being humiliated. McKenzie called it a "bold undertaking in pushing the Pipe" to the Cheyennes. McKenzie described how the following morning he departed with Rattle Snake for a neighbouring camp. Their impending arrival was notified by two Cheyennes who ran ahead. "We began our slow pace with the Rattle Snake and Mons'r Gissom, each with his pipe in one hand and the Branch of Chockcherry with the fat Meat on, in the other. – walking before us, and singing a lamentable song. The Branch and Meat an Emblem of Peace and Plenty; and the Pipe that of Social Union – Many were the ceremonies which we were obliged to observe."[83] This passage conveys cross-cultural understandings and what Mackenzie thought to be the meaning of these symbolic materials. With the pipe representing social union and the chokecherry branch with meat symbolizing peace and plenty, the fur traders advanced. They followed their interpreter Rattle Snake who led the procession with the appropriate "lamentable song." They were greeted by a chief who approached on a white horse with two hundred warriors. After embracing the Rattle Snake, the unnamed chief led them the final three miles to their camp while holding the ceremonial pipe in his right hand with "the end of the stem pointed to the Camp." McKenzie was only vaguely aware of what was going on, describing how the chief "sung or lament[ed] all the way, in a language which none of us could understand."[84]

At the camp, harangues were made to prepare "for the reception of the Pipe and Dancers," and respectable men were selected from both sides "to execute every formal motion of the Pipe and adopted Son." The "Son" was sent naked and crying to Le Borgne, his new master, who received him kindly and clothed him and performed numerous ceremonies with flowers, weeds, bull's heads, human skulls, bones, scalps, and other items. Finally, the adopted Son "began to Dance le grand Calmneti, and some of the G. Ven'trs came with small articles to trade and lay them down."[85] This passage suggests similarities between ceremonial pipe and adoption ceremonies. Other aspects such as nudity, human bones, and scalps are features that escaped the mention of ethnographers at the turn of the twentieth century such as Alice Fletcher's detailed study of the Pawnee Hako, which describes the ceremonial pipe adoption ceremony and nearly one hundred associated songs.[86] It is clear that in the case of McKenzie and Mr Gissom, pipe ceremonies were central to establishing the necessary social relationships for trade. They proved a crucial entryway to establishing peaceful and proper relations. Fur traders had some grasp of these ceremonies and their differences between Indigenous cultures. They clearly understood some of the protocol and symbolism but also took risks and learned as they went, relying heavily on Indigenous allies and guides for help meeting with new

Indigenous Nations. Pipe ceremonies, songs, and dances had to be navigated, forming a major component of the alliance-making process on the Great Lakes and northern Plains.

While visiting a camp of Cree and Assiniboine near the NWC post of Fort Alexandria, Daniel Harmon was invited to a war dance. The appearance of the warriors impressed him and he described the thirty dancers as "all clothed with the skins of the Antelope, dressed, which were nearly as white as snow; and upon their heads they sprinkled a white earth, which gave them a very genteel appearance."[87] Harmon described the dance in remarkable detail, both its movements and music:

> Their dance was conducted in the following manner. A man, nearly forty years of age, rose with his tomahawk in his hand, and made, with a very distinct voice, a long harangue. He recounted all the noble exploits which he had achieved, in the several war parties with which he had engaged his enemies; and he made mention of two persons, in particular, whom he first killed, and then took off their scalps; and for each of these, he gave a blow with his tomahawk against a post, which was set up, expressly for that purpose, near the center of the tent. And now the musick began, which consisted of tambourines, and the shaking of bells, accompanied by singing. Soon after, the man who had made the harangue, began the dance, with great majesty; then another arose, and joined him; and shortly after, another; and so on, one after another, until there were twelve or fifteen up, who all danced around a small fire, that was in the centre of the tent. While dancing, they made many savage gestures and shrieks, such as they are in the habit of making, when they encounter their enemies.[88]

This Cree and Assiniboine war dance closely resembles the dances of eastern Indigenous peoples in the striking of a wooden post in the centre of the circle. Tambourines and bells would have been obtained from the fur trade and were shaken to provide rhythm for the dance. For Harmon, the duration was most extraordinary: "In this course, they continued, for nearly an hour, when they took their seats, and another party got up, and went through with the same ceremonies. Their dancing and singing, however, appeared, to be a succession of the same things; and therefore after having remained with them two or three hours, I returned to my lodgings; and how long they continued their amusement, I cannot say."[89]

Whether or not Indigenous peoples visiting the forts were able to perform their war dances inside or outside the gate was often based on the proclivities of the post-master. At the NWC's Fort Alexandria, Daniel Harmon described a trading party that had stopped by the fort. They had apparently been on the warpath for some time: "Agreeably to the custom of the country, I gave them a few trifling articles, not as a reward for having been to war, but because they have done us honour, as they think, by dancing in our fort."[90] Harmon, like other savvy fur traders, did not want to risk alienating allied warriors and hunters who would return with more furs. He knew future profits were at stake. Allowing the trading party to dance inside the fort, Harmon understood the performance was an honour and he reciprocated with gift-giving.

George Nelson reported being presented with war dances frequently while working for the NWC. On 7 June 1809, he described an Anishinaabe war dance, an occurrence he characterized as "nothing strange." He described how they "come + dance war dances before our house door, + Mr Cameron gives them some tobacco + vermillion as he strikes at the Poteau [Post] saying that he was at two different battles + was wounded in one."[91] The Indigenous warrior's narrative of courage and sacrifice was conveyed clearly enough for Nelson to describe in his journal. The gifts of tobacco and vermilion had symbolic and spiritual importance to Anishinaabe culture, and were part of the material diplomacy with the French.[92] The visual spectacle may have been restricted by walls and palisades, yet the drumbeats and singing would have travelled over fences and walls. In other words, for fur traders, war dances and their accompanying songs were part of their work experiences and they sometimes occurred right outside of their living quarters.

War songs and dances were often mentioned alongside a particularly important cultural institution that developed in the fur trade, weddings *à la façon du pays* or according to the "custom of the country." Personal relationships and business interests were intertwined for fur traders, for whom it was common to find a wife in the local Indigenous community, forming a partnership that was often vital for their survival and commercial success. The fur trader John Long described the procedures of marriage in a section of his journal devoted to the subject of courtship. According to him, permission to marry had to be requested from the Indigenous woman's father. Speeches were given and ceremonies were observed before the man provided a feast to the woman and her entire family. After this, they, according to Long, "dance and sing their war songs."[93] The recounting of personal histories and demonstrating physical prowess would have served to familiarize new family members. Although the context was a marriage ceremony, this would have reinforced kinship-based military commitments.

Fur trade wedding ceremonies exhibited distinct styles and variations within the broader cultural exchange. In the Plateau-Basin region of the west, Ross Cox witnessed an elaborate wedding ceremony between a Métis hunter named Pierre Michel and a Salish woman. This account emphasizes the transformative rituals she underwent, receiving instructions from the older women and her uncle, and undergoing the physical transformations associated with adopting European dress and style. "A procession was then formed by the two chiefs, and several warriors carrying blazing flambeaux of cedar, to convey the bride and her husband to the fort. They began singing war songs in praise of Michel's bravery, and of their triumphs over the Blackfeet. She was surrounded by a group of young and old women, some of whom were rejoicing, and others crying. The men moved on first, in a slow and solemn pace, still chanting their war-like epithalamium. The women followed at a short distance; and when the whole party arrived in front of the fort, they formed a circle and commenced dancing and singing, which they kept up about twenty minutes. After this the calumet of peace went round once more, and when the smoke of the last whiff had disappeared, Michel shook hands with his late rival, embraced the chiefs, and conducted his bride to his room."[94] In this ceremony, the outsider male was welcomed into the woman's kinship network. His feats and bravery were recognized and commemorated by the community through songs. The ceremonialism of marriage in this case involved a procession, singing, dancing, and pipe ceremonies immediately outside the gates of the trading post. Here again, war songs and dances fulfilled roles associated with forming partnerships and strengthening social relations.

The Haudenosaunee who worked for the fur trading companies sometimes found opportunities to practise their war dances. One remarkable example is when the HBC was threatened with violent confrontations on the northwest coast. In response, fur traders encouraged war songs and dances from their Haudenosaunee colleagues. On 16 June 1828, when preparing to leave Fort Vancouver and facing a potentially hostile encounter with the Clallems, "the Iroquois went through a war dance in character before the hall door."[95] When the time came to depart, the Iroquois, "Owhyhees" (Hawaiian) and "Chunook" (Chinook), all part of the HBC contingent, "painted themselves." This implied that these diverse peoples became united in their preparations for battle. The war dance was known to foster courage and a commitment to fight and was at this time of vulnerability called upon by the fur traders.

The writings of fur traders highlight the prevalence of music and dance in unexpected ways. Ceremonial pipe dances and war dances played prominent roles not only between Indigenous peoples, but in colonial diplomacy and trade with the French and then British. Fur traders described these dances among many Indigenous Nations, and documented them serving a variety of different functions. Their accounts sometimes demonstrate an eye for detail, and many successful traders adopted an open and pragmatic approach in their regard. Beginning diplomatic relations with pipe ceremonies that included songs and dances was common. Rather than functioning to make peace and war, ceremonial pipe and war dances in the context of the fur trade both strengthened alliances and trading relationships. After William Johnson adopted the ceremonial pipe and war dances to secure Indigenous allies in the 1750s and 60s, many fur traders participated in these forms over the following decades as part of the diplomatic protocol that accompanied trade. The Haudenosaunee brought their traditions with them into the northwest, serving as a frame of reference and comparison for fur traders. Overall, one can conclude that their accounts acknowledge the central role of ceremonial pipe and war dances in fostering the social relationships necessary for successful trade.

Soundways from Montreal
to La Cloche

The St Lawrence fur trade required most personnel in the summer season. Bales and barrels of goods had to be paddled and portaged from Montreal to the western depots of Michilimackinac and Fort William, with most voyageurs returning to Montreal before the winter freeze-up. The majority of their time was spent travelling. English-speaking fur traders hired voyageurs out of Montreal to transport their goods. These voyageurs were drawn from rural French Canadian families living around the island of Montreal and further afield in the St Lawrence and Trois Rivieres,[1] some of whom had prior experience as *coureurs de bois* and knowledge of the Ottawa River and route west. While the number varied, on average perhaps 10 per cent of the canoe crews were Indigenous, mostly Mohawk from Kahnawake. Those in the canoes travelled and worked together in close quarters. The journey west, though stretching over thousands of kilometres, consisted of a relatively narrow path of well-trodden territory. For the voyageurs, this terrain was laden with symbols and landmarks that helped convey its meaning and history. The landscape shaped the journey, and the rituals, stories, and songs of the voyageurs were laden with the lore and wisdom of those who had come before.

Over the last few decades, historians have focused inwards on sensations of the body, and outwards toward analyses of the environment. Environments evoke emotions, associations, and meanings that resonate in deeply personal ways. The intersection of people and place has been studied with an eye for the multiplicity of narratives and significances that differ between individuals and cultures.[2] Historians of immigration early recognized the significance of the portability of human communities, and recent writings in mobility studies have promoted further awareness among historians.[3] Cultural theorist Stephen Greenblatt proposed five goals in his *Cultural Mobility: A Manifesto*. Two of particular relevance are to "identify and analyze the 'contact zones' where cultural goods are exchanged," and to identify how these locations contributed to a "sensation of rootedness."[4] These goals provide relevant considerations and objectives of fur trade mobility history. With canoes, riverbanks, and portages as contact zones, what emerges is a rootedness generated by passing through.

The term *soundscape* was introduced by Canadian composer and scholar R. Murray Schafer around 1970. While he does not get much recognition from historians, he developed a germane body of work on historical soundscapes. He introduced useful terms such as *soundmark,* which is "derived from *landmark* to refer to a community sound which is unique or possesses qualities which make is specially regarded or noticed by the people in that community."[5] An example of this might be found at the narrows of Lake Manitoba, named after the Cree word "*Manitobou bou,*" or "narrows of the great spirit," because of the sounds produced there.[6] While soundmark, like soundscape, is a useful concept, it has the danger of downplaying agency and different perceptions. It emphasizes physical sound rather than people's responses and cultural understandings of place. A critique of this "acoustic ecology" approach was articulated by ethnomusicologist Steven Feld. His term *acoustemology* combines the words "acoustic" and "epistemology" to connote sound as a way of knowing and listening as a way of accessing knowledge.[7] While acoustic ecology emphasizes the landscape, *acoustemology* focuses on "the experience and agency of listening histories, understood as relational and contingent, situated and reflexive."[8] It carefully considers reception and sound as a mechanism of learning. In this paradigm, music functioned as an "intimacy-making bridge," forging social bonds in a variety of contexts.[9]

Soundways are the methods and understandings of sound-making customs. This concept is underutilized in the literature yet appears most suitable for the context of the fur trade. On the highly travelled Ottawa-Matawa-French River route from Montreal to the Great Lakes, soundways consisted of gunshots, vocalizations, prayers, oral stories, and songs. Produced by guns and human voices, they varied by crew and were subject to change over time. Yet the canoe-based St Lawrence fur trade that flourished from the 1600s produced a storied canoe culture of travel over this route that continued until at least the mid-nineteenth century. Soundways followed unwritten yet culturally prescribed rules, serving to mediate understandings of proper human engagement with the landscape, its history, and its meaning. Individual responses and understandings were embedded in group dynamics. Preceding the age of audio and video recording, these soundways must be reconstructed from written fragments of history, oral culture, and folksongs.

The soundways of the voyageurs emphasized the vulnerability of the individual to the powers of dangerous forces, whether human or supernatural. The voyageurs performed vocational rites of passage at specific locations along the route. The long and somewhat uneasy history of *coureurs de bois* in close quarters with their *bourgeois* continued in the nineteenth century with the voyageurs and their masters.[10] The predominance of French Canadians as voyageurs in the Montreal trade brought a vernacular Catholicism that intertwined with Indigenous influences. Mock baptisms occurred along the route to the northwest, initiating voyageurs into new realms of occupational status. They also reinforced notions of reciprocity, highlighting the bourgeois' dependency on and obligations to his men.[11] The works of cultural theorists concerning rites of passage and ritual are useful here, including Victor Turner's discussions of liminality.[12] The primary accounts of fur traders sometimes reference performativity in the canoe brigades, revealing what Stephen Greenblatt might call "the reenacted 'cultural archive.'"[13]

Soundways marked significant locations along the route from Montreal to the Great Lakes. Some resembled "contact zones" as defined by Mary Louise Pratt, as "social spaces where disparate cultures meet, clash, and grapple with each other."[14] The Ottawa River was one such prime contact zone, where different peoples, whether Algonquin, Odawa, Nipissing, Mohawk, or French Canadian, had overlapping understandings of the same geography. These were articulated variously through place names and sounded responses. Keith Basso emphasized how it is on "communal occasions – when places are sensed *together*," that expressions of "symbolic relationships" and proper conduct appear.[15] English-speaking fur traders often interpreted the meaning and significance of places by listening to the explanations of their guides and voyageurs. Place names, interpretations, and their transmission placed "flexible constraints on how the physical environment can (and should) be known, how its occupants can (and should) be found to act."[16] Relationships to place were expressed, represented, and enacted through stories and songs, providing meaning. They were, as Basso puts it, "woven into the fabric of social life, anchoring it to features of the landscape and blanketing it with layers of significance."[17] On the route westward from Montreal to the Great Lakes, important locations were acknowledged with particular soundways. Routines of travel were paused and resonated with layers of meaning. Rituals mediated interpretations of the landscape and demarcated regional transitions and rites of passage. Geographical and historical knowledge was layered onto the collective experience through the aural realm, constituting a cultural script acted (and re-enacted) from the moment of departure.

Departure

Montreal had served as the hub of the Great Lakes' fur trade since the late seventeenth century. The rapids of Lachine divided the St Lawrence, serving as the loading and departure point for canoes headed into the interior. At the southwestern tip of the island of Montreal was St Anne's, the small town and church that for centuries was the last settlement visited by the canoe brigades before travelling up the Ottawa River. In Arnold van Gennep's classic three-phase rites of passage model, "preliminal rites" serve as the initial phase to displace individuals from their previous lives.[18] In the Montreal fur trade these manifested at two locations, the rapids of Lachine and St Anne's church. At both, ritualized soundways produced a pattern of departure that reinforced connections with the French Canadian community and the Catholic Church.

For many voyageurs, the departure at Lachine was the last time to say goodbye to friends and family. This departure was an annual event in early May of considerable social significance. When John MacDonald of Garth described his first departure west in a canoe brigade in 1791, he recounted the "great event," with a "crowd of friends and spectators were there to witness our departure."[19] George Nelson vividly reported the sights and sounds: "In May each year we would see numbers of young men, each one with his bag, containing a few of the most necessary articles of clothing; on his back, with a paddle & 'setting pole' in his hand, bidding 'Farewell' (alas! How many for ever!) to relations & friends."[20] Canoe travel was dangerous, and the gravity of the departure was symbolically acknowledged. Most men would return in the autumn, others would stay in the interior for years, and others would never return. The soundscape resounded not only with the sounds of crying but with singing. The young men "Embarking in their bark Canoes, with tears in their eyes & singing as if going to a banquet!"[21] The sources do not provide which songs were sung, only suggesting that they augmented the solemn mood and reflected the prolonged social separation and dangers ahead. Paddling out into the Lac des Deux Montagnes, the fur trade canoes paddled away from the emotional scene, leaving those on shore behind.

The first stop was the small Catholic church on the southwest corner of the island of Montreal. St Anne, the mother of the Virgin Mary and protector of fishermen and sailors, was customarily prayed to for safe water travel. She long held a special significance to those who visited New France, from Jacques Cartier to the Jesuits.[22] Sainte-Anne-de-Beaupré is a small town and church about thirty-five kilometres northeast of Quebec City and the site of focused devotion from the early seventeenth century. There, boats would customarily fire their cannons while passing the church to receive protection against the dangers of the river.[23] Alain Corbin has explored how the sounds of church bells "sacralized" territorial space in early modern Europe, with communities eagerly establishing themselves within earshot. Catholic theologians ascribed to bells the "power to open a path for the good angels from heaven and ward off the creatures of hell."[24] France was known as the country of "ringing towns" because church bells were one of the most prominent features of the soundscape. This was replicated in New France. Montreal was established in 1642 by the Societé de Notre-Dame as the religious settlement "Ville-Marie." Over the following decades, other Catholic religious orders such as the Sulpicians arrived. By the eighteenth century, St Anne's on the southwestern tip of Montreal was situated on the edge of French settlement, where the sounds of ringing Catholic church bells ended.

Expressions of Catholic devotion and prayers for safe passage characterized the soundways at St Anne's. The descriptions written by Protestant English-speaking fur traders about the customs of French Canadian and Haudenosaunee crews were distanced by the vectors of race, class, and religion. Two distinct representations of the voyageurs' departures emerge in the written record, characterized as either noble and pious, or wild and vulgar. Jonathan Carver, one of the early English traders to travel with French Canadian voyageurs on the route up the Ottawa River in the early 1760s, described having no choice but to participate in the "custom to be observed, on arriving at Saint-Anne's." Omitting mention of donations, prayers, or hymns, he instead cites the custom of distributing eight gallons of rum to each canoe, a gallon for each man, intended to last the duration of the voyage yet normally consumed on the spot. "The saint, therefore, and the priest, were no sooner dismissed, than a scene of intoxication began." Singing and fighting lasted the night until the crew departed the following morning.[25] In contrast, the Presbyterian John MacDonald provided a different description, "land[ing] at St. Anne where the men paid their devotion to their titular saint."[26] When Roderic MacKenzie departed in June of 1789, he wrote: "St. Ann's church was the last church on our route, and the *Voyageurs,* in consequence, generally drop a piece of money into a box there, as an offering, to secure the protection of '*La Bonne Sainte Anne*' during their absence, and I, with a view to do as the people of Rome do, joined my mite to that of the rest of the crew."[27] These examples demonstrate a range of responses by fur traders to the rituals of departure and soundways of the voyageurs at St Anne's. They also suggest that the English-speaking fur traders sometimes participated in the ceremonies of the voyageurs at the outset of the journey.

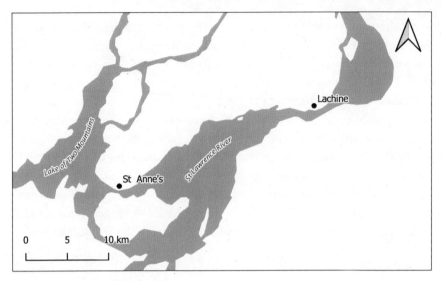

Fig. 5.1 St Anne's and Lachine

A richly descriptive account of this custom was provided by Captain George Back in the early 1830s. He wrote that on "coming abreast of a village, near which stood a large cross, a few paces from the church, the more devout of the *voyageurs* went on shore, and, standing in a musing posture, implored the protection of the patron saint in the perilous enterprise on which they were embarked; while their companions, little affected by their piety, roared out to them to *'s'embarquer,'* and paddled away to the merry tune of a lively canoe song."[28] This description reinforces and disrupts the portrayal of devout and pious voyageurs offering prayers to their patron saint. This and other primary accounts from the fur trade do not emphasize the singing of hymns by voyageurs departing St Anne's, but rather committing individual acts of devotion and prayer. This differs from the romanticized depiction of Irish poet Thomas Moore who passed through in 1804 and whose "A Canadian Boat Song" enshrined the famous line "We'll sing at St. Anne's our parting hymn!"[29]

If Lachine served as a place of reckoning about mortality, so did St Anne's. The soundways here were pervaded by a sense of tragedy. John Macdonell reported that his brigade arrived and "found the Priest saying mass for one Lalonde, who had been drowned, by the mens account, one hundred and ten leagues above this place."[30] St Anne's was where prayer, commemoration, and mourning occurred for those who passed away at various locations along the perilous journey. Victor Turner emphasized that rituals rarely dissolved social divisions but could "create solidarity in the few parts of society shared by all."[31] In this case, boundaries of race, class, culture, and language were to some degree bridged through worship and prayer. Departure here was most characterized by their sounds. The "sacralized" space marked by ringing church bells, the blessings of the priest, and the individual recitation of prayers indicated Christian ceremony, even if not all members of the brigade participated. Departing was ritualized into acts that acknowledged the importance of the Catholic Church and the significance of leaving it behind.

Much nationalist French lyric and poetry was written in the mid to late nineteenth century emphasizing Catholic piety and virtuousness as the hallmarks of French Canada.[32] This may be the origin of a song sometimes cited as being sung shortly after departure entitled "Quand un Chretien Se Determine à Voyageur" (When a Christian Decides to Voyage). It takes the form of advice given from experienced voyageurs to young *mangeurs de lard* (porkeaters), warning of the physical dangers and difficulties caused by the elements, the mosquitoes, and the spiritual dangers to the soul.[33] This composition bears traces of literary origins and was first published in the 1860s.[34] No references have been located in the written records of fur traders or travellers describing it on the Ottawa River route before 1840, thus it may well be a later composition.

Canoe Travel

Canoes were sites of socialization. Mobility provided access to the series of meaningful locations and soundways along the route. Travel entailed a routine and social dynamic that restructured hierarchies and leadership roles. Corresponding to what Victor Turner described as the "liminal period" in a rite of passage, canoe travel shifted from a structured hierarchical society to "an unstructured or rudimentarily structured and relatively undifferentiated" community who "submit together to the general authority of the ritual elders."[35] In the canoe brigades, these were the guides, bowsmen, and steersmen. Known as the *bouts*, they were the most experienced and well-paid voyageurs, forming an elite who commanded the canoes while leading the crews through ritual progressions. They started the paddling songs and at specific locations recounted oral stories. One such place was a "curious cave" on the side of a hill on the north side of the Ottawa River about which Alexander Henry (the elder)'s crew told "marvellous tales."[36]

Devotional rites played a prominent role throughout the journey. Daniel Harmon described his crew taking off their hats and making the sign of the cross often. At least one man in each canoe "repeat[ed] a short prayer" whenever they entered a new river or passed crude gravesites erected along the shore for deceased voyageurs. This was a frequent occurrence, invoked "at almost every rapid which we have passed, since we left Montreal." Harmon commented that the voyageurs "say their prayers more frequently" on the river "than when at home."[37] This may not have been true, but these customs illustrate that they acknowledged the risks and dangers of the journey as well as the memory of voyageurs who had passed with a distinctly Catholic response.

One of the *bouts* was responsible for driving and directing the men and was known as the guide. John McLean described how the guide roused the men each morning with the call "Lève, Lève!" If the men did not wake up and tie their beds quickly, "the tents go down about their ears, and they must finish the operation in open air."[38] John Henry Lefroy, a scientist travelling in a canoe brigade in the 1840s described how the voyageurs lay down after supper "until the cry of *lève! lève!* turns us out before three in the morning." For him, the mornings were unpleasant, as "the discomfort of this mode of travelling is chiefly a want of time for washing, dressing and so on."[39] A similarly critical opinion is provided by Robert Ballantyne, who described how at the "first blush of day" he was awakened by "the loud halloo of the guide, who with the voice of a Stentor gave vent to a '*Lève! lève! lève!*' that roused the whole camp in less than two minutes."[40] Ballantyne worked for the HBC for six years from ages sixteen to twenty-two, and his subsequent career as a writer is evident in his description of this auditory custom:

At the first peep of day our ears were saluted with the usual unpleasant sound of "*Lève! Lève! Lève!*" issuing from the leathern throat of the guide. Now this same "*Lève*" is in my ears a peculiarly harsh and disagreeable word, being associated with frosty mornings, uncomfortable beds, and getting up in the dark before half enough of sleep has been obtained. The way in which it is uttered, too, is particularly exasperating; and often, when partially awakened by a stump boring a hole in my side, have I listened with dread to hear the detested sound, and then, fancying it must surely be too early to rise, have fallen gently over on the other side, when a low, muffled sound as if some one were throwing off his blanket would strike upon my ear, then a cough or a grunt, and finally, as if from the bowels of the earth, a low and scarcely audible "*Lève! Lève!*" would break the universal stillness, growing rapidly louder, "*Lève! Lève! Lève!*" and louder, "*Lève! Lève!*" till at last a final stentorian "*Lève! Lève! Lève!*"

brought the hateful sound to a close, and was succeeded by a confused collection of grunts, groans, coughs, grumbles, and sneezes, from the unfortunate sleepers thus rudely roused from their slumbers.[41]

These descriptions convey an idea of how guides administered soundways every morning, influencing the daily sensory progression of the fur traders and voyageurs while travelling. They also reveal something of the divide between the English-speaking fur traders and the French-speaking voyageurs on the journey. While the latter conducted and regulated canoe travel, the English-speaking merchants and masters sat passively. Once the group had embarked, the *bouts* would exercise their leadership role by steering the canoes and controlling the labour primarily through the *chanson d'aviron* or paddling songs, something that will be examined in Chapter 6.

"Petit Rocher": *La Complainte de Cadieux*

Approximately halfway along the Ottawa River portion of the journey was a site of special significance. The route was dramatically blocked by Grand Calumet Island and the ferocious rapids that surrounded it. The carrying place here was called the *portage de sept chutes* because it bypassed seven waterfalls. It was the first long portage on the journey westwards. According to Alexander Mackenzie, it was 2,035 paces long over a "high hill or mountain."[42] This trail hosted the dramatic history of a young voyageur left behind by his crew while fleeing an Iroquois war party. His gravesite was maintained along the path, and his "death song," which he supposedly composed and wrote on tree bark while dying, was routinely sung by the voyageurs at this location. This soundway is richly documented in the written record. It was described by numerous fur traders and collected by folklorists and musicologists. Its tale of abandonment, miracle, and death was regularly recounted here with songs and oral stories, reinforcing the importance of this location.

George Nelson provided an account of the oral story in 1802.[43] According to his version, in 1759, a canoe of voyageurs was returning home from the upper countries and on this portage encountered a "large party" of Iroquois warriors who "immediately set up their frightful War yell & pursued." The Canadians jumped into their canoe and were taken over the rapids. Remarkably, they made it through without suffering any damage. When the Iroquois made it to the end of the portage, they saw "a tall woman in white robes standing in the bow of the Canoes." They perceived this as representing the "protection of a

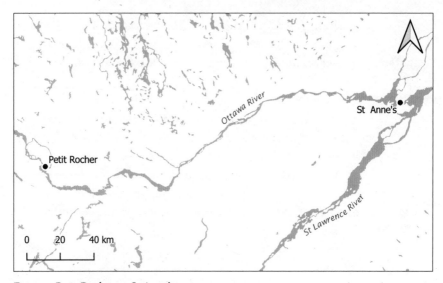

Fig. 5.2 Petit Rocher to St Anne's

divinity" and abandoned their pursuit. Nelson's men informed him that "they saw a woman, they believed to be the Virgin Mary, conducting the canoe." At the end of this description, Nelson related that "one unfortunate creature" who had a bruised heel had hidden in the bushes and was left behind, and when a canoe from Montreal returned ten days later they found him dead "in a hole he had himself dug out with [a] paddle."[44] Without naming the voyageur or describing the song, Nelson recounted the events he learned about while on the portage.[45]

Travelling in 1821, Dr John Bigsby related another version while passing through this location. He emphasized the song over the story. The carrying place circumvented a dangerous set of rapids that set the "scene of one of the most beautiful of the Canadian boat-songs. I have heard it repeatedly, but did not take it down. It is supposed to have been found inscribed on the bark of a birch-tree a little above the Falls."[46] In Bigsby's account, the voyageurs were saved by "Mary, the Virgin Mother, who immediately appears to them in a rainbow amid the spray of the cataract, and beckons them onwards – to leap the fall." They were spared from harm altogether, except for "one unhappy man" who had left the canoe. This account differs from Nelson's in certain details. The antagonists are here described generically as "hostile Indians," and the apparition of Mary beckons the canoe over the falls instead of being perceived after the fact.

Also in 1821, Nicholas Garry, the new deputy governor of the HBC, described reaching Grand Calumet Island. After observing the cross that marked the voyageur gravesite, he related how "many years since" a canoe of *coureurs de bois* became engaged in battle with hostile "Indians," landing on this island. They were pursued and forced to hastily re-embark, running the rapids and leaving behind an injured man. On their return, they found that he was dead. "They then buried him in this Spot and he became a sort of Saint." Garry mentions that while the voyageur "could neither read nor write many songs and phrases are extant which, it is said, he composed."[47] Here the story of the miraculous escape through the rapids recurs. While the Virgin Mary does not appear in this version, Garry emphasized that the doomed voyageur himself was "a sort of Saint." Passing voyageurs offered their prayers to him and sang his song.

The details of this narrative are quite different when described by J.G. Kohl in the 1850s. His appears to be the earliest to record the name of the voyageur as "Jean Cayeux." According to this version, he was said to be on a hunting trip on the Ottawa River near Grand Calumet Island with his family when he was suddenly surrounded by the Iroquois. His wife and children took the canoe while Cayeux was left behind on a rock in the middle of the river. As the canoe passed through the rapids, his wife and children held their hands in prayer. This is when "a white form appeared in the bow of the canoe," which was recognized as the "blessed Virgin." The Iroquois pursued the family to the next French fort, after which they returned to Grand Calumet Island. Here, they chased Cayeux through the forest. Eventually eluding his pursuers, with his final energy Cayeux constructed a shelter of branches and dug himself a Christian grave. Finally, "he erected a cross, and he cut and carved on the wood his complainte, the entire history of his tragic fate. (So, at least, my Canadians asserted. They believed they sang the very song composed by Cayeux on his death-bed, but I imagine they could only have been some short allusions to his end.) The wooden cross soon rotted away, but the copy of his complainte is saved. And the cross has been repeatedly renewed up to the present time, and the Voyageurs still know the spot exactly."[48] Kohl's version maintained many elements of the narrative. The miraculous escape, the apparition of the Virgin Mary, the grave of the solitary voyageur, and the composition of his death song are all consistent with earlier accounts. Yet this version differs in its plot and many details. Was Jean Cadieux a voyageur working in the fur trade or simply on a hunting trip? It should be noted that this version, while detailed, was written decades later.

Story and song are often complementary elements of oral tradition. In this case, they intertwined into a magico-religious narrative about a miraculous escape and martyrdom. That the oral tradition revolved around a specific location was significant, as the voyageurs knew where Cadieux was supposedly buried and this helped keep the story alive. Passing the gravesite provided the signal to narrate and sing these elements of the cultural archive. Musically transcribed as early as 1863 and 1865, Cadieux's song has since been recorded in more than a dozen slightly different versions.[49] One version of 1863 was transcribed from "le vieux Morache, ancien guide." Morache introduced the song by relating it to the precise location along the route, as "on ne manque pas de s'arrêter au *Petit Rocher de la Haute Montagne*: qui est au milieu du portage des Sept Chutes, en bas de l'île du *Grand Calumet*."[50] Marius Barbeau published a version based on the widespread core narrative:

La Complainte de Cadieux, Coureur de Bois (ca 1709)[51]

Petit Rocher de la haute montagne,	Little Rock on the high mountain
Je viens ici finir cette campagne!	I have come here to finish this campaign!
O doux échos, entendez mes soupirs!	Oh, soft echoes, listen to my sighs!
En languissant, je vais bientôt mourir.	While languishing here, I will soon die.
Petits oiseaux, vos douces harmonies,	Little birds, your gentle harmonies
Quand vous chantez, me rattach' à la vie.	When you sing, it keeps me alive.
Ah! si j'vais des ailes comme vous,	Ah! If I had wings like you,
Je s'rais heureux avant qu'il fût deux jours	I would be happy before two days' time.
Seul en ces bois que j'ai eu de soucis,	Alone in these woods, I have worried
Pensant toujours à mes si cher amis!	Thinking always of my dear friends!
Qui me dira, ah! sont-ils tous noyés?	Who will tell me, Ah! have they all drowned?
Les Iroquois les auraient-ils tués?	Have the iroquois killed them?

Par un beau jour que,
    m'étant éloigné,
En revenant, je vis une fummée,
Je me suis dit: Qu'est-ce
    qui loge ici?
Les Iroquois m'ont-ils pris
    mon logis?
Tout aussitôt, je fus en embassade,
Afin de voir si c'était embuscade.
J'ai aperçu trois visages français,
M'ont mis le coeur d'une trop
    grande joi'.
Mes genoux pli'nt, ma faible
    voix s'arrête
J'ai tombé là. A partir ils
    s'apprêtent.
Je restai seul. Pas un qui
    me consol'.
Quand la mort vient, [pas] un
    [ne s'y] désol'.
Un loup hurlant vint près de
    ma cabane.
Voir si mon feu n'avait plus
    de boucane.
Je lui ai dit: Retire-toi d'ici,
Car sur ma foi, je perc'rai
    ton habit!
Un noir corbeau, volant à
    l'aventure,
Vint se percher tout près de
    ma toiture.
Je lui ai dit: Mangeur de
    chair humain',
Va t'en chercher autre viand' que
    la mienn'!
Prends ta volé, dans ces bois,
    ces marais.

On a nice day when I have
    gone far away,
On returning, I saw smoke,
I said to myself: who lodges here?

Have the Iroquois taken
    my home?
Immediately, I went in delegation
In order to see if it was an ambush
I saw three French faces,
My heart filled with
    great joy.
My knees shook, my feeble
    voice stopped.
I fell there. They were
    preparing to leave.
I stayed alone. No one
    consoled me.
When death comes, no
    one is sorry.
A wolf howled very close
    to my cabin
To see if my fire had any
    more smoke.
I said to him: Leave here.
Because on my faith, I see
    your clothing!
A black crow, flying for adventure,

Came to perch close to my roof.

I said to him: Eater of
    human flesh,
Go find flesh other than mine!

Take off, into the woods
    & marshes.

Tu trouveras plusieurs
corps iroquois.

You will find many
iroquois corpses.

Tu trouveras des tripes,
aussi des os.

You will find the tripes and bones.

Mange à ton saoul! Laisse-
moi en repos!

Eat until you're drunk! Let me rest!

Rossignolet, va dire à ma
maîtresse,

Nightingale go tell my mistress

À mes enfants qu'un adieu je
leur laisse

And my children farewell,

Que j'ai gardé mon amour
et ma foi,

That I have kept my love & faith

Que désormais, faut
renoncer à moi.

And from now on they must
forget me.

C'est aujourd'hui que le mond'
j'abandonne.

It is today that I leave this world.

Mais j'ai recours à vous, Sauveur
des hommes.

But I have recourse in you,
Saviour of men.

Très Sainte Vierg', ne
m'abandonnez pas!

Blessed Virgin Saint, ah! don't
abandon me.

Permettez-moi d'mourir
entre vos bras!

Let me die in your arms!

The opening line establishes the location of Cadieux's death at the specific site on the portage, at the "petit rocher de la haute montagne" (little rock of the high mountain). After lamentations and encounters with animals of symbolic importance, he implores the Virgin Mary not to abandon him. This represents Barbeau's "texte critique," representing the core narrative found in more than a dozen slightly different versions recorded in the nineteenth and early twentieth centuries. The textual differences between the various transcribed versions of this song are much less varied than the narratives in the fur trade accounts.[52] Perhaps this is because they were transcribed in the 1860s or after, and a uniform version had become established. Or perhaps the mnemonic qualities of melody, rhythm, and rhyme acted to preserve the song. Walter Ong suggests in his book *Orality and Literacy* that music could act "as a constraint to fix a verbatim oral narrative."[53] Either way, the lyrics are remarkably similar between versions.

Variations in the oral stories can be compared with the songs. The lyrics in stanza three imply that Cadieux was with a voyageur canoe, with his "cher amis" whom he worried might have drowned or been caught by the Iroquois. Yet his wife and children are also mentioned in the song lyrics, loosely supporting both story versions. Although it is impossible to determine in which ways the song changed over time, the extant versions are remarkably similar. Songs recorded or collected after the fur trade era by folklorists must always be treated skeptically, as they often promoted a particular moral, literary, linguistic, and historical agenda.[54] French Canadian folklorists Ernest Gagnon and Marius Barbeau stressed a particular version of French Canadian music, culture, and history. It emphasized family, community, and national values, Catholic devotion, and cultural continuity with medieval France.[55]

In the case of Cadieux's song, its origin story and repeated mention in the written record set it apart. Some of the collected versions have specific records of oral transmission. Marius Barbeau identified the version he recorded in 1918 as the oldest, with Ovide Soucy having learned it fifty years previous from his seventy-five-year-old uncle, dating it to the outset of the nineteenth century.[56] It was called by old voyageurs such as Morache the "*chant de mort du brave Cadieux*."[57] Its form has been identified as a *complainte*, canticle, or "Come-all-ye!"[58] Barbeau identified the features of its composition that set it apart from the folk and jongleur songs of France, in particular the decasyllabic metre with a masculine caesura at four feet. This revealed that the composer "avait quelque notion de l'art poétique des écoles."[59] The eleven stanzas closely follow the AABB rhyme scheme. The ascription of authorship to Cadieux, an illiterate voyageur, was crucial to the song's narrative and transmission, no matter how improbable. It may have been received skeptically by some, yet the lyrics confirm and reinforce the narrative.

The Virgin Mary is an integral aspect of all versions of the narrative. This is a testament to her prominence in the spiritual world of the voyageurs. Yet the emphasis within the song is mostly on supernatural encounters with animals. Anthropomorphized animals are a staple of medieval and early modern French folklore.[60] The song begins with Cadieux addressing the environment, bidding it to listen: "O doux échos, entendez mes soupirs!" The various animals represent omens of life and death. Cadieux asserts that the gentle harmonies of little birds kept him alive. He resists a howling wolf and black crow, both symbols of death. Finally, Cadieux asks the nightingale to tell his mistress and children about his tragic fate. The nightingale bird is only found in Europe and has been associated since classical times with laments and symbolizing tragic situations. This cultural vocabulary is representative of French folklore and is consistent with French Canadian themes explored by Barbeau and others.[61]

The three stanzas that mention the Iroquois are worthy of scrutiny. Alone in the woods, Cadieux imagines his friends and worries they may have drowned or the Iroquois may have killed them. When he sees smoke, he wonders if the Iroquois have found his lodge. The reference in stanza nine to the bones in the forest is cryptic and unexplained.[62] That the Iroquois are the antagonists of the narrative reflects the fur trade of New France. At various times in the seventeenth and eighteenth centuries, the Mohawk were at war with the French and laid ambush along the St Lawrence and Ottawa Rivers. Yet circumstances had changed dramatically by the late eighteenth century. Now, Mohawk from Kahnawake made up a substantial portion of the canoe brigades that ascended the Ottawa River. French Canadians and Haudenosaunee alike signed contracts with the various Montreal trading outfits. Yet the song of Cadieux not only survived in this period, its fame seemingly grew. Its lessons about the dangers of separation in the wilderness and the river served as guidance for young voyageurs throughout the post-conquest fur trade era.

Cadieux's *complainte* was rooted at a particular place in the landscape that was given new life with every passing brigade. Voyageurs would take the song with them, in its melody, music, and morality, as they progressed beyond. When Morache narrated the story and song to the French Canadian folklorist Taché, he related it specifically to its location on the portage. He emphasized that "Chaque fois que les canots de la compagnie passent au *Petit Rocher*, un vieux voyageur raconte aux jeunes gens l'histoire de Cadieux; les anciens voyageurs qui l'ont déjà entendu raconter aiment toujours à l'entendre, quand ils ne la redisent pas eux-mêmes." The song was collected and published in numerous editions as "Petit Rocher," or "Petit Rocher de la Haute Montagne," which was a reference to the specific location that triggered its story and performance on the portage.

"Listening" to the fur trade reveals Grand Calumet Island as a significant location. It was surrounded by a dramatic series of roaring rapids. These necessitated a long portage – the longest until that point when headed west from Montreal – some days' travel away from the security of the St Lawrence settlements. Cadieux's tale crystalized fears that manifested from vulnerability. Emphasizing the danger posed to voyageurs "left behind," the story stood both as a history and as a parable, depicting the suffering of a voyageur separated from his crew, "poor Cadieux." Facing the terror of hostile Iroquois and scavenging wolves, he found solace only in the mercy of the Virgin Mary and death itself. This frightening story relayed with the song's tragic tone etched a powerful memory in the minds of voyageurs and fur traders. It was part of the "religico-magical rites" that were integral to the voyageurs' culture, which have been described as a response to "the dangerous and frequent tragedies in their jobs."[63] The *complainte* of Jean Cadieux is a rare instance where we can listen and hear with confidence what was familiar to fur traders centuries ago. This song and story explained the significance of the most remarkable portage on the Ottawa River route.

Just to the west of Grand Calumet Island was another important location. After passing through Lake Coulonge and the dramatic Rivière Creuse, or Deep River, with its high cliffs on the north end, a low sandy beach emerges to the south.[64] This was a well-established location where ritual "baptisms" for those who had never passed along the Ottawa River took place, known as the "Pointe aux Baptêmes." In 1686, Chevalier de Troyes mentioned it and the custom of baptizing those who had never passed before.[65] Alexander Henry (the elder) in the 1760s described the long beach emerging far into the river, "a remarkable point of sand, stretching far into the stream, and on which it is customary to baptize novices."[66] Historian Carolyn Podruchny has interpreted these rituals as cultural performances marking "thresholds crossed," as voyageurs physically entered new landscapes and socially new occupational identities and stages of manhood.[67] This was where the pre-Cambrian shield was dramatically encountered. This new landscape characterized much of the subsequent journey west, representing not only a visual change but an auditory one. Hard shorelines and cliffs echoed sounds made on the water and along the shore.

Places of ritual baptism are where the voyageurs exerted their agency and power. They were treated with drinks, or else masters were served the humiliation of a rough dunking. Why did fur traders so readily undergo ritual baptisms?[68] Fur traders did not typically write favourably about being subjected to the demands of their subordinates. These customs mirror those of sailors who demanded drinks from those who had never before passed certain places of significance, or else they were subjected to various uncomfortable treatments. Those who did not meet expectations could be sure, according to Daniel Harmon, of "being plunged into the water, which they profanely call, baptizing."[69] This location along the Ottawa River functioned as a meaningful point of transition as well as place of rest. It may have been therapeutic to stop for a drink after passing the particularly long portage at Grand Calumet Island, with its frightening story and mournful song of Cadieux still on the mind. That the landscape noticeably changed here made it a place of natural significance. The voyageurs' songs would now reverberate off the rocky shores of the Ottawa, Mattawa, and French Rivers.

Points of baptism were also places of play. Perhaps the most important such place was to the northwest of Lake Superior at the height of land. This marked another dramatic transformation in the landscape. Edward Umfreville passed this location in 1784 and spoke of "Paying my Baptême here," providing his crew with an obligatory dram.[70] Alexander Henry (the younger) recounted how in 1800 on the first day after departing Grand Portage, the voyageurs stopped to enjoy their regale at a "delightful meadow" where there was "plenty of elbow-room for the men's antics," a description that suggests play and perhaps dancing.[71] Crossing the height of land signalled a new watershed, and the significance of this natural boundary was well respected. John Macdonell's account is the richest. He recounted how he was "instituted a *North man* by *Batême* performed by sprinkling water in my face with a small cedar Bow dipped in a ditch of water and accepting certain conditions," including perpetuating these ceremonies and never kissing a voyageur's wife against her will. Though Macdonell believed that "the intention of this Bâptême being only to claim a glass," the ceremony itself was meaningful in a variety of ways and was marked by the sound of firing guns in an "Indian manner." The production of Indigenous soundways at this significant location on the journey west is highly symbolic. It announced a different cultural space and different social practices.[72]

While the portage on Grand Calumet Island was famous for Cadieux's lament, other portages were also associated with lamentful music. At the forks of the Ottawa and the "Petite Rivière" (Mattawa), treacherous rapids and white-water presented many hazardous obstacles. Two portages nearby possessed musical associations and dangerous reputations. Alexander Mackenzie described these as "Portage Pin de Musique" and "mauvais de Musique." Mackenzie does not explain these names aside from the comment that this was a path "where many men have been crushed to death by the canoes, and others have received irrecoverable injuries."[73] In the mid-1810s, Ross Cox described the portage "called Mauvaise de la Musique, the road of which is extremely awkward and dangerous." Recounting a story told to him by his voyageurs, Cox related that "a few years before, a man while carrying a canoe fell against a large rock, by which his head was completely severed from his body. His grave is in the middle of the pathway."[74] Nicholas Garry also mentioned it, and while the precise names of these two portages vary in the accounts, they represented two notable "musical" portages on the route between Montreal and the Great Lakes.[75] The evidence of the associated story and gravesite suggests a similar pattern to that of Cadieux. In the context of particularly dramatic environmental features, gravesite markers were powerful visual symbols of tragic history and present danger. They greatly influenced interpretations of place.

They triggered an auditory response, whether prayers spoken under the breath, stories told, or songs sung. While the evidence did not reveal whether these "musical" portages were associated with another *complainte* similar to Cadieux's, the evidence suggests meaningful soundways may have been practised.

Transitioning to the Great Lakes

A very significant transition on the journey westwards was the emergence into the Great Lakes. Natural features signalled a momentous change. The narrow channels of the French River opened into Georgian Bay. The relative protection of the woods and cliffs gave way to an open expanse of fresh water that stretched as far as the eye could see. The winds and waves were dramatically stronger and bigger as canoes emerged from the French River and travelled along the north shore of Georgian Bay. The propensity for powerful winds and large waves to overturn a canoe or push it up against the rocky islands and jagged shoreline represented a real danger. To the west of the French River, "Point Grondine" or "Grumbling Point" was exposed to the open expanse of Georgian Bay. It was named as it was due to the "sound of the waves splashing through the rocks."[76] The "grumbling" that was produced was a naturally occurring soundmark, and auditory reminder of the force of the winds and waves on Georgian Bay. For canoes heading west, this stretch of open water marked a dramatic transition. They headed for the narrow straits and shelter of Shebahonaning, what would become known as Killarney.

After passing through this narrows, canoes travelled northwest toward Little La Cloche Island. Here there was another important narrows that yielded a degree of shelter from the winds and waves. This was the location of an important soundmark. Alexander Henry (the elder), in his account from 1 September 1761, confirmed having "reached an island, called La Cloche." He explained the place name, describing how it is "because there is here a rock, standing on a plain, which, being struck, rings like a bell."[77]

To Anishinaabeg peoples, these "ringing" or "sounding" stones have long been held in sacred reverence.[78] Similar culturally significant "rock gong" sites have been identified and investigated in Africa,[79] yet research in Canada on the subject is much more limited.[80] The Anishinaabemowin designation for these stones is *Sinmedwe'ek*, or *Mishomis*, meaning grandfathers.[81] The name *La Cloche* appears to derive from the era of the French fur trade. Henry's account suggests this place was named before the mid-eighteenth century. "La Cloche" indicates the French associated the sound of the rocks with church bells from an early date. It also suggests there was only one. Alexander Henry described

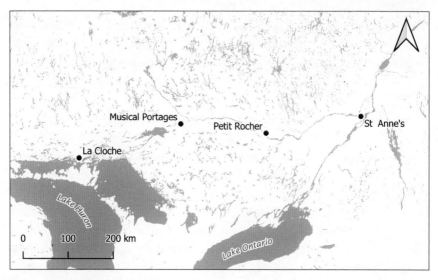

Fig. 5.3 La Cloche to St Anne's

a single sounding boulder, as do other accounts based on oral histories, while some recount a single boulder surrounded by seven smaller ones that all rung when struck.[82]

The degree to which the ringing stones influenced the soundscape around Little La Cloche Island is difficult to ascertain. It seems to have been a defining feature of the area for Anishinaabe peoples as well as fur traders. Oral histories collected from Anishinaabe elders in the twentieth century describe how their ceremonial ringing was used to announce special events of importance. This included noteworthy occasions such as the passing of a chief. It also served as an alarm system to warn of the approach of enemies from the south, as they made their way around Little La Cloche Island to the north channel. According to oral traditions, the ringing stones could be heard as far as the north shore of Manitoulin Island, east to Lake Nipissing, and south to Parry Sound.[83] The stones were honoured as other-than-human ancestors, and presented with gifts and tobacco offerings. It was believed that *sinmedwe'ek* imparted special powers and knowledge through sounds, forming a connection to the spirit world.[84] Scholars have investigated how this site long served as an important location of social, economic, and spiritual passage.[85]

In 1788, E.E. Gother Mann, captain of the Royal Canadian Engineers, toured Lake Huron and sketched a map with "La Cloche" noted. It is the only significant landmark depicted along the "rocky and barren" north shore

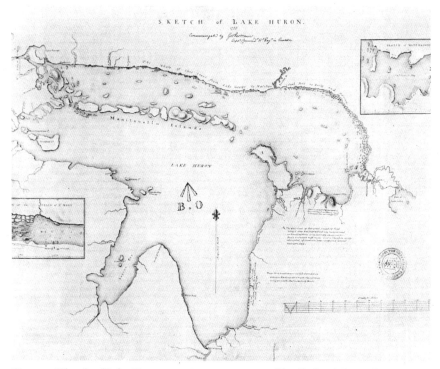

Fig. 5.4 "Sketch of Lake Huron, 1788: circumnavigated by Gother Mann, Capt. commanding Royal Engineers in Canada." La Cloche is named in small script close to the north shore and directly above the fleur de lys marker pointing to magnetic north. Along the north shore is inscribed "The whole of this Coast from Lake George to Matchadesh Bay is Rocky and Barren."

between the French River and Sault Ste Marie. This soundmark was emphasized by the St Lawrence fur trade. It was mentioned by Roderic McKenzie of the NWC in 1789. Not only was it passed by canoes travelling along the north shore of Georgian Bay; it was commemorated with the name of the local trading post. In the 1790s, Fort La Cloche was constructed nearby on a small bay on the northeast corner of Great La Cloche Island.[86] Soon after, it was moved across the water to the north shore. This place name was extended beyond Great La Cloche Island to the La Cloche mountain range that runs along the north channel.

How were the ringing rocks or Sinmedwe'ek perceived by fur traders? Unfortunately, the documentary record is too thin to get an understanding. We can surmise that it played into conceptions of place as the area was known to fur traders as "La Cloche." This is close to where Alexander Henry (the elder) was

Fig. 5.5 "La Cloche," in a postcard from the 1920s.

received by an Anishinaabe community with civility and kindness in 1761 until it was revealed he was English.[87] He then put on the clothing "usually worn by such of the Canadians as pursue the trade into which I had entered," adopting the voyageurs' sash, loose shirt, blanket coat, and red cap, and smearing his face and hands with dirt and grease.[88] Henry adopted the look and manners of the French fur traders before him. We do not know what kinds of soundways they practised or experienced here. We can assume that they would have been aware of the site due to the name La Cloche, which after the 1790s was the trading post in close proximity. To the Anishinaabeg, Sinmedwe'ek were ancestors and living members of the community. For fur traders, bells symbolized the Catholic church and Christendom, and perhaps evoked religious associations. In Anna Jameson's historic account, when travelling along the north shore in 1836–67, she wrote that this "place derives its name from a large rock, which they say, being struck, vibrates like a bell. But I had no opportunity of trying the experiment, therefore cannot tell how this may be … the Indians regard the spot as sacred and enchanted."[89] That this site's sacred reverence was recognized by an outsider such as Jameson suggests it was likely known as such by fur traders as well.

The journey between Montreal and the Great Lakes progressed through a series of culturally significant soundmarks and soundways. Important locations elicited responses in the voyageur canoes that provided interaction with and interpretation of the landscape. Histories, mythologies, and social significances were transmitted through songs and oral stories. These were directly linked to distinct places in the landscape. Soundways drew canoe crews together and provided meaning for their journeys. They marked major points of interest and transition. Grand Calumet Island was one such location, with its *petit rocher de la haute montagne* that was simultaneously a place, a song, an oral story, and a gravesite. The fur trade developed cultural practices and understandings that were layered over existing Indigenous practices and understandings of significant locations, such as at La Cloche. Fur traders and voyageurs practised a highly ritualized form of travel that was sensitive to place and replete with soundways.

6

Paddling Songs;
Chansons D'aviron

"*nous avons déserté*" (we have deserted)[1]

Que nous mangions poul's grass's
    et des pigeons lardés
	When we ate fat chickens
	    and pigeons

Que nous allions voir les fill's
    bien tard après souper
	When we went to see the girls,
	    well after supper

Que nous fumions la pip' comm'
    des jeun's cavalier.
	When we smoked the pipe,
	    like young knights

These are lyrics from a voyageur song transcribed on the water by Edward Ermatinger in the 1820s. It has a curious but perhaps not uncommon history. It is about three soldiers deserting the army for the love of a woman, and it appears to be derived from an early modern French marching song. Its existence in the paddling song repertoire of the York Factory Express canoe brigade that travelled between Hudson Bay and the Pacific Ocean in the 1820s, where it was likely transcribed, seems improbable. This chapter will explore the similarities between marching songs and paddling songs, including the origins of this and other voyageur paddling songs Ermatinger recorded on the water. Rather than merely reproducing the folk songs of France, the voyageurs adapted the *laisse* structure to suit their purposes, devising new choruses and lyrics such as these to extend the verse. The vast distances travelled and rhythmic nature of the work produced songs of great length that served key practical functions and provided an outlet for distinct cultural expressions.

Signals of Movement

Indigenous peoples often *heard* fur traders coming. Singing provided an audible signal of approaching canoes, with the sound of voices rising and falling on the water. Certain Cree peoples preserved their ancestors' "descriptions of the Frenchmen singing on the way down the Nelson."[2] Singing usually signalled departure or arrival. John Macdonell described one such arrival at Grand Portage where "the beach was covered with spectators to see us arrive, our canoe went well and the crew sung paddling songs in a vociferous manner."[3] Like discharging firearms, singing assumed a friendly reception. There were instances when unwitting voyageurs singing in their canoes alerted those who wished to do them harm. John McLean recalled when at Fort St John on the Peace River in 1805, "The men, altogether unconscious of the fate that awaited them, came paddling toward the landing-place, singing a voyageur's song, and just as the canoe touched the shore a volley of bullets was discharged at them, which silenced them for ever. They were all killed on the spot."[4] This is the most dramatic example found to date, yet it illustrates the potential mortal danger faced by fur traders. Competition between trading companies was often fierce. Indigenous peoples at times saw fur traders as unwelcome visitors and threatened them at the trading posts or while travelling. There were places of notorious danger, such as the Great Lakes immediately following the Seven Years' War, or on the northern Plains in Snake and Blackfoot territory in the early nineteenth century.[5] Yet there are few recorded incidents of fur trade canoes being ambushed.

Singing broadcasted the movement of people and goods. Surveilling competitors' activities was an integral part of the fur trade. Mathew Cocking, a York Factory employee and inland English trader, described the manoeuvrings of himself and Robert Davey to counter "the Pedlars" (the Montreal traders). His journal conveys careful observations of their movements. He described when they were "taking their Canoes out of the Water," and "when they perceived a Pedlers Canoe coming across."[6] Singing on the water highlighted valuable information about the comings and goings of personnel and cargo.

Among the primary accounts, Robert Ballantyne most vividly described the travelling canoe brigades at their peak with the NWC:

No less than ten brigades (each numbering twenty canoes) used to pass through these scenes during the summer months. No one who has

not experienced it can form an adequate idea of the thrilling effect the
passing of these brigades must have had upon a stranger. I have seen four
canoes sweep round a promontory suddenly, and burst upon my view;
while at the same moment, the wild, romantic song of the voyageurs,
as they plied their brisk paddles, struck upon my ear, and I have felt the
thrilling enthusiasm caused by such a scene: what, then, must have been
the feelings of those who had spent a long, dreary winter in the wild
North-West, far removed from the bustle and excitement of the civilised
world, when thirty or forty of these picturesque canoes burst unexpectedly upon them, half in shrouded in the spray that flew from the bright,
vermilion paddles, while the men, who had overcome difficulties and
dangers innumerable during a long voyage through the wilderness, urged
their light craft over the troubled water with the speed of reindeer, and
with joyful hearts at the happy termination of their trials and privations,
sang with all the force of three hundred manly voices, one of their lively
airs, which, rising and falling faintly in the distance as it was borne, first
lightly on the breeze, and then more steadily as they approached, swelled
out in the rich tones of many a mellow voice, and burst into a long
enthusiastic shout of joy![7]

This description suggests the hardships inherent in fur trade travel and the
emotion involved in completing a voyage. These were the dramatic moments in
the fur trade's annual cycle, which is why they were so often described. From the
historical evidence it is clear that singing was an essential component of canoe
travel, setting the march, controlling the pace, and synchronizing the strokes.
The voyageurs extended their songs over long durations by stitching together
well-known segments of folksong verse and improvising additional lines at the
end. The voyageur paddling songs transcribed by Edward Ermatinger in the later
1820s are the best primary evidence of tunes and lyrics to these inescapable work
rhythms. They indicate that there was room for creativity, improvisation, and
the expression of voyageur identity within the framework of established folk
songs. The voyageurs sang about scenarios of abundance, comfort, feasting, and
intimacy with women. This reflected their uncertain food supply and extended
periods away from loved ones. The songs simultaneously evidenced an unfailing
voyageur *gaité* and revealed deep anxieties. Paddling songs expressed the voyageur
vocational identity yet often transcended divisions of language, race, and class.
Their origins can be located in the *chansons en laisse* brought from France in
the seventeenth century, but were adapted with different extensions and new
choruses. Folklorists sterilized and interpreted them as lively relics of medieval

France, while their manifestations in the fur trade canoes served as an important platform for individual and group expression.

Songs on the Water

In the primary accounts of colonial encounters, boat songs are among the first musical genre mentioned. On his third journey to the Arctic in the 1570s, Martin Frobisher encountered Inuit singing as they paddled their skin kayaks out to his ships. Instead of a skirmish or violent encounter, he described how they mimicked the English rowing songs, keeping "time and stroke to any tune which you shal sing."[8] This exchange of paddling songs on the water constituted one of the first recorded interactions between Europeans and Indigenous peoples in the far north. The rhythm of the song resonated across cultural boundaries, providing a framework for communication and interaction without interpreters. Frobisher reported that "they will rowe with our Ores in our boates, and kepe a true stroke with oure Mariners, and séeme to take great delight therein."[9] At the outset of the seventeenth century, Samuel de Champlain encountered a group of Indigenous peoples off of Nauset Harbour who "launched a canoe, and eight or nine of them came out to us singing."[10] More such accounts were produced in the eighteenth century, with William Beresford transcribing and publishing an Indigenous song he heard sung frequently on the water before trade in Sitka Sound.[11] Despite these early accounts indicating encounters with the paddling songs of Indigenous peoples, they are few and far between in the publications of anthropologists and ethnomusicolologists.[12]

The reliance of British capital on French Canadian labour had profound cultural implications. It meant that the *chansons d'aviron* or paddling songs that the French had adapted to canoe travel in the seventeenth century became associated with the post-conquest fur trade, when the St Lawrence trade networks extended across the continent. For overwintering fur traders, hearing paddling songs signalled the end of the long quiet winter. Ross Cox characterized this season as when the voyageurs "again chanted forth their wild and pleasing *chansons à l'aviron*."[13] Despite this straightforward characterization of *joie de vivre*, voyageur songs have a surprisingly politicized history. The *coureurs de bois* have been associated with the national identity of French Canada for centuries.[14] Numbering in the hundreds by the 1680s, they adopted Indigenous technologies such as canoes, moccasins, and snowshoes to travel incredible distances through the interior waterways.[15] Their extended departures from French society made them a focal point of colonial anxieties about maintaining "order and authority," as they escaped the surveillance of church and state.[16] The historical archetypes of the *habitants* and *coureur de bois* have been regarded as central to French Canadian identity, with the latter associated with "freedom" and "independence."[17] The image of an idyllic French Canadian social type has been carefully curated since the folklorists of the mid-nineteenth century. As a result, the voyageurs' historic song tradition has been presented from a nationalist and Catholic perspective.

Most writing from the mid-nineteenth century onwards presents the image of the *coureurs de bois* and voyageurs singing joyous folk songs that were popular in the St Lawrence and old France. One of the best historians of voyageur songs, Grace Lee Nute, wrote in 1931 that we are "obliged in the main to hear the voyageurs of our imaginations singing the folk songs that were current among *all* Canadians."[18] It is true, as we shall see, that the roots of the voyageur repertoire originated from the wave of seventeenth-century French immigration to the St Lawrence valley. Yet this characterization is insufficient. Many of the most distinctive characteristics of the *chansons d'aviron* during the fur trade, such as their military character, their bawdiness, Indigenous influence, and their propensity for extension over long durations, have been downplayed or omitted in published folk song collections.

Historiography and Folk Song Collections

How the nation is represented has always been a central consideration of folk-lorists. As Ian McKay demonstrated with Helen Creighton's folk song collecting in the mid-twentieth century, the task of cultural selection and constructing the "folk" was inherently a "nation-building enterprise."[19] French Canadian folk song collecting began in earnest in the 1860s, a period of intense nationalism. At this time, Hubert La Rue, along with Abbé Henri-Raymond Casgrain, Antoine Gérin-Lajoie, and Joseph-Charles Taché founded *Les Soirées canadiennes*, which published assorted "collection[s] of national literature."[20] With the Province of Canada struggling politically and economically after the Rebellions of 1837–38, the crisis encouraged expressions of French Canadian nationalism and depictions of national identity. In the preface of Ernest Gagnon's influential 1865 *Chansons Populaires du Canada,* he wrote that French folk songs were durable icons of Francophone identity, like monuments made of granite or bronze, like the menhirs, dolmens, and cromlechs of Bretagne. Folk songs were interpreted as living relics of a long and illustrious history.[21] Gagnon and later folklorists presented French Canada as a time-capsule of pre-Revolutionary France and an embodiment of an essentialized Francophone identity.

In the post-Confederation era, Marius Barbeau looms large in this scholarship. As an anthropologist, folklorist, and musicologist who played a significant role in the development of the Canadian Museum of History, he was perhaps the most influential in collecting and presenting French Canadian folk songs to the Canadian public. The image that Marius Barbeau depicted was of traditional folk songs as ubiquitous in French communities across North America, "as familiar as barley-bread."[22] The rich singing culture of the French manifested regularly in the festivities, holidays, weddings, and special events that characterized social life.[23] According to Barbeau, French Canadians spontaneously adapted their songs to North America's distinct mode of transportation. "Picking up the paddle, the canoemen burst into song at once, the better to work in unison and keep their spirits from flagging."[24] This simplistic though charming explanation was commonplace for folklorists who collected songs and identified their origins in the distant past. In subsequent publications, Barbeau speculated on patterns of transmission and traced certain songs in the French Canadian repertoire as far back as the fourth and sixth centuries CE.[25] Barbeau described his interpretive framework at the end of his long career, writing the "language and folk traditions of ancient France followed the settlers and adventurers into the New World. Time, distance, and misfortune were not enough to blunt the racial patrimony of old; they only served to enhance its value as a solace in the wilderness. Songs, tales, and handicrafts survived the change and centuries, as if conserved under a white blanket of snow."[26] Barbeau repeatedly emphasized continuity with France over North American innovation. Rather than discussing Indigenous influences, he declared that folk songs were an important part of Francophone "racial patrimony." The presentation of this material was not designed to capture the full diversity of French Canadian folk culture, but rather to represent particular characteristics. Barbeau was explicit in his hopes that his collections would inspire "composers to create 'national' music."[27] Bridging anthropology, musicology, and folklore studies, he trained an entire generation of French Canadian scholars and his extensive collections are still widely cited.[28] Many of his interpretations have been implicitly or explicitly advanced.

Folkloric collections are where historians have turned for illustrative material. The two major English-speaking historians of the voyageurs are Grace Lee Nute in the early twentieth century and Carolyn Podruchny in the early twenty-first. Both rely on these sources. Grace Lee Nute laments that while many observers at the time wrote their impressions of these songs, few took the effort to record either their melodies or lyrics. Her chapter employs examples mentioned by fur traders such as "À La Claire Fontaine," "J'ai Trop

Grand Peur Des Loups," "Voici le Printemps," "Frit à L'Huile," "Le premier jour de Mai," and "J'ai Cueilli la Belle Rose" from versions collected and standardized by La Rue, Gagnon, and Barbeau. That an entire chapter of Nute's history of the voyageurs is devoted to their songs is a recognition of their importance. Self-referential songs such as "Parmi les Voyageurs," according to Nute, demonstrated "the class-consciousness of the voyageurs." Yet her version was first published by La Rue rather than something collected or transcribed during the fur trade.[29] Carolyn Podruchny's *Making the Voyageur World: Travelers and Traders in the North American Fur Trade* cites the same folklorists while advancing the historical analysis by identifying a number of social functions. Singing was integrated into daily routines, and songs combined Catholic and Indigenous influences to provide "a forum for pleasure and creativity" and express the voyageurs' unique identity.[30] Podruchny's work locates voyageur songs within the hegemonic social order, with paddling songs selected and started by the highest paid voyageurs, the *bouts,* setting the pace of travel and work for the group.

The scholarship of musicologist Conrad Laforte in the later twentieth century signalled a renewed scrutiny of voyageur song form as well as a reappraisal of its contents. His *Survivances médiévales dans la chanson folklorique* focused on the lyrical structure known as the *laisse,* sometimes called an "epic lay" in English. This versatile form "ont servi à de multiples usages," in social, children's, and marching songs. According to Laforte, the voyageurs were one of the key social groups "qui ont contribute le plus à la conservation de ces chansons."[31] The verse of these songs was characterized by a set number of syllables or "feet," around a caesura or pause. The final rhyme or assonance ending of each lyrical couplet was the same, hence "*laisse*" or "leashed" (AAAA).[32] These *chansons en laisse* have been further categorized into *chanson de métiers* (occupational songs), *chansons à réponse* (call and response), *chanson de rondes* (songs for round dances), and others. They alternate between a rhymed couplet and chorus. Laforte's investigation of this song form is exhaustive, while his assertions of "medieval" origins continues the emphasis of previous folklorists, a claim that has recently been scrutinized.[33]

The most historically minded analysis of the voyageur paddling song repertoire is Laforte's "Le Répertoire Authentique des Chansons D'aviron de nos Anciens Canotiers (Voyageurs, Engagés, Coureurs de Bois)." It makes two important points, the first concerning form and the second content. The first is a clarification of what kinds of songs were used as paddling songs. Laforte asserts that the *chansons d'aviron* alternated between a group chorus and a solo verse based around the *laisse*. These songs were distinct from the *complaintes* or ballads of the voyageurs which were often sung outside of the canoes by individuals instead of the entire group.[34] Both Nute and Podruchny reprint examples of *complaintes* and *chansons d'aviron* without clearly delineating differences in their form and function, or discussing how they might be analyzed differently as historical evidence. Voyageurs were compelled to sing the *chansons d'aviron* and paddle to the rhythm over long workdays. *Complaintes* were similar to ballads, often relating personal stories of misfortune. More recent collections such as Madeleine Béland's *Chansons de voyageurs, coureurs de bois et forestiers* provide examples of *complaintes* interspersed with paddling songs. Laforte on the other hand clearly distinguished these songs sung outside of the context of paddling from the *chansons d'aviron*.[35] He diverges from his predecessors in recognizing the prevalence of "comiques ou grivois" (comic or bawdy) lyrics, something virtually absent from the collections of La Rue, Gagnon, Barbeau, and Béland, but supported by the historical evidence from the fur trade.[36]

Primary Sources: The Ermatinger Collection

Dozens of travellers and traders commented on the songs of the voyageurs, and at least four collections were transcribed from the canoes of the fur trade. One is mentioned by John MacTaggart in his publication about Canada in 1826–28. He published only small lyrical samples and never the full collection he claimed to possess.[37] Another collection was transcribed by Edward M. Hopkins, who lived near Lachine and documented nine French Canadian paddling songs, all possessing the *laisse* form.[38] This collection is not from a fur trader and was written at the relatively late date of 1861, taken apparently from the voyageurs of governor George Simpson, an elite group of self-styled "hommes choisis! Les plus beaux chanteurs du monde," whom J.G. Kohl described as singing "the merriest songs."[39] This collection, while valuable, may not be representative of the common paddling song repertoire employed at the height of the fur trade.

The most valuable collections were compiled by musically proficient fur traders W.F. Wentzel and Edward Ermatinger. The former's collection survived until the late nineteenth century when it was described by the editor L.R. Masson as "mostly obscene and unfit for publication."[40] It seems to have disappeared from Library and Archives Canada around the outset of the twentieth century, which an archivist suggested may have been due to the "rubric of moral turpitude."[41] This leaves the most valuable extant collection of voyageur songs that of fur trader Edward Ermatinger. It remained in his family's possession in Portland Oregon until it was lent to the Public Archives of Canada in 1943. It was subsequently published by Marius Barbeau in the *Journal of American Folklore* as "The Ermatinger Collection of Voyageur Songs (ca. 1830)."[42] Ermatinger retired from the fur trade in 1828, and these songs were likely transcribed before that date rather than 1830 as Barbeau's title suggests. These eleven songs with lyrics and musical notations represent the richest collection of paddling songs from the fur trade era. They represent the best source available for studying the *chansons d'aviron*, providing insights into the voyageurs' repertoire and how these songs functioned on the water.

Ermatinger was a fairly prominent name in the fur trade. Lawrence Ermatinger was a Swiss-born merchant and partner in the firm Trye and Ermatinger of London England who arrived in Montreal soon after the British conquest and became involved in trading goods to Michilimackinac and Grand Portage. His son Charles Oakes worked for the HBC while another son, Lawrence Edward, became assistant commissary-general in the British army. Lawrence Edward's sons Edward and Francis both entered the fur trade with the HBC in 1818, engaging until 1828 and 1853 respectively.[43] Edward received a formal education in England in languages and music, providing him with relatively rare skills to transcribe voyageur songs. Over the course of his life he was a fur trader, businessman, politician, and writer.[44]

In the brief introduction to the published Ermatinger collection, Barbeau emphasized historic continuity with the songs of French-speaking communities in the St Lawrence and France. He asserted that these songs are of the "common stock of traditional folk songs" transmitted across the Atlantic from approximately 1640 to 1680, the period of most intensive migration to the St Lawrence from France. He described the songs as "alive and variable," sometimes deviating from the "original pattern," and constantly shaped by the "mannerisms of individual singers." Indeed, in their form as *chanson en laisse*, and in their motifs and narratives, the Ermatinger collection evidences remarkable continuity with the folksongs of the St Lawrence. All the songs in the Ermatinger collection have been collected in some version by folklorists in Quebec and France, sometimes with dozens or even hundreds of variations documented. Yet in his treatment, Barbeau neglected to investigate how the familiar repertoire was modified and adapted. Interestingly, the Ermatinger collection demonstrates unique choruses and extended verses. Cultural creations of the fur trade are interwoven into the narratives of knights, love, pastorals, flowers, and nightingales. Like much folkloric material, what seems innocent on the surface often contains allegorical meanings with sexual innuendo. A few lyrics directly express lewd sensory desires.

Paddling songs were adapted to various tempos. Mid-nineteenth-century ethnographer J.G. Kohl conducted a thorough analysis of how voyageur songs functioned on the water. He observed and interviewed voyageurs, learning that paddling songs were subdivided based on the speed of work by "'chansons à l'aviron,' 'chansons à la rame,' 'chansons de canot à lége,' and so on." Songs were chosen because they functioned well at particular tempos, with *lége* the fastest and *rame* the slowest. Yet Kohl suggested that all these categories of paddling songs were ultimately very similar, with the differences "less in the character of the song than in the time and tact of the melody."[45] The *laisse* seems to have underpinned the various paddling songs that were subdivided according to tempo and working context. The songs in the Ermatinger collection are based on core narratives that were brought from France in the seventeenth century, and are well-known French *chansons en laisse*. The Ermatinger collection demonstrates that the choruses of these old songs were variable and prone to refashioning, while there was room for adaptability in the verses and improvisation to extend the song.

Functioning of the Chansons D'aviron

The observations of travellers and traders indicate that singing was the crucial device that coordinated paddles aboard the fur trade canoes. The largest *canots du maître* could have a dozen or more paddlers, while the smaller *canot du nord* had four to six.[46] The canoes often travelled in flotillas or brigades, and the "call" had to be issued loudly to unify the movement of all the paddles together. The brigade's guide or leading bowsman or steersman issued this vocal cue with the first line or two of verse, selecting the song and setting the pace. The group sang the response and commenced paddling to the tempo.[47] The call established the melody and rhythm that was mimicked by subsequent singers.[48] It needed to provide recognizable lyrics so that everyone, even the inexperienced *mangeurs du lard,* could quickly join in. Singing synchronized the paddles of the voyageurs as marches synchronized the legs of soldiers. Each individual conformed his movements to the rhythm of the song or else would fall out of step or stroke. If that occurred, it had the potential to disrupt the movements of others ahead and behind. The song acted as the primary mechanism of synchronicity.

Marching songs are similar to paddling songs in both form and content. Fur traders who travelled thousands of kilometres by canoe such as George Simpson and Alexander Ross referred to canoe travel as a "march."[49] One NWC employee wrote in his journal about the time he "could not march on the river."[50] John McDonnell described distances by "days march by water,"[51] while Duncan M'Gillivray related how Athabasca men prided themselves on "expeditious marching."[52] This terminology was a figure of speech, yet it acknowledged the similarities between paddling and marching. Most of the voyageur paddling songs recorded by Edward Ermatinger possess the 2/4 time signature of a march.[53]

The structure of paddling songs was revealing. Though started by the *bouts,* the songs could take on a life of their own. Different singers could cycle into the verse, each singing their own rhymed couplet. Alexander Ross described a "particular voice being ever selected to lead the song," suggesting different singers started the songs or led the solo couplets alternating with the group chorus.[54] Nicholas Garry recorded "one man leading, the other[s] joining chorus and all paddling to Time."[55] Continual cycling between verse and chorus meant the narrative advanced slowly. Each new couplet repeated the last line and followed with a new line in the same rhyme scheme. This structure contained power dynamics, as the call was typically issued by the most senior, prestigious, and well-paid voyageurs, the guide, bowsman, or steersman.[56] The call could initiate a grueling pace, reflecting their wishes rather than those of the crew. The lower status *mangeurs du lard* might have their turn singing as soloists, yet they would have little opportunity to slow the pace once the song began. Barking orders, singing the "call," and leading the paddling songs were such important tasks that *bouts* could receive more pay if they had strong voices.[57] They could also lose their position if their throat or voice failed them during a voyage.[58] Singing then, was an essential mechanism for the group and provided a way for individuals to distinguish themselves. Singing operated to reflect and maintain the social order, while it also offered an arena for individual expression.

The Ermatinger collection reveals how the voyageurs adapted the early modern *chansons en laisse* repertoire over long distances. Between short breaks, known as *pipes,* the voyageurs paddled for an hour or two on average.[59] Paddling songs got the paddles moving, set the pace, and synchronized them on the water. After a few minutes, they were not absolutely necessary. Yet some accounts indicate that paddling songs were extended as long as necessary between *pipes.*[60] Kohl witnessed the songs functioning on the water and identified features that seemingly escaped later scholars. He observed that "The principal virtue of these songs appears to be their length."[61] They were not only long but "remarkably long," he wrote, arguing they were impossible to record in their entirety.[62] He described their transcription as akin to cutting "off half a yard as a specimen" because the songs "must last, if possible, for a whole river, or at least a lake."[63]

This conceptualization is more helpful and contextually accurate than those provided by folklorists who "collected songs" as if they were short discrete entities. Voyageur songs were adaptable, fluid, and necessarily extendable.

Lyrics

The first question is to consider whether the Ermatinger collection was representative more generally of voyageur paddling songs. Edward Ermatinger did not leave an explanation as to why he recorded the songs that he did. It may be that they were the most common during his time travelling with the voyageur canoes in the 1820s.[64] He may have selected these songs because they were the most representative, or perhaps they were his favourite. Certainly there were more paddling songs that he heard that he did not transcribe into this collection. It is possible to cross-reference the Ermatinger collection songs with other primary accounts. This method suggests that the first and third song, "J'ai trop grand peur des loups" and "M'envoient à la fontaine" were the most popular *chansons d'aviron* in the collection and voyageur repertoire more generally. Both are referenced numerous times in the written record before 1840.[65] Only two other voyageur songs possess as many references: "Trois Beaux Canards" (also known by the choruses "en roulant ma boule" and "v'la bon vent") and "Rosier Blanc," which are not found in the Ermatinger collection.[66] This suggests that the Ermatinger collection contained some of the most frequently referenced and historically utilized voyageur paddling songs.

Viewed together, these songs contained allegories and euphemisms that provided layered meanings. Animal species, birds, flowers, and fountains constituted the characters and locations of the narratives, possessing double meanings and symbolic significances. How these meanings changed over time and space has generated heated debate among scholars.[67] Robert Darnton has stressed the "complexity and multiplicity inherent in symbolic expression," demonstrating how folk motifs were nuanced and could possess a variety of meanings. Others have argued for a more straightforward interpretation of symbolic vocabularies.[68] The ecclesiastical authorities of New France complained about the "double meanings" latent in the discourse of young men and the lower orders.[69] The narratives of the Ermatinger collection's paddling songs still possess these characteristics. Scenarios of marriage, hunting, and family life are interwoven with knights, fountains, sheep, shirts, trees, and singing nightingales, all rich folkloric symbols. These fall into thematic categories of French Canadian folk songs delineated by Laforte and others who have suggested their deeper meanings.[70]

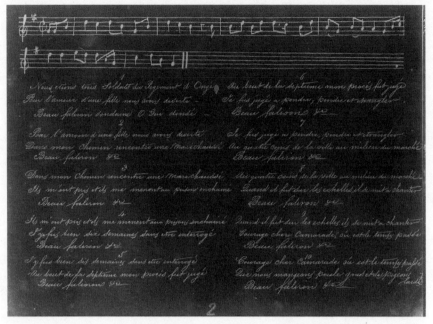

Fig. 6.1 From the collection of fur trader Edward Ermatinger, recorded ~1827–30, "Folk songs, French-Canada, ca. 1830."

"Trois beaux canards" was one of the long-standing and favoured voyageur songs. Its core narrative displays its feudal origins. It consists of the "fils du roi" (son of the king) hunting with his giant gun, shooting at the black (bad) duck, but hitting the white (good) duck. He is chastised: "Le fils du roi tu est mechant!" (Son of the king you are so mean!). To the fur traders, surrounded by singing voyageurs, this expression of playful hostility toward the "son of the king" may have been unnerving. Direct expressions of class consciousness appear to be absent in the extant voyageur repertoire, and yet this symbolic language from the feudal past was carried forwards and may have wielded some symbolic power against fur trader overlords.

The Ermatinger collection reveals that the voyageurs used three different methods to extend paddling songs over long durations. The first was linking sequences of verse that could be "leashed" because they shared the same rhyme or assonance ending. An example of this can be found in "mes blancs moutons garder," which possesses eleven lines of verse before transitioning into the first four lines of "c'était une vieille grand-mère."[71] The verse in both cases conforms to the rhyme/assonance ending of {é}, allowing for the easy interchange of long sequences. These interlinked verse narratives both possess a metre of fourteen syllables and depict pastoral themes. This suggests that rather than singing distinct songs with fixed texts, voyageurs could sing a series of verse segments sharing a common rhyme scheme to the same (or different) chorus. This kind of singing resembled quilt-work, interlacing segments of verse together to suit the necessary duration.

The second method of extending songs was to break the unified rhyme scheme and introduce a new rhyme-assonance ending. This method is evident in four of eleven songs in the Ermatinger collection.[72] New rhyme schemes were introduced, which could be continued or revert to the original.[73] Even in these examples where the *laisse* is broken, it is retained for long sequences. The Ermatinger collection suggests that while this method could be used to prolong the action, the tendency was to continue the rhyme scheme established at the outset.

The final method that the voyageurs used to extend their singing over long durations was by rhyming simple and repetitive lines onto the end of the verse. This provided an opportunity for customization and creativity. In his publication of the Ermatinger collection, Barbeau suggests the songs' "vitality," how they were "alive and variable," yielding slightly "to the mannerisms of individual singers and the utilities they served."[74] Yet it went beyond that, as these songs reveal the mechanisms for extension. Rhyming simple and repetitive lines onto the end of a verse is known as anaphora.[75] In these cases, each phrase begins similarly or identically, facilitating the enumeration of details onto an established structure around a common theme. Anaphoric endings are found prominently in the lyrics of four songs in the Ermatinger collection. This kind of material is largely omitted in the published folk song collections of Gagnon and Barbeau. They would have thought it was extraneous, idiosyncratic, and in many cases, inappropriate. Yet this appears to be where voyageurs had the greatest opportunity for creativity, fashioning lyrics that directly related to their vocation.

Of the four songs that contain extensions of verse through anaphora, all extend beyond the core narratives published by folklorists in the St Lawrence. They include "j'ai trop grand peur des loups" and "m'envoient à la fontaine," as well as "nous avons déserté" and "le rossignol y chante." They represent examples of voyageur expression quite different from the pretty imagery of nightingales and ducks, presenting instead bawdy fantasies of sensory gratification.

"j'ai trop grand peur des loups" (I am too scared of wolves)[76]

A la maison accoutumé	At the accustomed house
A la maison du boulanger	At the house of the baker
Ya du bon pain pour y manger	There's good bread to eat
Ya du bon vin pour y trinquer	There's good wine to toast
Et des bons lits pour nous coucher	And good beds for us to sleep upon
Des joli's fill's à nos côtés.	With beautiful girls at our sides

"nous avons déserté" (we have deserted)[77]

Que nous mangions poul's grass's et des pigeons lardés	When we ate fat chickens and pigeons
Que nous allions voir les fill's bien tard après souper	When we went to see the girls, well after supper
Que nous fumions la pip' comm' des jeun's cavalier.	When we smoked the pipe, like young knights

"m'envenant à la fontaine" (I am going to the well)[78]

On y prend de la carpe, aussi de l'éturgeon	Catching carp, and also sturgeon
Aussi des écrevisses, qui vont de reculons	Also crayfish, who move backwards
Tout comme ces jeun's filles qu'on leur prend les tétons	Just like the young girls, whose breasts (or nipples) we grab
Quand on sait bien s'y prendre, on les tire du fond.	when we have a good hold, we pull them from the depths

"le rossignol y chante" (the nightingale sings)[79]

Faudrait qu'un petit vent pour abattre tes fleurs	In need of a small wind to knock down your flowers
Faudrait qu'un bel amant pour avoir tes faveurs!	In need of a good lover to have your favours
Faudrait qu'un voyageur pour y gagner ton coeur!	In need of a voyageur to win your heart!

The voyageurs' extended lyrics most often intertwined longings for food and intimacy. These songs were a mechanism for expressing and managing real concerns. Hunger and loneliness were commonly experienced by those working in the fur trade. The voyageurs sang about food and drink that were generally unavailable, from baked bread to fat chickens and wine. Proper beds for sleeping were a comfort that the voyageurs relinquished for the duration of their travels. Lyrics about sleeping often included sexual innuendo. References to women ranged from chivalrous to salacious. Those expressed in "le rossignol y chante" demonstrate a romantic proclamation and approach. The final lyrics of "m'envenant à la fontaine," on the other hand, transform sexual innuendo into outright assault. In this case, what may have been sung playfully appears sinister on the printed page, particularly when assessed alongside histories of colonial sexual violence.[80]

These songs are based on recognizable folk songs in the French Canadian repertoire, and Ermatinger's versions may be compared with those transcribed elsewhere. The immense repository of French Canadian folk songs in the Archives de Folklore at the Université Laval in Quebec contains dozens of versions of "j'ai trop grand peur des loups" and "m'envenant à la fontaine." These versions suggest that the endings collected by Ermatinger were indeed distinct. The most common ending for "j'ai trop grand peur des loups," often entitled "trois cavaliers," is a misadventure whereby the protagonists sleep in a chicken coop. One version playfully ends with: "Moi je coucherai avec la mariée, Toi, tu coucheras dans le poulailler, les poules, les coqs riront de toi."[81] Various comical scenarios are presented in the other variations, for instance sleeping next to "une grosse mouton," or sleeping while "Un gros coq d'Inde et à tes pieds."[82] Other scenarios inside the chicken coop include sleeping with "Les poules, les oies ferent sur toi."[83] The worst depicts trying to sleep while being scratched by rats and pecked by chickens on the nose.[84] The version in the Ermatinger collection, on the other hand, inverts the misadventure into an exceptionally idealistic ending, with the protagonists receiving beds, partners, food, and drink.

"M'envoient à la fontaine," often titled "fille au cresson" or "la fontaine est profonde" has been collected in dozens of variations in both France and Quebec. Many of the standard endings depict a fishing scenario, such as "Aussi des écrevisses, Qui vont de reculons, Ah! dites-moi donc, la belle, L'écrévisse c'est-y bon? On y coupe la tête, le restant en est bon, embrassez-moi, la belle, Après ça nous en irons."[85] In other examples, the final lines do not relate to women but only the topic of food. For instance, one common variation ends with the lines "Quel poisson lui prend-on? On y prend de la carpe, Aussi de l'eturgeon, Ah! dites-nous, la belle, Ah! quelle sauce nous l'mange-t-on?, Yon le mange a la sauce, Et faite au beurre, a l'ognon."[86] The version in the Ermatinger collection, on the other hand, contains overtly sexual language. Of all the versions of paddling songs documented, this one captured by Ermatinger is the most *grivois*.

"Nous avons déserté," the second song of the Ermatinger collection, is a more curious manifestation. It is certainly much less well known in the French Canadian folk song repertoire. This song does not seem to appear in the published collections of Gagnon and Barbeau. In researching its origin, a striking clue is provided in its opening line: "nous etions trios soldats, du regiment d'Ongé." This is a curious reference as no such place exists. In a version collected by E.M. Massicotte, the lyric is "nous étions trios soldats, du regiment dernier."[87] This seems to be a dead end, yet it is clearly a soldier song. The Ermatinger lyric suggests it came from a specific regiment of the colonial French army. To my delight, at the Bibliotheque Nationale's Department de Musique in Paris I discovered a very similar marching song from the military regiments of Angers, France. Of course, "D'Ongé" is a corrupt transcription of "d'Angers." The journey this song took from western France to the York Factory express brigade is tantalizing cultural history.

Eleven versions of this song have been catalogued under the name "Le Déserteur que l'on s'apprête à pendre." These are transcribed in various collections and catalogued in volume 2 of the exhaustive *Répertoire des Chansons Françaises de tradition orale*.[88] Ermatinger's version shares the same twelve syllable *laisse* (6F 6M). Although many of the details differ, the core narrative consists of a group of soldiers deserting the army for the love of a woman. Yet the lyrics at the end of the Ermatinger version are not found in the others. The version recorded by Massicotte ends with "Où est le temps passé, Où nous allions voir les filles, bien tard après souper, Il n'en faut plus parler."[89] The final line of the Ermatinger collection, on the other hand, presents the voyageurs as self-styled knights on horseback smoking their pipes. Structurally, this song could be adapted to the contexts of marching and paddling, and yet there is a deeper historical connection. The Troupes de la Marine and Carignan-Salières regiments periodically played an important role in seventeenth century New France.[90] Many soldiers retired along the St Lawerence, and their sons often became *coureurs de bois* or *engagés,* providing a direct link with the fur trade.[91] The *mentalité* of these two very different vocations appears to have been similar. Men marching to war or working in the fur trade were both away from home for extended periods of time and subjected to an insecure food supply in all-male company. Of all the versions reviewed, only the voyageur ending depicts an idealized and encouraging scenario that may have provided hope to weary paddlers.

The final song of our examination, "le rossignol y chante," is unique in expressing a self-conscious voyageur identity. "Faudrait qu'un voyageur pour y gagner ton coeur!" reflects a masculine bravado obsessed with courting women. The voyageurs were employed in a hierarchical, paternalist relationship in which they occupied the bottom position. They were not like wage labour, as they were indentured for long periods of time, and their vocational ceremonies were more akin to a guild. E.P. Thompson wrote that "class happens when some men, as a result of common experiences (inherited or shared), feel and articulate the identity of their interests as between themselves, and as against other men whose interests are different from (and usually opposed to) theirs."[92] While the voyageurs' songs display evidence of a distinct vocational consciousness, they do not establish an oppositional framework with company owners that is found in working-class songs of the nineteenth century. Thus, Nute's assertion of voyageur songs representing "class-consciousness" seems exaggerated. They reveal the vocational anxieties of scarcity and separation and insights into the voyageur *mentalité*. They reflect the insecurities of men who were required to leave family and loved ones for months or years at a time with tearful departures. The voyageur myth of the *chasse-galerie* reflects the *ennui* produced by the fur trade, whereby men bargain their souls with the devil to fly home in a canoe for a brief visit with their loved ones.[93] Paddling songs offered an ongoing forum of expression that allowed for escapist fantasies and daydreams of love, intimacy, food, and comfort. They sang of sensual fulfillment in the face of sustained deprivation.

On long journeys, food was often a matter of continual concern. Canoe travel was predicated on a much higher labour-to-cargo ratio than York boats, meaning that there were more mouths to feed and less room for provisions.[94] The voyageurs' physically demanding vocation produced notoriously large appetites. David Thompson estimated that his men ate at least eight pounds of meat each day.[95] For many of the routes northwest of Lake Superior it was impossible to carry sufficient food provisions. The hyper-dense and nutritious pemmican worked best, but some years it was scarce. Canoe brigades relied on Indigenous peoples and trading posts along the way for supplies.[96] Food was socially significant. It divided voyageurs into the lower status *mangeurs du lard*, who ate pork provisions on their roundtrips from Montreal, and the *hivernants* and *hommes du nord* who traversed from western Lake Superior to the distant northwest, frequently risking hunger and starvation while relying on meat from the hunt.[97] The fur trade produced many accounts of extreme privation, with the decades of the 1780s and 1810s representing periods of particular scarcity.[98] Kohl observed that nearly all of his voyageurs had experienced extreme hunger and were "almost always in a state of want."[99]

Singing was often interpreted as having a reinvigorating effect on the voyageurs. In this assertion, there seems to be a combination of fact and fiction. It certainly helped push voyageurs through fatigue and famine by keeping their paddles moving over long durations. Kohl described how the voyageurs "consider singing as specially necessary to give them fresh mental strength for the bodily exertion."[100] Elizabeth Simcoe described how "after a day of fatigue, where strong currents require peculiar exertion, they sing incessantly and give a more regular stroke with the oars when accompanied by the tunes."[101] Fur trader Nicholas Garry wrote that singing "appears to ease their Labours."[102] Ross Cox described how singing had an "enlivening" effect and "softens down the severity of their laborious duties."[103] As evidence he cites a brigade in "starving condition" singing the "'*chansons à l'aviron*' until day-break, to divert their hunger."[104] Alexander Ross described how singing helped voyageurs "keep for days and nights together on the water, without intermission and without repose."[105] John Howison travelled with voyageurs during the years 1818–20 and wrote that they were "inured to hard-ship ... toiling at the oar during the whole day, and lightening their labour with songs."[106] While these descriptions express classist condescension, they do, in fact, align with neuroscience that suggests singing releases endorphins and serotonin.[107] Singing may indeed have had the physical and psychological effect of enlivening voyageurs during long privations.

Conrad Laforte speculated that singing functioned as "une sorte d'évasion par l'imagination" (a kind of evasion for the imagination), allowing the voyageurs to overlook or ignore their conditions and surroundings.[108] The Ermatinger collection suggests that the escapism tended toward scenarios of abundance and favourable outcomes. Singing served as a distraction, but it also presented a mental refuge, as good times were imagined. There are some similarities with Indigenous hunting songs, which often included voicing or envisioning success. As we will see in Chapter 7, it was not unprecedented for voyageurs to conjure with Indigenous hunters. One fascinating account portrays voyageurs not only imagining but seemingly *willing* their desires into existence. In 1821, Nicholas Garry described a canoe brigade singing about varieties of alcohol and then stopping to drink water, with "the Imagination and spirit giving to it all the Qualities they have been vaunting."[109] With limited control over their actual provisions, the voyageurs sang about the abundance they desired in their paddling songs.

Many travellers depicted idyllic and happily singing voyageurs which eclipsed their hardships. Most first-hand accounts describe the excitement of departure or arrival rather than the arduous days of labour in-between. Men and women of the upper classes in the eighteenth and nineteenth centuries often interpreted the work songs of lower orders as indicators of simplicity and even happiness. This romanticism glossed over genuine hardship and suffering. Consider Irish traveller Isaac Weld's description of voyageurs "singing merrily" after having paddled the entire night.[110] Similar appraisals were recorded concerning the songs of slaves in the American south in the early nineteenth century.[111] As a result, the primary accounts convey an unrealistic perception of ever-content and joyous voyageurs. This is reflected in the historiography, with Grace Lee Nute writing that the songs "lightened the work and were the natural expression of such an effervescent race of men as the French Canadians admittedly were."[112] Carolyn Podruchny wrote that one of the two major functions of voyageur singing was to provide "a forum for pleasure and creativity."[113] These appraisals may have some truth, but the apparent *gaieté* of paddling songs often served to mask undeniable suffering. Pleasure was a byproduct of songs used to manage the march, often carrying the men through extended periods of exertion and privation.

The Chorus

The voyageur chorus was most often remarked by observers. Alternating with the verse produced a "rising and falling" effect on the water.[114] John J. Bigsby described hearing the singing of an approaching canoe brigade as far as six miles away while surveying Drummond Island in 1820.[115] It was certainly the chorus he heard first. Those inside the canoes described the choruses as "powerful," "noisy," and "roaring."[116] Ballantyne described the departure of the spring brigade from York Factory with a "cheering song from the men in full chorus."[117] The chorus on the water tied the canoes together and enabled the group of singers to be extended. Anna Jameson described the voyageurs in her canoe singing with another canoe "joining in the chorus."[118] Colin Robertson described how his canoe met with another on Lake Bourbon near Norway House in July of 1819, forming a brigade when "the men of both canoes join[ed] in the chorus."[119]

The choruses of voyageur songs, in general, were simple and incredibly adaptable, with many possessing dozens of chorus variations. Many of the most well-known songs, such as "en roulant ma boule" and "v'la bon vent," are distinct chorus variations of the same song, "trois beaux canards," which has been collected in over one hundred different versions.[120] Unsurprisingly, the two most widespread songs from the Ermatinger collection, "j'ai trop grand peur des loups" and "m'envoient à la fontaine," have the most choruses associated with them. Thomas Moore transcribed a chorus of the former in 1804 as "A l'ombre d'un bois je m'en vais jouer, A l'ombre d'un bois je m'en vais dancer."[121] Another recorded from the lips of voyageurs is "L'on, lon, laridon daine, Lon ton, laridon dai."[122] "M'envoient à la fontaine" possesses perhaps even more chorus variations, including that collected by Barbeau: "dondaine, don, Dondaine, dondaine."[123] The chorus of "mon père a fait bâtir maison" is clearly built for the paddle: "Fringue, Fringue, sur la rivière, Fringue, Fringue, sur l'aviron." Other voyageur choruses also mentioned the paddle: "C'est l'aviron qui nous mène, qui nous mène, C'est l'aviron qui nous mène en haut."[124]

Vocables are nonsemantic syllables combined rhythmically for their sound rather than content and were frequently employed in these choruses. They appear in many folk song genres and singing cultures all over the world.[125] Ernest Gagnon quoted a sixteenth-century French scholar who described the "infini d'interjections qui se trouvent dans les chansons populaires," such as "lirompha, dada, etc."[126] While on paper they appear curious, when sounded they are easy to learn and repeat. In the Ermatinger collection, vocables can be found in the chorus of five of eleven songs and evidence a distinct style. Songs whose choruses consist of vocables include "la chasse au perdreau": "gai faluron malurette, O gai! faluron maluré"; "le rossignol y chante": "beau faluron ma dondaine, O gai! faluron ma dondé"; "nous avons déserté": "beau faluron dondaine, O gai dondé!" Songs with some vocables in the chorus include "m'envenant à la fontaine": "la violette dondén,' la violette dondé" and "mes blancs moutons garder": "digue dondèn', jeune fille à marier."[127] The frequent repetition of vocables such as "faluron" and "dondèn" suggests their special significance. Kohl observed that vocables were nearly interchangeable in voyageur paddling songs, as he heard a long song whose refrain was "Ma dondon, ma dondette," while the second time he heard it, it was "Ma luron, ma lurette."[128] Beyond merely being favoured by the voyageurs for their sound, Kohl observed that "'Dondon' and 'luron' were popular names for girls, sweethearts, &c."[129] The vocables found in the Ermatinger collection appear to be variations of these and perhaps conveyed similar meanings.

Indigenous peoples may have influenced voyageur songs in this realm of nonsemantic expressions or vocables.[130] Indigenous peoples across North America used vocables prominently in the lyrical content of their songs.[131] This was clearly a "pre-contact" characteristic. As fur traders encountered the diversity of Indigenous singing, the prevalence of vocables was likely to have been observed. In general, songs with vocables may have had a "widening the circle" effect so to speak, allowing for people from diverse cultural and linguistic backgrounds to join in. Ted Gioia suggested that the proliferation of vocables in sea shanties was due to "constant borrowing across linguistic barriers."[132] Although vocables can be found generally in the French Canadian folk song repertoire, they occur more frequently in the Ermatinger collection.

The chorus presented an image of unity within the brigades. While most voyageurs were French Canadians from the St Lawrence valley, by the early nineteenth century there were increasing numbers of Indigenous peoples in their ranks. There were significant numbers of Iroquois from Kahnawake and Kahnesatake in the Montreal canoes.[133] Alexander Ross described them participating in the paddling songs, although he stated that they preferred hymns.[134] When Father Aubert travelled from Montreal to Red River in a voyageur canoe, he described his crew of two Iroquois and four French Canadians as experienced voyageurs with voices "doués de fort belles voix et sachant par coeur le répertoire de toutes les chansons canadienne."[135] By the mid-nineteenth century, according to Ross, most voyageurs were mixed ancestry or Métis.[136] Yet outsiders had difficulty distinguishing and delineating between the backgrounds of men aboard the canoes.[137] Experience and employment rather than race or cultural background determined whether the French Canadian or Indigenous voyageurs were *mangeurs du lard* or *hommes du nord*. The NWC's and HBC's rigid structure relegated all voyageurs to the status of servants, while the masters, officers, factors, and clerks were demarcated as non-labourers.[138] Control of singing reflected hierarchy within their ranks, yet the communal paddling songs presented an image of solidarity and connected the men in co-operation, bridging cultural divisions to foster and express a cohesive voyageur identity.

A retired voyageur interviewed in the late nineteenth century recalled the social inclusivity of paddling songs. In his experience of over forty years working in the fur trade, he had developed an extensive musical vocabulary, claiming "Fifty songs could I sing." He prized how well he could sing with others in particular. He boasted that he "could carry, paddle, walk and sing with any man I ever saw."[139] Vocalizations that resulted from polyglot and culturally diverse crews singing together were labelled, in culinary terminology, as "rubbaboos." Robert Kennicott described how "Rubbaboo is a favorite dish with the northern voyageurs, when they can get it. It consists of pemmican made into a kind of soup by boiling in water … Any queer mixture gets that name among the voyageurs. When I try to speak French, and mix English, Slavy and Louchioux words with it, they tell me 'that's a rubbaboo.' And when the Indians attempt to sing a voyaging song, the different keys and tunes make a 'rubbaboo.'"[140] This reference suggests that cultural intermixtures of melody and lyrics were commonplace enough to have their own name. A musical analysis of the Ermatinger collection indicates that the tunes possess a relatively narrow melodic range, with most of the songs employing only five or six notes of the scale.[141] This limited range would have contributed to the ease of group participation and served to "widen the circle." All voyageurs, whether they were considered "good" singers or not, were expected to contribute and sing while paddling.

Precious few documented paddling songs truly reflect the polyglot nature of the fur trade. One is derived from the St Lawrence's "southwest" trade and contains Indigenous words. Its final phrases, while undoubtedly Indigenous, have not been translated according to Barbeau or to my knowledge:[142]

Dans l'Mississippi ya des sauvagesses, (Bis)
Des souliers brodés, Des mitassës rouges,
Des poudramiskis, Pour bacawiner.
(On the Mississippi there are *sauvagesses*.
Their embroidered shoes, their red leggings,
Des poudramiskis, Pour bacawiner.)

In Anishinaabemowin, "poudra" can mean powdered, and "misk" is the initial morpheme for red.[143] *Poudramiskis* might refer to ochre or vermilion. This would be consistent with the previous line's emphasis on finery. It also aligns with the prominence of red ochre in the Indigenous cultures of the Mississippi. It is not clear what *bacawiner* means. "Baac" can mean "opening," while "Bakinaage" means s/he wins, and "Bakinawaan" means s/he "beats" him/her in Anishinaabemowin.[144] Quill embroidered moccasins and "mitassës rouges," or red leggings, were well-known styles sometimes remarked by fur traders on their journeys around the Great Lakes. Alexander Henry (the elder) adopted these leggings himself in 1761 to blend in with the Indigenous-French Canadian fashion. He described how "my legs were covered with *mitasses, a* kind of hose, made, as is the favorite fashion, of scarlet cloth."[145] Voyageur songs with Indigenous lyrics demonstrate the degree to which Euro-Canadian fur traders became familiar with Indigenous languages and the degree to which their cultures intertwined.

Paddling songs offered an important forum for early expressions of Métis identity. Many mixed ancestry descendants from fur trade partnerships in the Great Lakes to Red River corridor worked in the canoe and boat brigades of the NWC and HBC.[146] One such man, Pierre Falcon, worked in a fur trade canoe when he was young and eventually became known for his lyrical talents as the "bard of the prairies."[147] His most famous composition is "chanson de la grenouillère" or "la bataille des sept chênes" documents a Métis perspective of the Battle of Seven Oaks in 1816. Like the *chansons d'aviron*, it employs the unified rhyme scheme of a *laisse*.[148] The Battle of Seven Oaks is frequently interpreted as the foundational moment of Métis national consciousness.[149] Falcon's rhymed couplets helped preserve and disseminate news of the incident which produced only one casualty among the Métis-NWC contingent and twenty among the HBC including governor Semple.[150] Because this song uses the *laisse* form it could easily be applied as a paddling song. It may well have been, although the earliest description of it taken on the water appears to be from the 1860s.[151] A significant number of voyageur songs or *chansons en laisse* were maintained by Métis communities in Manitoba in the twentieth-century, including many of the most popular historic paddling songs of the fur trade.[152] That voyageur musical culture, itself a mixture of old French and Indigenous influences that developed over centuries of fur trade interactions, influenced early expressions of Métis identity is not surprising. The Métis national anthem bore the influence of voyageur paddling songs and described the moment of greatest conflict in the British North American fur trade.

To a remarkable degree, voyageur paddling songs inspired English-speaking fur traders and the merchant elite of Lower Canada. Widely referenced for their romantic quality when observed on the water, paddling songs were generally written about favourably even by those who could not understand the lyrics. To the English ear, they signalled order, regularity, and movement, which also signalled profit. Peter Grant wrote that it was "pleasing to see them ... singing in chorus their simple melodious strains and keeping exact time with their paddles."[153] For Alexander Ross, singing was synonymous with labour. He described how they "renew their labors and their chorus."[154] Fur traders sometimes learned these songs and performed them outside of the canoes. At early nineteenth-century meetings of the Beaver Club, a prominent group of Montreal fur trade elite, the opening ceremonies began with the "animated song of the voyageur."[155] James Hughes described the club's meetings with the gentlemen arranging themselves on the floor and imitating the actions of paddling, "shouting at full voice the inspiring boating songs."[156] Due to their social exclusivity, Podruchny has interpreted these reinterpretations as representing the bourgeois "distancing themselves from their workers," casting them as "exotic curiosities," and serving to display their "sense of manhood" to the other merchants.[157] Yet the incorporation of *chansons d'aviron* rather than "Canadian Boat Songs" styled on Thomas Moore's popular English glee, indicates that authenticity was a source of pride for the veteran fur traders who met in the Beaver Club.

Voyageur paddling songs developed recognition and cachet among Anglophones on both sides of the Atlantic in the first few decades of the nineteenth century. Countless travellers through the British North American colonies described their romantic effect. Inspired by real *chansons d'aviron*, the Irish poet Thomas Moore composed the popular "A Canadian Boat Song" as a three-voice glee set to piano accompaniment. It and the genre of Canadian Boat Songs it inspired differed in almost every regard from real voyageur paddling songs.[158] Yet the popularity of this genre allowed fur traders to leverage access to the real paddling songs when they returned to metropolitan society. When in Montreal attending a dinner hosted by William McGillivray, physician John Bigsby recorded that his host performed "a wild *voyageur* song." McGillivray's rendition might be called rough-refined, singing with one hand on the piano and the other imitating the movement of the paddle. While it would have sounded completely different, this would have demonstrated how the melody and paddling were synchronized on the water. The song was "le premier jour de Mai." Bigsby reported that Mr McGillivray "sang it as only a true *voyageur* can do, imitating the action of the paddle, and in their high, resounding, and yet musical tones." The sense of authenticity was enhanced with the delivery, as his "practised voice enabled him to give the various swells and falls of sounds upon the waters, driven about by the winds, dispersed and softened in the wide expanses, or brought close again to the ear by neighbouring rocks." Though he was indoors, Bigsby interpreted the song as representing an outdoor voyageur experience and reflecting nature itself. As the voyageurs were sometimes reported to have done, McGillivray finished his performance "with the piercing Indian shriek."[159] Of the entertainment provided by his host at this elite dinner party, Bigsby was clearly impressed.

As described, canoe travel was institutionalized with voyageur paddling songs, and these could accentuate or bridge class divides. There are some accounts of fur traders singing along with the paddling songs. When Benjamin Frobisher was being transported in a canoe after nearly starving to death, Samuel Wilcocke interpreted it as a benchmark of strength that he "could soon occasionally join his men in the chorus of some *voyageurs* boat songs."[160] This passage suggests that this was not an infrequent occurrence when fur traders were healthy. Some accounts reveal insights into what paddling songs meant and how they impacted fur traders. When Thomas Verchères de Boucherville set out as a clerk with the NWC in 1803 he was only eighteen years old. Unlike some of the clerks hired by the Montreal merchants, he understood French, although he had difficulty with the voyageurs' particular dialect and vocabulary of "jargon." Verchères wrote that "Our guide was called Larocque; the steersman's name was Robillard; both were famous *chanteurs de voyage.*"[161] Verchères appreciated how effective these *bouts* were in starting the voyageur songs. Their steersman "sang from morning till night with really remarkable spirit, always giving us something new and in harmony with the occasion." According to Verchères, "He was a model voyageur in this respect, and in many others as well." Verchères wrote that because they had "no fear of meeting an enemy," the "music kept time with the movement of the oars and we made astonishing progress."[162]

Yet over the course of the long voyage, the *chansons d'aviron* would have a deeper impact on Verchères. He described their influence as heightening latent emotions and serving as a vehicle for their expression:

> A youth of eighteen, and never before away from the paternal home for any long journey, I understood next to nothing of the bárbaric jargon of the voyageurs nor did I know anything of their habits and manner of life. Alone with them in this frail craft, only now did I begin to reflect upon the folly which had induced me to share such an adventure. The prospect of a seven years' engagement, with no hope of drying the tears of my poor mother, who was even now grieving over my waywardness, was almost more than I could bear, and my restless fearlessness was fast giving way to the cravings of nature, when the sonorous voice of the steersman began to intone the words of the merry song "Where are we going to sleep tonight?" and I was about join in the reply "At home as ever, laridondee," when I found myself chasing back a flood of tears.

Instead of a good bed in a warm and comfortable room there was only a tent for covering and a couch upon the bare earth. But I soon mastered my grief and at the second refrain was ready to join with the others, only in place of the usual words I sang "My dear tent as ever." By the time we arrived at Sault Ste Marie my homesickness was beginning to abate somewhat although I was still far from cured. For two days I had been unable to eat food of any kind, and of all the maladies I have ever experienced, this was one of the most painful.

The significant lyric for Verchères was "à la maison accoutumé," which is one of the prominent lines of "j'ai trop grand peur des loups," the first song of the Ermatinger collection. It almost brought Verchères to tears because of the emotions welling inside regarding his prolonged separation from home. That a clerk like Verchères was so moved by paddling songs, describing their effects at length and singing along himself, demonstrates that they could resonate widely. Singing was a major way that men who were forced to work closely together for long periods commiserated. Paddling songs were a practical necessity, but they could still elicit a tremendous emotional response.

For fur traders travelling in voyageur canoes, songs were an inevitable consequence of the mode of transportation. Many expressed appreciation for this particular genre of work song, whether or not they understood the lyrics or participated in singing. It was sung and appreciated at the exclusive Beaver Club parties in Montreal. Beyond a cherished custom on approaching and departing areas of significance, the paddling songs of the voyageurs fulfilled several crucial functions on the water. They started the march and set the pace of travel, synchronizing the paddles of all the men. The long working hours in the canoes of the voyageurs ensured that singing operated as the predominant musical forum, facilitating bonding among crews and allowing for cross-cultural exchanges. The existence of idealized scenarios and bawdy lyrics at the end of the songs in the Ermatinger collection evidence working class, if not necessarily class-conscious, expressions. Singing about the things they often did not have – ample food and physical intimacy – seemed to keep the voyageurs paddling over the long distances. The existence of Indigenous lyrics in some of these songs demonstrates how this intercultural forum produced new cultural products. These include the songs of Métis voyageurs such as Pierre Falcon, who worked in the canoes of the fur trade and wrote the Métis national anthem. Rooted in the old traditions of French folk songs, new creations arose from the diversity of people and circumstances of the fur trade.

Indigenous Hunting
and Healing Songs

The following fur trade account describes Anishinaabe birch bark musical scrolls known as *Wiigwaasabak*:

> Their songs are delivered in *Notes,* impressed or drawn on bark, in the form of hierlographics, and thus taught, and being hierlographics ... no two are alike, it therefore requires time to learn them; that is, any *one* of them: for those notes are not like ours, *marked* with regular bars &c, so that one Gamut serves for all; but with them, each one may said to be itself a Gamut.
>
> However, I have reason to think that they are regular and uniform; for many years ago, when I was still scarcely more than a boy [i.e., working as a fur trader in what is now northern Wisconsin in 1802–04], I rem[em]ber throwing away the contents of one of these medicine bags in which there were several strips of Bark covered with these Notes. An indian happened to be by – he took one up and with the Point of his knife placing it on one of these began to sing, moving the knife regularly as children do when they begin to learn their a, b, c. This surprised me a little at the time, for the indian was a stranger and had but lately arrived from his own lands that were several hundred miles off. After laughing at and ridiculing him as is the custom with us, I asked how he could make them out? "The same," said he, "as you do to *reckon* (i.e., read) your *papers.* See, this one is (meant for) the *Thunder;* that, the Earth, &c, &c, but I only know a few of these songs: the possessor of this bag knew a great deal – he was a great Medecine man, i.e., Doctor" &c.[1]

George Nelson described his conviction that *Wiigwaasabak* formed a distinct but comparable system of musical notation with its own rules and logic. He was more favourable in his attitude toward Indigenous cultures when he was writing his memoirs than when a youthful fur trader. It is not clear how he came into possession of the medicine bag, but he indicated he was "throwing away" its contents, and he initially ridiculed the Indigenous man singing. Yet this performance convinced him that the Anishinaabe hieroglyphics or pictographs constituted a "regular and uniform" system of musical notation. Nelson's description constitutes an early account of Anishinaabe birch bark musical scrolls. Considerable study was devoted to this topic in the twentieth century by ethnomusicologists such as Francis Densmore and anthropologists such as Ruth Landes and Selwyn Dewdney.[2] Yet none of these scholars appears to have reviewed the written record of the fur trade. Nelson's passage demonstrates how fur traders could produce valuable descriptions of Indigenous culture a century before anthropologists. Nelson learned through a knowledgeable informant that these songs had been possessed by a great doctor. He may have been associated with the Midéwiwin, or Grand Medicine Lodge, an important aspect of traditional Anishinaabe spirituality that he and other fur traders would describe.

Fur traders observed diverse Indigenous hunting and healing song traditions. These topics were, after all, relevant to their commercial success. Some fur traders had a personal interest in hunting and medicine. Their business was invariably influenced by the success of the hunt and the health of the Indigenous community with whom they traded. Hyperfocused on the supply of pelts and meat, fur traders often described the methods of Indigenous hunters. These descriptions are a testament to the traditional Indigenous use of songs in communicating with animal spirits. The health of the Indigenous community was of direct concern to fur traders who relied upon and sometimes lent credit to its members. Fur traders described when Indigenous hunters fell ill, and sometimes observed traditional healing methods that prominently included song. As fur traders brought medicine chests to trading posts near Indigenous communities in the late eighteenth century, there was a meeting of medicines, and an exchange of healing techniques. There resided a practical desire within some fur traders to understand these procedures in form and function. Explorer-fur traders travelling in close contact with Indigenous peoples and those working *en déroine,* that is, travelling to trade with and temporarily live alongside Indigenous communities, most frequently described the songs and ceremonies of hunting and healing. These practices, whether they were Anishinaabe, Cree, Dene, or others, sought to engage with unseen forces through song. Indigenous songs were conduits to harnessing and manifesting spiritual power seen as essential to the success of hunting and healing endeavours. This chapter will examine the descriptions of Indigenous songs and ceremonies that fur traders witnessed while working closely with Indigenous peoples.

Hunting Songs

Indigenous cultures pursued a wide variety of strategies in procuring food, yet all traditionally pursued hunting. Because fur traders were not generally self-sufficient, they relied on the partnership and success of Indigenous hunters, a fact whose historical significance was first stressed by Harold Innis. According to Arthur Ray's appraisal, "Innis clearly appreciated the central role aboriginal people played in the enterprise," a departure from previous Eurocentric interpretations.[3] Ray's work greatly elucidated the significance of Indigenous peoples in the fur trade. He demonstrated how the Cree and Assiniboine integrated the fur trade into their seasonal rounds of gathering in the summer on the Plains for the bison hunt and dispersing in the winter to the woodlands for smaller scale hunting.[4] When the act of hunting is examined in its totality from conception and preparation to completion and processing, it becomes obvious that it was about much more than killing an animal. A hunter was supported by his community, and he was expected to provide for it. Sharing meat reinforced kinship ties and group solidarity.

Hunting was interwoven into the cultural fabrics of diverse Indigenous communities. To Algonquian speakers, many song and dance types referred to or described animals. Hunters used singing in their preparations with a rattle or drum accompaniment to "conjure" the hunt and facilitate its success.[5] Among the Dene, animals, particularly the caribou, held a place of great importance in songs and stories.[6] Anthropologist Richard Preston made the following observation about the Cree:

> The songs serve a role in my total field experience that is central and revealing, and it is appropriate that I use them here to focus on an area of personal symbolisms in the use of cultural patterns. The cultural patterns are those of hunting, involving caribou, bear, beaver, and others. The personal symbolisms are the expression of emotion that are manifested not in the action of hunting but in the symbolic forms of song and narrations. I do not wish to imply that the expression of emotions in the acts of hunting contrast with the expression of emotions in the acts

of singing. They are better defined as complementary forms of expression, for songs may be an integral part of, and contribute instrumentally to the success of the hunt. Songs symbolically express the emotions that go with hunting, but they serve as more than a symbolic substitute for hunting. When hunting is accompanied by singing, the songs add power to the ability of the hunter. In an essentially mental or spiritual way, the songs influence the animals, making the hunt more successful.[7]

Fur traders encountered these cultural traditions of hunting and described them at length. They often learned about the hunter's methods, which in turn revealed something about their spiritual relationships with animals.

David Thompson began his fur trade career working with the Cree in the 1780s and 1790s. Early on he recognized the importance of dreams and visions to Indigenous hunting. The Cree "have recourse to Dreams and other superstitions" he wrote, giving hunters "important knowledge." Thompson identified one particular individual by name and wrote in detail about the songs he heard "early every morning": "One of my best acquaintances, named 'Ise pe sa wan,' was the most relied on by the Natives to enquire into futurity by conjuring; he was a good hunter, fluent in speech, had a fine manly voice; and very early every morning, took his rattle, and beating time with it, made a fluent speech of about twenty minutes to the Great Spirit and the Spirits of the forests, for health to all of them and success in hunting; and to give to his Poo wog gin, where to find the Deer, and to be always kind to them, and give them straight Dreams, that they may live straight."[8] Thompson spoke from knowledge gained living with the Cree community and its members, and his understanding of the language allowed him to state the content of these episodes somewhat credibly. Through vocalizations and the rattle, the hunter's prayers were directed to both the deer spirit and the Great Spirit.

In her research among the Cree of northern Manitoba, Lynn Whidden interviewed Cree hunters in the late twentieth century who recalled the importance of the drum to hunting. It was associated especially with periods of scarcity and hunger: "So the drum would be used to help the hunt. And an old man would be called upon to use the drum and to sing. And so he would sing about big game like beaver, deer. That's how the hunt got better."[9] By drumming, the man would "know where the game was," and he would tell the young men where to hunt.[10] Drumming and singing accomplished specific tasks and were here remembered for their functionality. There were even accounts of the old men singing and drumming all night to influence the wind.[11] As Whidden observed, "the value of a song was in its correct use," and Cree hunters stressed the importance of getting the words right to be successful.[12]

When food was in short supply, fur traders sometimes became closely acquainted with their hosts' hunting practices. In George Nelson's first years trading west of Lake Michigan in 1802–04, his Anishinaabe hosts and French Canadian crew occasionally approached starvation. At a certain point, Nelson decided to encourage local hunters to "make their medicine." He accomplished this through a gift of tobacco: "but more by incitement I give some tobacco to the Commis & one of his brothers an old man to make their medicine (as they call it) or prayers to kill something – particularly bears for there are but very few other animals here."[13] Tobacco and ritualized smoking accompanied the hunting ceremonies. Nelson provided a detailed description of the sounds and emotional tone of the proceedings. He had never witnessed the ceremony executed with such solemnity, which he attributed to the distressing circumstances. "Altho' this is not the first time that I've seen them & been with them while at these ceremonies, yet I never seen any carried on in so grave & serious (& I believe I may say solemn) a manner – not the least noise – giggling – whispering or laughing as is most usually their custom – but here silence was only interrupted long & low speeches – songs & beating upon a piece of stick with each of the three men two small drumsticks painted – they sung many songs & several very handsome ones if we may judge of them by their tunes – quite different from the usual strain of their songs they would frequently sing 'till near day; & in short conduct the whole of their ceremonies in a manner by far more consistent than many of us Christians do in our churches – if I may be allowed to make the Comparison … we were frequently invited to these ceremonies."[14] Nelson's frequent observations provided him with familiarity and admiration for Anishinaabe hunting songs.

Nelson described specific instances of Indigenous hunters singing to improve the hunt. He described how one hunter found that "the others with their medicine & other ceremonies could not get any thing," so he "set up all this last night ('till quite day light) alone singing, beating the drum & harangueing & smoking" in preparation to kill a bear the next day. If a hunter was not successful, another could make their presence and intentions known through song. Hunting songs thus sent a signal to the community and fur traders alike regarding hunting preparations. Nelson wrote how hunters "frequently conjured, i.e. prayed & sang, & laid out all their most powerful nostrums, to kill bears."[15] During a period of prolonged difficulty and famine, Nelson related the activity of one particular Anishinaabe hunter named Le Bougon or "Chubby." He had apparently killed another man in the autumn and now attributed the failure of his hunt to becoming "polluted" by this event. "How many appeals, what beating of drums, singing, smoking &c. &c. Still to no purpose" Nelson remarked.[16] Hunting songs were employed to ensure success in the hunt by interacting with unseen spiritual forces.

On another occasion, Nelson described the elaborate preparations of a hunter: "At dark, he began, laying out & exposing all his nostrums, roots, herbs, & dolls, to Pray (harangue), sing, beat his immense large drum, & smoke. He kept close to it the whole night. At Sun rise he gave a cry to attract attention, & accosted the others 'old man, naming le Commis, you will find a large Bear, after much trouble in that wind fall, on the opposite Side of this Creek. You, young man, to the Commis Son, you will follow your fathers track 'till you have passed the 2 Small lakes – you will see a Fir tree thrown down by the wind, beyond that is another wind fallen tree, by the root of which you will a young one, his first year alone. I also have one up this river'! And, if I remember right, he *gave* one to Le Commis elder brother, who was with us."[17] Here the medicine man sang and beat his "immense large drum" as a part of the ceremonial preparations. This undoubtedly attracted much attention, as the auditory signal was transmitted all night. The community would have heard it when they slept. Perhaps it shaped their dreams. The cry in the morning to "attract attention" gathered the community and connected them to the hunting process. The medicine man sought to predict the behaviour of animals. If done correctly, Nelson suggested they would give themselves to the hunters. "This is so strange, & so out of the way that I will ask no one to beleive it … yet, *I sayit is true,* beleive who may," wrote Nelson, "those who will not beleive the Gospel will still less credit this," but they had a "Splendid feast at night" and for several nights afterward.[18] This passage suggests that Nelson was not only fascinated by the hunting ceremonies but believed they contributed to success.

Hungry fur traders sometimes imitated Indigenous hunting songs. Nelson recorded how one day he and the voyageur Sorel "proposed to imitate the indians conjuring." He described how they "speechifyed, sang, beat the drum, smoked & danced." This description highlights fur traders imitating Indigenous music specifically to be successful in the hunt. "Sorel, he who sang the best, imitating them, would run to the chimney yelling 'something shall be cooked in that place' – part indian, part french & English – 'tomorrow, tomorrow, at latest, I smell it.'"[19] This suggests that mimicry and singing ability were valued, and that musically inclined individuals may have been more capable crossing the cultural divide and singing in an Indigenous language. The multi-lingual aspect is particularly fascinating, as the fur traders were combining their energies to imitate the medicine men. When le Commis brought sides of moose he had killed the next day, both Nelson and Sorel attributed it to their conjuring. Sorel in particular, a French Canadian, gained recognition for his abilities "and was frequently called upon after this." Hence a fur trader could become respected within the Indigenous community for the efficacy of his hunting songs. While Sorel was known as a strong singer, Nelson records that he eventually lost "his *influence*."[20] Similar occasions may have led other overwintering fur traders to investigate Indigenous drums, rattles, and hunting songs.

Duncan Cameron wrote about Anishinaabeg hunters north of Lake Superior around Lake Nipigon. "Whenever they intend going out to hunt the moose or the reindeer," he wrote, "they conjure and beat the drum a long time the night before." He indicated that this had the intended purpose of "charming any animal they may then find." For Cameron, these preparatory ceremonies were striking in both their frequency and duration. He noted their attribution of success: "Whatever good luck they have, is attributed to their drum and Medecine bag."[21] It was obvious to Cameron that there was no separating music and hunting. He was clearly struck by the ceremonial forms, the use of the drum, the medicine bag, and long durations of song. While he only scratched the surface of their meaning, he did fully realize their importance to the Anishinaabe conception of success in hunting.

Feasts before the hunt were sometimes called "medicine feasts." At times fur traders were able to participate in these community events. While his Anishinaabeg hosts apparently excluded women and children, fur traders such as Cameron had "often been invited to those grand feasts, and as it would be exceedingly insulting to refuse such an invitation, I always had to accept." With little choice in the matter, Cameron felt that "the politeness bestowed on me amply repaid by the foolish capers I was obliged to cut to perform my share of the ceremony."[22] Recognizing it would be socially unacceptable to refuse to attend, Cameron demonstrated that he was an observant if reluctant participant. "They call their 'Medecine' or conjuring feasts, at which they observe a number of ridiculous ceremonies, such as eating without a knife, striving who can finish his share first, dancing, walking so many times around the fire, retiring one by one in rotation, and several other foolish ceremonies too tedious to insert here."[23] Despite his opinions of these proceedings, Cameron was nonetheless frequently invited to these feasts. He attended and participated because otherwise he risked insulting his hosts and hurting his business.

John Tanner worked with various fur trading companies in the Red River and Lake of the Woods districts during the 1810s. As a boy, he was captured from the frontiers of Kentucky and adopted by an Anishinaabe family. His Anishinaabe name was "Shaw-Shaw-Wa Be-Na-Se" or "The Falcon," and he gained a reputation for his hunting abilities. At the point when his community was reduced "nearly to starvation," Tanner was called upon to conduct a medicine hunt. Tanner related how he "had recourse, as a last resort, to medicine hunting. Half the night I sung and prayed, and then lay down to sleep."[24] His ensuing description is one of the most detailed from the era:

> I saw in my dream a beautiful young man come down through the hole in the top of my lodge, and he stood directly before me. "What," said he, "is this noise and crying that I hear? Do I not know when you are hungry and in distress? I look down upon you at all times, and it is not necessary you should call me with such loud cries." Then pointing directly towards the sun's setting, he said, "do you see those tracks?" "Yes," I answered, "they are the tracks of two moose." "I give you those two moose to eat." Then pointing in an opposite direction, towards the place of the sun's rising, he showed me a bear's track, and said, "that also I give you." He then went out at the door of my lodge, and as he raised the blanket, I saw that snow was falling rapidly. I very soon awoke, and feeling too much excited to sleep, I called old Sha-gwaw-ko-sink to smoke with me, and then prepared my Muz-zin-ne-neen-suk, as in the subjoined sketch, to represent the animals whose tracks had been shown me in my dream.[25]

Attracted by songs and prayers, the spirit entered the lodge while Tanner was dreaming, guiding him to the animal tracks. Tanner's narrative is extraordinarily detailed, rich, and extremely rare in the annals of the early nineteenth century.[26] Nanabozho, the Anishinaabe cultural hero and trickster figure, is invoked: "The songs used on occasion of these medicine hunts have relation to the religious opinions of the Indians. They are often addressed to Na-na-boo-shoo, or Na-Na-bush, whom they intreat to be their interpreter, and communicate their requests to the Supreme. Oftentimes, also, to Me-suk-kum-mik O-kwi, or the earth, the great-grandmother of all. In these songs, they relate how Na-na-bush created the ground in obedience to the commands of the Great Spirit, and how all things for the use, and to supply the wants of the uncles and aunts of Na-na-bush, (by which are meant men and women,) were committed to the care and keeping of the great mother. Na-na-bush, ever the benevolent intercessor between the Supreme Being and mankind, procured to be created for their benefit the animal whose flesh should be for their food, and whose skins were for their clothing."[27]

Tanner related an occasion in the late winter after a long stretch of unsuccessful hunts. His overwintering party was reduced to "extreme hunger." He finally spotted a moose, and just as he was creeping near, his best dog broke free and scared it off. He sacrificed the dog that night to feed his family, and at this point other starving Indigenous families called on Tanner "to make a medicine hunt": "I accordingly told Me-zhick-ko-naum to go for my drum, and as preparatory to the commencement of my prayers and songs, I directed all my family to take such positions as they could keep for at least half the night, as, after I began, no one must move until I had finished. I have always been conscious of my entire dependence on a superior and invisible Power, but I have felt this conviction most powerfully in times of distress and danger. I now prayed earnestly, and with the consciousness that I addressed myself to a Being willing to hear and able to assist, and I called upon him to see and to pity the sufferings of my family. The next day I killed a moose, and soon after, a heavy snow having fallen, we were relieved from the apprehension of immediate starvation."[28] Tanner stated the drum was the most essential item for conducting a medicine hunt, with "prayers and songs" intertwined components. It was to the success of these ceremonial efforts that the hunt and a change of weather were attributed. Tanner's upbringing in Anishinaabe society set him apart from most fur traders. His participation in medicine hunts reveals the extent to which songs and drums played a central role in their hunting traditions.

When William Apess of Pequot origin travelled along the southern Great Lakes in the 1810s, he described how Indigenous hunters "chanted the wild beasts of prey with their songs." This was transformed in a recently published version of his memoirs to "[en]chanted the wild beasts of prey with their songs," changing the connotation.[29] The new wording implies animals were enchanted by songs, while the original suggests instead animals chanted into being. This better aligns with the conception of animals summoned or "conjured" by songs.[30] A recent survey of scholarship argues that music touched "virtually all aspects" of hunters' lives, with the conclusion that no people "value music more highly or embrace its social and symbolic uses with greater fervor and vitality."[31] Among the most prominent types of Indigenous songs that fur traders described were related to hunting. Edward Ermatinger in the 1820s could identify songs associated with the hunt, recording in his memo book and journal how a hunting party returned "singing the song expressive of having killed."[32] Because of the fur traders' regular interactions with Indigenous peoples, they gained various understandings of their cultures. Their vocation was focused on furs, and the products of Indigenous hunters were of central importance to their survival and enterprise. The music that was associated often drew their attention.

Midéwiwin

The Midéwiwin, Medicine Society, or Grand Medicine Society developed in the northeastern woodlands and Great Lakes regions among Anishinaabe peoples. Its widespread prominence during the period of study is supported by the fur trade record. It played a role in many fur traders' lives and interactions with Indigenous communities. Whether it was a pre-contact or post-contact development has been the subject of scholarly disagreement. Ojibwe scholars Edward Benton-Banai and Basil Johnston considered it to be the traditional religion of the Anishinaabeg.[33] Anthropologists such as Harold Hickerson interpreted it as a response to the devastation and crisis caused by European diseases, alcohol, and Iroquois attacks in the seventeenth century.[34] Anthropologists Irving Hallowell and Ruth Landes published their observations of the Midéwiwin, with the former studying the Saulteaux of Berens River in Manitoba, while the latter focused on the Ojibwe of Minnesota and Northwestern Ontario and closely related practices of the Potawatomi, Sauk, and Dakota.[35] Recent scholarship interprets the Midéwiwin as a historic shift in worldview away from individual dreams and visions as the source of power in Ojibwe society to the Midéwiwin's inherited knowledge systems and traditions.[36] Eventually it faced adversarial missionaries, government agents, and settler society, and became increasingly secretive. Yet aspects of it were historically accessible to fur traders, in particular the initiation ceremonies of new members. These records are valuable because they pre-date the interference of settler society and suggest the Midéwiwin's widespread proliferation during height of the fur trade.

According to Ojibwe scholar Basil Johnston, the Midéwiwin was a way to commemorate the gift of knowledge from the animal and plant worlds through ceremony. The celebration of the gift of medicine is known as the Midéwiwin, which is probably a contraction of the word "Mino" (good) and "daewaewin" (hearted), but might also mean "the sound" or "sounding." Drums were used in the ceremonies to summon the spirit of well-being. Rattles were shaken to dispel the spirit of ailment and suffering.[37] Songs with the power to attract animals were owned by individuals and sung before hunting expeditions.[38] These ceremonies often included the use of medicine bundles, drums, and/or rattles.[39] The Midéwiwin ranks or orders were associated with specific ceremonies and techniques that initiates learned as they advanced. Each level was associated with specific ceremonial song scrolls and performances.[40] The spiritual focus is evident in the name of "Mah nee doo wigi wahm (Spirit Lodge)."[41] It is clear from the records of the fur traders that the Midéwiwin initiation ceremonies were prominent affairs in the community. This is where fur traders witnessed first-hand its operation and mechanics, which frequently involved the use of songs. While their description of the ceremonies often revealed their prejudices, the fur trade record nonetheless preserves documented occurrences and some ethnographic details.

Alexander Henry (the younger) described the ceremonies he observed at Red River in the early nineteenth century. He was struck by the gender dynamics of the Midéwiwin and the admissibility of both men and women. On one occasion, Henry "found the Indians were busy employed in making the Grand Medicine." He described it as "a ceremony generally performed every spring, when they all meet and when there is always some novice to be admitted into the mysteries of this grand and solemn affair." Henry described them as semi-public events, identifying the new inductees as "two young men … a woman and M. Langlois's Girl." Unlike the European norms of separate spheres and gender-exclusive orders, Henry hinted at the impropriety of such mixed arrangements and the mysterious ceremonies and rites. He described the "many curious circumstances reported concerning the admittance of women into this Great mystery of mysteries. The most ancient and famous for the art among the men, it is said, have every privilege allowed them with a novice and are granted every favour they wish to enjoy."[42] These observations were not directly obtained but rather gathered from what was "said," whether from an Indigenous or Euro-Canadian source is unknown. Yet it is obvious that the Midéwiwin was mostly shielded from the eyes and ears of Henry. This did not stop him from sharing and speculating on what little he did know.

Fur traders were sometimes informed about the Midéwiwin by the Indigenous peoples with whom they were trading. From his 1804–05 journal in the Cross Lake, Snake River area, Thomas Connor mentioned how an Indigenous trading party referenced the "Mittay Ceremony" alongside a special request for rum. He responded with hostility, "refused & abused them as they deserve."[43] It is not clear why he thought such a response was appropriate, although he may have been disappointed by their trade. Another fur trader

A. McLellan reported the occurrence of a "Scautoux" or Saulteaux man cutting off a horse's tail on the same day as the making of the "Grande Medicin."[44] The insinuation seems to be that it was taken for use in the ceremonies. These references suggest that some fur traders only knew about the Midéwiwin through word of mouth, and in these cases associated it with material losses. Yet there is no evidence that these fur traders themselves understood or witnessed the society's ceremonies.

Others with extended careers sometimes became more intimately acquainted. These fur traders tended to be more sympathetic to Indigenous peoples and cultures. NWC employee George Nelson acknowledged that it took him years to acquire any real understanding of the Midéwiwin. In one of his later journals, he stated that he "admired a good deal, having now a far better idea of their Theology, & understand their language also much better than I did 13 years ago when I saw them the first time."[45] Writing from Tête-au-Brochet in 1819, Nelson described how the Anishinaabe were "very busy in preparing for the meetaywee, to initiate two men & a woman in their Brotherhood, confirmation, whatever it may be termed." He spent considerable time observing the proceedings. He wrote that he "passed a part of the night in looking at them, having been invited; & to day I went to see them go through the initiation."[46] This opportunity for amateur ethnography resulted from a disruption of schedule due to inclement weather. This is a common theme in the records of the fur trade, as more extensive passages and descriptions were often written on days waylaid.[47] Nelson stressed his familiarity and respect for these proceedings toward the end of his career in 1819. His attendance was cut short in this case: "unfortunately the wind changed all of a sudden to the N.E. & I took my leave of them just as they began their preparatory Dance and speeches."[48] The constraints of northern travel and trade dictated that favourable weather conditions had to be utilized due to the short travelling season.[49] In this instance, Nelson suspended his observations yet still provided an account.

Fur trader Peter Grant's records suggest that even at the outset of the nineteenth century, the Midéwiwin was at least partially a secretive society. Grant worked for the NWC for most of his career from 1784 until 1805 at Red River, Lac La Pluie, and Sault Ste Marie. From his two decades of experience trading mostly with Anishinaabe peoples, he produced what Masson described as the "most complete and elaborate" NWC partner account on North American Indigenous peoples.[50] In Grant's opinion, the ceremonies of the Midéwiwin could be compared with European traditions: "The *Mitewie* is a mysterious ceremony, rather of the nature of our Free Masonry, but with this remarkable difference that both sexes are equally admitted as members." These gender norms were shocking to Grant. He recognized that candidates for initiation had to be respected members of the community. New initiates were expected to give presents, which was a "requisite to constitute the meeting of the Order." From his observations, the society seldom or never met for ceremonies except for when a candidate was to be initiated. Yet this was likely the most socially prominent aspect of the Midéwiwin and the only one to which he was invited.

Grant described the initiation ceremony in detail. A sizable lodge was constructed with several long poles suspended like a scaffold on which the various presents of the initiates were displayed. There was an opening procession before the men and women seated themselves at the opposite ends of the lodge. The singing, drumming, and dancing that was interwoven throughout the ceremonies is evident in the following description: "All the members, dressed and painted as on all great occasions, go to this lodge in procession and preceded by drums, and, rattles. They take their seats indiscriminately on each side of the lodge, the men on one side, and the women on the other. The oldest and most considerable men generally begin the ceremony by singing and beating the drum. After beating the drum for a considerable time, one of the fraternity gets up and gently dances right opposite the music, and, by degrees, a whole group of dancers join, keeping exact time with the drum and, when heartily tired, quietly sit down in their places and smoke their pipes, without observing any particular ceremony. After breathing a little, the drummers summon up the dancers again, and the new members are allowed to join the dance."[51]

Beginning with the elders and slowly incorporating the newcomers, the dance possessed a unified step and continued for a long duration, until the dancers were "heartily tired." Grant described this ceremony as continuing "with very little variation for the greater part of the day." At a certain point, the drums were "laid aside for a moment." Smoking ensued, during which "a general silence prevails in the lodge."[52] The silence was broken when one of the members rose with his medicine bag, holding it before him and "running with a short quick step" around the lodge, uttering unfamiliar and "unintelligible sounds as he proceeds." "After parading two or three time around in this manner, he shakes his bag with great dexterity, makes a push with it towards one of the members and immediately retires to his seat. The person pointed at pretends to be affected in an extraordinary manner; he groans, inclines his head in a languishing manner on his breast, or falls prostrate on the earth; he sometimes, indeed, contents himself with a little jerk backwards of the head, but always muttering something to himself, expressing his gratitude to the person who gave him the pretended shock. The same cheat is carried on until every member present has acted his part, and the newly adopted member properly instructed in the mystery."[53]

This description focuses on a medicine bag, with the various actions harnessing and displaying its power. It contains many details that appear to be based on repeated observations. Grant stresses that while only members and new initiates were allowed inside the lodge, the veil of secrecy was not absolute. Outsiders were permitted to stand at the door and watch: "none but members ever presume to enter the lodge; the others are permitted to stand at the door and look at the performers as long as they please." According to his description, the powers of the medicine bags were never doubted, even by those standing outside like Grant did. The cultivation of a favourable impression about their powers seems to have been a main function of the ceremony. According to this description, outsiders "never presume to doubt the miraculous virtue of their medicine bags, and great pains are taken by those honorable members to improve such opinion."[54] While Grant acknowledged the high regard of the medicine bags, he had his suspicions and doubts about what he observed. While he had been granted access to witness the Midéwiwin initiation ceremonies, he was still an outsider who did not understand or appreciate its deeper spiritual and social significances.

These accounts demonstrate varied observations and responses to the Midéwiwin. In almost every case, fur traders became acquainted by witnessing the initiation ceremony of a new member. This was a prominent event in the community to which the fur traders were often invited or permitted to observe. To witness such occasions usually entailed living with or near an Indigenous community. Travellers passing through were rarely so fortunate. When the artist Paul Kane reached the Red River area, he related entering a "medicine lodge," where he encountered four chiefs "sitting upon mats spread upon the ground gesticulating with great violence, and keeping time to the beating of a drum."[55] As Kane was an uninvited guest, he described how "something, apparently of a sacred nature was covered up in the centre of the group, which I was not allowed to see," and "they almost instantly ceased their 'pow-wow,' or music, and seemed rather displeased at my intrusion."[56] This kind of culturally insensitive behaviour would have been unlikely in the fur trade, as it would have hurt the relationship with the Indigenous community and worked against the interests of the fur trader. This might explain why I have found no such examples, even though there are many descriptions of the Midéwiwin.

Conjuring Ceremonies

If Midéwiwin initiation ceremonies were accessible to fur traders, the dramatic public displays known variously as "spirit lodge," "shaking tent," or "shaking lodge" formed another window into Indigenous spirituality. This was a divination ritual whereby spirits were invoked by the man inside the lodge or tent and interacted with directly by community members. Fur traders sometimes observed and described these ceremonies in detail. Anthropologists have documented spirit lodges being constructed in very particular ways, for instance that they were typically constructed from eight poles that were twelve to fourteen feet in length. Fur traders recorded more variety and often fewer poles. Perceiving the ceremony from the outside, fur traders focused on the lodge and its sounds, describing singing, vocalizations, and musical instruments.

Alexander Henry (the elder) witnessed a spirit lodge ceremony in the vicinity of Sault Ste Marie in the immediate aftermath of the Seven Years' War. This was before the Treaty of Niagara in 1764 when the British formally made peace with the Anishinaabeg of the Great Lakes. His remarkable description includes the construction of the lodge and the ceremony itself. Moose skins were hung over a frame of five poles of five different species of timber ten feet in length and eight inches thick that were planted in the ground in a circle four feet in diameter. The poles were buried one foot deep and bound together at the top. The ceremony began in the evening. Nearly the whole village convened, and fires were lit around the lodge. When the "priest," as Henry called him, entered the lodge, it began to shake and numerous voices were heard. This was followed by a long silence before one particular voice, whom the audience identified as the "Chief Spirit, the TURTLE," arrived. Henry described what he heard. "New sounds came from the tent. During the space of half an hour, a succession of songs were heard, in which a diversity of voices met the ear. From his first entrance, till these songs were finished, we heard nothing in the proper voice of the priest; but, now, he addressed the multitude, declaring the presence of the Great Turtle, and the spirit's readiness to answer such questions as should be proposed."[57] Questions were asked about the intentions of the English and if the Anishinaabeg would be received as friends if they went to Fort Niagara to meet William Johnson. The spirit replied that their canoes would be filled with presents, including blankets, kettles, guns, gunpowder, shot, and barrels of rum, and every man would return safely to his family. Henry documented the enthusiastic response as "a hundred voices exclaimed, 'I will go, too! I will go, too!'"[58] This passage indicates the prevalence of the spirit lodge in the civic life of Anishinaabe communities. Henry would not be the last fur trader to describe these ceremonies in detail.

David Thompson's long working career produced many descriptions of Indigenous cultures and spiritual practices. He described what he termed the "conjuring box" ceremony of the Cree and Ojibwe based on the actions of his acquaintance Ise Pe Sa Wan in the 1790s. While later observers often called these ceremonies "shaking tent" based primarily on a visual description, Thompson used instead conjuring box, suggesting the function and auditory components. Ise Pe Sa Wan began with a "sweating bath," followed by the construction of a lodge from four long poles sixteen feet in length placed in a square in the ground three feet apart.[59] Five feet above the ground, four cross pieces were tied to the poles and three feet above these four more were tied. The sides of the entire structure were covered or "dressed" in leather deer skins. After having his hands, arms, and legs tied together, Ise pe sa wan was placed inside with his rattle. Thompson described how silent anticipation heightened the sensations of onlookers as they prepared for the ceremony to begin: "All is now suspense, the Men, Women, and Children keep strict silence; In about fifteen, or twenty minutes; the whole of the cords, wrapped together are thrown out, and instantly the Rattle and the Song are heard, the conjuring box violently shaken, as if the conjuror was actually possessed." In this account, singing and shaking of the rattle were the dominant auditory features. Thompson continued in his description, writing that "sometimes the Song ceases, and a speech is heard of ambiguous predictions of what is to happen. In half an hours time, he appears exhausted, leaves the leather box and retires to his tent, the perspiration running down him, smokes his pipe and goes to sleep."[60] The importance of the occasion to the community is obvious from Thompson's comments about their participation and strict silence. The impression on Thompson is apparent in the details he recorded, from its preparation to finish.

While literate fur traders sometimes described such demonstrations of Indigenous spirituality, it is not clear to what degree the curiosity was shared by the men in their charge. Yet Thompson's records suggest that his HBC labourers were indeed interested. He related an occurrence when "five Scotchmen were with me on some business we had with the Natives," and they observed a conjuring box being erected. They all watched the preparations as "no business could be done until this was over." When the Scotsmen perceived the conjuror about to be tied, "they said, if they had the tying of him, he would never get loose." This was communicated by Thompson to the Cree, "who readily agreed the Scotchmen should tie him: which they did in the usual way, and they placed him in the conjuring box; quite sure he could not get loose; In about fifteen minutes, to their utter astonishment, all the cords were thrown out in a bundle, the Rattle, and the Song in full force, and the conjuring box shaken, as if going to pieces; my men were at a loss what to think or say." This remarkable passage demonstrates the observation and interaction with the Cree ceremony by those involved in the fur trade. The prejudices of the HBC men led to their "astonishment" at the outcome. The outcome became the subject of religious interpretation. According to Thompson, "The Natives smiled at their incredulity; at length they [the 'Scotchmen'] consoled themselves by saying the Devil in person had untied him, and set him loose."[61] While this language suggests that Thompson did not himself attribute a supernatural cause, it does suggest how Indigenous spiritual traditions were interpreted by fur traders through a Christian worldview.

John McDonnell observed spirit lodge ceremonies in the Red River area in 1793–95. Like other fur traders, he largely focused on superficial aspects and the lodge itself that housed the ceremony. His description uses the French Canadian term *jongleur* and interestingly highlights the role of the drum and rattle, using Indigenous terms: "This spirit never appears but in the *jonglerie*, a small circular appartment raised a man's height, inclosed with raw hides and bound with thongs. Into this place the juggler is thrust, sometimes tied neck and heels, and a few minutes after, the Tabou and Chichiquoi begin beating and he kicks the cords that bound him out of the juggling place, though no person is seen within. The *jonglerie* is about three feet in diameter."[62] John McDonnell suggested that the man inside the lodge beat the tambour with the rattle, combining the sounds of the two instruments. A "familiar spirit," visited the "juggler" who answered questions "generally as dark and ambiguous as those of the ancient oracles among the heathen, and which may be interpreted in many different ways." This description from the 1790s reveals a fur trader's understanding of the materials, procedures, and terminology of the spirit lodge ceremony.

Duncan Cameron described a version of this ceremony while working with Anishinaabe peoples on Lake Nipigon. He termed the practitioners "conjurers" while the voyageurs called them "jongleurs." He recognized the importance of this ceremony, as it was the one the "conjurors are most proud of" and whose main purpose was to "foretell future events." The conjurer entered the lodge with only a rattle while another sat outside to decipher and interpret the sounds. Cameron described the sounds resonating from inside the lodge. "He then begins to make a terrible noise in the language the bystanders cannot understand, and himself neither, probably, and shakes his rattle, imitating the noise of different animals. This part of the performance being over, he answers the questions which may be put to him and which generally relate to the return or whereabouts of absent friends for whose safety they may have been uneasy."[63] While it is not clear to what degree Cameron understood Anishinaabemowin, he described the wide array of questions and answers received, stating that the conjurors "are never at a loss with an answer, and will tell you with the greatest assurance or impudence what they are doing at the time." Cameron's comments about interpretation reveal the degree to which he and the voyageurs witnessed these ceremonies: "Some of the Canadians, who are almost as superstitious as the Indians themselves, will swear that they most distinctly heard two voices in the jonglery, alluding to the Devil, whom they suppose to be at the bottom of it." Cameron affirms that he "often listened and never could hear the old gentlemen's voice."[64] Cameron's comments reveal that he and the voyageurs working in the area observed and tried to understand these ceremonies, even if they fell into the familiar pattern of incredulous fur traders and superstitious voyageurs.

This differs significantly from the interpretations of George Nelson, the fur trader who perhaps contemplated and documented these ceremonies most carefully. He prefaced his passage on the subject by stating that all human societies have forms of conjuring and desire to foresee the future. He related the story of an anonymous NWC fur trader who desired to know the whereabouts of an Indigenous group expected to arrive but who were delayed. While the ceremony was underway, a "young half-breed" who was skeptical of the ceremony was encouraged by the Indigenous community to see for himself. The man "entered one of these conjuring *huts* … He raised the bottom of the *casement* and entered, but as he was not below, he rose on his feet and felt for him, but [the conjuror was] not to be found. However he was *paid* for his curiosity: there was a dreadful fluttering within, but especially about his head, his hair flying about in his face as if in a tempest and frequent appearances of small lights before his eyes which ever way he turned: he bawled out and asked those without what was the matter with him: he became afraid and walk'd out as quick as he could. Very shortly after they heard the same cries of pain, faintly, at first, but the voice soon entered. The *Conjuror* said he was carried to where the people were; 'they are all asleep at such a place and tomorrow will be here' &c. He said there were 4 (spirits) of them that carried him off: each held him by the *little finger* and *little toe!*"[65] This passage suggests the spirit lodge was used to determine the location of distant groups, and these ceremonies were sometimes actively investigated and described by those involved in the fur trade.

Far from dismissing such a story, George Nelson reaffirmed the veracity with his observations. He stated that "surely a man may believe his senses," speaking to both the visual and auditory evidence that affirmed it in his mind. "A man tied, wound up in a blanket, or Skin equally soft: here he is held by one, two, or 3 men – he slips out of the blanket and presents himself before you free, leaving the cords &c *untied* in the blanket: you hear him Speak, and perhaps 20 other voices besides, all at the same: again he is bound as a criminal, rather indeed as a Pig, crumpled into a heap and thrust in to his *hut;* at the very instant of his entrance the hut shakes as if ten thousand devils were for pulling it to pieces: you enter this, find the man absent, hear a fluttering about your ears, or see a vast number of small lights resting on the hoops that hold the poles together: immediately after you are out you hear the man speak within again; you look again and feel for him, but hear him talking at a distance, what can this be but supernatural agency?"[66] This description is a remarkable and fascinating example of a fur trader closely examining the spirit lodge ceremony and being convinced of its mystery and power.

The above examples speak to the degree to which some fur traders observed and interacted with spirit lodge ceremonies. It is a telling omission that anthropologists such as Richard Preston cite early Jesuit missionaries and some explorers in their literature reviews but omit the records of fur traders.[67] This is likely because they were unaware of the depth of these records and the degree to which fur traders lived closely alongside Indigenous communities and described these ceremonies. Fur traders and voyageurs alike were interested in these spiritual events. In many respects, the audience participated in and validated the performances, and the conjurors served the community with valuable information. Their descriptions highlight the widespread distribution of these ceremonies among Cree and Anishinaabe communities in the late eighteenth and early nineteenth centuries. Songs, voices, and auditory features were central to the functioning and reception of spirit lodge ceremonies and were described by fur traders.

Wabanowiwin

An Anishinaabe spiritual movement known as Wabanowiwin began around the turn of the nineteenth century northwest of Lake Superior. It is referred to in the journals of fur traders with some variation as *Wabbano* or *Wah Bino*. This term may have originated from the Algonquian word for ritual or in Anishinaabemowin from "what is represented by the east."[68] Its practitioners have often been described for their spectacular handling of fire and burning objects.[69] Their ceremonies were attempts "to influence the manitos of game animals."[70] Most sources indicate that the ceremonies occurred mostly in the spring, similar to the Midéwiwin.[71] Anishinaabe groups that were dispersed over the winter then congregated. This was undoubtedly an Indigenous religious movement, yet the fur trade influenced its material culture. The genesis of *Wabanowiwin* has been pinpointed to the Lake of the Woods region sometime around 1796. This was along the heart of the Montreal fur traders' route west and around the height of the competitive fur trade with the HBC.[72] This religious tradition responded to scarcity among fur-bearing animals, an issue that was greatly exacerbated due to pressures from the St Lawrence and Hudson Bay fur trade. Large game animal scarcity in the Great Lakes region contributed to Anishinaabe migrations westward during this period.[73] The fur trade records detail how Wabanowiwin's practitioners employed not only fire but music to foster spiritual power for healing and hunting.

During his first year with the NWC in 1797–98, David Thompson overwintered near Lake of the Woods. That first season he witnessed the Wabanowiwin. While waiting for the river to clear of ice, Thompson devoted space in his journal to provide "some information on the Religion and Ceremonies of these people." He recorded how "of late a superstition had sprung up, and was now the attention of all the Natives. It appeared the old Songs, Dances and Ceremonies by frequent repetition had lost all their charms, and religious attention; and were heard and seen with indifference."[74] The new spiritual path sought to assist the hunt. Thompson reported how two or three medicine men, "after having passed some time in a sweating cabin, and singing to the music of the Rattle," dreamt of the new spiritual rites.[75] He proceeded with a detailed account of how "they saw a powerful Medicine, to which a Manito voice told them to pay great attention and respect, and saw the tambour with the figures on it, and also the Rattle to be used for music in dancing: They also heard the Songs that were to be sung." Remarkably, Thompson's account focused not only on the visions but on the sound in the dreams. In Anishinaabe tradition, dreams were commonly ascribed as an important source of songs.[76] Dreaming and singing were primary ways of interfacing with the spirits or *manitous*. The structure of the religion was also devised during these dreams. "They were to call it the Wahbino: It was to have two orders; the first only Wah bino and second Kee che Wah bino; and those initiated to bear the name of their order (fool, or knave) Every thing belonging to the Wah bino was sacred, nothing of it to touch the ground, nor to be touched by a Woman."[77] Its origins and the subject of its practitioners' dreams was communicated to Thompson. Wabanowiwin appears to have developed with two orders that fostered the sanctity of its materials and methods, and unlike the Midéwiwin it barred women from participating.

Thompson turned his attention to the drums. Based on the visions and "guidance of the Wah bino sages," special "tabours were made" of a circular frame eight inches deep and a foot and a half wide. These were covered with "fine parchment," according to Thompson, by which he meant tightly stretched hide. On these were painted symbolic figures in red and black. According to Thompson, from these "were suspended many bits of tin and brass to make a gingling noise."[78] These pieces of tin and brass were likely cut from European trade goods such as kettles and pans. These metal pieces were integrated onto the drums and became associated not only with their design but their sound. Thompson noticed that the rattle had a peculiarly ornamented handle, and the drumsticks were flat, carved, and painted with figures. "The Mania became so authoritative that every young man had to purchase a Wahbino Tambour; the price was what they could get from him." Not only were specialized drums made, but "figured dances were also sold." While Thompson expressed concern about the Wah bino proponents "getting rich on the credulity of others," he ultimately labelled these practices as "harmless" "mummery." "Since there must be some foolery," he wrote, "this was as harmless as any other."[79] Yet Thompson's account indicated that he was an active observer. He asked an Anishinaabe chief what he thought about this new religious practice, to which he looked at Thompson "full in the face, as much as to say, how can you ask me such a question."[80]

Thompson goes on to describe a dance associated with Wabanowiwin. When a "Kee chee Wah bino Man" arrived, he made a speech about the power of the Wabano. A dance immediately proceeded. Thompson reported seating himself on the ground, while five young men arrived who were painted above the waist: "The Wah bino Man began the Song in a bold strong tone of voice, the Song was pleasing to the ear, the young Men danced, sometimes slowly, then changed to a quick step with many wild gestures, sometimes erect, and then, to their bodies being horizontal: shaking their Tambours, and at times singing a short chorus. They assumed many attitudes with ease, and showed a perfect command of their limbs. With short intervals, this lasted for about an hour." This extraordinary description includes Thompson's appraisal that these songs were pleasing to the ear and included a chorus. He was praise-worthy of the dance, the control it required, and the diversity of movement it displayed. Thompson inquired into its meaning. He was informed that these songs were meant to control the animals. "By what you have seen, and heard," he was told, "they have made themselves masters of the Squirels, Musk Rats and Racoons' also of the Swans. Geese, Cranes and Ducks." Not all animals fell under their influence, as Thompson inquired about bison, moose, and red deer, but he was informed that these "Manito's are too powerful." He did encounter some from the community who viewed "the Wah bino as a jugglery between knaves and fools," but ultimately reported that for a "full two years it had a surprising influence over the Indians, [who] too frequently neglected hunting for singing and dancing."[81] Yet these practices would not have been viewed as such by the Anishinaabe practitioners, as they were intended to improve success in the hunt.

While Thompson ultimately viewed singing and dancing as peripheral to hunting success, the new religion emphasized the connection. Like other fur traders, Thompson relied on French Canadians with more experience for much of his information. Mr Cadotte informed Thompson that although he spoke the Anishinaabe language, he could not understand any of the phrases in these songs, "only a chance word."[82] This led to speculation between Thompson and Cadotte that they must have "a kind of mystical language among themselves; understood only by the initiated." While Thompson viewed its novelty as the main source of its popularity, he may have been influenced by Mr Cadotte's opinion that most of the Wabano singers were "idle Men and poor hunters." Yet their very endeavours through their songs and dances were intended to improve the hunt. Somewhere between Rainy River and Lake of the Woods, Thompson described several large lodges containing forty to fifty families who became "enamoured of the Wahbino Song and Dance." Thompson was critical of this development, stating that "so many dancing together they too often became highly excited and danced too long." Some made drums with strings of animal bones from mice, squirrels, frogs, and birds' claws, and when struck the strings of bones changed positions. Their shapes and alignments "pretended to tell what was to happen."[83] Thompson described the spectacle of long poles tied from tree to tree, on which were carefully hung the sacred *Wabano* medicine bags and tambours of each man.[84]

On one occasion, when Thompson was taking a measurement with parallel glasses and quicksilver, his Indigenous acquaintance declared his "Wah bano" was strong. Thompson took this to mean "By what you are doing, you give to yourself great power, my Wahbino can do the same for me." Thompson responded that "the Great Spirit alone was strong, your Wah bino is like this," and he held up a pinch of sand and let it fall.[85] According to the account, that night, the wind disrupted the pole on which the tambours and medicine bags were tied, making them fall to the ground. To add insult as they lay there, "the Dogs had wetted them," a sacrilege that challenged their aura of spiritual power. How could the sacred medicine bags and drums suffer such treatment? As news of this accident spread, Thompson reported that "the sensible men took advantage of it; and by the following summer nothing more was heard of the Wah bino Medicine."[86] Yet despite this assertion, Wabanowiwin indeed continued to be practised and spread further afield.

Alexander Henry (the younger) described the arrival of Wabanowiwin in the vicinity of the Red River in late October of 1800. A man named Mimintch came to trade, bringing the new drums and instructions about the new songs and ceremonies. He introduced these to Henry's Indigenous hunter, whose activities were of practical interest and concern: "He has given my hunter an elegant Drum trimed [sic] with all the ceremonies of the Wabbano medicine." This new drum was accompanied by "a number of different medicines and songs concerning that ceremony." These constituted "articles of superior value and high consideration amongst those people."[87] While Henry does not indicate precisely what materials lined the edge of the drum, it is possible it included refashioned bits of metal. Henry was suspicious of Mimintch, apparently because he brought only a few furs to trade and, despite his debts, requested alcohol. Henry feared Mimintch's intent was to "debauch my hunter away." As a result, Henry actively tried to obstruct his influence.

Yet the Wabanowiwin was a cultural phenomenon that Alexander Henry (the younger) would again encounter. A few months later, on an unseasonably warm day in late January, he described a scene of games and songs among the Saulteaux and Assiniboine. The women played "Coullion" on the ice and the men played "Platter," while others were "beating the drum to keep chorus with their Wabbano songs." This description, like earlier ones, suggests group choruses were characteristic of the songs of the Wabanowiwin. Yet this example occurred further west and included the Assiniboine. While the warm weather may have provided the opportunity for outdoor recreation, spring was still a long way off, and hunting was "out of the question at this season of the year."[88] Thus, this occasion of ceremonies and songs occurred well before the onset of the hunting season. On 27 May 1802, Henry described a group "Making the Wabbano" after a meeting of the Midéwiwin.[89] This evidence suggests Wabanowiwin was practised in the winter as well as springtime and was not seen to conflict with the Midéwiwin.

Henry's account makes it clear that Wabanowiwin songs were used not only in conjunction with hunting but also with healing. He relates a story from the local Indigenous community whereby a woman had been shot in the back and a man named Auguemance had tried to heal her. Henry learned how Auguemance "by means of his art in medicine and his superior knowledge of the Wabbano, he had extricated a bit of Iron from out the back of his patient which had given her much relief, but that by means of his conjuration he found she had some piece of hard metal in her neck, which baffles all his powers of medicine to extract. He was now exhausted all his skill in vain, has sung all his grand medicine and Wabbano songs, and beat his drum both day and night for some time past, but still the bit of metal does not appear. He however does not dispair and hopes to get it out, there being only that now, which prevents her recovery." Henry interpreted the actions of Auguemance to be merely "a trick of the fellow to get more property."[90] Yet he understood that Wabanowiwin was used in the healing ceremony as an aid. Interestingly, Henry here indicated Midéwewin songs were sung alongside Wabanowiwin songs in the attempt to heal.

John Tanner's testimony sheds light on the spread of Wabanowiwin across the prairies. Tanner recounts seeing a man in the distance carrying two large "Ta-wa-e-gun-num," or "Waw-be-no" drums: "As we were one day travelling through the prairie, we looked back and saw at a distance a man loaded with baggage, and having two of the large Ta-wa-e-gun-num, or drums used in the ceremonies of the Waw-be-no."[91] This image reflects the incredible determination of this spiritual movement's practitioners, as well as the centrality of its drums. Tanner asserted that some of the older and more respected Anishinaabe considered it "a false and dangerous religion," yet he indicated it was still "fashionable" (and spreading) by the 1830s. Tanner compared its mechanics to the Grand Medicine Society: "The ceremonies of the Waw-be-no differ very essentially from those of the Metai, and are usually accompanied by much licentiousness and irregularity." Providing a detailed account, Tanner described how the Wabbano practitioners used a frame drum, rather than the hollowed log drum of the Midéwiwin: "The Ta-wa-e-gun used for a drum in this dance, differs from the Woin Ah-keek, or Me-ti-kwaw-keek, used in the Me-tai, it being made of a hoop of bent wood like a soldier's drum, while the latter is a portion of the trunk of a tree, hollowed by fire, and having the skin tied over it. The She-zhe-gwun, or rattle, differs also in its construction from that used in the Me-tai."[92] The drums of the Wabanowiwin were thus more portable, with Tanner comparing them to a European "soldier's drum."

Unlike prior descriptions, both men and women are described as participating in the ceremonies, and Tanner provided a long description of the dances that incorporated elements of juggling and fire-throwing: "The initiated take coals of fire, and red hot stones in their hands, and sometimes in their mouths. Sometimes they put powder on the insides of their hands, first moistening them, to make it stick; then by rubbing them on coals, or a red hot stone, they make the powder burn. Sometimes one of the principal performers at a Waw-be-no, has a kettle brought and set down before him, which is taken boiling from the fire, and before it has time to cool, he plunges his hands to the bottom, and brings up the head of the dog, or whatever other animal it may be which had been purposely put there. He then, while it remains hot, tears off the flesh with his teeth, at the same singing and dancing madly about. After devouring the meat, he dashes down the bone, still dancing and capering as before."[93]

This passage suggests that initiates of the Wabanowiwin combined song and dance with demonstrations of immunity to extreme heat. Tanner attributed this ability not to the potency of their songs, but to the herbs employed to neutralize their pain and heal their burns: "They are able to withstand the effects of fire and of heated substances by what they would persuade the ignorant to be a supernatural power, but this is nothing else than a certain preparation, effected by the application of herbs, which make the parts to which they are applied insensible to fire. The plants they use are the Wa-be-no-wusk, and Pe-zhe-ke-wusk. The former grows in abundance on the island of Mackinac, and is called yarrow by the people of the United States. The other grows only in the prairies. These they mix and bruise, or chew together, and rub over their hands and arms. The Waw-be-no-wusk, or yarrow, in the form of a poultice, is an excellent remedy for burns, and is much used by the Indians, but the two when mixed together seem to give to the skin, even of the lips and tongue, and astonishing power of resisting the effects of fire."[94]

Like the Midéwiwin, the Wabanowiwin focused to a large degree on healing rites, the use of herbs, and their ceremonial application alongside appropriate songs and dances. The cultural and material influence of Wabanowiwin is palpable in the accounts of fur traders. They lived alongside Indigenous peoples and were concerned with the procedures of hunting and healing. Wabanowiwin developed at the height of fur trade competition along the trade route to the northwest and appeared to have represented an aesthetically innovative yet spiritually "traditionalist" system. Its songs may have borne some witness to European musical influence regarding vocal style, chorus, and materials. Yet their application in facilitating hunting and healing through song and dance was distinctly Indigenous. Fur traders witnessed and described these traditions that they endeavoured to comprehend.

Healing Songs

As the previous examples have demonstrated, fur traders often became familiar with Indigenous use of song and dance as mediums with the spirit world. Since the early eighteenth century, fur traders had a special relationship with Indigenous medicine men. HBC representatives made special gifts to prominent medicine men who arrived at their posts as part of trading parties. They would be taken "singly with their wives into a room where they are given a red leather trunk with a few simple medicines such as the powders of sulphur, bark, liquorice, camphorated spirit, white ointment, and basilicon, with a bit of diachylon plaster."[95] This exchange expanded the medicines available to healers in Indigenous societies. This trading ceremony can be seen as an acknowledgement of their special role in Indigenous societies and was part of the broader exchange of survival methods and materials upon which the fur trade was predicated. Fur traders often learned how, what, and where to hunt in the local area from Indigenous hunters. They wanted the communities they traded with to do well in order to provide good returns the following season. Thus, the good health of the Indigenous community was in the best interest of fur traders. Many fur traders brought with them mathematical and scientific instruments, and quite a few had significant interests in science and medicine.[96] The fur trade introduced Indigenous peoples to the medicine chests of the trading posts while fur traders became familiar with Indigenous healing practices that often involved song.

Alexander Henry (the elder) travelled throughout the Great Lakes and over the height of land to Lake Winnipeg and the Saskatchewan River in the late eighteenth century, noting healing songs among various Indigenous peoples he encountered. He wrote that "in all parts of the country, and among all nations that I have seen, particular individuals arrogate to themselves the art of healing."[97] From his observations, medicine men were customarily materially recompensed for their services by the community. On one occasion, several elder chiefs invited Henry to witness the healing ceremony of a girl around twelve years of age because he too was seen to possess healing powers. The invitation was interpreted as a "compliment ... paid to myself, on account of the medical skill for which it was pleased to give me credit." This can be seen to reflect the larger phenomenon whereby fur traders served as early bearers of European medicines to Indigenous communities. Henry begins with a description of "whom the French call *jongleurs,* or jugglers" or the "physician (so to call him)" sitting on the ground with a bucket of water and bones resembling a swan's wing. The following description reveals a healing ceremony that interspersed singing with the sounds of the rattle:

> In his hand, he had this *shishiquoi,* or rattle, with which he beat time to his *medicine-song* ... After singing for some time, the physician took one of the bones out of the basin: the bone was hollow; and one end being applied to the breast of the patient, he put the other into his mouth, in order to remove the disorder by suction. Having persevered in this as long as he thought proper, he suddenly seemed to force the bone into his mouth, and swallow it. He now acted the part of one suffering severe pain; but, presently finding relief, he made a long speech, and after this, returned to singing, and to the accompaniment of his rattle. With the latter, during his song, he struck his head, breast, sides and back; at the same time straining, as if to vomit forth the bone. Relinquishing this attempt, he applied himself to suction a second time, and with the second of the three bones; and this also he soon seemed to swallow. Upon its disappearance, he began to distort himself in the most frightful manner, using every gesture which could convey the idea of pain; at length, he succeeded, or pretended to succeed, in throwing up one of the bones. This was handed about to the spectators, and strictly examined; but nothing remarkable could be discovered. Upon this, he went back to his song and rattle; and after some time threw up the second of the two bones. In the groove of this, the physician, upon examination, found, and displayed to all present, a small white substance, resembling a piece of the quill of a feather. It was passed round the company, from one to the other; and declared, by the physician, to be the thing causing the disorder of his patient.[98]

The audience played a vital role in observing the healing ceremony. Like the others, Henry was keenly attuned to the materials and movements of the medicine man. Henry stated that most in the community believed these physicians could cause as well as cure disorders. In this instance, the patient died the next day, yet Henry became convinced of the medicine men's abilities to cure small wounds: "With regard to flesh-wounds, the Indians certainly effect astonishing cures. Here, as above, much that is fantastic occurs; but the success of their practice evinces something solid."[99] Acknowledging their ability to heal wounds, Henry asserted that the medicine men's "reward may generally be said to be fairly earned, by dint of corporal labour."[100] When a man with an axe wound was brought into the fort at Sault Ste Marie, Henry observed an Anishinaabe healer retrieving his "*penegusan,* or medicine-bag," and through his procedures and operations produced an effective remedy.[101] While Henry found Indigenous healing ceremonies novel and astonishing, he was convinced to at least some degree of their efficacy.

Samuel Hearne devoted five pages of his journal from 1769–72 to Indigenous practices of medicine. Hearne used the term "doctor" to describe the Cree medicine men he encountered on his voyages.[102] He described observing a man with a "dead palsey" or "paralytic stroke" that rendered him affected down one side from the crown of his head to the sole of his foot. Internal afflictions prevented him from eating food and reduced him to a mere "skeleton." After he was placed inside of a large "conjuring house," the Cree doctor arrived. He "offered to swallow a large piece of board, about the size of a barrel-stave, in order to effect his recovery." One side of the board was painted with an animal, and the other a representation of the sky. Hearne observed with astonishment and skepticism the medicine man swallowing the board and offered some praise: "they must be allowed a considerable share of dexterity in the performance of those tricks, and a wonderful deal of perseverance in what they do for the relief of those whom they undertake to cure."[103] Yet Hearne's incredulity was noted by his Cree hosts. They responded with humour: "some of them laughed at my ignorance, as they were pleased to call it; and said, that the spirits in waiting swallowed, or otherwise concealed, the stick." Hearne's Cree guide Matonabbee, near the Prince of Wales's Fort, insisted to Hearne "in the strongest terms" that he had seen a medicine man swallow a child's cradle, folding it easily into his mouth, and pulling it back out again unscathed. Hearne described consciously putting aside his skepticism and becoming "very inquisitive about the spirits which appear to them on those occasions, and their form."[104] He was told that the spirits appeared in various shapes, with each conjurer having his own "peculiar attendant." The spirit present when swallowing the wood typically appeared in the shape of a cloud. Hearne thought this very "a-propos to the present occasion," remarking: "I must confess that I never had so thick a cloud thrown before my eyes before or since."[105] Hearne's difficulty reconciling what he saw and heard only increased when he began to inquire into the practices and discuss them with the Cree.

Part of what Hearne had difficulty reconciling was the gender dynamics. He described communal healing rituals and how both men and women healers typically worked almost naked. To the original medicine man's efforts was added that of five other men and an old woman "all of whom were great professors of that art." Stripping themselves "quite naked," Hearne described how all of these practitioners "began to suck, blow, sing, and dance, round the poor paralytic." They continued for a full three days straight, "without taking the least rest or refreshment, not even so much as a drop of water." Pushing the limits of human endurance, at the end of this ceremony their mouths were so parched with thirst that they were black, with throats so sore they could not speak. From Hearne's perspective their suffering seemed somewhat feigned, yet he observed that they had made themselves "almost as bad as the poor man they had been endeavouring to relieve … for they lay on their backs with their eyes fixed, as if in the agonies of death." The patient would certainly have been vaguely aware of the communal efforts to battle his affliction and may have found it encouraging regardless of the outcome.

This man's health was of particular significance to Hearne because he was a crucial member of his travelling party. His condition had important implications on the journey's success. It was with obvious relief that Hearne reported the man's remarkable transformation. "And it is truly wonderful, though the strictest truth, that when the poor sick man was taken from the conjuring-house, he had not only recovered his appetite to an amazing degree but was able to move all the fingers and toes of the side that had been so long dead. In three weeks he recovered so far as to be capable of walking, and at the end of six weeks went a hunting for his family. He was one of the persons particularly engaged to provide for me during my journey; and after his recovery from this dreadful disorder, accompanied me back to Prince of Wales's Fort in Jun [sic] one thousand seven hundred and seventy-two; and since that time he has frequently visited the Factory."[106] While documenting his remarkable transition, Hearne explains that the man never regained all his former characteristics, something that might be explained by his brain injury. Yet the apparent efficacy of the ritual clearly troubled Hearne. He wrote that "the apparent good effect of their labours on the sick and diseased is not so easily accounted for," positing an explanation that resembled the placebo effect. "Perhaps the implicit confidence placed in them by the sick may, at times, leave the mind so perfectly at rest, as to cause the disorder to take a favourable turn; and a few successful cases are quite sufficient to establish the doctor's character and reputation: But how this consideration could operate in the case I have just mentioned I am at a loss to say; such, however, was the fact, and I leave it to be accounted for by others."[107]

David Thompson relates the story of an Anishinaabe medicine man from the shores of Lake of the Woods in 1798–9. This account invokes the "Man Eater (a Wee te go)," otherwise known as *windigo*, the cannibal figure invoked in numerous Indigenous stories and narratives. Thompson described how in a council meeting, the father of a man accused of being a *windigo* was chastised for not contacting a medicine man sooner for his son. At an early stage, the ailment might have been dispelled "by sweating" and the medicine man's "songs to the tambour and rattle might have driven away the evil spirit, before it was too late."[108] Thompson reported the council's decision that the *windigo* should be put to death, with the man having admitted his strong desire to eat his sister. The evil spirit thought to create cannibalistic desires could be driven away by the medicine man's songs with the drum and rattle, yet once an individual was thought too far gone, this remedy was deemed insufficient. This conception of mental illness and its cure involving a medicine man interfacing with unseen spirits through songs was learned and written down by Thompson.

The first fur traders to travel and work in the far northwest of the continent around the turn of the nineteenth century documented healing songs among Athapascan-speaking communities. In Alexander Mackenzie's journals and letters, he remarks on the good health of these peoples and their relative lack of diseases and ailments. He briefly summarized the methods he observed practised by their medicine men: "binding the temples, procuring perspiration, singing, and blowing on the sick person, or affected part."[109] While limited, Mackenzie provided an early account. George Keith would spend many more years living and working in this region, recording more detailed descriptions. Writing between 1807 and 1817 from the Mackenzie River and Great Bear Lake departments, he described the healing ceremonies of the "Beaver Indians," or Dane-zaa.

> When the men are in violent pain and fearful of dying, they generally must have a confessor or one of the *jongleurs* to whom (as the only means of recovery held out to the patient by the latter,) they publicly unbosom themselves without reserve and declare all their evil doing. Previous to confession, the mystical cord, ornamented with loon necks, stripes of mink and other skins, claws of the eagle, and a variety of rare and elegant bird feathers, must be attached across the lodge, a little elevated from the ground; over this, the penitent occasionally throws

himself upon his belly and the juggler embraces this opportunity of singing, sucking, &c, and performing his mystical gestures and incantations, and singing a gentle reprimand at each avowed offence against moral rectitude. They are remarkably humble and submissive during this ceremony and ordeal.[110]

From Keith's observations, the Dane-zaa relied on songs, either sung or hummed, alongside various actions to effect cures: "They know nothing of medicinal roots or herbs, so that, except singing their sick Song, or rather humming one, biting, pulling with their Teeth and sucking the parts affected." This comment may reflect the fact that Keith lacked a deep understanding of Dane-zaa medicine. He witnessed some ceremonial aspects but remained ignorant about their use of medicines. However, his records reveal that Indigenous peoples in the region regularly applied to the HBC for this purpose. When they were near the trading post "they always apply for some medicine which is always given gratis."[111] This gift-giving of medicine helped solidify the reciprocal relationship and may have held deeper significances for the Dane-zaa.

Ross Cox was a fur trader with the American Fur Company and the NWC in the early 1810s. He worked for some time among the Chinookan peoples of the west coast. He described how when sickness was detected in a man, he was laid on his back, "while a number of his friends and relations surround him, each carrying a long and a short stick, with which they beat time to a mournful air which the doctor chants, and in which they join at intervals."[112] This description appears to depict a more communal approach to the healing ceremony than those taken from Indigenous peoples in the western Subarctic, Plains, or eastern regions. The healing techniques were taken to their greatest extent, according to Cox, when a man would climb on the roof of the house, "which he belabours most energetically with his drum sticks, joining at the same time with a loud voice the chorus inside." With the singing both inside and outside of the house, kneeling over the patient, pushing on his stomach, and performing various manoeuvres, the cries of the man were "drowned by the doctor and the bystanders, who chant loud and louder still the mighty 'song of medicine.'" Cox identified distinct stanzas in the songs, at the end of which the medicine man seized the patient's hands, joining them together and blowing on them. While the healing song continued, the medicine man alternately pressed and blew until a small white stone was produced out of the patient's mouth.[113] This method of curing by ceremonially removing a small object from the patient resembles other descriptions somewhat, such as that

recorded by Henry at Sault Ste Marie, and the techniques associated with the
sacred megis shell in the Anishinaabe Midéwiwin.[114]

As we have already seen, George Nelson was an observant and relatively
open-minded fur trader with years of experience who inquired into Anishinaabe
spirituality and ceremonies. He recognized that the medicine man's deeply
spiritual relationship with plants and herbs included close observation of their
effects, with distinct classifications and usages: "Roots and herbs also ... such
as are medicinal, appear, and teach their votaries their respective Songs – how
they must do, what ceremonies they must perform in taking them out of the
Ground, their different applications, &c. &c."[115] Nelson's understanding of
Anishinaabe culture was deep enough that he understood the importance of the
songs in the usages and protocols of engagement as well as distinguishing each
plant in the mind of the medicine man. During apprenticeship, "he is shown
all the roots, herbs, plants &c, and is taught the respective song (of each) or of
any particular one or number, or such as only grow in the climate he inhabits.
Both the songs and the Plant, herb, &c, are so indelibly imprinted on his mind
(or memory), tho' he had never seen them before, or should not happen to
meet with any of them for years afterwards, yet on his first view, he immediately
recognizes them, and every circumstance that had been instructed him, as if he
had passed a regular apprentiship."[116] What is unusual is that Nelson discussed
these concepts from a number of angles, demonstrating that he was not merely
repeating what one informant had told him, but rather was grappling with the
underlying cosmology and spiritual beliefs that explained that the songs were
connected to both the plant and the associated spirit: "As far as I can learn,
every different root, herb, plant, mineral, Spirit (or whatever you may please
to term this latter) have each their respective songs; and which they must
sing ... When they sing, those of their *familiars* who instructed this Song,
whether to the one who sings, as having learnt it from himself (i.e., Familiar)
or having been handed to him; he is said to attend, invisibly, of course, and
perform that which he promised this (medicine, supposing it is one) should
effect ... Hence it is they always sing when they attend on a desperately sick
person, amongst themselves."[117] Though he conceded he did not have a perfect
understanding, Nelson did convey something of the traditional Anishinaabe
usage and conception of songs used in healing ceremonies alongside roots,
herbs, and plants.

As with other accounts, Nelson provided his perspective on the auditory
qualities and musicality of healing songs. While he appreciated them somewhat,
he indicated that they were outside of the conception of music for pleasure. He

also testified to the virtuosity: "These songs are a dull monotony; for tho' they have a few variations and are hi[gh] and low, and the transition sometimes so very sudden that it requires a particular command of the throat to sing them; and to *me*, so difficult that I should I believe require a 7 years apprenticeship even with Esculapius (but I believe it is *Pluto* or *Pan* who teaches the songs) himself, for me to learn them, and there is certainly no musick in them; tho' some few that I've heard many years ago, passing a winter with them, I found pleasing enough; but perhaps more from the *solemnity* with which all was going on was I struck, than any thing else: indeed we had great reason to be solemn, for we were dreadfully pinched by hunger."[118] This account is remarkable both for its candid appraisal and estimation of the time necessary to master the songs of the medicine men. Nelson recognized that songs were a fundamental component of the Anishinaabe use of medicinal plants and herbs and were central to healing ceremonies.

While fur traders' opinions of Indigenous hunting and healing songs ranged from critical to appreciative, and their beliefs in their efficacy ranged from skeptical to convinced, what is most important is that they described these ceremonies in such detail. Unlike the later activities of missionaries, Indian agents, and medical professionals, fur traders did not interfere with traditional Indigenous hunting and healing practices. While their bringing of medicines to the trading posts may have augmented and expanded the healing practices of certain Indigenous communities, they did not actively displace or restrict traditional Indigenous practices in any way. They did not typically try to teach a new set of religious songs to replace traditional Indigenous spirituality, as missionaries did. In many ways, fur traders were like ethnographers conducting fieldwork and documenting aspects of Indigenous ways of life, albeit ones that concerned them. Yet fur traders were also agents of change. Their influence broadened the hunting techniques and medicines available to Indigenous peoples. Indigenous music was impacted to at least a small degree, for instance with pieces of metal from trading goods refashioned for use on garments and drums. The underlying logic of hunting and healing songs, to engage with unseen forces and spirits, was sometimes explicitly acknowledged by fur traders. Supernatural explanations of their successes were sometimes advanced by voyageurs, while masters tended to be more skeptical. They expressed a diversity of views and often acknowledged the role of medicines and herbs in addition to the ritualistic aspects of healing ceremonies. What is of most historical significance is not the array of reactions or expressed opinions of fur traders, but rather that these descriptions form a notable component of their written record. Indigenous hunting and healing ceremonies prominently incorporated music, capturing the attention of fur traders working in or near the community. They took note because the health of Indigenous peoples had a direct influence on their success. If the Indigenous communities who traded at the post were suffering, so too would the fur traders in both provisions and pelts. Thus, the propensity for fur traders to describe these Indigenous ceremonies arose largely from practical considerations and concerns rather than mere ethnographic curiosity. Yet the records left by fur traders preserve important details about traditional methods and understandings of Indigenous hunters and healers.

Music of the Trading Posts

How musical was the fur trade? A historian might answer this question by only reviewing the primary sources of written evidence. An ethnomusicologist might answer by studying contemporary traditions and speculating on historical roots. Indeed, ethnomusicologists have conducted fieldwork in Métis and First Nations communities across northern and western Canada, revealing a widespread "old-time" fiddle music culture with associated step dancing (often called "jigging") whose origins are attributed to the fur trade. This overall style combines both European and Indigenous approaches to playing the fiddle and dancing. The geographic extent of this "hybrid" fur trade-derived music is extensive. It has been studied among the Omushkego Cree of Hudson Bay, the Athapascan people of the Yukon, and the Métis of Red River.[1] These fiddling traditions bear witness to Scottish, French Canadian, and Orkney origins, reflecting the predominant cultures that brought their fiddles and tunes to the trading post network at the height of the fur trade in the decades around 1800. A close examination of the primary accounts indicates that European musical instruments were traded by Montreal merchants and the NWC especially before the amalgamation with the HBC in 1821. This trade supported the development of a vigorous music and dance culture throughout the trading post network. Secular instrumental dance music was central to "fur trade society." Dances celebrated successes, holidays, and special events. The trading posts were the nodes around which this dance music tradition flourished. It mostly consisted of jigs and reels played on fiddles, sometimes accompanied by other instruments such as flutes or Indigenous drums. This dance music tradition played an important role in bridging divisions of culture, class, gender, and company at the height of fur trade competition. After the amalgamation of 1821, it was increasingly restricted by the reforms of the HBC and an expanding Christian missionary presence. Yet, by then, the fur trade had produced syncretic music and dance styles that took root and flourished outside of the walls of the trading posts.

In the written record from 1760 to 1840, references to music and social dance are generally few and far between. This is understandable given the material limitations that fur traders faced. It was a rough profession that entailed the transport of materials over long distances and difficult terrain. Paper and ink were precious, good writing surfaces were scarce, and the opportunity to write was often limited. Many of the records that were made at the time have been lost or destroyed. Some fur traders kept personal diaries or wrote memoirs. The HBC mandated that its fur traders keep post journals, while most of the Montreal outfits did not. In post journals, typically brief entries describe business operations, listing work details and material transactions. Music, dance, and other recreational activities were rarely described unless particularly noteworthy or relevant to business. In personal diaries and memoirs on the other hand, passion for music and dance is sometimes vividly recorded. After the 1821 merger of the HBC and the NWC, some fur traders expressed dismay with the restrictions placed on musical occasions and dances by the regime of governor George Simpson. Yet these traditions had become so interwoven into the operations of the fur trade that it was difficult – nearly impossible – to deny them entirely. Indeed, instrumental music and social dance continued to serve an important, if more limited, role at the trading posts until at least the mid-nineteenth century.

Trading Posts as Sites of Musical Exchange

In the seventeenth century, Europeans brought their musical traditions to North America. L'Ordre de Bon Temps or Order of Good Cheer is the infamous social club created on the suggestion of Samuel de Champlain in 1606 for the French to pass the winter in good health with activity and entertainment that prominently featured food and music.[2] In the St Lawrence, "two violins, for the first time" apparently appeared at the wedding of the daughter of the seigneur of Espinay, M. Couillar in 1645.[3] The first "ball" was documented at the home of Louis Théandre Chartier de Lotbinière in 1667. The Jesuits who described it stated "may God grant that it do not become a precedent," representing well the missionaries' habit of criticizing social dances, both European and Indigenous.[4] In Hudson Bay, the first recorded instance of a bowed string instrument is attributed to Charles Bayley, the first governor of the HBC. He had a "violl and shell and strings" sent to him from London in 1678.[5] That he wanted a musical instrument to keep him occupied through the long winter evenings is unsurprising. What is surprising is that he was a Quaker, a Christian sect often critical of recreational music. Yet the historical evidence suggests that the first governor of the HBC introduced stringed instruments to Hudson Bay.

The earliest known description of a dance on Hudson Bay is a 1749 account from Moose Factory: "Having three Fidlers in the Factory, viz. Geo. Millar, Willm. Murray and James Short, our people celebrated the Evening with Dancing and Signing, and all were very merry."[6] This suggestive if short description is quite an anomaly in the annals of the HBC during the first century and a half of its existence. This event seems to have been recorded due to the rarity and excitement of having three fiddlers together at a trading post at the same time. It suggests that violins were by this time sporadically making their way to the trading posts as the possessions of individuals. There appears to have been a great appetite for fiddle music and dancing among fur traders, an all-male workforce. In the writing of musicologists on the origins of North American fiddle music, there is a long interval between this example in 1749 and a subsequent written description of a dance at an HBC post. Lederman and Mishler next cite an example from York Factory in 1843, while Wilkins cites a dance at Moose Factory in 1911.[7]

Yet what of the period from the 1760s to the 1840s? This crucial timeframe encompassed the conquest of New France, Pontiac's Rebellion and subsequent Treaty of Niagara, expansion of the fur trade to the southwest and northwest of the Great Lakes, the American Revolution, intense commercial competition across the north, the emergence of the Métis people, the amalgamation of 1821, monopoly under the HBC, and finally the arrival of missionaries in significant numbers. This period of rapid expansion and intense activity is too important to be overlooked. It is undoubtedly more difficult to find references to music in the Hudson Bay trade than the St Lawrence trade before 1821. In most documentation and correspondence of the employees of the HBC, references to music and dancing are conspicuously absent. Many "Bay men" presented an image of sober industry and religious piety in their journals and correspondence. Mathew Cocking on 29 September 1776 related that he "Read Divine Service for the Day."[8] The HBC's Joseph Hansom described the "heavey claps of Thunder till Noon," and added that he "Read divine Service" on Sunday 26 July 1778.[9] In the daily Journal of Occurrences maintained at each trading post, descriptions of pastimes are limited or nonexistent. In the Journal of Occurrences at York Factory from 1818 to 1819, the only entries that suggest ceremonies or rituals are Sunday's "read prayers."[10] In the journal for Edmonton House from 1819 to 1820, the cultural activities on New Year's Day, 1 January 1819 are only suggested with the following terse description: "People passed the day in Amusement. Mild Weather, Wind West."[11] I suspect the amusements included music and perhaps dancing, but it is impossible to know for certain given the limitations of the written record. The following year, the journal entry describing New Year's Day celebrations reads "The people passed the day in Conviviality."[12] No further details are given, and there is no indication regarding music or dance. One might be inclined to think HBC post life was devoid of music.

Due to the often busy work schedule at the posts on Hudson Bay, some accounts indicate that there was scarcely any time for leisure pursuits, especially in the summer months. James Hargrave described in letters written at York Factory from the 1820s to the 1840s that from five in the morning until eleven at night throughout the summer he was completely busy with duties that required "the utmost stretch of thought and exertion of body."[13] The nights provided only a few hours of rest, "all too little for repose." During the winter, deskwork occupied the hours from daylight until bedtime. Saturday was passed in hunting or walking, and Sundays were "sacred days," reserved for quiet contemplation and perusal of the bible. The gentlemen are described as enjoying quiet games and reading. "Our short days are whiled away in easy employment at the desk, – and we beguile the tedium of the long winter evenings by a Game at Backgammon, Chess or Whist – enlivened by a bottle of wine, or should the pensive mood prevail a well stocked library furnishes food for the mind in profusion besides which I have annually a chest full of Books Newspapers & Reviews from London, containing every thing most attractive in the literary world."[14] Yet there was likely more music and dance at the posts on Hudson Bay than is indicated in the HBC archives. Parks Canada recently uncovered a painted board from a depot building at York Factory dating to approximately 1800 that features a vivid depiction of a fiddler.

There is more evidence of musical instruments making their way into the St Lawrence fur trade. A rich variety of violins, viols, lutes, guitars, flutes, spinets, organs, and even harpsichords made their way to New France, mostly imported into the homes of the elite. For instance, intendants Jacques Raudot and Antoine-Denis Raudot were known for concerts at their residence from 1705 to 1711. Intendant Claude-Thomas Dupuy from 1725 to 1728 owned two bass viols, a portable spinet, and a twelve-stop organ.[15] Not everything was imported from Europe, as viols and violins were made in the French colony, as well as possibly guitars.[16] With relatively few written references to musical

Fig. 8.1 Painted panel ca 1800, York Factory depot building.

instruments and dances beyond those of the balls held by officials, it is difficult to assess the degree to which these instruments influenced anyone other than the elite. Violins (fiddles in the folk idiom) transcended class divisions, finding a place not only in the homes of *seigneurs*, but also of *habitants*. New France's expansive fur trade produced long-term relationships with eastern Indigenous peoples that led to many undocumented exchanges of instruments and music. This is clear from references such as the following from Warren Johnson in the Mohawk valley in 1760–61: "I heard an Indian playing many European Tunes, & pretty well on the Fidle."[17]

This example foreshadows the kind of intercultural musical exchanges that manifested across fur-trading country over the next century. Fiddle music most often transcended the social divisions of people in the fur trade. It was a key recreational platform for socialization, business, and pleasure. It was an important part of the relationship obligations maintained between masters and their servants and voyageurs. It was central to how many fur traders initiated and maintained relationships with Indigenous women and interacted with their communities. Which of these functions fiddle music and dance was fulfilling largely depended on the season and occasion. At the summer rendezvous and Christmas–New Year's celebrations, it was a core component of the large gatherings and annual celebrations. Throughout most of the year, it operated on a smaller and more local scale.

The scattered references in the written record demonstrate that dancing played a central role in social activities at the big trading hubs in the western Great Lakes such as Michilimackinac, Grand Portage, and Fort William. In the spring, fur traders travelled from trading posts throughout the interior of the continent to meet with those arriving from Montreal at these trading hubs. These rendezvous produced large gatherings of peoples from diverse linguistic and cultural backgrounds. The dances allowed the significant merchants and fur trading partners to socialize and make connections. Peter Pond left an early description of such a summer rendezvous at Michilimackinac. During the day, the "Good Company" were amusing themselves at billiards, while the "vulgar" were apparently off fighting. Pond recounts that he was "Dansing at Nite with Respectabel Parsons [sic]."[18] In the winter, music and dancing played a different yet no less crucial role. In a letter from 27 April 1778, John Askin described the previous months at Michilimackinac: "We have passed Our Winter as agreeably as the place would admit of a Dance every week."[19] We know from other documentation that Askin ordered violins and strings, suggesting fiddle music at the dances.[20] These weekly dances over the winter and spring would have provided recreation, physical activity, and entertainment for masters and servants. It would have improved working relationships in the long run, offering an opportunity for male bonding within each household. Compared to the population increases they witnessed during the summer rendezvous, numbers at the trading hubs were modest during these quieter months.

In a letter from Michilimackinac dated 22 June 1778, the trader John Askin complained that the newly arrived shipment from Montreal did not contain the violins he had ordered. Askin's pleading tone is noteworthy. His following statement well encapsulates the situation of fur traders overwintering: "The things from England are really well choose & please me much, however a fiddle which I had mentioned in that memoir is left out, & tho' such an omition can be of no consiquence to persons who can supply the want at the next Shop, it is so different here, that I would not for ten Guineas it had not come, please purchase one for me at Montreal without fail let the price be about £6 Halifax, I sent you a memord. this Spring in which a fiddle was mentioned, that one is also to come, its for an other person, please do not forget a quantity of strings with the fiddles."[21]

Musical interactions also occurred outside the gates. While rarely commented on in the written record, there are a few precious examples describing the diverse music that occurred outside of the walls of the trading posts. Jean-Baptiste Perrault worked as a voyageur in the fur trade for over three decades. He described the scene outside of the gates of Michilimackinac upon his arrival in mid-July 1787. It was marked by an array of auditory stimulus, as "cris de joie" (cries of joy) and cannon fire were followed by the sounds of Indigenous instruments: "tambours, flûtes, chicheigiven, joints aux chants de la voix, rendoient un son mélodieux" (drums, flutes, rattles, joined in the singing voice, rendered a melodious sound).[22] Layered overtop were the sounds of a group of British soldiers led by Captain John Dease who marched to the council house, "la troupe sous les armes au son du tambour" (the troops under arms and sound of the tambour).[23] In this poly-musical environment, the British military drums beat near Indigenous drums. They were different musics serving different functions for different peoples converging around the trading post. The soundscape bore witness to the plurality of presence and intentions. This moment was likely not unique, but on this occasion, it was recorded.

Grand Portage was the key trading hub at the western end of Lake Superior that dominated the northwest trade. A few years before the NWC was forced by the international boundary to transfer their operations to Fort William near modern-day Thunder Bay, Daniel Harmon described a remarkable dance on 4 July 1800. While occurring in the summer, it was not quite the summer rendezvous. Many Indigenous women accompanied the fur traders as dancing partners: "the gentlemen of the place dressed, and we had a famous ball, in the dining room. For musick, we had the bag-pipe, the violin and the flute, which added much to the interest of the occasion. At the ball, there was a number of the ladies of this country; and I was surprised to find that they could conduct with so much propriety, and dance so well."[24] This passage is notable for the diversity of instruments and the participation of Indigenous women – "ladies of this country" – as dancing partners. Harmon compliments them for conducting themselves "with so much propriety," reflecting their familiarity with European dances and suggesting their frequent inclusion. That the musical instruments were described with such enthusiasm and appreciation suggests that this much variety was the exception rather than the norm. Bagpipes, like the drums and fifes that found their way to trading posts, brought with them military associations. These would not have found their way into the sophisticated balls of the St Lawrence. Nonetheless, Harmon describes the event as a "famous ball." With the unusual array of musical instruments and intercultural dancing partners, this was a different type of ball created from the distinct elements available at this particular time and place.

Yet this dance was not the only one that occurred within the walls of Grand Portage that day. Harmon included in his journal an important detail that might be overlooked. He mentioned that Indigenous men were permitted to dance inside the fort during the day, stating simply: "The Natives were permitted to dance in the fort." The fur trader's journals often provide transactional details about what transpired to the company's material investments. It seems to be in this light rather than in a moral way that Harmon mentions that after the dance the Indigenous men were given a gift of "thirty-six gallons of shrub." They departed the fort to consume it.[25] What is most significant here is that the Indigenous group was permitted to dance inside the fort during the day. While no explanation is provided, the gesture appears to be one of respect. It may have symbolically served as an acknowledgement of their relationship and status as important trading partners. The Indigenous presence was not only seen but felt through the auditory vibrations of their songs.

At the smaller trading post dances, the circle of inclusion was extended more readily. Sometimes the men of the trading post would dance together; other times they would invite those from a neighbouring post or the local Indigenous community. This recreation provided warmth and laughter and served as a bulwark against feelings of isolation and homesickness. Smaller posts and winter camps brought the fur traders closer to Indigenous communities. As we will see in the following examples, song and dance served as a crucial coping mechanism for fur traders in combatting loneliness, feelings of dislocation, and long durations of cold indoor confinement in small quarters while overwintering. Vigorous dances to instrumental music – usually the fiddle – often served as the centrepiece for the celebration of seasonal holidays, weddings, birthdays, and baptisms. These smaller celebrations necessitated intermingling at close quarters and served to reduce rather than reaffirm social distinctions, as the gentlemen often danced alongside voyageurs and servants.

Overwintering was a significant emotional burden for many. Daniel Harmon wrote in his journal about his struggles and difficulties while fur trading and living in a "solitary place." He was camping for weeks away from the trading post in 1803 with a small assortment of goods. He desperately missed his old acquaintances, expressing "almost regret" at becoming a fur trader and leaving them behind. He hoped to "one day enjoy, with increased satisfaction, the society of those friends, from whom I have for a season banished myself."[26]

Reluctant at first to take an Indigenous wife, he wrote that it was preferable, "in this part of the world," "to have a female companion, with whom [to] pass ... time more socially and agreeably, than to live a lonely life."[27] Harmon did not describe himself taking up a musical instrument. But he did report that his companion Mr Goedlike "plays the violin, and will occasionally cheer our spirits, with an air." Without this companion, Harmon's experiences would have been much different and devoid of music. Harmon writes that "most of our leisure time, which is at least five sixths of the whole" was spent on "reading, and in meditating and conversing upon what we read."[28] Yet having a musician influenced the emotional state of the group and was a luxury worthy of note.

So dear, it seems, was dancing to so many fur traders that fierce commercial rivalries were sometimes put aside to engage in this activity. Daniel Harmon reported a situation at Riviere à la Souris or Mouse-River near the Qu'appelle valley in what is now Saskatchewan, where establishments of the NWC, XY Company, and HBC existed within close proximity. He described how customarily they would dance together every Sunday. Harmon reported on Monday 27 May 1805: "Last evening, Mr Chaboillez invited the people of the other two forts to a dance; and we had a real North West country ball." Harmon was something of a teetotaler, and more concerned with commenting on the insobriety than the specifics of the music or dance. He described how "three fourths of the people had drunk so much, as to be incapable of walking straightly, the other fourth thought it time to put an end to the ball, or rather *bawl*." Even after such a long night, the next morning Harmon was invited to breakfast at the HBC house with Mr McKay, and that evening was invited "to a dance." This one, he was keen to note, "ended more decently, than the one of the preceding evening."[29] Sharing the duty of hosting, dances were part of the regular interactions between fur traders at these trading posts.

Usually, dances appear in the written record due to some special event. Archibald McLeod described a dance held the day after Easter Sunday on 6 April 1801. It is unclear if the dance was to commemorate the holiday or the fact that one of the men from the Shell River Fort had brought his violin. Yet the men's condition was unenviable: "Cold &. blowing hard, the people are some cutting fire wood others hauling, some for Gum &. others working at the Batteau. Several of the people are ill with severe Colds. One of the Shell river men having brought his Violin with him the people danced all night."[30] It is remarkable that the men of the trading post had the energy and desire to dance, given their state. Yet even facing these brutal working conditions, most accounts indicate that fur trade dances finished at a late hour or even daybreak.

Marriages were often commemorated with dancing. The Montreal merchants and fur traders of the NWC inherited the French custom of marrying-in to Indigenous communities. This stood in sharp contrast with the HBC where intermarriages were forbidden for employees until quite a late date.[31] Yet such prohibitions were deemed unrealistic by some fur traders once the HBC began to move inland to compete with the NWC. Nor'Westers George Nelson and Daniel Harmon were reluctant to take wives but eventually did so anyway. Nelson's journal entry for this momentous occasion is brief but suggests that the marriage was the reason for a dance: "A ball was given on the occasion by W.C. (W. Cameron)."[32] Nelson insinuated in his journals that wedding ceremonies were sometimes celebrated excessively. He mentioned that Mr Seraphin had at least three dances to celebrate his wedding. The third may have been held due to the availability of a musician: "We were obliged to leave off and prepare for a dance (which is now the third) in honour to Mr Seraphins wedding. Mr M Donald played the violin for us + Mr Seraphin played the Flute alternately."[33] In this case, instrumental music performed on the flute by the groom and the violin by a colleague was used to celebrate the marriage.

Departures and arrivals were the most significant events at the trading posts. Both were customarily marked with dances. No matter the exhaustion of crews, a collective effort was made to dance the night before departure and the night of arrival. George Nelson described an occurrence at his trading post near the River Dauphine when bad weather delayed a departure, and a dance was held even though the men were exhausted: "The weather is such to inritely [sic] prevent the departure of the Gentlemen: the wind was very high; + many heavy showevers. –We idled away our time uselessly though we had a great necessity of making good use of it. We had a dance last night, but soon left it over as all hands were tired + very sleepy."[34] The consumption of alcohol was usually associated with these dances. At the arrival of an unnamed NWC partner at Fort Dunvegan in 1806, "the Men of Mr McLeod's Canoe began to drink this evening, and danced till 10 O'clock."[35] On a weekend in 1808, not much sleep was had when "At about 10 A.M. M Donell sets off after having spent the night with us dancing."[36] This kind of extreme commitment to dancing is common in the fur trade records.

Post-masters were expected to provide provisions at dances. Sometimes there was an implicit threat issued by the servants in a similar manner to the ritual baptisms of canoe voyages. Celebrated holidays included All Saints and St Andrew's Day at the beginning and end of November respectively, which were sometimes commemorated by the ceremonialism of erecting maypoles and raising flags.[37] Daniel Harmon related how on St Andrew's Day at Fort Alexandria, the servants appeared at the master's door early in the morning, presenting him with a cross. Meanwhile "a number of others, who were at his door, discharged a volley or two of muskets."[38] With this dramatic announcement, Mr McLeod invited them into the hall where they "received a reasonable *dram*, after which, Mr McLeod made them a present of a sufficiency of spirits," which were expected to last the rest of the day, to be consumed in men's quarters. In the evening, "they were invited to dance in the hall; and during it, they received several flagons of spirits. They behaved with considerable propriety, until about eleven o'clock, when their heads had become heated, by the great quantity of spiritous liquor which they had drunk, during the course of the day and evening. Some of them became quarrelsome, as the Canadians generally are, when intoxicated, and to high words, blows soon succeeded; and finally, two battles were fought, which put an end to this *truly genteel,* North Western ball."[39] This example suggests how the post-master orchestrated the celebrations by hosting the dance, issuing provisions of alcohol, and how the voyageurs were invited into the hall, a regulated social space, for the dance in the evening. The men pressed their superiors for the holiday, beginning symbolically with the presentation of a cross and the volley of firearms outside of the master's room in the early morning. The account of Archibald McLeod presents a similar pattern with the day beginning with the ceremonial presentation of the cross. He then summarized his gifts of alcohol to his men, first in the morning and then two quarts of High Wines in the evening mixed with water and sugar. Subsequently, "they danced, till three oClock in the morning to Frisés singing."[40] As in other accounts, alcohol consumption was mentioned alongside dancing. In this case, a musical instrument was not available, and the dance was held to the vocal music of Frisé, presumably a voyageur.

The major holiday season occurred between Christmas Eve and the New Year. Typically, a tremendous effort was made to celebrate. Co-operation and expressions of goodwill between rival fur traders often ensued. Overwintering at the southern end of Lake Winnipeg in 1810, George Nelson arrived two days before Christmas at fellow NWC partner Duncan Cameron's fort. Nelson was the first to arrive: "Satur 22 Sund 23rd. I arrive this evening at Fort Aleaxr [Alexander][41] where I find Mr Cameron with all his family in the best of health + spirits – No one is yet arrived here except myself – therefore no news."[42] The weather the following day was bad, delaying the arrival of company. Two days after Christmas on Thursday 27 December 1810, "while all hands were busy dancing Mr Dougald Cameron arrived with two men Bousquet from

Lac du Huard about 10'Oclock last night."[43] Arriving midway into the dance, the newcomers immediately joined the celebrations. That these men would be celebrating at all is remarkable, considering Nelson's following comment: "no news of any Consequence unless I remark the old predominant Complaint of this Department – Starvation."[44] This example suggests that the precise date of the celebration was less important than the arrival and gathering of company during the holiday season, in which merriment and dancing were made a priority above all other considerations.

Archibald McLeod hosted a New Year's party at Fort Alexandria in 1801, attracting traders and hunters from as far as Red River and Fort des Prairies, near modern-day Winnipeg and Edmonton, respectively. It is clear from McLeod's account that the dance was extremely diverse, not only comprising servants of the company and voyageurs but also retired voyageurs and Iroquois: "Hoole &. La Couture arrived from Swan River, &. Le Mire with them … people from Fort des Prairies, Red River, Swan River, Free Men, &. Iroquois, in all 38 Men including my own men I likewise gave them ½ Foot Tobacco each man, they danced & sang all day &. night, but had no quarrels, one of ye G.P. kegs of H.W. contained only 20 Qts."[45] This example demonstrates how significant numbers of fur traders, voyageurs, and Indigenous men might gather from numerous posts in a region to celebrate and dance together. Despite the copious amount of high wines provided by McLeod, this account suggests that they did so successfully. McLeod's comments indicate the draw of holiday celebrations, the distance travelled, the diversity of the people involved, and the centrality of dance as the primary cross-cultural activity. Linguistic, ethnic, and class divisions appear to have been overlooked as diverse people undertook long journeys to attend such functions.

Dancing culture was so central to trading post life that people found alternatives when musical instruments were unavailable. George Nelson described New Year's Day in 1809: "Mr McDonell gives a genteel feast to all hands. And for the first day of the year we have beautiful weather. We dance at night, and Ausgé sings for us as a mean substitute for the fiddle."[46] Ausgé, the voyageur who accompanied Nelson, applied his vocal cords to the task and sang the dance tunes that are here unnamed. Perhaps the singing consisted of tunes with no lyrics, or perhaps he sang the *chansons à repondre* often used for dancing in the St Lawrence.[47] Similar descriptions are recorded elsewhere, for instance by Edward Ermatinger at Carlton House in 1826. "To make up a deficiency in the Musical dep't," Ermatinger wrote, "Madamne Husprenant and G. Poivez were kind enough to write their voice, which the latter accompanied by beating on a Tin Pan, and the dancing went on until a late hour."[48] Here cookware was repurposed to serve as a percussion instrument for the vocalists. It is easy to see how spoons might be employed in a similar manner, although I have come across no such references in the fur trade record from 1760 to 1840.

The large trading hubs on the west end of the Great Lakes were more clearly stratified by class than the smaller posts. In the case of Fort William, the great hall served as the venue for the gentlemen's dining and after-dinner dancing. This location is significant. Dining rooms have been examined by scholars as culturally significant spaces in distinguishing and affirming social status and hierarchy.[49] Dining manners and table etiquette served as displays of class and social standing. Physical comportment and grace of movement played an important role in the display. The great hall of Fort William provided the venue for both dining and dancing. It was a socially exclusive space. Servants, voyageurs, and Indigenous peoples were not permitted to enter except at the invitation of the post-master. As historians have remarked, there were surprisingly cordial and familiar relations between servants and masters in the fur trade. There was rarely enough personnel at any given trading post to maintain strict social boundaries, even Fort William. Exclusivity was likely maintained even less than the written record suggests.[50]

Of the nearly four decades of the NWC's predominance (~1780–1820), the only extant diary recorded by a NWC partner during an annual rendezvous is that of Simon McGillivray in 1815.[51] During that significant year, tensions between the NWC, HBC, and the Selkirk settlers at Red River had flared. The "Pemmican Proclamation" was provokingly issued by the HBC's Miles MacDonell in 1814 and restricted the export from the Red River area of this crucial food source necessary for the canoe brigades. Some of the Red River settlers had travelled to Fort William and a dance was organized by the masters of the NWC "given in the evening to the Colonists, the Ladies of the Fort & ca. and all is fun & good humour. Our officers appear in uniform for the first time and dancing kept up till daylight."[52] The "Ladies of the Fort" are again inferred to be the Indigenous wives of the fur traders. Miles MacDonell was under "house arrest" in an adjacent bedroom. From his confinement, he recorded in his own words how "there was a ball to which all the Settlers from Red R. & their women were asked. The Servants of the N.W. Co. thought that they had a good a right to be at the ball as the Settlers, went there in a body & continued to the end. There was not much drinking but they danced reels incessantly & made a dreadful noise. I could not get a wink of sleep."[53]

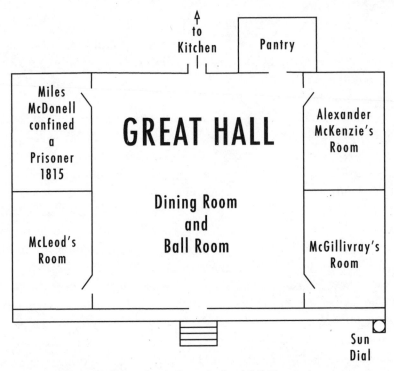

Fig. 8.2 Plan of Fort William, sketch drawn by Lord Selkirk, 1816.

Writing with obvious resentment, MacDonell could only imagine the scenes of revelry occurring on the other side of the wall. He recorded that the servants of the NWC danced reels loudly until daybreak. These were likely of the "Scotch Reel" tradition whose two main types of dance were with a partner in longways form or solo with different steps.[54] The jigs and minuets mentioned by John Lambert as equally popular with fiddlers in the St Lawrence are here not mentioned, nor are the distinctive strathspeys and hornpipes that might be expected from Scottish fiddlers.[55] According to MacDonell's description, only reels were danced. This may or may not have been true. It may well have been, or it may have been noted to demonstrate the crudeness of the NWC. The officers were, after all, mingling and dancing with their *servants!* MacDonell's description connects the servants' presence with the settler women, although the servants of the NWC found their way into the gentlemen's dances more regularly than MacDonell supposed. McGillivray's brief entry for the following day includes the detail that the evening passed off "jovially – songs & ca.," although the previous night's dance had lasted until daybreak.[56] An inclusive and vibrant musical culture is here represented, even during this tense year, with the NWC masters hosting visitors and their servants to dance reels in the ballroom of Fort William.

Another important NWC trading post was on Lac la Pluie (Rainy Lake). While northwest of Lake Superior, its proximity to Fort William and location on the route to Red River meant that it was much better connected and provisioned than other posts in the interior. When Ross Cox passed through in 1817, he encountered "a number of gentlemen, guides, interpreters, and *engagés,* some outward-bound, and others belonging to various departments destined for the interior." He stayed at this hub for a week waiting on an arrival from Fort William and for the men to be deployed to their various overwintering posts. During this time, Cox remarked that he consumed luxuries such as cakes, tea, and coffee, rare delicacies greatly appreciated after years of employment around the smaller posts. Not only was there plentiful food, but there was bountiful music.[57] Cox's appreciation is as apparent as his description is vibrant: "We had two excellent fiddlers; and as several of the gentlemen had wives, we got up three or four balls, in which the exhilarating amusement of the 'light fantastic toe' was kept up to a late hour in the morning. We walked through no lazy minuets; we had no simpering quadrilles; no languishing half-dying waltzes; no, ours was the exercise of health; the light lively reel, or the rattling good old-fashioned country dance, in which the graceful though untutored movements of the North-West females would have put to the blush many of the more refined votaries of Terpsichore."

While labelling the dances as "balls," Cox explicitly rejected the "lazy minuets," "simpering quadrilles," and "languishing half-dying waltzes" that were associated with balls in eastern settlements. Cox suggested that these genres were effeminate and aristocratic and were bypassed for the rigorous "exercise of health," characterized by the "light lively reel" and the "rattling good old-fashioned country dance." These likely consisted of partner dances characterized by chain, round, and figure-eight floor patterns, while the Scotch reels allowed for solo performances and opportunities to "dazzle onlookers with a number of fancy steps more or less in place."[58] Cox described the "graceful though untutored movements" of the Indigenous women, paying them a compliment while also suggesting that their conduct and etiquette would offend Christian sentiments. In this prominent forum of interaction, dancing brought the gentlemen, servants, and Indigenous women surrounding the post together in recreation and socialization.

Ross Cox described a summertime gathering outside of Fort William. He was struck by the incredible diversity of those assembled: "Most part of the *voyageurs,* soldiers, Indians, half-breeds, &c., were encamped outside the fort in tents, leathern lodges, mat covered huts, or wigwams. On inquiry, I ascertained that the aggregate number of the persons in and about the establishment was composed of natives of the following countries: viz. England, Ireland, Scotland, United States of America, the Gold Coast of Africa, the Sandwich Islands, Bengal, Canada, with various tribes of Indians, and a mixed progeny of Creoles, or half-breeds. What a strange medley! Here were assembled, on the shores of this inland sea, Episcopalians, Presbyterians, Methodists, Sunworshippers, men from all parts of the world, and whose creeds were 'wide as the poles asunder.'"[59]

The years after 1812 witnessed a diversification in the personnel of the fur trade, with the inclusion of Hawaiian (Sandwich) Islanders and Irish American personnel, such as Cox, from the American Fur Company. Rather than segregating into groups based on ethnicity, language, or religion, the diverse peoples seem to have engaged in lively interactions outside the fort. Cox described how "immediately around the fort the scene was enlivened by animating groups of women, soldiers, *voyageurs,* and Indians, dancing, singing, drinking, and gambling; in their features comprising all the shades of the human species, and in their dress, all the varied hues of the rainbow."[60] The cross-cultural interactions of soldiers, voyageurs, and Indigenous men and women often consisted of song and dance. We are not granted details as to what was sung or which instruments were employed, yet this is one of the best first-hand descriptions of the diverse gatherings outside of the forts' gates during the summer rendezvous.

The trading post network supported many musicians. Fur traders could request supplies, practise their musical instruments, and host dances. Some fur traders gained a reputation for their musical talent. A long-standing overwintering partner of the NWC in the Athabasca region named Willard-Ferdinand Wentzel played the violin. He lived and worked for twenty years around the Subarctic posts of Slave Lake and Great Bear Lake. Wentzel's journal and letters reveal anguish at his perceived banishment from civilization. Suffering emotional privations and periodic starvation during his long tenure in some of the most distant trading posts of the northwest, he wrote in his letter to McKenzie on 30 April 1811: "I am quite alone at the Fort, not even an animal to keep me company. Such are the vicissitudes of fickle fortune! A place where I had never great cause to complain! But, to use an Indian phrase, *Cooloo,* I am still alive, why should I complain."[61] In the next statement, Wentzel hinted that one of his main coping mechanisms was music. On this occasion, he was desperate for new music to play on his fiddle: "Could I persuade myself that my little friend Johnny would recollect me, I should request a few new tunes of him for which I would make any return in my power. I have some music to which he is welcome by only sending a note, for I have entirely given up the flute and only scrape, now and then, on the fiddle. I beg you will please remember me to him."[62] John Franklin stopped in at Wentzel's trading post on his 1820s polar expedition, consulting on Indigenous customs, language, and survival in the far north.[63] Wentzel was apparently quite the host, and Franklin described him as "an excellent musician!"[64]

Instruments

As previous pages illustrate, instrumental music was a highly valued social pursuit interwoven into the fabric of the fur trade. It was employed alongside the most significant social events of the year. Musical instruments made their way to the trading posts through a variety of mechanisms alongside supporting materials such as strings and songbooks. The fur trade network was extensive, and instruments had to be paddled and portaged long distances. From the earliest times, this factor limited the import of larger musical instruments. In the seventeenth and early eighteenth centuries, the French imported and traded large numbers of *bombardes*, small double-reed woodwind instruments.[65] The archaeological record suggests that perhaps even more prolifically traded and more durable were jaw harps (referred to as "Jew's Harps") by the late eighteenth century. Jaw harps have been uncovered by archaeologists at numerous excavation sites around historic trading posts. One such example was excavated from the Rossdale site near Fort Edmonton. It is described in the Royal Alberta Museum's excavation summary as the "first evidence of European recreational activities on the site during fur trade times."[66] This is a considerable honour for such a small piece of metal. Musical instruments in the fur trade were generally of two types: medium-sized instruments such as violins and flutes carried with and kept in the private possession of fur traders, and those stocked in the inventories of the trading posts such as jaw harps and violin strings.

Jaw harps were popular small instruments that proliferated throughout Europe and much of the world during the industrial revolution. A Prussian army deserter in the late eighteenth century brought German Saxon manufacturing techniques to England, establishing the Troman firm and helping Birmingham England emerge as the top world producer of these instruments in the nineteenth century.[67] Rarely described by fur traders in their accounts of the trading post dances, jaw harps seem to have been purchased by servants and voyageurs and traded with Indigenous peoples. They were simple, durable, and produced a characteristic "twang." John Howison travelled from Montreal to Lake Ontario in the second decade of the nineteenth century. He described an encounter with

Fig. 8.3 Excavated jaw harps from the HBC and NWC era around 1810–13. The left (broken) is from Fort White Earth and the right from the Rossdale site near Fort Edmonton.

a Haudenosaunee man who had fought alongside the British in the War of 1812, and who got their attention with "war whoops" performed "in great style." Having gained an audience with Howison's group, the man "seemed anxious to exert his powers still further, and accordingly took two Jews harps from a little bag, playing upon each alternately."[68] The sounds of the war whoop and jaw harps were central to this cross-cultural encounter. Starting with an Indigenous vocalization, attention shifted to the smallest musical instrument imported in large numbers by the fur trade. In the hands of the Haudenosaunee man, this event was worthy of note to Howison and his party.

Fur trade inventories from 1760–1840 do not exist for most of the Montreal merchants. The NWC's extant inventories are patchy, but the final two years before amalgamation with the HBC are comprehensive. The snapshot from 1820–21 provides us with prices and stock from this time and some indication of what would have been carried by the NWC during the previous decades of operation. The inventories reveal insights into the distribution and pricing of goods. Jaw harps were carried in two materials, iron and brass. The Lake of Two Mountains inventory lists "2 Gross" (288) Iron "Jew's Harps" worth 13s 6p and four dozen (48) Brass "Jew's Harps" worth 6s.[69] The unit price of the iron harps in this district works out to be 0.56 p while brass harps were nearly triple that value, at 1.5 p each. Many of the inventories do not distinguish which kind of harp is for sale, although iron appears to be the more common variety. At Fort William, Lake Winnipeg, and Lake Athabasca, jaw harps were valued at 1.16p and 1.17p each, more than twice the price as at Lake of Two Mountains near Montreal. The relatively low price of 1p in the Columbia department on the west coast seems to be a result of their prolific numbers in that inventory.

Table 8.1 Jaw harps at North West Company trading posts, 1821

Location	Number of harps	Total value (£)	Price per unit (£)
Lake of Two Mountains[1]	iron: 288 (24 doz) brass: 48 (4 doz)	iron: "/13/6 brass: "/6/"	iron: "/"/0.56 brass: "/"/1.5
Columbia Dept.[2]	323 (26 11/12 doz)	1/6/11	"/"/1
Fort William[3]	75 (6 ¼ doz)	"/7/3	"/"/1.16
Athabasca Dept.[4]	44 (3 2/3 doz)	"/4/3	"/"/1.16
Bas de La Riviere[5]	6 (1/2 doz)	"/"/7	"/"/1.17
Fort Alexander[6]	6 (1/2 doz)	"/"/7	"/"/1.17

1 "Lake 2 Mountains Inv. Cont.," *North West Company Account Book 1821,* 132.
2 "Columbia River Inventory Continued," *North West Company Account Book 1821,* 12.
3 "Fort William Inventory Continued," *North West Company Account Book 1821,* 169.
4 "Athabasca Inventory Continued," *North West Company Account Book 1821,* 5.
5 "Bas de la Riviere Inventory Cont.," *North West Company Account Book 1820–1821,* 170.
6 "Fort Alexander Inventory Continued," *North West Company Account Book 1821,* 110.

Table 8.2 Violin strings at North West Company trading posts, 1820–21

Location	Number of sets	Total value (£)	Price per set (£)	Price per string (£)
Fort William (1820)[1]	33	3/11/6	"/2/2	"/"/6.5
Fort William (1820)[2]	25 ½	5/2/"	"/4/"	"/1/"
Fort William (1821)[3]	80	4/"/"	"/1/"	"/"/3
Athabasca (1820)[4]	2	"/4/4	"/2/2	"/"/6.5
Athabasca (1821)[5]	3	"/6/6	"/2/2	"/"/6.5
Columbia River (1820)[6]	2	None listed	–	–

1 "Fort William Inventory Cont.," *North West Company Account Book 1820,* 14.
2 "Amount brot. forward," *North West Company Account Book 1820,* 15.
3 "Fort William Inventory Continued," *North West Company Account Book 1821,* 176.
4 "Atha Quip. Inventory Cont.," *North West Company Account Book 1820,* 72.
5 "Athabasca Inventory Continued," *North West Company Account Book 1820–1821,* 50.
6 "Amount Bt Forw," *North West Company Account Book 1820,* 261.

Violin or fiddle strings are listed in inventories of the NWC during the years 1820–21. There was a large stock of violin strings at Fort William, which would have supplied people and trading posts throughout the region. The prices for violin strings in 1820 at Fort William varied from 6.5p to 1s per string, suggesting that two different varieties were available. Considerable fluctuations in price are demonstrated by the records, as the following year violin strings were listed at the same location for only 3p. In the Athabasca department, the price per string remained on the high end at 6.5p. In every case, between 1820 and 1821, the cost of purchasing a single violin string was many times higher than buying a jaw harp. The average price of a single violin string of the cheaper variety was around 6p, while a jaw harp was around 1p. The contrast is stark. One violin requires four strings – a total price of 24p or 2s – and this is required in addition to the violin itself. We can infer that playing the violin would have been prohibitively expensive to many except the officers and clerks of the trading posts.

Two violins have been located in the NWC inventories from 1820–21. These suggest that the NWC did indeed transport and sell them, albeit in limited numbers. One is listed for one pound at the English River (or Churchill River) post[70] while the other is listed with a bow for two pounds in the Columbia department.[71] These were luxury items and very expensive considering the salary of most people working in the fur trade. The only other musical instruments identified in the inventory lists are two tambourines listed at the Lake of Two Mountains post in 1821 for 1s apiece.[72]

The most comprehensive account of musical materials held at any trading post before 1840 is Edward Ermatinger's list of instruments and sheet music inside a "parcel" at Fort Vancouver in 1826. This remarkable document lists a duet for the flute, six duets for the violin, one duet of an overture, an instruction book for the violin, and two songbooks of "Scotch Reels." This list includes "1 Duet for two Flutes – Laubersolerz, 6 Duet for violins Viotte, 1 Duet Overture to Lodoiska, 1 Instruction for Violin, 2 Old Books Scotch Reels- Sundry Sheets Psalms, my air Kind Deaice, 1 Small Bugle no mouth piece … 1 violin bow." It is striking that both "high" and "low" music are here represented, with classical pieces alongside folk tunes. There are books for solo players (introduction books), duets, and social dances for large groups. It is notable that there are so many duets. Ornate compositions for two instruments were obviously learned and performed at the trading posts, yet in order for this to happen there had to be two musicians with instruments who could read musical notation. Duets would have served as a platform for intimate one-on-one interaction and social bonding between fur traders. They could also be performed for others as entertainment, or at a dance. The books of Scotch reels suggest that fiddle tunes played at the social dances were not only transmitted through the oral folk tradition but were also supplemented with printed music. The bugle with no mouthpiece and violin bow demonstrate that musical materials, even if discarded, were still valuable and kept together in parcels.[73]

Musical instruments and orders were often personally arranged. In Edward Ermatinger's *Memorandum Book of 1821–22*, he reminded himself to "send home for … goulding & co. Pegs & violin."[74] In his book *Memorandums for 1823*, Ermatinger makes more notes to "send home" for musical instruments, this time for "a Fife and a Third Flute or G. Flute."[75] By 1826, Ermatinger seems to have been communicating with his brother Francis and assisting other fur traders to procure musical supplies from Montreal. He made a note "To write my Brother about Mr McLeans Violin."[76] Ermatinger continued supplying music to fur traders after he retired in 1828. The following year, in 1829, Thomas Dears wrote to Ermatinger from Thompsons River indicating that he would like to "make a small purchase of some of your Music."[77] Writing from New Caledonia in 1830, John Tod mentioned receiving some of Ermatinger's sheet music from his brother Francis.[78] Ermatinger ordered new flute springs for Tod, in addition to violin strings, pegs, and bridges.[79] This variety of musical material went far beyond what was stocked on the shelves of the trading post. Clearly significant were these networks of acquisition, connecting the distant trading posts with musical merchandise in Montreal.

The enormous difficulty and expense in obtaining violins and parts inspired some people to craft their own in and around the trading posts. This activity certainly occurred more than is recorded in the written record, as many carpenters, labourers, and Indigenous craftsmen would not have left any record beyond the instrument itself. Some literate fur traders, such as Thomas Dears at Fort Connelly in what is now central British Columbia, did leave a record. In 1833, he reported that his three-year-old daughter sang along when played "life let us cherish" "upon a violin I have made and it amuses me sometimes."[80] This account is noteworthy because it provides the name of a known traditional tune, one composed in 1795 and adapted to English as a popular waltz in Britain and America. It was a tune often used in quadrilles or square dances for the basket figure.[81] While Dears does not get into details about the construction of his violin, it was likely made from wood foraged from around his trading post on Bear Lake.

There was a tradition on Hudson Bay of Indigenous men carving their own fiddles since at least the 1840s. The description of a Christmas ball at York Factory in 1843 by Robert Ballantyne is one of the most elaborate and detailed. Here he described the fiddle and dance traditions where they persisted longest with the HBC, at the Christmas balls. He notes the centrality of Scottish reels in a multi-cultural dance:

> On several benches and chairs sat all the Orkneymen and Canadian half-breeds of the establishment, in their Sunday jackets and capotes; while here and there the dark visage of an Indian peered out from among their white faces. But round the stove-which had been removed to one side to leave space for the dancers- the strangest group was collected. Squatting down on the floor, in every ungraceful attitude imaginable, sat about a dozen Indian women, dressed in printed calico gowns, the chief peculiarity of which was the immense size of the balloon-shaped sleeves, and the extreme scantiness, both in length and width, of the skirts. They were chatting and talking to each other with great volubility, occasionally casting a glance behind them, where at least half a dozen infants stood bolt upright in their tight-laced cradles. On a chair in a corner near the stove sat a young good-looking Indian, with a fiddle of his own making beside him. This was our Paganini; and beside him sat an Indian boy with a kettle-drum, on which he tapped occasionally, as if anxious that the ball should begin.[82]

Fiddles and fiddlers were in demand at the trading posts because of the popularity of its music and step dancing traditions. Most fur traders hailed from Scotland, the British Isles, or the St Lawrence, areas where these forms were very popular during this period. Yet here the musicians were Indigenous, likely the "homeguard" Omushkego Cree from around York Factory. The homemade fiddle and kettle drum, in Indigenous hands, were used to play and accompany Scottish reels for dancing. The end product was something novel, reflecting the cultural diversity, exchanges, and collaboration common in the dances of the fur trade.

Sheet Music

The evidence of sheet music in the fur trade is fragmentary, yet it is safe to say that a good amount passed through the trading post network. Like musical instruments, sheet music was carefully stored with personal possessions.

Fur traders took these possessions into the trading posts when they started working there and usually took them out once they moved on. The larger trading posts developed libraries, yet most of their contents before the 1840s are unknown. In the lists of books that do exist from this period, music books are absent.[83] It is again in the personal correspondences and papers of individual fur traders that reference to sheet music exists. For instance, a piece of correspondence from John Askin in 1778 revealed that he was not only purchasing violins from Montreal but importing sheet music from Detroit, writing in a letter to Sampson Fleming, "many thanks for your Country Dance Book."[84] This presumably served him well during his weekly winter dances at Michilimackinac, and may have influenced fur trade dances in the area more broadly. In the 1810s, Ross Cox revealed in his memoir that his NWC canoe brigade travelled with a small library. This included a book of hymns and two unnamed songbooks.[85] While it is unknown whether these books were for voice or instrument, their inclusion in the small travelling library signals their importance. Taken together, the historical evidence suggests that both "high" classical music and "low" fiddle music entered the trading post repertoires via song sheets and music books.

Edward Ermatinger's private notebooks provide details and further evidence of his role in trafficking in musical materials, including sheet music, to trading posts. In the *Memorandum Book from 1821–22*, he writes to "Send home for M.R. King's general treatises on Music & c." He ordered flutes and fifes in 1823, alongside an "Instruction Books for the Flutes."[86] These books of sheet music came at a considerable cost. "Music Book Borin" is listed at four shillings.[87] In Ermatinger's order from 1829, he lists "the Paid Dance for Music" as costing twelve shillings, while "5th music 4 Songs" is listed for six shillings.[88] These were significant prices that underscore the class component of musical literacy in the fur trade. Sheet music not only came at a considerable cost but required the formal training and musical literacy that most servants, voyageurs, and Indigenous musicians did not have. This is not to say that they could not be exceptional musicians of the first rate. But song books and sheet music would have likely introduced new tunes that spread beyond the owner and potentially ended up in the repertoires of fiddlers.

The waltz arrived in the Hudson Bay fur trade directly from Europe in the fall of 1819. Fittingly, it was brought by Swiss and German settlers that landed at York Factory en route to Red River. They brought both the sheet music and the dance, staying long enough at York Factory to make a big impression. John Tod had been working with the HBC since 1811 and remembered this occasion as particularly noteworthy.[89] That evening, a memorable musical encounter

manifested that was recalled in vivid detail decades later. The fur trader Edward
Ermatinger quickly learned how to play the waltzes on his violin: "It was the
first time in my life that I had witnessed a Waltz dance – what with the heart
stirring strains of Your violin [Edward Ermatinger] – the agile, but graceful
movements of the Swiss peasant girls, in their neat modest dresses, and the
beautiful time they all Kept to Your music, on the rough hewn floor of that old
Colony Store – My whole Soul became fascinated in the novelty of the Scene –
novel it certainly was to me, who had never Seen Such a Sight before – In all
this excess of admiration however, Young as I was, mind You there was nothing
approaching in the slightest degree to any thing inimical to a virtuous feeling."[90]

This noteworthy event took place at York Factory due to the arrival of the
Red River settlers and the presence of a young Edward Ermatinger who was an
avid musician and violinist. The dance was hosted in the storeroom rather than
the dining hall. The next day, the musicians retired to an old guardroom. After
Ermatinger and Tod played their instruments with an unnamed German man,
he left them a transcribed collection of waltzes. This remained in the fur trade
for decades and had an influence on the musical life at various trading posts:

> Undoubtedly for the first time in the historical records of the eternally
> frozin regions of H Bay, that had appeared on its bleak, ice-bound
> coast – On the evening succeeding that of the dance, having discover'd
> that the Father of the amiable Louisa whom probably You still remem-
> ber, was an amateur on the flute, we all three played together in the old
> Guard room, and at parting for the night the old gentleman presented
> me with a half bound music book, containing a large collection of
> German Waltzes – Nearly one-third of the said book however, had been
> merely cross lined – A considerable part of which You, afterwards, filled
> up with Your own compositions, and copies from other music, that had
> been sent to You by Your own Father – Amongst the former is the much
> admired "H Bay March." These, and many others, in Your own hand
> writing, have all been Sacredly preserved, and in my possession to this
> day, and, should my successors obey my injuctions, will be found in my
> coffin when dead.[91]

This is the earliest description found to date of the waltz in the Hudson
Bay fur trade. It arose from the unusual circumstance of Red River colonists
arriving on an uncommon and unwise (as it turned out) route for settlement.
Yet their arrival in the 1810s influenced not only the political and commercial

dynamics of the fur trade but also its musical culture. Their time at the trading posts and then Red River represented a significant new cultural influence in fur trade country. The Swiss and German immigrants provided lessons and partners for dancing on this occasion and untold others. They transmitted a new dance style that had gained popularity in Europe over the previous decades. The songbook acquired from this occasion remained in the possession of Edward Ermatinger and then John Tod through the 1820s to 1840s, and as it moved from the Northern Department to New Caledonia its pages accumulated musical compositions. The most noteworthy of these from a historical perspective seems to have been Lawrence Ermatinger's own "Hudson Bay Company March."[92] This song and the book itself has unfortunately not been located and is absent from the Tod family fonds at the Archives of British Columbia. It would be a major source of information about the music history of the fur trade. Perhaps, in accordance with Tod's wishes, he was indeed buried with the songbook.

The Birth of the Métis, Amalgamation of 1821, and De-institutionalization of Fiddle Music

The arrival of the Selkirk settlers in the 1810s had a number of profound implications for the fur trade and Indigenous peoples living around Red River. Métis national identity was first articulated against the backdrop of this settlement and the HBC decrees that challenged traditional Indigenous livelihoods and the viability of the St Lawrence fur trade. The Red River settlement caused various disturbances to the operations of the Montreal merchants, specifically the NWC. Red River was at the centre of their trans-continental trading post network, and it relied on the pemmican produced in that area for the voyageurs who manned the canoe brigades. HBC governor Miles MacDonell's 1814 Pemmican Proclamation was a desperate attempt to save the settlement by outlawing the export of pemmican by anyone in the area. This was a drastic and disruptive measure that inevitably led to confrontation. The Battle of Seven Oaks two years later occurred when HBC governor Semple rode out with a party of twenty men to intercept a NWC caravan. Pierre Falcon's "chanson de la grenouillère" documented the ensuing battle and complete annihilation of Semple's party. It has remained a centrepiece of Métis national consciousness and is still sung as the Métis national anthem.[93] The song presents the perspective of the "bois-brûlé" – an early self-designator of the Métis – as an Indigenous people with rights to the land. In opposition, the HBC and Selkirk settlers had arrived "pour piller notre pays." Métis national consciousness was articulated explicitly against the HBC's proclamations and settler encroachment. After 1821, the HBC imposed monopoly and restrictions against free trade, providing an ongoing rallying point for Métis national identity. Similarly, Métis fiddle music and "jigging" flourished against the backdrop of increasing restrictions by the HBC. These musical traditions eventually became subdued at the trading posts, yet continued outside of the walls and remained central to Métis culture.

The biggest single disruptive influence on the music culture of the fur trade was that of governor George Simpson. When he first arrived from London in 1820, he was forced to learn not only the economics of the fur trade but also its customs. Much to his chagrin, he discovered a generous and inclusive music and dance culture that seemed to pervade every gathering. This is something he would come to consider an extraordinary encumbrance on business. In 1820, Simpson hired canoemen around Montreal, including Mohawk guides. His journal entry for August 1820 revealed his reservations about engaging these men, writing that "Their terms are most extravagant." Yet Simpson records how he "Gave the people a dance in the Evening."[94] "Giving a dance" meant hosting with all the attendant obligations: time to dance, liquor to drink, and sometimes food to eat. Simpson soon began to employ it strategically. For instance, on Sunday 1 October, Simpson noted in his journal "our provisions are very scarce," yet he "Gave the people a dance in the evening."[95] Perhaps the dance cheered the mood and took the men's minds off their suffering and need for provisions. Yet this night of merriment had predictable consequences, with Simpson recording the next day "The debauch of last night has rendered some of the men unfit for service to day."[96] According to Simpson's calculations, this encumbrance on productivity was to some degree counterbalanced by increased liquor sales. He stated that if he had "a good stock of spirits it would work down their extravagant wages, the small quantity sold last night amounts to £43."[97] Dances could divert the men from their dissatisfaction and hunger while proving a captive market for liquor sold at inflated prices.

Dances were a key social arena for business manoeuvring. They served as a reward for the servants and opportunity for the fur trader to further his interests. In his first season, Simpson overwintered at Fort Wedderburn on Lake Athabasca in the shadow of the NWC's larger and better situated Fort Chipewyan. He wrote candidly about promising his men a dram and dance to entice them to do things they were reluctant to do. On 28 October 1820, with their stock of provisions reduced to four bags of flour, Simpson wrote that "if the Lake does not soon set fast, I fear we shall be exposed to serious privations."[98] Yet in his efforts to better compete with the NWC, Simpson determined that a new building had to be constructed on a rock outcropping near the water behind their fort. He wrote that "it is a difficult undertaking for the people in their present half famished state, I however pointed out the necessity of the measure, and promised them a Dance when finished if they would commence operations tomorrow, (Sunday) which after a dram they cheerfully agreed to do."[99] Promising a dance and alcohol to entice his malnourished servants to continue working, Simpson effectively got what he wanted. He understood that dances held great favour among his men and used this to his advantage. Dances were important social occasions for the exchange of information and gossip, as well as the re-engagement of employees. In a telling passage, Simpson made clear his expectations if a dance was to be provided: "Pray gain all the information you can about the movements of the enemy, and what their strength, intentions and prospects are. If it is absolutely necessary to be at the expense of giving the people a dance & drink, it may be a good opportunity of re-engaging them." In his estimation, the costs associated with hosting the dance might be worthwhile if it meant re-engaging the best men. In this period, there was a real danger that the most skilled and valuable employees would be lured away by the competition.

Due to dancing's central role in interactions with the NWC over this fateful winter of 1820–21 and Simpson's record-keeping, it can be traced in some detail. In October, Simpson had his men arrest Simon McGillivray, collaring him and locking him inside Fort Wedderburn. He would remain confined inside the HBC fort until the night of 4 December 1820, when he was dancing reels with his wife, and managed to escape.[100] The inherently loud and distracting atmosphere of the dance, with its accompanying inebriation, undoubtedly facilitated his escape. For the remainder of the winter, Simpson depended on the full allegiance and efforts of his men. He catered to their customs over the holiday season, including on New Year's Eve or Hogmanay to the Scots: "The Festivities of the New Year commenced at four O'Clock this morning when the people honoured me with a salute of Fire arms, and in half an hour afterwards the whole Inmates of our Garrison assembled in the hall dressed out in their best clothes, and were regaled in a suitable manner with a few flaggon's Rum and some Cakes; a full allowance of Buffaloe meat was served out to them and pint of Spirits for each man; the Women were also entertained to the utmost of our ability. In the course of the day St. Picquè & Rondeau contrary to Mr Keith's instructions paid us a visit ... the people have been enjoying themselves with a dance and seem much gratified by the attentions paid them."[101] From the employees' perspective, this day was a welcome reprieve from work and the deprivations endured over the previous months on Lake Athabasca.

Yet rather than the anticipated outcome, Simpson expressed frustration the following day. There was not an immediate return to normal productivity. He reported that "our people have been in a state of intoxication all day and very troublesome." However, it was necessary to "humour them at present," he wrote, "as I am anxious to renew their engagements without delay." While their productivity had declined for days due to the festivities, Simpson needed to remain benevolent to secure the men's allegiance. He could not be too rigid in the allowance for time off work, space inside the trading post buildings, and provisions necessary for holiday festivities. Simpson understood that alcohol worked both to the benefit and detriment of the company's interests, placating servants and serving to recuperate their wages, even while contributing to inefficiency. As his supply of rum depleted, Simpson expressed regret at the lost profits. The holiday season impressed upon him that his employees seemed "inclined to part with a considerable proportion of their superfluous money."[102] Simpson was willing to give the men a dance, but it is clear that commercial competition and the profit motive were always at the forefront of his mind.

After the amalgamation of the HBC and NWC in 1821, the musical culture of the trading posts faced increasing obstacles and operational adversities. Occasions for instrumental dance music were restricted. A dual-pronged assault was led by economically and morally minded reforms. Despite this mounting intolerance, personal writings indicate that music continued to play an important role in the lives of fur traders, especially during winter holidays and in smaller and more informal settings. Many fur traders continued to keep their instruments with them at the trading posts, providing recreation during the long and isolating winters. Yet it appears music re-oriented from a collective focus involving the various people of the post and vicinity to more exclusive musical interactions between fur traders. In John Tod's very first letter to Edward Ermatinger after the latter had retired in 1828, he complained about the changes being wrought on the culture of the fur trade. In particular, he bemoaned the new attitude toward music. He reminisced on younger days with Ermatinger, "when we could indulge in our favourite and delightful amusement – music – and when the pleasing sound of a Violin & Flute used to be considered no crime nor looked upon with the digree [sic] of severity we have sometimes witness'd since our separation."[103] Tod's correspondence to Ermatinger reveals that he continued to cherish his flute and sheet music, keeping them close at hand when working at different posts.[104] At a more solitary post on McLeods Lake in 1826, Tod wrote of making music with a "fellow labourer in the vineyard," a Sekani woman. He wrote that if he is "condemned to lead a few more Years of solitude here I may probably commence practicing again on the violin – my fellow labourer in the vineyard is possessed of an excellent ear for music & never fails to accompany me on the Flute with her voice when I take up the instrument – I shall not trouble You with any order at this time."[105] Here is a rare instance of a fur trader describing in writing how he was making music with an Indigenous woman. With Tod playing the flute and the Sekani woman singing, a musical relationship was formed that crossed cultural boundaries. It seemed to hold a special significance for Tod. When Ermatinger replied to Tod's letter and further inquired "what is become of the girl who used to sing at McLeods Lake," Tod responded that "in plain language she still continues the only companion of my solitude – without her, or some other substitute, life, in such a wretched place as this, would be altogether insupportable."[106] Here is the pattern of an overwintering fur trader using music as a way to connect with the people around him to overcome loneliness and isolation.

Music seems to have been practised more often in the smaller buildings at trading posts after the amalgamation of 1821. For instance, Ballantyne reported that when he visited Norway House in the 1840s, it was the clerk's house that was periodically overtaken by musical activity. He described "many a happy hour" spent on the clerk's bed listening to songs and stories, describing how "the loud laugh, uproarious song, and sound of the screeching flute or scraping fiddle, issued from the open doors and windows."[107] John Tod described in a letter the acoustics of a small room at Oxford House that resonated favourably with the flute and violin. He declared that "one of the rooms here is so admirably adapted for the sound of a violin and Flute, (both on which I still continue to make a noise occasionally) that I have frequently been tempted to make use of them in course of this last winter."[108] This kind of mindfulness toward favourable acoustic spaces suggests their importance to musically inclined fur traders such as Tod, who described a small room in the trading post rather than the main hall.

After the amalgamation of 1821, large dances still occurred on special occasions and holidays. Although Fort William's importance declined dramatically, it remained an important post and was visited by fur trader Robert Ballantyne in the 1840s. The post-master "turned out to be an impressive player of Scottish reels on the violin."[109] Mentioning that both his companion and the post-master were "genuine Highlanders," Ballantyne identified the music of the influential Scottish fiddler Niel Gow. He described distinctive melodic ornaments such as trills and the dance styles of the reel and strathspey. Yet remarkably, the post-master is described as self-taught, presumably having spent much of his leisure time at the fort practising: "This post-master turned out to be a first-rate player of Scottish reels on the violin. He was self-taught, and truly the sweetness and precision with which he played every note and trill of the rapid reel and strathspey, would have made Niel Gow himself envious. So beautiful and inspiriting were they, that Mr B--- and our host, who were both genuine Highlanders, jumped simultaneously from their seats, in an ecstasy of enthusiasm, and danced to the lively music till the very walls shook, much to the amusement of the two ladies, who having been both born in Canada, could not so well appreciate the music. Indeed, the musician himself looked a little astonished, being quite ignorant of the endearing recollections and associations recalled to the memory of the two Highlanders by the rapid notes of his violin." Due to the music's powerful effect, more songs were demanded. The musician had little choice but to continue performing for his guests. Many of the dances required partners, and the gentlemen "sent over to the men's houses" for the French Canadian wife of Pierre Lattinville and her two daughters, who were known to reside close-by.[110] They arrived shortly at the ball room,

and after much coyness, blushing, and hesitation, at last stood up, and under the inspiring influence of the violin, we

Danced till we were like to fa'
The reel o'Tullochgorum!

And did not cease till the lateness of the hour, and the exhaustion of our musician, compelled us to give in.[111]

Musically inclined post-masters were often recognized and appreciated for their talents. When John Henry Lefroy set out on his journey to find the Magnetic North in 1843, he reported in a letter from Fort Simpson on the Mackenzie River that in the north, music "is rather a favourite pursuit."[112] In a following letter he writes that "Mr McLean is a good flute player." He attributed this to the extreme isolation McLean had endured for years: "he had need of some resource." "There have been and are," Lefroy reported, "some excellent and even first rate musicians in the country."[113]

Yet countervailing forces and policies were introduced in the early 1820s that operated to suppress music and dance at the trading posts. When George Simpson became governor of an amalgamated company in 1821, he worked to promote efficiency and reduce what he deemed unnecessary expenses through a program known as "retrenchment."[114] He laid off much of the French Canadian and Métis workforce, including many of the most experienced voyageurs.[115] The number of employees was reduced by over 50 per cent between the years 1821 and 1825, from 1,983 to 827.[116] He simultaneously took a series of steps to limit what he considered the wasteful spending associated with dances. The HBC's council minutes from 1822–24 laid the groundwork for "trimming personnel rolls" and regulating the retirement of servants and families. The council insisted with "vigour" that "education and religion be integrated into post family life," not only for its own sake but because trading posts were increasingly being visited by members of the clergy.[117] In his journal from 1824–25, Simpson complained that the fur traders, in passing through Norway and Cumberland House were in the habit of "indulging themselves in taking a few holydays at the Establishments."[118] He condemns the "heavy expence" that attended these amusements and the prolonged work stoppages that ensued. Precious hours were wasted and "extra provisions are consumed" when "Balls are given and the business frequently neglected."[119] Simpson made his position against regular dances clear, and yet it was not so easy to stop the deeply engrained customs of the fur trade.

The reason Norway House at the north end of Lake Winnipeg was singled out was that it increased in importance after amalgamation. It became somewhat similar to the trading depots in the western Great Lakes that had served as places of rendezvous during the summer months. The dances linked to these occasions became aggressively targeted by Simpson. "The Establishment of Norway House alone has occasioned more expence," Simpson wrote, "in this way since the Coalition than the profits of its Trade would defray."[120] It was not just the material expenses but also the wasted travel time that concerned Simpson. In a letter from Simpson to John McLeod on 7 July 1826, he affirmed that "no supplies of any kind be delivered" except from the orders of Mr McTavish in an attempt to address the "irregularity in the affairs" that had occurred "for several years past." Simpson reiterated that although it now served as a depot, "it is perfectly understood that none of the expenses usually connected with Depot such as public messes, balls, etc, etc. are to be incurred there and that Craft make no longer stay there than sufficient to arrange their baggage or cargoes."[121] Now that the HBC had a monopoly, it could enforce such rules that disrupted the time-honoured social traditions of the fur trade. Arrivals and departures had long been celebrated with dancing. So too the summer rendezvous that brought men from the coasts into contact with those from the interior. So too the celebrations marking significant arrivals, weddings, and reunions. These were to be no more.

The council minutes of the HBC's Northern Department in 1825 demonstrate a move toward policies that promoted Christianity and "proper" moral conduct. Particular scrutiny was applied to the servants of the company and Indigenous peoples. Minute 107 concerns goods allotted to Indigenous children who had left their parents to join the HBC's Missionary Society school. Minute 108 commits generally to promote positive values in Indigenous peoples, with "industry encouraged, vice repressed, and morality inculcated. Spirituous Liquors gradually discontinued."[122] The final ten minutes were designed to inculcate "religious improvement" throughout Rupert's Land, including provisions stating "Immoral habits checked – opposites encouraged," and a re-affirmation that "divine service [is] to be read Sundays."[123] There is no acknowledgement of the dances that were often held on Sundays at trading posts in years prior.

Dances were also curtailed during the holiday seasons. Writing from Fort Garry in 1827, J.G. McTavish described the celebrations as considerably restrained compared to those of the previous era: "the days are gone by when such assemblies were enlivened by the song and the dance, the soul drenched in wine, or the carcass snugly consigned to oblivion below the board. Wonderful indeed are the conquests of psalm singing and amazing its power in giving an edge to the blunted conscience." A different mentality and morality had prevailed, evident in McTavish's dry comment about the zealous "dotards" who "will tell you gravely that the high-way to hell runs through the mazes of a Highland Reel."[124] This is the most memorable comment regarding the restrictions placed on fiddle music and dance at the trading posts in the 1820s. Reels, the most popular genre of music played at fur trade dances, was specifically identified for its corrupting effects. It was considered dangerous to the soul. That reels tended to be popular among the lower classes certainly may have contributed to this assessment. In the context of the fur trade, reels had been the best vehicle for uniting fur traders with voyageurs, servants, and Indigenous peoples, bridging divisions of race, class, and gender. This inclusive activity was now being actively censured.

The expanding influence of Anglican, Methodist, and Catholic Oblate missionaries undoubtedly hastened this transformation. Between the 1820s and 1840s, missionaries worked and travelled throughout the trading post network. Red River became a hub of Christian missionary activity. The Church Missionary Society (CMS) was founded in 1799 by the Clapham Sect of the Church of England, establishing themselves at Red River with the Reverend John West.[125] This presence helped transform the soundscape of Red River. While travelling on the river on a Sunday in 1825–26, Rev. Jones reported seeing "on a stage, not 18 inches from the water, a party of Half Breed young women singing 'Walls's Hymns.'"[126] Reverend J. Smithurst reported Indigenous girls singing near Red River on 26 June 1840: the "tune was the hundredth, Shirland, and Auburn, the girls alone singing the soft parts, in the latter tune which had a fine effect. All was managed with the utmost exactness not a note wrong and sung in very correct time."[127] Similarly, Mr John Roberts reported hearing "Guide Me O Thou Great Jehovah," coming from the "Indian Church" at Red River on 19 July 1842.[128] The Red River school imported a number of music books, for instance *Watt's Divine and Moral Songs*, *Nursery Rhymes*, *Hymns for the Infant Mind*, and others.[129] The sons and daughters of fur traders were now likely to be exposed to Christian religious music. People from the trading posts around Red River were recruited to join the choirs of the missionaries. For instance, on 1 November 1846, "There were eight of the singers from the Fort here to join with my singers...I am also wishing my singers to chant the 95th and 100th Psalms in the morning service, and the 67th in the evening service. I shall be able to teach them this the better now they have heard the Fort singers Chant."[130] On 28 December of that same year, Smirthurst hosted singers from the Indian Church and the fort, passing the evening "singing over a variety of sacred Music, consisting of Psalm tunes, Chants and Anthems."[131] While the epicentre of activity was at Red River, missionaries dispersed throughout the trading post network.

The fiddle and dance tradition that developed in the fur trade before 1821 now faced institutional constraints and a critical missionary presence. Yet for young Métis people growing up in and around the trading posts, there were still opportunities to participate in music and dance. The history of Peter Erasmus demonstrates how a young Métis man in the early to mid-nineteenth century inevitably got caught up in the fiddle music and dance culture of Red River. He dictated his memoirs near the end of his life, and they represent an early and valuable Métis primary source. He was the son of a Danish man who fought in the battle of Waterloo and settled at Red River with his Métis wife. Peter Erasmus was born in Red River in 1833, growing up playing the fiddle as a teenager in the 1840s. Eventually obtaining a violin of his own, he practised whenever he had the chance away from his work and duties. He played the fiddle at dances, he said, less for the love of the music and more in hopes of being socially accepted. This is a revealing remark and suggests that Erasmus did not consider himself particularly talented. He recalled at that time in Red River, "there were many French Métis people who were wonderful violinists."[132] Taking a job freighting goods for the HBC, Erasmus commented that while there was "little idle time for me that winter for dancing and parties ... I managed to squeeze in a few."[133] He recounts that while staying with his aunt and uncle at The Pas, he restricted himself to playing "church music" on the violin. This reflects the missionary influence, as playing Christian music may have been how he could still practise his instrument while avoiding scrutiny. When he was twenty years old, Erasmus enrolled for the ministry at Red River. Although prohibited from attending dances, he found ways to bypass the rules to occasionally attend and perform on his fiddle. Yet he was always worried he would be caught, which suggested the severity of the issue. While in his third term, he received a letter from the chief factor of the HBC offering him a job with Rev. Mr Woolsey at Fort Edmonton, as guide and interpreter. Erasmus took the position, describing how on arriving in the 1850s, he was greeted by "people singing hymns and praying." He had encountered the "Pigeon Lake Indians," who had been instructed in music by Reverend Rundle. This depiction of the trading post soundscape is very different than those described in previous decades. Christian hymns became a prominent part of musical interactions and the soundscape around the trading post.

Yet evidence of the old fur trade dances did surface over the winter holidays. Erasmus described how everything transformed on Christmas Eve in 1856. Visitors and dog sleds arrived from great distances. Although Mr Woolsey held "strong views against dancing," Erasmus was granted permission to attend if he promised not to consume liquor. Erasmus had heard of "unrestricted convivial times at these Christmas gatherings" in the past. Yet he reported that "there was no evidence of excess that day."[134] He reports that the musicians had little time for rest between songs that night. His musical services were requested even though "there were plenty of fiddlers among the French Metis people from Lac Ste. Anne." In true fur trade fashion, the dance lasted until daybreak. Many people then faced a difficult situation: "after dancing all night they had to run behind dogs for another forty miles before they would have any rest or sleep."[135] The holiday celebrations at Fort Edmonton in 1856 seem to have retained much of the character of earlier fur trade celebrations, even with the nearby presence of Methodist and Catholic missionaries. Yet by this time, fiddle

Fig. 8.4 Red River jig illustrated in *Harper's New Monthly Magazine*, 1860.

music and dancing were commonly practised in Métis households outside of the official auspices of the trading posts. Métis traders such as Johnny Grant described the social pressure to dance at gatherings in homes, especially the dances that took place to celebrate weddings. In his memoirs he mentioned meeting musicians and that he "loved to dance," although he stopped in his older years.[136]

Fiddle music and dance traditions introduced by the fur trade not only flourished in Métis communities, but also First Nations. Among the Gwich'in of Alaska and the Yukon, Cree of the Hudson Bay, and Saulteaux of Lake Winnipegosis, syncretic styles of fiddle music and dance combining European and Indigenous influences were still practised until the late twentieth century.[137] In each case, the fur trade was identified as when the fiddle music and associated step dancing were introduced and took root. The oldest tunes in each repertoire are attributed to this era. There are differences in the styles of fiddling and dances based on the Indigenous culture and the community's distinct history, yet there are also similarities. Indigenous musical influences found in all three fiddle repertoires include tunes with extended introductory phrases and endings, unique phrase lengths with a particular propensity for phrases of five beats in length, an asymmetric number of phrases, repeating yet variable motifs, and tunes rearranged with the high part first and low part second. Scottish reel step-dancing traditions underpin the various dancing practices, yet there is also a strong French Canadian influence, especially in the Yukon and Manitoba, suggesting that French Canadian voyageurs served as a conduit for much of the original repertoire. Gwich'in, Cree, and Anishinaabe dance steps and musical influences are integrated into each respective tradition. These examples indicate that the repertoire that developed during the fur trade remained vibrant for generations of musicians. A long-lived fur trade in these regions may have contributed to their continued existence in the late twentieth century. Yet what is clear from these studies is that the traditions introduced during the fur trade to a large degree became Indigenized, changing and incorporating new elements over time.

Distinct styles developed at each location with a particular syncretic blend of local culture and history. Cree fiddlers on Hudson Bay were strongly influenced by fiddling traditions from the Orkney Islands, reflecting the HBC's distinct labour history. Cree fiddle dances amalgamated British square dance patterns and traditional Indigenous step dancing, and integrated step dances within set dances.[138] Tunes were associated with specific dances, such as "Waap Shuu Daow" (The Rabbit Dance), "Mo Kujakash" (The Red Sucker Dance), and "In Chuuk Hegan" (The Otter Dance), all of which were named after animals and integrated their distinct movements.[139] Interestingly, according to fiddler James Cheechoo, it was usually the children of mixed marriages that picked up the fiddle and continued these traditions in Cree communities.[140] In the Saulteaux community of Ebb and Flow on the west side of Lake Winnipegosis, both European and Indigenous influences were documented among the old-time fiddle and dance tradition in the 1980s. French Canadian influence was strong in the older repertoire, as seen in features such as the propensity for single note bowing, ornamentation, double stops, open-string drones, and foot-tapping patterns involving both feet.[141] Tunes introduced during the fur trade are most identified by their asymmetric phrasing, a feature found both in Québecois and Indigenous music.[142] While the set and step dancing traditions that once accompanied fiddle music had become infrequent by the 1980s, older players still referred to tune types by the associated dance. This was still, after all, dance music. In the older players, the memory of fiddle music at community dances remained strong. These traditions played an important role in many communities' social fabric until at least the last decades of the twentieth century.

The Red River Métis fiddling style is the most well-known syncretic musical form that developed during the fur trade. It was transported far and wide through the fur trading networks. The Red River colony was remarkably culturally diverse during the first few decades of the nineteenth century. French Canadian and mixed-ancestry voyageurs and freemen as well as Scottish fur traders and settlers contributed to this vibrant musical form. A strong French Canadian influence is evident in the fiddle style in the ways previously described, while much of the repertoire has Scottish origins. The most popular form of music and dance in the fur trade was Scottish reels, and these are prevalent in the Red River Métis repertoire. The "Red River Jig" is, in fact, a reel, not a jig. The term "jigging" is applied to this and other types of step dancing, deriving from the French *giguer*. The "Red River Jig" can be performed by couples or solo individuals step dancing with both basic and fancy steps.[143] The origins of this popular tune are contested and variously described. It seems to have Scottish origins and was likely brought out west by the voyageurs in the early 1800s. This is the story told by Frederick Genthon, HBC fur trader at Moose Lake who lived long enough to be recorded playing the "Red River Jig" in the twentieth century.[144] Another narrative is that the "Red River Jig" was composed by fiddlers gathering at the forks of the Red and Assiniboine Rivers, with the central involvement of the Desjarlais family.[145] On the other hand, there is a popular and closely related Quebecois equivalent known as "La Jig du Bas Canada" or "La Grande Gigue Simple." In 1980, Roy Gibbons collected ten versions of the "Red River Jig" played by Métis fiddlers in Saskatchewan and Alberta, and ten versions of "La Grande Gigue Simple" by Francophone fiddlers in Quebec, concluding that it originated in the east and was modified in the west.[146] It was certainly disseminated around the trading post network and became integrated in repertoires far beyond Red River.

Evidence of the fiddle and dance tradition in Gwich'in communities first appears in Robert Kennicott's journal from 1861.[147] Travelling with HBC canoe brigades from Fort William to Fort Yukon, Kennicott was a naturalist hosted by the company who, among other things, described a ball held at La Pierre's House near Fort Yukon the day after Christmas. The Orkneyman post-master James Flett hosted the dance, and it was attended by "the largest number of whites ever seen at La Pierre's House, besides a dozen or so of Indians." Kennicott described the dancing curiously as "a Louchioux dance, a form of exercise which is decidedly calculated to promote the rapid circulation of blood."[148] Kennicott's description of the dance revealed that the figures were "Scotch reels of four, and jigs." From Kennicott's perspective, the best dancers were Indigenous – likely Gwich'in – a boy and wife of a man from La Pierre's House. This indicates the degree to which Indigenous dancers played a central role in the fur trade dance tradition. For musical instruments, they utilized the typical combination of an old fiddle paired with the simple percussion of an "old tin pan."[149]

Mishler's study of the Gwich'in concluded that English, French Canadian, Scottish, and Orcadian traditions were undoubtedly introduced before the 1860s.[150] Fort Yukon was only established in 1847 by the HBC, decades after Simpson began his reforms in the 1820s. That these traditions were introduced to Gwich'in communities by fur traders in the mid-nineteenth century demonstrates that the HBC at this time still served as an institutional vector for the dissemination of secular fiddle music and dance. In Alaska and the Yukon, the Gwich'in called the "Red River Jig" "Jig Ahtsii Ch'aadzaa." It was performed by one couple on the floor at a time, with everyone else standing around watching and waiting for their turn. The dance had a formal opening and the lead couple usually included one of the older men of the group. One of its great appeals was the opportunity it provided for exhibitionism, as creative or skilled steps generated applause and cheers from the crowd.[151] An alternate form of this dance occurred when an individual man or woman took to the dance floor, performing their regular and fancy steps for the crowd. This style was practised by the Turtle Mountain band of Ojibwe, Métis in North Dakota, and others.[152] This seems to be the style described by Robert Kennicott in 1861 among the Gwich'in, commenting that its tune played continuously and that "all seemed to enjoy it very well."[153] That these traditions brought by the fur trade resonated in a meaningful way for generations after its decline is remarkable. It is a testament to the cultural interconnections and recreational exchanges that brought people from diverse backgrounds together for centuries.

The trading post network from 1760 to 1821 provided the institutional basis for the origins of syncretic fiddle and dance genres. Music and dance were central to the operation of the fur trade, interwoven into nearly every aspect and occasion of significance. This included large dances to celebrate the summer rendezvous, to more intimate music making while overwintering. Music and dance were pursued regularly and especially to commemorate weddings, holidays, and special occasions in the working lives of those at or near the trading posts, such as arrivals and departures of people and cargo. The violins and sheet music that made their way through the trading post network were primarily brought as the personal property of fur traders. Yet before the amalgamation, the NWC had supplied musical instruments such as jaw harps, violins, and strings to their trading posts across northern North America. Descriptions by fur traders are often brief but mention the voyageurs, servants, and Indigenous peoples who were deeply intertwined with these dancing traditions. With trading posts serving to host such festivities, fur trade dances regularly brought together diverse peoples in sustained exchanges of intangible cultural heritage. Syncretic fiddle and dance styles likely developed in many communities, but were well documented by ethnomusicologists among the Hudson Bay Cree, Red River Métis, and Yukon Gwich'in. In each of these communities, Indigenized fiddle and dance styles developed out of the fur trade. While many of the most popular songs are variations of Scottish tunes that arrived over two hundred years ago, there are many adaptations and Indigenous influences in their performances. These fiddle and dance styles sprouted in communities near the trading post networks, yet after 1821 the institutional support for fiddle music and dance declined. Fur traders faced increasing obstacles due to economic reforms and missionary activity. While the trading post network continued to play a diminished role in supporting and disseminating fiddle music and dancing, these traditions carried on and continued outside of the trading posts.

Conclusion

By listening to the fur trade, we become attuned to how relationships manifested and were maintained on an individual and group basis. We can hear
that the fur trade entailed much more than merely exchanging material goods.
Encounters had to be navigated, relationships had to be formed, and trust had
to be built. Power relations and cultural influences extended in both directions
between Europeans and Indigenous peoples, and up and down the social
ladder between masters and servants. Soundways and musical performances
were a key platform that brought the diverse people of the fur trade together.
Indigenous hunters used firearms to salute with trading posts. Experienced
voyageurs led paddling songs. Fur traders, servants, voyageurs, and Indigenous
peoples played reels on the fiddle and danced to its music. In cross-cultural
encounters, singing and dancing were primary forms of interaction. When
the words of religious songs were not understood, their solemnity was. While
many aspects of the musical encounter were successfully navigated, there were
instances of unfamiliarity and misunderstanding. Fur traders who spent years
living near Indigenous communities and with Indigenous peoples were more
likely to become acquainted with their culture and describe it in their written
records. Getting along required a frequent renewal of relationships and cultural
protocol that often involved singing and dancing.

Today, the decaying foundations of most trading posts across northern
North America convey a profound sense of silence. A few historical sites
have resurrected an echo of their former life, but it is usually quite different
than how it would have sounded in the past. Many people are not aware of
their existence, or that their town or city was built on or near the location
of a historic trading post. The prevailing traditional image of the Canadian
north, established by the Group of Seven and others, presents an image of
a harsh and barren landscape. It is devoid of an Indigenous presence.[1] It is

also devoid of the vibrant fur trade history that resounded for centuries. The fur trade was anything but silent. It burst with ceremonial gunfire, echoed with singing voices, and thundered with stomping feet. Both Europeans and Indigenous peoples had their own distinct musical cultures and soundways that collided and mixed in an often noisy affair. It is impossible to literally listen to this fur trade. But by attempting to, we hear key aspects of the shared history between Indigenous peoples and Euro-Canadians. Fiddle music and step dancing derived from the fur trade remained strong in many communities across Canada until the late twentieth century.

James Anderson was a fur trader who worked around the north including Moose Factory in the early twentieth century. In his published memoirs, he wrote that "there was no very great exchange of social activities between the Indians and the whites, excepting for the fairly numerous dances which took place whenever the Indians would congregate at the post."[2] He identified these activities as still occurring in the summer as well as the holiday winter season. Anderson described how "to the tune of two fiddles and one Indian drum dancing as commenced at eight in the evening and carried on to the small hours of the morning ... the *pièce de résistance* at the dance was the good old Red River jig, as for the rest of the Indian rabbit and duck dances, besides quadrilles and square dances."[3] The remarkable longevity of this musical tradition is evident, with instruments, songs, and dances that blended European and Indigenous culture over the centuries. This tradition is documented in the National Film Board of Canada's fascinating but somewhat problematic *The Fiddlers of James Bay.* It continues in the twenty-first century by old-time Cree fiddlers.[4]

During the height of the fur trade, the soundscape was most fundamentally transformed by gunpowder. Cannons produced loud booms that the Omushkego Cree initially associated with thunder. This changed with the ongoing presence of HBC ships and establishment of trading posts with cannons and supplies of guns and gunpowder. Cannons and muskets were institutionalized by fur traders for their sound-making abilities. They served as saluting mechanisms for arrivals and departures and signalling systems. The conduits of the fur trade provided the avenues by which arms and ammunition were supplied throughout the vast territories from the Great Lakes and Hudson Bay across the Prairies and Subarctic to the west coast. The auditory reports that travelled long distances were useful tools of communication, not only for fur traders but also by servants of the companies and Indigenous peoples. Gunpowder signalled the presence of fur traders wherever they went, accompanying ritual baptisms, arrivals, and holiday celebrations at the trading posts.

In the hands of Indigenous peoples, gunshots developed distinct auditory customs that, in turn, influenced fur traders. People who interacted in the fur trade often communicated and celebrated with their muskets.

Music and dance figured prominently in cross-cultural encounters. Indigenous peoples sang and danced with the intent to welcome, honour, entertain, and occasionally discourage fur traders who were passing through or overwintering in their territory. Fur traders described the role of music and dance in establishing peaceful relations, alliances, and trade with a wide range of Indigenous cultures. Their remarkable passages describing what they observed were partly fuelled by curiosity and partly by pragmatism. They recognized that ceremonies, songs, and dances were significant to the diplomatic protocol and ongoing relations with the Indigenous communities with whom they were establishing alliances and trade. Fur traders often interpreted dances less for aspects of musical culture and more for what they revealed about social and gender dynamics. The performances they described provide a crucial record of the diverse cultural traditions of Indigenous North America before settler colonialism. Fur traders' writings serve as windows into Indigenous cultures, yet they are often tinted by the authors' preconceived notions and prejudices, and thus should be read "against the grain."

Fur traders were required to navigate Indigenous treaty-making protocol. Calumet pipe ceremonies proved a crucial mechanism for establishing peaceful relations and trading relationships in the St Lawrence's southwest and northwest trade. Whether or not the ceremony was associated only with smoking rituals, as it was for some Indigenous Nations in the northern Plains and western Subarctic, or whether it was accompanied by elaborate songs and dances enacting peace-making, adoption, and renewal as it was for others, pipe ceremonies were central to the expansion of the fur trade in North America. The Haudenosaunee and Anishinaabeg brought not only their ceremonial pipe dance traditions with them into the northwest but also their war dances. These served as platforms of social engagement with other Indigenous peoples in northern North America. In the context of the fur trade, both ceremonial pipe and war dances served to strengthen alliances and trading relationships. Both were part of the cultural fabric of trading and alliance-making and had a considerable influence on the soundscape of the fur trade.

The fur trade brought European military instruments in and near Indigenous communities. While used to convey military signals and orders on the battlefield, the disciplinary associations of drums, bugles, and bagpipes were transformed in the fur trade. They became part of the soundways of arrival, providing music for dances, and serving as objects of curiosity during cross-cultural encounters. They still produced a commanding and imposing effect. They may have been imported into the fur trading networks in the greatest numbers during periods of war from the Seven Years' War until the War of 1812. Yet they also served a conspicuous role in governor George Simpson's tours and interactions with HBC servants and Indigenous peoples. Simpson utilized musical instruments to impress and enhance his aura of authority. Military instruments were repurposed for ceremonies and recreation in and around the trading posts. Familiar to both Europeans and Indigenous peoples, drums were a potent conduit for cross-cultural musical interactions. Musical instruments served as important points of contact and interaction and involved two of the "deepest" senses, hearing and touch.

Rituals of sound punctuated the canoe voyages between Montreal and the western Great Lakes. Significant locations were commemorated with sounded responses. These traditions served to bond crews and convey histories, myths, and cultural significances at specific sites. Soundways provided meaning, structure, and belonging on the long and often dangerous journeys. The gravesite of Jean Cadieux at Grand Calumet Island on the Ottawa River was one such significant site that revealed something of the voyageurs' *mentalité* and magico-religious beliefs. The associated story and song stressed vulnerability and deep-seated anxiety about being left behind. These soundways and the ritual baptisms along the river marked various stages of removal from eastern civilization, and often included Indigenous characteristics. Landscape features that produced or augmented sounds were important to how fur traders conceptualized and interacted with places along the way.

Overwintering at trading posts and trading *en déroine* brought fur traders into intimate relations with Indigenous peoples. It allowed them the opportunity to observe aspects of musical culture in the daily life of communities. While some fur traders were skeptical about Indigenous hunting and healing songs, others became convinced of their efficacy. The fur trade disseminated cultural influences and expanded the availability of sound-making materials. People produced new methods of sound and music making. While fur traders did not possess the systematic descriptive methodologies of trained ethnographers, their descriptions are valuable because of their early date, proliferation, and detail. Unlike the missionaries and Indian agents that followed in the nineteenth century, they did not attempt to change, restrict, or prohibit traditional Indigenous music and culture. Instead, they were often observers and even participants. It was not mere curiosity that spurred their descriptions, although there was that too. They realized their relations with the Indigenous community influenced their profits and livelihoods. They observed Anishinaabe religious traditions such as the Midéwiwin and Wabanowiwin in various communities. This challenged later nineteenth-century depictions of a monolithic and unchanging "primitive" Indigenous culture. The written record of the fur trade presents an alternate ethnographic archive. In some cases, it contradicts later descriptions that naturalized the influence of settler society and missionaries.

Canoe travel in this period was characterized by and predicated on the *chansons d'aviron*. Singing was essential to its operation, starting the march, synchronizing the paddles, and controlling the pace. The voyageurs extended their songs over long durations by stitching together well-known segments of verse and improvising additional lyrics around the *laisse* form. Within the framework of inescapable work songs, the Ermatinger collection indicates that there was room for creativity, improvisation, and the expression of voyageur identity. Subject to an uncertain food supply and extended periods away from loved ones, the voyageurs sang about scenarios of abundance and comfort, characterized by feasting and intimacy with women. Superficially they conveyed an unfailing *joie de vivre*, but they also revealed deep anxieties and insecurities. Their origins may have been with the *chansons en laisse* that arrived with French immigrants in the seventeenth century, yet they were adapted with novel extensions and new choruses. The canoe brigades were multi-cultural, and the paddling songs had the ability to transcend divisions of language, race, and class. Old voyageur songs remained part of the folk repertoire not only in Quebec, but also Francophone and Métis communities across western Canada.[5]

The pre-1840s fur trade produced a vigorous dance culture based around the music of the fiddle. Dances commemorated holidays and special occasions in the lives of those working at or near the trading posts. Music and dance were among the favourite collective pastimes, and they provided emotional and psychological support for many overwintering fur traders. They formed a recurring social activity that functioned to strengthen relationships and reciprocal bonds and build trust. Music and dance characterized cross-cultural interactions between the fur trade's diverse peoples. Class distinctions played a role at the summer rendezvous at the large depots of the western Great Lakes, yet for the most part music and dancing broke them down. At the smaller posts throughout the year, music and dance provided important occasions for bridging divisions of culture, class, gender, religion, and company. Before the amalgamation of the HBC and NWC in 1821, they were plentiful and integrated into the regular operations of trading posts.

The demand for musical instruments and sheet music in the fur trade was supplied through personal and commercial arrangements. Certain suppliers, such as Todd, McGill, & Co., and certain fur traders, such as Edward Ermatinger, had a wide influence in this regard. The NWC supplied musical materials such as violins, violin strings, and jaw harps to trading posts across North America. Both the cultural and material dynamic of the fur trade spawned the development of a music and dance culture that was characterized mostly by Scottish reels on the fiddle. This music was also popular in Scotland and the St Lawrence at the time, yet fur trade dances planted the seeds of fiddling traditions that would continue across North America long after the decline of the fur trade. The "Red River Jig" emphasizes individual displays of step dancing, resembling one of the two main approaches of dancing to Scotch reels in the eighteenth century. Yet the inclusion of different steps, for instance, hops, stomps, and other manoeuvres that strongly resemble Indigenous dance steps, indicate that this syncretic style developed in cross-cultural interactions and represents a truly hybridized form of music and dance.

Fiddle music and step dancing are today cherished as one of the core features of Métis national identity. The historical musical exchanges that took place during the fur trade underpin the development of Métis music and dance, yet are more broadly historically significant in constituting conversations, interactions, and activities between numerous Indigenous peoples and non-Indigenous peoples. Music and dance brought together diverse peoples in a wide variety of contexts, over an enormous geography, for a long period of time. This legacy represents an important part of the intangible cultural exchange of the fur trade that fostered cooperation and trust building, rather than the exclusive history of any one people or nation. Scottish, English, Indigenous, French Canadian, and Métis peoples alike participated in hybridized music and dance forms centred around the fiddle. Music and dance were central to the ethnogenesis of the Métis and continue to serve as markers of their history and cultural identity. Other communities also maintained syncretic fiddle and dance styles from the fur trade era. Violins manufactured in Britain or Scotland became infused with new meanings over time, sometimes becoming identified as "Métis" after centuries of use in fur trade families.[6] Communities from northern Quebec and Ontario to British Columbia and the Yukon until very recently possessed traditions of fiddle music and step dancing that initially arrived during the fur trade.

As historical descriptions provide a different kind of qualitative value, I have avoided theoretical discussions of musical synchronicity and convergence. Yet cross-cultural diffusion, juxtaposition, and fusion, all three stages of musical contact and invention, are documented in the written record.[7] The fur trade provided all of the necessary circumstances for the sharing and development of new soundways and musical traditions. By the 1820s, musical forms were pursued and developed outside of the trading posts, while the winter holidays remained a time of festivity and dancing. The dedicated dancing culture that had developed in the previous decades to celebrate weddings, holidays, arrivals, and departures was slowly curtailed. Traditions that were planted and sprouted during the fur trade grew in kitchens and community halls from Quebec to the Northwest Territories.

The field of fur trade studies has transformed entirely since Harold Innis wrote his economic history of early Canada. His near-exclusive concern for tracing economic and material exchanges has become the exception in the historiography. The social and cultural turn in the 1970s and the emergence of ethnohistory shifted the focus away from the fur traders and toward their servants and Indigenous peoples. The backgrounded and simplistic portrayals of Indigenous peoples that had previously been the norm have been reversed, and their crucial and nuanced roles and interactions serve as ongoing subjects of study. There has been an emphasis in the last few decades on tracing the development of a unique "fur trade society" and Métis ethnogenesis. These discussions have often placed too much emphasis on race and not enough on culture.[8] When culture is analyzed, the shared heritage of the fur trade – the fiddles, jigging, sashes, and canoes – emerge as crucial interfaces for the many peoples and cultures that interacted.

A recent collection of essays on the fur trade begins with the assertion that "material objects have always been central to the fur trade." Exchanges of felt hats, furs, blankets, and kettles constituted the "raisons d'être of centuries of trade between Europeans and Indigenous peoples in northern North America."[9] Yet material exchanges were accompanied by cultural interactions, both of which were significant and served as forces of change. This book attempts to fill a lacuna in the social and cultural investigation of the fur trade by "listening" to the past. Hudson Bay and the St Lawrence formed the two major conduits of the fur trade into northern North America. From the mid-eighteenth to the mid-nineteenth centuries, these entryways provided the main commercial and social linkages between Europe and eastern North America and the northern Plains, western Subarctic, northwest coast, and Plateau and Basin regions. The British fur trade extended across what is now certain northern States and the entirety of Canada. The distinct music and dance culture that developed has lingered variously in modern-day communities, preserving an echo of the remarkable reverberations that once sounded across this landscape.

Notes

Preface

1   Hutchinson, "Evans, James."

Introduction

1   Chappell, *Narrative of a Voyage to Hudson's Bay*, 55.
2   Ibid., 58.
3   There is no word "pillitay" in the Inuit language. The closest approximation is "pitaaqta," or "pilauqta," both meaning, more or less, "give us something." Personal Correspondence, Ittinuar, 27 March 2019; Chappell, *Narrative*, 102–3.
4   Ibid.
5   Ibid., 109–10.
6   Brown, *Ethnohistorian in Rupert's Land*, 23–46.
7   Podruchny, *Making the Voyageur World*, xii.
8   Mackenzie, "An Account of the Athabasca Indians by a Partner of the North West Company,"
9   This changed with the 1821 merger of the companies, after which more Indigenous peoples and French Canadians were employed by the HBC.
10   Middleton, *Pontiac's War*, IX.
11   Rich, *Montreal and the Fur Trade*, 68–74.
12   Ibid., 84–5.
13   Colpitts, *Pemmican Empire*, 38–9; Ray and Freeman, "*Give Us Good Measure*," 57.
14   Podruchny, *Making the Voyageur World*, 183–4; Rich, *Hudson's Bay Company*, Vol. 3, 713.
15   Child, *Holding Our World Together*, 40–1.

16   Henry, *Travels & Adventures*, 16.
17   Rich, *Montreal and the Fur Trade*, 92–3.
18   Woodcock, "Cuthbert Grant."
19   Ens and Sawchuk, *From New Peoples to New Nations*, 87–8; Chartrand, *Pierriche Falcon*.
20   Den Otter, *Civilizing the Wilderness*, 103–34, 163–91.
21   Grabowski & St-Onge, "Montreal Iroquois *engagés* in the Western Fur Trade, 1800–1821," 23–58.
22   Burley, *Servants of the Honourable Company*, 2–5; 96–105.
23   Pritzker, *A Native American Encyclopedia*; Waldman, *Encyclopedia of Native American Tribes*.
24   Anderson, *Crucible of War*, 617–32.
25   Borrows and Coyle, *The Right Relationship*, 17.
26   Richter, *Trade, Land, Power*, 120.
27   Clendinnen, *Dancing with Strangers*, 8.
28   Van Kirk, "*Many Tender Ties.*"
29   White, *The Middle Ground*, X.
30   White, "'Give us a Little Milk," 60–71; Ray and Freeman, "*Give Us Good Measure*"; Pulsipher, "Gaining the Diplomatic Edge"; Baldwin, "200 Years of Treaty Annuities."
31   Taylor, *The Divided Ground*; White, *The Middle Ground;* Havard. *The Great Peace of Montreal of 1701;* Witgen, *An Infinity of Nations*; McDonnell, *Masters of Empire.*
32   Taylor, *The Divided Ground*, 27, 158; White, *The Middle Ground*, 20, 373; Richter, *Trade, Land, Power*, 33, 73; Havard, *The Great Peace*, 25, 126, 137; Witgen, *An Infinity of Nations*, 206; McDonnell, *Masters of Empire.*
33   Van Kirk, "*Many Tender Ties*," 115, 128; Brown, *Strangers in Blood.*
34   Ray, *Indians in the Fur Trade.*
35   Miller, *Compact, Contract, Covenant*, 15.
36   Harvey, *The Theatre of Empire*, 25.
37   Stephen, *Masters and Servants*, xix.
38   The dig at the *fils du roi* arises in perhaps the voyageurs' most widespread paddling song, "Trois Beaux Canards."
39   This definition comprises the first chapter title in his classic 1973 study; see Blacking, *How Musical Is Man?*, 3–31.
40   Perea, *Intertribal Native American Music in the United States*, 3–5.
41   Small, *Musicking*, 2.
42   Tomlinson, *Singing in the New World*; Woodfield, *English Musicians in the Age of Exploration;* Agnew, *Enlightenment Orpheus.*
43   Sagard-Theodat, *Histoire du Canada*, Vol. 1, 173–4. Translation from Parkman, *Pioneers of France in the New World*, 392.
44   Fornasiero and West-Sooby, "Cross-Cultural Inquiry in 1802," 28.

45 Rotstein, "Trade and Politics: An Institutional Approach," 1–28; Rotstein, "Innis: The Alchemy of Fur and Wheat," 6–31; Ray and Freeman, "*Give Us Good Measure.*"

46 Van Kirk, "*Many Tender Ties,*" 36–7.

47 Ray and Freeman, "*Give Us Good Measure,*" 55.

48 White, "Give Us a Little Milk," 60.

49 Witgen, *Infinity of Nations*, 131–2.

50 Willmott and Brownlee, "Dressing for the Homeward Journey," 60.

51 Diamond, *Native American Music in Eastern North America*, 10.

52 Ibid.

53 Turgeon, "The Tale of the Kettle."

54 Nassaney, *The Archaeology of the North American Fur Trade*, 108.

55 Hu, "Approaches to the Archaeology of Ethnogenesis."

56 Sawatzky, "The Biography of the Pierre Bruce Fiddle."

57 McLeod, *Five Fur Traders of the Northwest*, 170.

58 Van Orden, *Music, Discipline, and Arms in Early Modern France*, 36.

59 Erasmus, *Buffalo Days and Nights*, 43

60 Diamond et al., *Visions of Sound;* Diamond, *Native American Music in Eastern North America.*

61 Owings, *Indian Voices*, 97; Browner, *Heartbeat of the People.*

62 Wilkins, "The Fiddlers of James Bay," 65–7.

63 One well known old-time fiddler from the community is James Cheechoo, who released his CD *Shay Chee Man* in 1998. It has ten traditional fiddle tunes that long accompanied dances in the Cree community.

64 Barman, *Iroquois in the West*, 142.

65 McDonald, *Peace River*, 4.

66 Barbeau, "The Ermatinger Collection of Voyageur Songs (ca. 1830)."

67 Laxer, "Row, Brothers, Row."

68 Nute, *The Voyageur;* Podruchny, *Making the Voyageur World.*

69 Laforte, "Le Répertoire Authentique des Chansons D'aviron de nos Anciens Canotiers," 145–159n.

70 Barbeau, "Voyageur Songs of the Missouri."

71 Chartrand, *Pierriche Falcon, the Michif Rhymester.*

72 Smith, *Listening to Nineteenth-Century America*, 6.

Chapter One

1 Bird, *The Spirit Lives in the Mind*, 47–9.

2 Ibid.

3 This was something learned at Ki-ni-ki-moo-sha-wow, meaning "barren or treeless headland," or Cape Henrietta Maria, ibid.; Brown, *Ethnohistorian in Rupert's Land*, 33.

4 Chappell, *Narrative of a Voyage to Hudson's Bay*, 120–1.

5 Champlain, *The Works…*, 66.

6 Ibid.

7 Ibid., 7.

8 Bohr, *Gifts from the Thunder Beings*, 136.

9 Given, *A Most Pernicious Thing*.

10 Silverman, *Thundersticks*.

11 Ibid., 23.

12 Rich, *The Fur Trade and the Northwest to 1857*, 39.

13 Carlos and Lewis, *Commerce by a Frozen Sea*, 59.

14 Rich, *The Fur Trade and the Northwest to 1857*, 31.

15 Ibid., 55.

16 Ibid., 97.

17 Bird, *The Spirit Lives in the Mind*, 47–9.

18 Chappell, *Narrative of a Voyage*, 120–1.

19 Schafer, *The Tuning of the World*, 25.

20 Rath, *How Early America Sounded*, 13–6.

21 Ibid.

22 Bird, *The Spirit Lives in the Mind*, 47–8.

23 Ibid.

24 Smith, *The Island of the Anishinaabeg*, 2.

25 Pomedli, *Living with Animals*, 193–218.

26 Brown and Brightman, "*The Orders of the Dreamed*," 109.

27 Ibid., 112.

28 Ibid., 2, 30–7, 41, 66.

29 Ibid.; Smith, *The Island of the Anishinaabeg*, 67.

30 Child, *Holding Our World Together*, 40–2.

31 Tanner, *A Narrative…*, 123–4.

32 Smith, *The Island of the Anishinaabeg*, 99.

33 Ibid.

34 Ewers, *Indian Life on the Upper Missouri*, 12.

35 Ibid.

36 Ray, *Indians in the Fur Trade*, 73.

37 Ibid., 19–21.

38 White, *The Middle Ground*, 136.

39 Gooding, *Trade Guns of the Hudson's Bay Company*, 19.

40 White, *The Middle Ground*, 138.

41 Silverman, *Thundersticks*, 132.

42 Ibid.

43 Russell, *Guns on the Early Frontiers*, 103; Bohr, *Gifts from the Thunder Beings*, 136–7.

44 Russell, *Guns on the Early Frontiers,* 104; Gooding, *Trade Guns of the Hudson's Bay Company,* 57.

45 Bohr, *Gifts from the Thunder Beings,* 194–7.

46 Beardy and Coutts, *Voices from Hudson Bay,* 10, 127.

47 Russell, *Guns on the Early Frontiers,* 127.

48 Silverman, *Thundersticks,* 11.

49 Ibid., 12.

50 Ibid.

51 Innis, *The Fur Trade in Canada,* 190–1.

52 Ibid., 192–3.

53 Ibid., 193.

54 Silverman, *Thundersticks,* 264.

55 Ibid.

56 McDonald, *Peace River,* 20.

57 Alexander Mackenzie, *The Journals and Letters of Sir Alexander Mackenzie,* 366.

58 Ibid., 390–1.

59 Ibid., 376.

60 Ibid., 387.

61 Ibid., 390.

62 Jobson, *Looking Forward, Looking Back,* 41.

63 Witcomb and Tiret, *Dictionary of Nautical Terms,* 587.

64 The British Army employed odd numbers up to twenty-one, while even-numbered salutes were reserved for funerary functions. See Boatner, *Military Customs and Traditions,* 48.

65 Pond, *Five Fur Traders of the Northwest,* 50.

66 Carver, "Captain Jonathan Carver's Journal," 9–10.

67 Nelson, "No. 5" Journal, June 1807–Oct. 1809, September 1808, 207–8.

68 Tanner, *A Narrative,* 195–6.

69 Ibid., 196–7.

70 Ibid.

71 Quoted in Ray and Freeman, *"Give Us Good Measure,"* 55.

72 Ibid., 59.

73 M'Gillivray, *The Journal of Duncan M'Gillivray,* 30.

74 Ross, *Beyond the River and the Bay,* 49–50.

75 Porter, "James Porter's Slave Lake Journal of 1800–1," 95.

76 The underlining appears in the original source. Unknown, "Northwest Company Papers: Indian Ledgers, Etc. [Typescript.]," 104.

77 Mackenzie, *The Journals and Letters,* 240.

78 Rich, *The Fur Trade and the Northwest to 1857,* 179.

79 Mackenzie, *The Journals and Letters,* 193–4.

80 Sturgis, *The Journal of William Sturgis,* 32.

81 Douglas, "Diary of a Trip to the Northwest Coast," 41–3, 50.

82 Gibson, *Otter Skins, Boston Ships and China Goods*, 113–4.

83 Ermatinger, "Notes and Correspondence on the Expedition to the Clallem Tribe 1828," 2–3.

84 Simpson, *Simpson's Athabasca Journal*, 74–5.

85 Longmoor, "Journal of the Most Remarkable Transactions and Occurrences …," 317.

86 McDonald, *Peace River*, 41.

87 Garry, *The Diary of Nicholas Garry*, 50.

88 MacMillan, *The North-West Company*, 26, 35.

89 McDonald, *Peace River*, 41.

90 Tanner, *A Narrative*, 270.

91 Ibid., 147–9.

92 MacGregor, *Peter Fidler*, 98.

93 McDonald, "Autobiographical Notes of John McDonald of Garth …," 22.

94 McKenzie, "'Reminiscences'…," 17–8.

95 Malhiot, "A Wisconsin Fur-Trader's Journal, 1804–05," 192.

96 Mackenzie, *The Journals and Letters*, 281.

97 Garry, *The Diary of Nicholas Garry*, 32.

98 Ibid.

99 Connor, *Five Fur Traders of the Northwest*, 251.

100 McDonell, *Diary*, 99–100.

101 Podruchny, *Making the Voyageur World*, 61–2.

102 Smith, "Of the Remarkable Occurrences," 187.

103 Podruchny, *Making the Voyageur World*, 62–3.

104 Ibid., 61–3.

105 Alexander Mackenzie, *The Journals and Letters of Sir Alexander Mackenzie*, 248.

106 Ibid.

107 Podruchny, *Making the Voyageur World*, 174–81.

108 Henry (the Younger), *Journal of Alexander Henry the Younger 1799–1814*, 125.

109 Wentzel, "W.F. Wentzel's Journals of 1804–7," 197.

110 Ibid., 292–3.

111 McDonald, "Autobiographical Notes of John McDonald of Garth …," 21.

112 Simpson, *Simpson's Athabasca Journal*, 204–5.

113 Van Kirk, "*Many Tender Ties*," 128–9.

114 For the history in Saskatchewan, see Jackson, "Political Paradox."

Chapter Two

1 Levitin, *This Is Your Brain on Music*, 249; Levitin, *The World in Six Songs*, 21, 86, 92. Oxytocin: 51, 98, 198, 232, 263, 305–6, 319; endorphins: 89, 99, 101; serotonin: 76, 99, 101, 307.

2 Cameron, "Singing with Strangers," 88–90.

3 Henry, *Travels & Adventures In Canada and the Indian Territories*, 300–1.

4 Ibid., 302.

5 Ibid.

6 Willmott, "Shape, Rattle and Roll."

7 Mackenzie, *Voyages from Montreal Through the Continent...*

8 Ibid., 183.

9 Ibid., 194.

10 Mackenzie, *Voyages*, 340–1.

11 Fraser, *The Letters and Journals of Simon Fraser 1806–08*, 97.

12 Van Kirk, "*Many Tender Ties*," 45–52.

13 Fraser, *Letters and Journals*, 99–100.

14 Ibid.

15 Ibid., 102–3.

16 Ibid., 104–5.

17 Ibid., 108–9.

18 Lutz, *Myth and Memory*, 61–3.

19 Thompson, *The Writings of David Thompson*, xxx.

20 Thompson, *Columbia Journals*, 144.

21 Ibid.

22 Ibid., 147.

23 Ibid.

24 Ibid., 148–9.

25 Ibid., 150–1.

26 Ibid., 151–2.

27 Ibid., 153.

28 Ibid., 165.

Chapter Three

1 Diamond, *Visions of Sound;* Browner, *Heartbeat of the people;* Matthews, *Naamiwan's Drum.*

2 Vennum, *The Ojibwa Dance Drum*, 13, 61;

3 Skaggs and Nelson, *Sixty Years' War for the Great Lakes, 1754–1814.*

4 Rich, *The Fur Trade and the Northwest to 1857*, 186–92.

5 Miller, *Compact, Contract, Covenant*, 79–99; *Indian Treaties and Surrenders, from 1680 to 1890.*

6 Benn, *Native Memoirs from the War of 1812*, 159–60.

7 Innis, *Peter Pond*, 3.

8 Barnes, *A History of the Regiments & Uniforms of the British Army*, 101.

9 Ibid., 100–1.

10 Langley, *The Eighteen Manoeuvres for His Majesty's Infantry*, 20.

11   "March," *Grove Music Online.*

12   These tunes may have served pragmatic functions on the battlefield, but they also provided nation-states with symbols of imperialism around which citizens could rally; see Richards, *Imperialism and Music.*

13   Merritt, *On Common Ground,* 244.

14   Ibid., 245.

15   O'Keeffe, *Musical Warriors,* 9.

16   *Exercise for the Foot,* 44.

17   Ibid., 15.

18   Foucault, *Discipline and Punish,* 6–7.

19   Orden, *Music, Discipline, and Arms in Early Modern France,* 188, 207.

20   "Last Post" would later be adopted for the funerals of fallen soldiers and commemorations.

21   Hawks, *Orderly Book and Journal of Major John Hawks,* 28–9.

22   Walhausen, *L'Art militaire pour l'infanterie;* Montgommery, *La Milice française.*

23   Norris, *Marching to the Drums,* 37, 54–79.

24   Brumwell, *Redcoats,* 101.

25   Herbert, *Music & the British Military in the Long Nineteenth Century,* 85.

26   The orders of "Bayonets to be fixed," "Shoulder," "take post in battalion," "first caution," "recover your arms," "to the Right-about," "march," "halt," "order your arms," and "take care to perform the manual exercise" are conveyed variously through a "roll upon the drum," a "flam on the drum," "a ruffle of the Drum," or "a troop" on the drum. *Exercise for the Foot,* 12–15.

27   Cooper, *A Practical Guide for the Light Infantry Officer,* 97–8. Cooper's manual demarcates the basic commands, such as "to advance," "to retreat," "to halt," to "cease-firing," and "to assemble," that had become standardized with the British army by the turn of the nineteenth century.

28   Forming for battle was signaled by the drumbeat "*to arms,*" while the signal to halt was the "*retreat.*" These were read aloud on the U.S. Schooner *Ariel* on 26 September 1813, "All signals will be immediately repeated by all the drums of the line"; Brannan, *Official Letters of the Military and Naval Officers of the United States,* 219.

29   Henry, *Travels & Adventures,* 78–9.

30   Carl Benn writes that "The beating probably consisted of the playing of reveille and morning duty calls." Benn, *Native Memoirs,* 131.

31   Skaggs and Nelson, *The Sixty Years' War for the Great Lakes, 1754–1814;* Taylor, *The Divided Ground;* Taylor, *The Civil War of 1812.*

32   Foucault, *Discipline and Punish,* 10–1.

33   Brumwell, *Redcoats,* 100.

34   Thompson, *A Bard of Wolfe's Army,* 166.

35   "March," *The Harvard Dictionary of Music,* 487.

36   Apess, *Native Memoirs,* 107.

37 Ibid.

38 Ibid.

39 For instance, in Peter Moogk's "The Liturgy of Humiliation, Pain, and Death: The Execution of Criminals in New France." Moogk, "The Liturgy of Humiliation, Pain, and Death," 89–112.

40 In 1757, the British Secretary of War Lord Barrington ordered the raising of a Highland Battalion "which is to Consist of Ten Companies of Four Serjeants, Four Corporals, Two Drummers, and One Hundred Effective Private Men in each Company, besides Commission Officers." Drummers are here less than two percent of the total force; Thompson, *A Bard of Wolfe's Army*, 111. A later eighteenth-century infantry manual from 1794 suggests that there should be one drummer for each company of thirty privates, three officers, two sergeants, and three corporals: approximately 2.5 per cent of each company. Langley, *The Eighteen Manoeuvres for His Majesty's Infantry*, 21. When the 78th Foot disbanded in Quebec in August 1763, their names were taken on subsistence rolls, revealing that of the 887 men, twenty were drummers. This sample tally comes at the end of six years campaigning in North America, with drummers representing 2.25 per cent of the total force. Thompson, *A Bard of Wolfe's Army*, 222.

41 Johnson, *The Papers of Sir William Johnson*, 325.

42 Ibid., 235, 236.

43 Ibid., 287.

44 Special thanks to Carl Benn for pointing me towards this evidence.

45 Corbiere and Philips, "A Dehe'igan (Drum) from Manitoulin Island," http://www.native-drums.ca/index.php/Scholars/Deheigan?tp=a&bg=1&ln=e, accessed 25 December 2019.

46 Diamond, *Native American Music in Eastern North America*, 132.

47 "Lake of 2 Mountains Inv. Cont," 1820–1, 133.

48 Chappell, *Narrative of a Voyage to Hudson's Bay in His Majesty's Ship Rosamond*, 201–2.

49 Merriam, *The Anthropology of Music*, 314; Nettl, *The Study of Ethnomusicology*, 440–1.

50 Wilkins, "The Fiddlers of James Bay," 65; Bird, *The Spirit Lives in the Mind*.

51 Wilkins, "The Fiddlers of James Bay," 65–7.

52 Whidden, *Essential Song*, 16.

53 Henry, *The Journal of Alexander Henry the Younger 1799–1814*, 184.

54 "Letter from R. Miles to Edward Ermatinger," 296.

55 Barnes, *The Uniforms & History of the Scottish Regiments*, 99.

56 Cooper, *Light Infantry Officer*, 98.

57 Ibid.

58 Parkman, *Montcalm and Wolfe*, 248.

59 Tod, "Ermatinger, Edward. Papers of Edward Ermatinger," 69.

60 Barnes, *The Uniforms & History of the Scottish Regiments*, 260.

61 "The piper has had many ups and downs in the matter of official approval," writes military historian R.M. Barnes, and "drummer" was used instead of "piper" to escape censure. See ibid.

62 James Thompson indicated that the piper could serve numerous roles, reporting that while staying in Donaghadee before crossing they were "awaken'd by one of our Regimental Pipers sounding the 'Alarm'!" A house was on fire on other side of town, and men were roused from their slumber by the emergency call on the pipes, rushing over to assist. Thompson lists three pipers: Privates McIntyre, Macdonald and MacCrimmon; see Thompson, *A Bard of Wolfe's Army*, 119.

63 Barnes, *The Uniforms & History*, 261.

64 Ibid.

65 Thompson, *A Bard of Wolfe's Army*, 198.

66 Ibid.

67 Ibid., 199–200.

68 Harmon, *A Journal of Voyages and Travels in the Interior of North America*, 14–17.

69 Ens, *Homeland to Hinterland*, 52.

70 Raffan, *Emperor of the North*, 186, 290.

71 McDonald, *Peace River*, 2.

72 Cunningham, *Leisure in the Industrial Revolution, 1780–1880*.

73 McDonald, *Peace River*, 7.

74 Ibid., 2.

75 Ibid., 4.

76 Ibid.

77 Keillor, Archambault, and Kelly, "Pow Wow Songs of Northern Style," 374–7.

78 McDonald, *Peace River*, 24.

79 Ibid., 28.

80 Newman, *Company of Adventurers*, 446–7.

81 McDonald, *Peace River*, 14.

82 Ibid., 15–16.

83 Ibid., 26.

Chapter Four

1 This topic has seen a recent revival of interest. See Dowd, *War Under Heaven*; Middleton, *Pontiac's War*; Widder, *Beyond Pontiac's Shadow*; the classic work on the subject is Parkman, *History of the Conspiracy of Pontiac*.

2 Shannon, *Iroquois Diplomacy on the Early American Frontier*; White, *The Middle Ground*, 269–366.

3 Harris, "Arthur J. Ray and the Empirical Opportunity," 256.

4 Miller, *Compact, Contract, Covenant*, 33–66.

5 La Potherie, "Adventures of Nicolas Perrot, by la Potherie, 1665–1670," 76–7.

6 Ibid., 84–5.

7 La Potherie, "Adventures of Nicolas Perrot," 86.

8 The anthropological scholarship on this topic is vast. For an overview see Turnbaugh, "Calumet ceremonialism as a nativistic response," 685–91; Blakeslee, "The origin and spread of the calumet ceremony," 759–68; Hall, "The evolution of the calumet-pipe," 37–52.

9 Paper, "Cosmological implications of pan-Indian Sacred Pipe Ritual," 99–101.

10 Ibid.

11 Witgen, *An Infinity of Nations*, 168–213.

12 White, *Middle Ground*, 21–2; White, "*Give us a Little Milk*," 60–7.

13 Jolliet and Marquette, *Early Narratives of the Northwest*, 243–7.

14 Ibid., 245–7.

15 Ibid., 245–6.

16 Ibid., 246.

17 Ibid., 247–8.

18 White, *The Middle Ground*, 21.

19 Calloway, *One Vast Winter Count*, 237.

20 Havard, *The Great Peace of Montreal of 1701*, 135–7, 187.

21 Ibid., 111.

22 See Havard, *The Great Peace of Montreal of 1701*, 224. To establish this claim he cites La Potherie and Charlevoix: La Potherie, *Histoire*, 2:14; Charlevoix, *Histoire*, 1:264 and 3:212–13.

23 Calloway, *One Vast Winter Count*, 237–8.

24 Rogers, *A Concise Account of North America*, 224.

25 Ibid., 224–5.

26 White, *Middle Ground*, X.

27 Witgen, *Infinity of Nations*.

28 Miller, *Compact, Contract, Covenant*, 33–66.

29 Alfred, *Wasáse*, 19.

30 Allen, *His Majesty's Indian Allies*, 12.

31 Gwyn, "Johnson, Sir William."

32 O'Toole, *White Savage*, 57.

33 Johnson, "The papers of Sir William Johnson," 781.

34 Ibid., 852.

35 Ibid.

36 Ibid., 810.

37 Ibid., 866.

38 Ibid., 667.

39 Ibid., 937–9.

40　Anderson, *Crucible of War*, 240.

41　Taylor, *The Divided Ground*, 73.

42　Shoemaker, "Categories," 51–75; Axtell, "Babel of Tongues," 15–60.

43　Johnson, "The papers of Sir William Johnson," 168.

44　Ibid., 291–2.

45　Henry, *Travels & Adventures In Canada and the Indian Territories*, 24, 252–3, 42–7.

46　Carver, "Captain Jonathan Carver's Journal," 38.

47　Ibid., 38–9.

48　Carver, *Travels Through the Interior Parts of North America*, 266–7.

49　Ibid.

50　Ibid., 268–9.

51　Ibid.

52　Hemphill, *Bowing to Necessities*, 77–9; Orden, *Music, Discipline, and Arms in Early Modern France*.

53　Carver, *Travels Through the Interior Parts of North America*, 267.

54　Ibid., 269.

55　Ibid.

56　Ibid., 270.

57　Gist, *Christopher Gist's Journals*, 53–4.

58　Ibid.

59　Long, *Readings in Canadian History*, 293–4.

60　Ibid., 294–5.

61　Ibid.

62　Long, *Readings in Canadian History*, 294.

63　Ibid., 64–5.

64　Ibid., 64–6.

65　Perrault, *Jean-Baptiste Perrault*, 70–2.

66　Ibid., 64–5.

67　Thompson, *The Writings of David Thompson*, 281–3.

68　Ibid.

69　Malhiot, "A Wisconsin Fur-Trader's Journal, 1804–05," 211.

70　Ibid.

71　Grant, "The Sauteux Indians," 336–7.

72　Ibid., 336–7.

73　Ibid., 335–6.

74　Ibid.

75　Ibid.

76　Henry, *Travels & Adventures*, 252–3.

77　Ibid., 259–61, 286.

78　Mackenzie, *The Journals and Letters of Sir Alexander Mackenzie*, 182–3.

79 Ibid., 136–8.
80 McKenzie, "Chs. McKenzie," 14–15.
81 Ibid.
82 Ibid.
83 Ibid., 17.
84 Ibid., 18.
85 Ibid., 35–6.
86 Fletcher, *The Hako*, 24.
87 Harmon, *A Journal of Voyages and Travels in the Interior of North America*, 44.
88 Ibid., 44–5.
89 Ibid.
90 Ibid., 55–6.
91 Nelson, "Journal 1 Sep. 1808–31 Mar 1810."
92 McDonnell, *Masters of Empire*, 185.
93 Long, *Early Western Travels*, 174–5.
94 In this case, the woman apparently relinquished her "leathern chemise, the place of which of which was supplied by one of gingham, to which was added a calico and green cloth petticoat, and a gown of blue cloth"; Cox, *The Columbia River*, 143.
95 Ermatinger, *Notes and Correspondence on the Expedition to the Clallem Tribe 1828*, 2.

Chapter Five

1 Greer, *Peasant, Lord, and Merchant*, 180.
2 Tilley, *A Phenomenology of Landscape*; Chamberlin, *If This Is Your Land, Where Are Your Stories?*; Lane, *The Solace of Fierce Landscape*; Lane, *Landscapes of the Sacred*.
3 See, for example, Flynn, "Experience and Identity: Black Immigrant Nurses to Canada, 1950–1980," 381–398; Walker, *The History of Immigration and Racism in Canada*; Ma and Cartier, *The Chinese Diaspora*.
4 Greenblatt outlines the five points: 1. Mobility must be taken in a highly literal sense; 2. Mobility studies should shed light on hidden as well as on conspicuous movements of peoples, objects, images, texts, and ideas; 3. Mobility studies should identify and analyze the "contact zones" where cultural goods are exchanged; 4. Mobility studies should account in new ways for the tension between individual agency and structural constraint; 5. Mobility studies should analyze the sensation of rootedness; Greenblatt, *Cultural Mobility*, 250–2.
5 Schafer, *The Tuning of the World* (Toronto: McClelland and Stewart Limited, 1977), 274.

6   On Lake Manitoba where it narrows roughly halfway between its northern and southern extent, "the waves on the loose surface rocks of its north shore produce curious bell-like and wailing sounds, which the first Indian visitors believed came from a huge drum beaten by the spirit Manitou." Sacchetti, "Rock Gongs," 8–13.

7   Feld, "Acoustemology."

8   Ibid.

9   Feld, *Jazz Cosmopolitanism in Accra*.

10 Podruchny, *Making the Voyageur World*.

11 Podruchny, "Baptizing Novices," 2–3.

12 Turner, *The Ritual Process*; Turner, *Dramas, Fields, and Metaphors*.

13 Greenblatt, *Cultural Mobility*, 248.

14 Pratt, *Imperial Eyes*, 7.

15 Basso, *Wisdom Sits in Places*, 66, 109.

16 Ibid., 72.

17 Ibid., 110.

18 Gennep, *The Rites of Passage*, 21.

19 McDonald of Garth, "Autobiographical Notes of John McDonald of Garth …," 2.

20 Nelson, *My First Years in the Fur Trade*, 5.

21 Ibid.

22 Beaudoin, *L'Été Dans la Culture Québécoise XVII-XIX siècles*, 167–9.

23 Ibid., 168.

24 Corbin, *Village Bells*, xi.

25 Henry, *Travels & Adventures*, 16.

26 Garth, "Autobiographical Notes of John McDonald of Garth a Partner in the North West Company 1791 1816," 2.

27 McKenzie, "'Reminiscences,'" 7.

28 Back, *Narrative of the Arctic Land Expedition …*, 32–3.

29 This line had an influential impact on representing the voyageurs and French Canadians as simple and pious subjects against a rustic backdrop. See Moore, *A Canadian boat song*.

30 Macdonell, *Five Fur Traders of the Northwest*, 68.

31 Muir, *Ritual in Early Modern Europe*, 4.

32 The earliest recorded reference I have traced of this song is in *Les Soirées Canadiennes* from 1863. We must be careful because voyageur imagery was used by French Canadian intellectuals, poets, and singers in the St Lawrence, looking back from the mid-late nineteenth century on the pre-industrial era of lumbering and fur trade for romanticized national inspiration. See Grisé, "La Présence De Thomas Moore …," 48–71.

33 Podruchny, *Making the Voyageur World*, 93.

34 Béland, *Chansons de voyageurs, coureurs de bois et forestiers.*

35 Turner, *The Ritual Process,* 96.

36 Henry, *Travels & Adventures,* 29.

37 Harmon, *A Journal of Voyages and Travels …,* 9.

38 McLean, *Notes of a Twenty-Five Year's Service in the Hudson's Bay Territories,* 117.

39 Lefroy, *In Search of the Magnetic North,* 13.

40 Ballantyne, *Hudson's Bay or Every-Day Life in the Wilds of North America,* 75.

41 Ibid., 195.

42 Mackenzie, *Voyages from Montreal through the Continent of North America,* lxii.

43 Nelson, Journal "No. 1" (27 April 1802–April 1803), 11–12.

44 Ibid.

45 Ibid.

46 Bigsby, *The Shoe and Canoe,* 154–6.

47 Garry, *The Diary of Nicholas Garry Deputy-Governor of the Hudson's Bay Company,* 33.

48 Kohl, *Kitchi Gami,* 261–5.

49 La Rue, "Les chansons populaires et historiques du Canada," 371–2; Taché, *Forestiers et Voyageurs,* 158–68; Gagnon, *Chansons Populaire du Canada,* 200–8.

50 Taché, *Forestiers et Voyageurs,* 158–68.

51 My translation. French text from Barbeau, "La complainte de Cadieux …," 163–83.

52 Marius Barbeau conducts a thorough analysis of the variations between thirteen versions of the song. Differences are mostly attributable to variations in wording rather than meaning: ibid., 167–71.

53 Ong, *Orality and Literacy,* 62.

54 McKay, *Quest of the Folk.*

55 Jessup, Nurse, and Smith, *Around and About Marius Barbeau.*

56 Barbeau, "La Complainte de Cadieux," 178.

57 Taché, *Forestiers et Voyageurs,* 175.

58 Marguerite Béclard d'Harcourt, quoted in Barbeau, "La Complainte de Cadieux, coureur de bois (ca. 1709)," 182.

59 Ibid.

60 Darnton, *The Great Cat Massacre,* 9–72.

61 Barbeau, *Canadian Folklore.*

62 Barbeau, "La Complainte de Cadieux," 163.

63 Podruchny, *Making the Voyageur World,* 16.

64 Mackenzie, *Voyages from Montreal through the Continent of North America,* lxii.

65 Podruchny, "Baptizing Novices," 5.

66 Henry, *Travels & Adventures,* 25–6.

67 Podruchny, *Making the Voyageur World,* 16.

68 Podruchny, "Baptizing Novices," 165–95.

69 Harmon, *A Journal of Voyages and Travels in the Interior of North America*, 2.

70 Umfreville, "Journal of a Passage in a Canoe …," 48.

71 Henry the Younger, *The Manuscript Journals of Alexander Henry*, 8.

72 Macdonell, *Five Fur Traders of the Northwest*, 99–100.

73 Mackenzie, *Voyages from Montreal through the Continent of North America*, lxiv.

74 Cox, *The Columbia River*, 341.

75 Garry, *The Diary of Nicholas Garry*, 38; Cox wrote it as "portage des Pins de La Musique," Cox, *The Columbia River*, 341; George Heriot described them merely as numbered musical portages: "*portage premier musique*," and "*portage musique*," George Heriot, *Travels Through the Canadas, Containing a Description of the Picturesque Scenery on Some of the Rivers and Lakes; with an Account of the Productions, Commerce, and Inhabitants of Those Provinces. To Which Is Subjoined a Comparative View of the Manners and Customs of Several of the Indian Nations of North and South America*, 1st ed (1807; repr. Edmonton: M.G. Hurtig, 1971), 240–1.

76 Greenman, *Old Birch Island Cemetery and the Early Historic Trade Route*, 6.

77 Henry, *Travels & Adventures*, 33.

78 They have also been called "sin'dewe," as well as "Assin-mad-wej-wig." "Sounding" or "ringing" stones. The European interpretation that they sounded like "bells" is absent from the Anishinaabe designation, despite some claims that they can be translated as the "bell rocks." See Manitowabi, "Sinmedwe'ek," 444–58.

79 For examples in Africa see Fagg, *The Rock Gong Complex Today and in Prehistoric Times*; Conant, "Rocks that ring," 155–62; Vaughan, *Rock paintings and rock gongs among the Marghi of Nigeria*.

80 Sacchetti, "Rock gongs, bell rocks, ringing rocks, tocsin rocks – unknown in North America? Pity!" 8–14.

81 The translation as "bell rocks," can be found in McGreggor, *Wiigwaaskingaa*, 80.

82 Pearen, *Exploring Manitoulin*, 20–1; Gutsche, Chrisholm, and Floren, *The North Channel and St. Mary's River*, 27–9.

83 Manitowabi, "Sinmedwe'ek," 447–8.

84 Ibid.

85 Edwards, *La Cloche*.

86 "History of Fort la Cloche," *Hudson's Bay Company Archives*.

87 Henry, *Travels & Adventures*, 34.

88 Ibid., 34–5.

89 Jameson, *Winter Studies and Summer Rambles in Canada*, 389.

Chapter Six

1   Barbeau, "The Ermatinger Collection of Voyageur Songs (ca. 1830)," 153–4.

2   Whidden, *Essential Song*, 13.

3   MacDonell, *Five Fur Traders of the Northwest*, 92.

4   McLean, *Notes of a Twenty-five Year's Service in the Hudson's Bay Territories*, 142.

5   Malloy, *The Plains Cree*, 69–95.

6   Cocking et al. "Journal of Occurrences and Transactions at Cumberland House …," 167.

7   Ballantyne, *Hudson's Bay or Every-day life in the Wilds of North America*, 245–6.

8   Frobisher, *A True Discourse of the Late Voyages of Discouerie…*, 62.

9   Ibid.

10 Champlain, *The Works of Samuel de Champlain* vol. 3, 402–3.

11 Goodman, "Sounds Heard, Meaning Deferred," 41–2.

12 Frances Densmore published one such song from in her book *Chippewa Music*, entitled "In her canoe," and listed under *Love Songs*. Densmore, *Chippewa Music*, vol. 1, 183. Among the northern Cree, Lynn Whidden recorded a number of canoe songs, but most seem to be associated with constructing canoes rather than paddling; see Whidden, *Essential Song*, 139–40, 143; Densmore, *Music of the Indians of British Columbia*, 73–5.

13 Cox, *The Columbia River*, 227.

14 Hébert, "Identity, Cultural Production and the Vitality of Francophone Communities Outside Québec," 44–60.

15 Choquette, "Center and Periphery in French North America," 197–8.

16 Greer, *The People of New France*, 85.

17 Paquet and Wallot, "'Nouvelle-France/Quebec/Canada: A World of Limited Identities,'" 99.

18 Nute, *The Voyageur*, 104.

19 McKay, *Quest of the Folk*, 85.

20 La Rue, "Les chansons populaires et historiques du Canada," 321–84; La Rue, "Les chansons populaires et historiques du Canada," 5–72.

21 Gagnon, *Chansons Populaires Du Canada*, viii.

22 Barbeau, *Folk-Songs of Old Quebec*, 1; Barbeau and Sapir, *Folk Songs of French Canada*.

23 Barbeau, *Folk-Songs of Old Quebec*, 11.

24 Ibid.

25 These songs are *Saint Alexis* and *Dame Lombarde*, respectively; see Barbeau, *Canadian Folklore*, 2.

26 Barbeau, *Jongleur Songs of Old Quebec*, vii.

27 Smith, "Ethnomusicological Modelling and Marius Barbeau's 1927 Nass River Field Trip," 215.

28 Ibid.

29 Nute, *The Voyageur*, 143.

30 Podruchny, *Making the Voyageur World*, 89.

31 Laforte, *Survivances Médiévales dans la chanson folklorique*, 264.

32 A caesura is a pause near the middle of a line of poetic verse. As Alan Hindley and Brian Levy explain, the *laisse* possesses a single rhyme / assonance ending; "as the name implies, the lines … are 'leashed' together by this common assonance." See Hindley and Levy, *The Old French Epic*, 21–8.

33 Haines, "Marius Barbeau et le Moyen-Âge."

34 Laforte, "Le Répertoire Authentique des Chansons D'aviron de nos Anciens Canotiers," 145–59.

35 Ibid., 146–9; Béland and Carrier-Aubin, *Chansons de voyageurs, coureurs de bois et forestiers*.

36 Laforte, "Le Répertoire Authentique des Chansons D'aviron de nos Anciens Canotiers," 156; Lacroix and Laforte, "Religion traditionnelle et les chansons des coureurs de bois," 11–42.

37 MacTaggart writes "for I have all their *good boat-songs*, and mean to publish them with the music attached, without which they are useless." See MacTaggart, *Three Years in Canada*, 254.

38 "The Hopkins Book of Canoe Songs," 54–7.

39 Kohl, *Kitchi Gami*, 256.

40 Wentzel, *Les Bourgeois de La Compagnie Du Nord-Ouest*, 71.

41 This information was gleaned from a conversation with an archivist at Library and Archives Canada in October of 2011. It may have been lost in 1904 when a number of items were sold, or it may not have been transferred when the Masson papers were divided between LAC and McGill Library.

42 Barbeau, "The Ermatinger Collection of Voyageur Songs (ca. 1830)," 147–61.

43 Momryk, "Ermatinger, Lawrence."

44 Thomas, "Ermatinger, Edward."

45 Kohl, *Kitchi-Gami*, 255.

46 Ibid., 24–5.

47 The "call" is the introduction of the verse, and five songs of the Ermatinger collection possess a single line "call," followed by a *refrain inséré* (inserted refrain) before the second line of verse. The other six possess an uninterrupted two line "call." Ibid.; There are many descriptions of brigade departures, and they indicate both the bowsman and steersmen leading the singing.

48 In five of eleven songs in the Ermatinger collection, the call is a single line of verse, after which the brigade responds with an exact repetition or with the first line of the chorus. This *refrain inséré* (inserted chorus) breaks up the

soloists' rhymed couplet, providing for rapid alternation between individual and group. Six of the eleven songs in the collection possess a longer two-line call that alternates more slowly with the chorus.

49 Simpson, *Fur Trade and Empire*, 140; Ross, *The Fur Hunters of the Far West*, 293–5.

50 Unknown, "Northwest Company Papers: Indian Ledgers, Etc. [Typescript.]," 99.

51 McDonnell, "North West Company's Western Posts," 4–5.

52 M'Gillivray, *The Journal of Duncan M'Gillivray of the North West Company at Fort George …*," 14–5.

53 The 2/4 timing characterizes nine of eleven songs, while a faster paced 6/8 timing characterizes the other two. See Marius Barbeau, "The Ermatinger Collection of Voyageur Songs (ca. 1830)," 153–161.

54 Ross, *The Fur Hunters of the Far West*, 293.

55 Garry, *The Diary of Nicholas Garry Deputy-Governor of the Hudson's Bay Company*, 34.

56 Dunn, *History of the Oregon Territory and British North American Fur Trade*, 53.

57 Bigsby, *The Shoe and Canoe*, 134–5.

58 Ermatinger, *Edward Ermatinger's York Factory Express Journal …*," 106.

59 Podruchny references the account of Jean Henry Lefroy, a scientist travelling with a Hudson's Bay Company Brigade in 1843–44 to posit that *pipes* were taken "on average every two hours." Podruchny, *Making the Voyageur World*, 124; Grace Lee Nute wrote that three *pipes* covered approximately twelve miles, see Nute, *The Voyageur*, 58.

60 Rochefoucauld-Liancourt, *La Rochefoucault-Liancourt's Travels in Canada 1795*, 293.

61 Kohl, *Kitchi Gami*, 257–60.

62 Ibid., 256–8.

63 Ibid.

64 Ermatinger, *Edward Ermatinger's York Factory Express Journal*.

65 For "*J'ai trop grand peur des loups*" see Moore, *Odes, Epistles and Other Poems*, 133–4; Lanman, "The American Fur Trade."; For "*M'envoient à la fontaine*," see MacTaggart, *Three Years in Canada*, 256–7; Bigsby, *The Shoe and Canoe*, 322; Garry, *The Diary of Nicholas Garry*, 94–5.

66 For "Trois Beaux Canards," see Bradbury, *Travels in the Interior of America*, 12–13; Nicholas Garry's men sang "ye, ye ment" in place of "En roulant ma boule" in the second line of every stanza, "Tous du long de la Rivière" in the fourth, see Garry, *The Diary of Nicholas Garry*, 128; Mountain, *Songs of the Wilderness: Being a Collection of Poems…*, 51; for "Rosier Blanc," see Garry, *The Diary of Nicholas Garry*, 93–4; Kohl, *Kitchi Gami*, 258–60.

67 Robert Darnton and Roger Chartier debated how folkloric symbols functioned, with Chartier arguing for a relatively unambiguous and straightforward relationship between the signifier and signified (lion = valour), while Darton's position was that symbols work "as a mode of ontological participation rather than as a relation of representation." See Darnton, "History and Anthropology," 333; Chartier, "Text, Symbols, and Frenchness," 682–95.

68 Darnton, *The Great Cat Massacre*, xviii, 9–72.

69 An "Episcopal order" issued by New France Bishop La Croix de Saint-Vallier in 1691 condemned not only the "diverse gatherings dances and other entertainments … held on Feast Day sand Sundays, and sometimes even during the hours of Divine Service," but also "the young men and boys, [who] take the liberty to utter in all their gatherings unseemly discourse with double meanings, which causes in their beahviour a corruption which cannot be sufficiently deplored." See Jaenen and Morgan, eds. *Material Memory*, 34–5; Têtu and Gagnon, eds. *Mandements, letters pastorals et circulaires des Evêques des Québec*, 275–81.

70 Laforte, *Survivances Médiévales dans la chanson folklorique*, 171–7; Laforte, "Le Répertoire Authentique des Chansons D'aviron de nos Anciens Canotiers," 145–59.

71 Barbeau, *En Roulant Ma Boule*, 265.

72 Three of the eleven songs in the Ermatinger collection divert from the rhyme scheme established at the outset, although even in these cases most lines adhere to the original *laisse*. "mes blancs moutons garder," "c'est l'oiseau et l'alouette," "un oranger il y a," "le rossignol y chante." Barbeau, "The Ermatinger Collection of Voyageur Songs (ca. 1830)," 153–61.

73 Reverting back to the original rhyme scheme after a new one is introduced occurs in "un oranger il y a." Ibid., 157.

74 Barbeau, "The Ermatinger Collection of Voyageur Songs (ca. 1830)," 147.

75 Weare, "Anaphora," 50; Adams, *Poetic Designs*, 114–16.

76 Barbeau, "The Ermatinger Collection of Voyageur Songs (ca. 1830)," 153.

77 Ibid., 153–4.

78 Ibid., 154.

79 Ibid., 160.

80 Podruchny, *Making the Voyageur World*, 260–7, 283–6.

81 Collection of C.M. Barbeau, "Trois cavaliers fort bien montés / M'en Revenant de L'alendrie," recorded by Germaine L. from Mme J-Bte Leblond, from Ste-Famille, Montmorency QC, 1928, Archives de Folklore, Laval University (Ms no 167).

82 "Et des belles filles à nos côtés, Tu as menti, franc cavalier, Tu as couché dans l'poulailer, Une grosse mouton à tes côtés"; "Tu as menti gros cavalier,

Tu vas coucher dans l'poulailler, Les poules les coqs à tes côtés, Un gros coq d'Inde et à tes pieds." See Collection Anne-Marie Doyon, "Trois cavaliers fort bien montés, J'ai vu le loup, le r'nard passer," Archives de Folklore, Laval University (enreg no. 16).

83 "Dans la maison accoutumée? Tu as menti, franc cavalier, Tu coucheras dans l'poulailler, Les poules, les oies ferent sur toi." Collection Huguette Théberge, "Trois cavaliers fort bien montés," recorded from Madame R. Théberge, Saint-Hugues, QC, 1969 (bobine 2, enregistrement 100).

84 "Là nous coucherons dans le poulailler, Les poules te picocheront le nez, Là nous coucherons sous l'escalier, Les rats te grafigneront le nez." Collection J.T. LeBlanc, "Trois cavaliers fort bien montés / Par un beau soir, m'y promenant," Archives de Folklore, Laval University (ms no 591).

85 Collection E.Z. Massicotte, "La fille au cresson / M'envoye t'a la fontaine," Archives de Folklore, Laval University (MN 3023).

86 Collection of C.M. Barbeau, "La fille au cresson / M'envoie a la fontaine," Archives de Folklore, Laval University (MN 275).

87 Collection E.M. Massicotte, "Nous etions trios soldats / Le Deserteur Pendu," Archives de Folklore, Laval University (BM 537).

88 Coirault, *Répertoire des Chansons Françaises de tradition orale*, 361–2.

89 Collection E.M. Massicotte, "Nous etions trios soldats / Le Deserteur Pendu," Archives de Folklore, Laval University (BM 537).

90 Dechêne and Paré, *Le Peuple, L'État et la Guerre Au Canada Sous le Régime Français*; Eccles, "The Social, Economic, and Political Significance of the Military Establishment in New France," 1–22.

91 Devine, *The People Who Own Themselves*, 23–28, 34–37.

92 Thompson, *The Making of the English Working Class*, 9.

93 Beaugrand, *La Chasse Galerie, and Other Canadian Stories*.

94 York boats varied in length from twenty-seven to forty-two feet, with a freight capacity of three and a half or four tons (with a total capacity of six tons per boat) and a crew of six to eight oarsmen, while the *canots du maître* carried three or four tons freight but required a larger crew, typically eight to ten men, but sometimes as many as fourteen; see Beardy and Coutts, *Voices from Hudson Bay*, 130; Glover, "York Boats," 19–23; Macdougall, *One of the Family*, 41; Podruchny, *Making the Voyageur World*, 24–5; Nute, *The Voyageur*, 24.

95 Thompson, *David Thompson's Narrative, 1784–1812*, 319.

96 Podruchny, *Making the Voyageur World*, 234–40.

97 Ibid., 118–20.

98 Ens, "The Battle of Seven Oaks and the Articulation of a Metis National Tradition, 1811–1849," 95.

99 Kohl, *Kitchi Gami*, 72.

100 Ibid., 256.

101 Simcoe, *Mrs. Simcoe's Diary*, 63–4.

102 Garry, *The Diary of Nicholas Garry*, 96.

103 Cox, *The Columbia River*, 355.

104 Ibid., 343.

105 Ross, *The Fur Hunters of the Far West*, 295.

106 Howison, *Sketches of Upper Canada, Domestic, Local, and Characteristic*, 31.

107 Levitin, *This Is Your Brain on Music*, 249; Levitin, *World in Six Songs*, 21, 76, 86, 89, 92, 99, 101, 307.

108 Laforte, "Le Répertoire Authentique des Chansons D'aviron de nos Anciens Canotiers," 156.

109 Garry, *The Diary of Nicholas Garry Deputy-Governor of the Hudson's Bay Company*, 34.

110 Weld, *Travels through the States of North America …*, 51.

111 Epstein, "Slave Music in the United States before 1860."

112 Nute, *The Voyageur*, 28.

113 Podruchny, *Making the Voyageur World*, 89.

114 For instance, Ballantyne described the voices "rising and falling faintly in the distance." See Ballantyne, *Hudson's Bay or Every-Day Life in the Wilds of North America*, 245; Anna Jameson wrote that the songs were "animated … they all sing in unison, raising their voices." See Jameson, *Winter Studies and Summer Rambles in Canada*, 425; Henry M. Robinson described voyageur songs "rising and falling in soft cadences in the distance." See Robinson, *The Great Fur Land*, 31–2.

115 Bigsby, *The Shoe and Canoe*, 143–4.

116 MacTaggart, *Three Years in Canada*, 255; Head, *Forest Scenes and Incidents*, 343.

117 Ballantyne, *Hudson's Bay or Every-Day Life in the Wilds of North America*, 72.

118 Jameson, *Winter Studies and Summer Rambles*, 425.

119 Robertson, *Colin Robertson's Correspondence Book*, 90.

120 Prey, "Formation et Métamorphoses d'une chanson: *le Canard blanc*," thesis, Université Laval, Quebec, 1959, cited in Laforte, *Survivances Médiévales dans la Chanson Folklorique*, 66; Barbeau, *Trois Beaux Canards*.

121 Moore, *Odes, Epistles and Other Poems*, 133–4.

122 Lanman, "The American Fur Trade," 189.

123 Collection of C.M. Barbeau, "La fille au cresson / M'envoie a la fontaine," Archives de Folklore, Laval University (MN 275).

124 Barbeau, *Jongleur Songs of Old Quebec*, 138–141.

125 Koskoff, *The Concise Garland Encyclopedia of World Music*, 59, 105, 251, 300, 313, 323, 330, 334, 474, 574, 590, 636, 653, 657; Nettl, *Excursions in World Music*, 329.

126 Gagnon, *Chansons Populaires du Canada*, 62.

127   Barbeau, "The Ermatinger Collection of Voyageur Songs (ca. 1830)," 147–61.

128   Kohl, *Kitchi Gami*, 257–9.

129   Ibid.

130   Laxer, "A Reservoir of Voices," 62.

131   Keillor, Archambault, Kelly, *Encyclopedia of Native American Music of North America*.

132   Gioia, *Work Songs*, 126.

133   Grabowski & St-Onge, "Montreal Iroquois *engagés* in the Western Fur Trade, 1800–1821," 23–58.

134   Ross, *The Fur Hunters of the Far West*, 286.

135   For instance, when Pierre Aubert journeyed to Red River in 1845, he described his crew. "Notre équipage se composait de six hommes, dont deux Iroquois et quatre Canadiens, hommes rompus aux fatigues des voyages, doués de fort belles voix et sachant par coeur le répertoire de toutes les chansons canadiennes." (Our retinue was composed of six men, two Iroquois and four Canadiens, men broken to the fatigues of voyages, gifted with strong good voices and knowing by heart the repertoire of all the Canadian songs.) Aubert, *Missions de La Congrégation Des Missionnaires Oblats de Marie Immaculée*, 183–4.

136   Ross, *The Fur Hunters of the Far West*, 291.

137   Kohl, *Kitchi Gami*, 261; Podruchny, *Making the Voyageur World*, xii.

138   For analyses of the NWC and HBC labour models, see Podruchny, *Making the Voyageur World*, 136; Burley, *Servants of the Honourable Company*, 245.

139   Baker, "Lake Superior," cited in Nute, *The Voyageur*, 265.

140   This passage was recorded in Robert Kennicott's journal in January 1862 at La Pierre's House. See Kennicott, "Robert Kennicott," 133–226.

141   Barbeau, "The Ermatinger Collection of Voyageur Songs (ca. 1830)," 160–1.

142   Barbeau, "Voyageur Songs of the Missouri," 338.

143   Personal correspondence, Alan Corbiere, 2 April 2019.

144   Ibid.

145   Henry, *Travels & Adventures In Canada and the Indian Territories*, 111–2.

146   Ens, *Homeland to Hinterland*, 29, 46.

147   MacLeod, *Songs of Old Manitoba*, 1–2.

148   Ibid., 2–9; Jones, "Commonplace and Memorization in the Oral Tradition of the English and Scottish Popular Ballads," 97–112.

149   O'Toole, "From Entity to Identity to Nation," 143–179.

150   Chartrand, *Pierriche Falcon*.

151   Ens, "The Battle of Seven Oaks," 109.

152   Whidden, *Métis Songs*.

153   Grant, *Les Bourgeois de La Compagnie Du Nord-Ouest*, vol. 2, 313.

154   Ross, *The Fur Hunters of the Far West*, 293, 295.

155 The official meetings began with a calumet ceremony, a speech, and a French Canadian voyageur song according to the rules and regulation book. See Gray, "The Beaver Club, Rules and Regulations of the Beaver Club," 305; Podruchny, "Festivities, Fortitude, and Fraternalism."
156 Reed, *Masters of the Wilderness*, 70–1.
157 Podruchny, *Making the Voyageur World*, 146; Podruchny, "Festivities, Fortitude, and Fraternalism."
158 Laxer, "Row, Brothers, Row," 70–99.
159 Bigsby, *The Shoe and Canoe*, 119.
160 Wilcocke, *Récits de Voyages Lettres et Rapports Inédits Relatifs Au Nord-Ouest Canadien*, vol 2, 214.
161 Sadly, their surnames are not provided; see Verchères de Boucherville, *War on the Detroit*, 3.
162 Ibid., 169–70.

Chapter Seven

1 George Nelson, *Letter-Journal*, quoted in Jennifer Brown and Robert Brightman, *Orders of the Dreamed*, 58–9.
2 Landes, *Ojibwa Religion and the Midéwiwin*; Dewdney, *The Sacred Scrolls of the Southern Ojibway*; Densmore, *Chippewa Music*.
3 Innis, *The Fur Trade in Canada*, xii; see Bryce, *The Remarkable History of the Hudson's Bay Company*; Laut, *The Adventurers of England on Hudson Bay*.
4 Ray, *Indians in the Fur Trade*, 33.
5 Speck, *Naskapi*, 232; Martin, *Keepers of the Game*, 115; Densmore, *Chippewa Music*, 82–6.
6 Sandlos, *Hunters at the Margin*, 16.
7 Preston, *Cree Narrative*, 199.
8 Thompson, *The Writings of David Thompson*, 105.
9 Whidden, *Essential Song*, 17.
10 Ibid., 18.
11 Ibid., 19.
12 Ibid., xiv.
13 Nelson, *My First Years in the Fur Trade*, 143.
14 Ibid., 143–4.
15 Ibid.
16 Ibid., 145–6.
17 Ibid.
18 Ibid., 146.
19 Ibid., 153.
20 Ibid.

21 Cameron, *Les Bourgeois De La Compagnie Du Nord-Ouest*, Vol. 2, 262.

22 Ibid., 254.

23 Ibid.

24 Tanner, *A Narrative of the Captivity and Adventures of John Tanner*, 182–3.

25 Ibid.

26 Deloria, *The World We Used to Live In*, 16–41.

27 Tanner, *A Narrative of the Captivity and Adventures of John Tanner*, 184.

28 Ibid., 202–3.

29 Benn, *Native Memoirs from the War of 1812*, 116.

30 Pomedli, *Living with Animals*, 28.

31 Gioia, *Work Songs*, 25.

32 Ermatinger, "Old memo book and journal of Edward Ermatinger 1823–1830," 14.

33 Benton-Banai, *The Mishomis Book*, 74; Johnston, *Ojibway Heritage*, 80–93.

34 Hickerson, "Notes on the Post-Contact Origin of the Midewiwin."

35 Hallowell, *The Role of Conjuring in Saulteaux Society*; Landes, *Ojibwa Religion and the Midéwiwin*.

36 Angel, *Historical Perspectives on the Ojibwa Midewiwin*, 10–1.

37 Johnston, *Ojibway Heritage*, 83–4.

38 Densmore, *Chippewa Music*, vol. 1, 82–8.

39 Ibid., 51, 85.

40 Pomedli, *Living with Animals*, 3.

41 Blessing, "Medicine Bags and Bundles of Midewiwin," 127.

42 Henry, *The Journal of Alexander Henry the Younger 1799–1814*, 118–9.

43 Connor, *Five Fur Traders of the Northwest*, 260.

44 McLellan, "Northwest Company Papers: Indian Ledgers, Etc. [Typescript.]," 77.

45 Nelson, "Journals, 1802–1839," 12.

46 Ibid.

47 See for example, Thompson, *The Writings of David Thompson*, 231.

48 Nelson, "Journals, 1802–1839," 12.

49 Podruchny, *Making the Voyageur World*, 114–121.

50 This was drafted for Roderick Mackenzie's intended publication. Morrison, "Grant, Peter."

51 Grant, *Les Bourgeois De La Compagnie Du Nord-Ouest*, 361.

52 Ibid.

53 Ibid., 361–2.

54 Ibid., 362–3.

55 Kane, *Wanderings of an Artist Among the Indians of North America*, 47.

56 Ibid., 47–8.

57 Henry, *Travels & Adventures*, 161.

58 Ibid., 161–2.

59 Thompson, *The Writings of David Thompson*, 106.

60 Ibid.

61 Ibid.

62 McDonnell, *Les Bourgeois De La Compagnie Du Nord-Ouest*, 276–8.

63 Ibid.

64 Cameron, *Les Bourgeois De La Compagnie Du Nord-Ouest*, 264.

65 Nelson, "*The Orders of the Dreamed*," 83–4.

66 Ibid., 83.

67 Preston, *Cree Narrative*, 80.

68 Gough, introduction to Henry, *The Journal of Alexander Henry the Younger 1799–1814*, 73; Moreau, *The Writings of David Thompson*, 234.

69 Vecsey, *Traditional Ojibwa Religion and Its Historical Changes*, 191–2; Matthews and Roulette, "Fair Wind's Dream: Naamiwan Obowaajigewin," 264.

70 Moreau, *The Writings of David Thompson*, 234.

71 Angel, *Historical Perspectives on the Ojibwa Midewiwin*, 38.

72 Pomedli, *Living with Animals*, 7.

73 Peers, *The Ojibwa of Western Canada, 1780 to 1870*, ix, 7–8.

74 Thompson, *The Writings of David Thompson*, 231.

75 Ibid.

76 Densmore, *Chippewa Music*, V.

77 Thompson, *The Writings of David Thompson*, 231.

78 Ibid.

79 Ibid., 231–2.

80 Ibid., 232.

81 Ibid.

82 Ibid., 232–3.

83 Ibid., 233.

84 Ibid.

85 Ibid.

86 Ibid., 233–4.

87 Henry the Younger, *Journal of Alexander Henry the Younger 1799–1814*, vol. 1, 76.

88 Ibid., 108.

89 Ibid., 130.

90 Ibid., 109.

91 Tanner, *A Narrative of the Captivity and Adventures of John Tanner*, 121–2.

92 Ibid., 122–3.

93 Ibid.

94 Ibid., 122–3.

95 Ray and Freeman, "*Give Us Good Measure*," 59.

96 Binnema, *Enlightened Zeal*, 98, 153, 172, 196.

97 Henry, *Travels & Adventures*, 115.

98 Ibid., 115–17.

99 Ibid., 117–18.

100 Ibid., 115–16.

101 Ibid., 118–19.

102 Hearne, *A Journey from Prince of Wales's Fort in Hudson's Bay...*, 228–9.

103 Ibid.

104 Ibid., 230–1.

105 Ibid.

106 Ibid., 232.

107 Ibid.

108 Thompson, *The Writings of David Thompson*, 235.

109 Mackenzie, *The Journals and Letters of Sir Alexander Mackenzie*, 254–5.

110 Keith, *Récits De Voyages Lettres Et Rapports Inédits Relatifs Au Nord-Ouest Canadien*, 127.

111 Keith, "An Account of MacKenzie's River Department," 46.

112 Cox, *The Columbia River*, 178.

113 Ibid.

114 Trenk, "Religious Uses of Alcohol among the Woodland Indians of North America," 77.

115 Nelson, *The Order of the Dreamed*, 38.

116 Ibid., 56.

117 Ibid., 59.

118 Ibid., 59–60.

Chapter Eight

1 Wilkins, "The Fiddlers of James Bay"; Mishler, *The Crooked Stove-Pipe*; Lederman, "Old Indian and Métis Fiddling ..."

2 Fischer, *Champlain's Dream*, 215–16.

3 Thwaites, *The Jesuit Relations and Allied Documents*, vol. 27, 12.

4 Ibid., vol. 50, 14–15.

5 Arthur, Chapman, and Massey, *Moose Factory 1673 to 1947*, 5.

6 Bassett, "Christmas in the Fur Trade," 18–23.

7 Wilkins, "The Fiddlers of James Bay," 70; Lederman, "Aboriginal Fiddling," 323.

8 Cocking et al., "Journal of Occurrences and Transactions at Cumberland House by Mr. Matthew Cocking and Others, Commencing the 4th July 1776 and Ending the 4th July 1777 By William Walker," 93.

9   Hansom, "A Journal of the Most Remarkable Transactions and Occurrences at Cumberland House," 251.

10   Swain, "A Journal of Occurrences at York Factory," 21–3.

11   Binnema and Ens, *Edmonton House Journals*, 343.

12   Ibid., 372.

13   Hargrave, *Letters from Rupert's Land, 1826–1840*, 180.

14   Ibid., 97.

15   Keillor, *Music in Canada*, 63.

16   Ibid.

17   Johnson, "Warren Johnson's Journal 1760–1761," 203.

18   Pond, *Five Fur Traders of the Northwest*, 47.

19   Askin, *The John Askin Papers*, 68.

20   Askin, *Fur-Trade on the Upper lakes 1778–1815*, 251–2.

21   Askin, "Fur-Trade on the Upper Lakes 1778–1815," 251–2.

22   Perrault, *Jean-Baptiste Perrault Marchand Voyageur*, 66.

23   Ibid.

24   Harmon, *A Journal of Voyages and Travels in the Interior of North America*, 14–17.

25   Ibid., 14–15.

26   Harmon, *A Journal of Voyages and Travels in the Interior of North America*, 76.

27   Ibid., 118.

28   Ibid., 94.

29   Ibid., 107–8.

30   McLeod, *Five Fur Traders of the Northwest*, 170.

31   Van Kirk, *Many Tender Ties*, 29; Brown, *Strangers in Blood*, 51–110.

32   Nelson, "No. 5" Journal, June 1807–Oct. 1809, 206–7.

33   Nelson, "Journal 1 Sep. 1808–31 Mar 1810," 1.

34   Nelson, "Journal Nov 1807–Aug 1808," 42.

35   Unknown, "Northwest Company Papers: Indian Ledgers, Etc. [Typescript.]," 10.

36   Nelson, "Journal 1 Sep. 1808–31 Mar 1810," entry for Sunday, 9 September.

37   McDonnell, *Les Bourgeois De La Compagnie Du Nord-Ouest*, 285.

38   Harmon, *A Journal of Voyages and Travels in the Interior of North America*, 36.

39   Ibid., 36–7.

40   McLeod, *Five Fur Traders of the Northwest*, 135–6.

41   This fort was recently renamed from Bas-de-la-Rivière. See Brown, "Duncan, Cameron."

42   Nelson, "Journal 1 April 1810–1 May 1811."

43   Ibid.

44   Ibid.

45   McLeod, *Five Fur Traders of the Northwest*, 148.

46 Nelson, "Volume 1: Miscellaneous recipies, vocabularies, etc."

47 Laforte, *Survivances Médiévales dans la chanson folklorique*, 50–1.

48 Ermatinger, "Memoranda 1826," 33.

49 Muir, *Ritual in Early Modern Europe*, 134–40.

50 Brown, *Strangers in Blood*, 42–50.

51 Morrison, *Simon McGillivray's Fort William Notebook, 1815*, 4.

52 McGillivray, *Simon McGillivray's Fort William Notebook, 1815*, 30.

53 Ibid., 31.

54 Keillor, *Music in Canada*, 71–3.

55 Lambert, *Travels Through Canada…*, 173–4.

56 McGillivray, *The North West Company in Rebellion*, 31.

57 Cox, *The Columbia River*, 321–2.

58 Keillor, *Music in Canada*, 72.

59 Cox, *The Columbia River*, 333.

60 Ibid.

61 Wentzel, *Les Bourgeois De La Compagnie Du Nord-Ouest*, 107.

62 Ibid., 107–8.

63 Few of his recommendations and warnings were heeded on Franklin's disastrous journey.

64 Ibid., 71.

65 Keillor, *Music in Canada*, 63.

66 "Summary of Excavation Block 00–07," Royal Alberta Museum, (Borden: F; Pi-63; Catalogue #2127).

67 Troman, *Rowley and the Jews Harp*.

68 Howison, *Sketches of Upper Canada*, 130–1.

69 "Lake 2 Mountains Inv. Cont.," *North West Company Account Book 1821*, 132.

70 "Amount Brot Forward," *North West Company Account Book 1820–1821*, 25.

71 "Columbia Inventory Cont," *North West Company Account Book 1821*, 50.

72 "Amount Brot Forw," *North West Company Account Book 1821*, 133.

73 Ermatinger, "Memoranda 1826," 29–30.

74 Ermatinger, "1821/1822 Memorandum Book," 3.

75 Ermatinger, "Memorandums for 1823," 1.

76 Ermatinger, "Memoranda 1826," 16.

77 Dears, "Letter of Thomas Dears to Edward Ermatinger," 286–7.

78 Tod, "John Tod to Edward Ermatinger," 15.

79 Ermatinger, "Old Memo Book and Journal of Edward Ermatinger," 17–21.

80 Dears, "Ermatinger, Edward. Papers of Edward Ermatinger, 1826–1843," 292.

81 The Traditional Tune Archive, https://tunearch.org/wiki/Annotation:Life_Let_Us_Cherish, accessed 8 May 2020.

82 Ballantyne, *Hudson's Bay or Every-Day Life in the Wilds of North America*, 163–5.

83   Beattie, "My Best Friend," 1–31.

84   Askin, The John Askin Papers, 79, 87.

85   Cox, *The Columbia River*, 222–3.

86   Ermatinger, "Memorandums for 1823," 1.

87   The figure in the column for pence is unclear: it could be a 6 or 5 or 0, although 0 was customarily marked as ".

88   Ermatinger, "Memorandums for 1823," 21.

89   Wolfenden, "Tod, John."

90   John Tod, "John Tod to Edward Ermatinger," 124–5.

91   Ibid.

92   Tod, "John Tod to Edward Ermatinger," 104.

93   Ens and Sawchuk, *From New Peoples to New Nations*, 87–8; Chartrand, *Pierriche Falcon*.

94   Simpson, *Journal of Occurrences*, 7.

95   Ibid., 71–2.

96   Ibid., 72–3.

97   Ibid.

98   Ibid., 99.

99   Ibid.

100   Raffan, *Emperor of the North*, 117.

101   Ibid., 204–5.

102   Ibid., 205.

103   Tod, "John Tod to Edward Ermatinger," McLeods Lake, 27 February 1826, New Caledonia, 1.

104   Tod, "John Tod to Edward Ermatinger," New Caledonia, 10 April 1831, 21; Tod, "John Tod to Edward Ermatinger," Bas de la Rivier, Fort Alexander, 29 June 1836, 31; Tod, "John Tod to Edward Ermatinger," Thompsons River, 20 March 1843, 81.

105   Tod, "John Tod to Edward Ermatinger," McLeods Lake, 27 February 1826, New Caledonia, 4–5.

106   Tod, "John Tod to Edward Ermatinger," New Caledonia McLeods Lake, 14 February 1829, 8.

107   Ballantyne, *Hudson's Bay or Every-day Life in the Wilds of North America*, 125.

108   Tod, "John Tod to Edward Ermatinger," Oxford House, 15 July 1837, 37.

109   Ballantyne, *Hudson's Bay or Every-Day life in the Wilds of North America*, 253–4.

110   Ibid., 254.

111   Ibid.

112   Lefroy, *In Search of the Magnetic North*, 111.

113   Ibid., 115.

114 Burley, *Servants of the Honourable Company*, 5; Brown, *Strangers in Blood*, 199–211.

115 Ens, *Homeland to Hinterland*, 22.

116 Merk, *Fur Trade and Empire*, xlvi.

117 Brown, *Strangers in Blood*, 202–3.

118 Simpson, *Fur Trade and Empire*, 14.

119 Ibid.

120 Ibid.

121 Simpson, "Geo Simpson to John McLeod," York Factory, 7 July 1826, 52.

122 McLeod, "Minutes of Council of Northern Department, 1825," 33.

123 Ibid., 37–8.

124 Hargrave, Fort Garry, 20 January 1827, *Letters from Rupert's Land*, 78–9.

125 Stevenson, "The Red River Indian Mission School and John West's 'Little Charges,' 1820–1833," 133.

126 Jones, "Rev Jones' journal 1825–26."

127 Smithurst, "Rev J Smithurst's Jrnl July 1 1840 to 31 July 1840," entry for 26 June 1840.

128 Roberts, "Journal of Mr John Roberts."

129 Cowley, "Book order."

130 Smithurst, "Smithurst Journal Nov. 1 1846–July 31 1847."

131 Ibid., 28 December.

132 Erasmus, *Buffalo Days and Nights*, 6–7.

133 Ibid., 7.

134 Ibid., 41.

135 Ibid., 41–3.

136 Grant, *A Son of the Fur Trade*, 215, 271.

137 Mishler, *The Crooked Stovepipe*; Whidden, *Essential Song*; Wilkins, "The Fiddlers of James Bay"; Lederman, "Old Native and Metis Fiddling in Two Manitoba Communities."

138 Whidden, *Essential Song*, 43.

139 Wilkins, "The Fiddlers of James Bay," 74.

140 Ibid., 64.

141 Lederman, "Old Native and Metis Fiddling in Two Manitoba Communities," 8–9.

142 Ibid., 9–11.

143 Dueck, *Musical Intimacies and Indigenous Imaginaries*, 167–73.

144 Randall, "Genthon the Fiddler," 17.

145 Whidden, *Métis Songs*, 77.

146 Gibbons, *Folk Fiddling in Canada*, 71–114.

147 Kennicott, "The Journal," 108–9.

148   Ibid., 108.

149   Ibid., 109.

150   Mishler, *The Crooked Stovepipe*, 19.

151   Ibid., 65.

152   Leary, *Medicine Fiddle*.

153   Kennicott, "The Journal," 109.

Conclusion

1   O'Brian and White, *Beyond Wilderness*, 14.

2   Anderson, *Fur Trader's Story*, 22.

3   Ibid., 29.

4   Rodgers, *The Fiddlers of James Bay;* Cheechoo, *Shay Chee Man.*

5   Ferland, *Chansons à répondre du Manitoba.*

6   Sawatzky, "From Trade Routes to Rural Farm."

7   Mishler, *The Crooked Stovepipe*, 9.

8   Macdougall, "The Myth of Metis Cultural Ambivalence," 437.

9   Podruchny, Gleach, and Roulette, "Putting up Poles: Power, Navigation, and Cultural Mixing in the Fur Trade," 25.

Bibliography

Archives and Collections

BRITISH COLUMBIA
British Columbia Archives
A-B-20-V5. Francis Ermatinger. "Notes and Correspondence on the Expedition to the Clallem Tribe 1828."
A-B-40-D75.2. James Douglas. "Diary of a Trip to the Northwest Coast. April 22-October 2, 1840."
A-B-40-ER62.3. "Ermatinger, Edward. "Papers of Edward Ermatinger, 1826–1843."
A-B-40-M142A. Archibald Macdonald, 1790–1853. "Correspondence Outward. Transcripts."
A-B-40-M22K. John McLeod Sr. "Journals and Correspondence of John McLeod Sr. 1812–1844."

WINNIPEG
Hudson's Bay Company Archives
B.239/a/126. James Swain. "A Journal of Occurrences at York Factory." 1818–19.
E.12/5, E.12/6. Isobel Finlayson. "Journal en route from YF to RR, entry for Sunday 6 August 1840."
Microfilm Reel 5M6. North West Company Account Book 1820.
Microfilm Reel 5M9. North West Company Account Book 1820.
Microfilm Reel 5M10. North West Company Account Book 1820–1821.
Microfilm Reel 5M11. North West Company Account Book 1821.
Microfilm Reel 5M12. North West Company Account Book 1821.
Church Missionary Society (CMS)
C1/055/9. John Roberts. "Journal of Mr John Roberts."
C1/019/4B. "Book order." A. Cowley. 1842.

Microfilm Reel A77. Rev Jones, "Rev Jones' journal 1825–26."
Microfilm Reel A78. J Smithurst. "Rev J Smithurst's Jrnl July 1 1840 to 31 July 1840."
Microfilm Reel A79. J Smithurst, "Smithurst Journal Nov. 1 1846–July 31 1847."

TORONTO
Archives of Ontario

F471-1-0-6 B803021. Charles McKenzie. "Chs. McKenzie."

F471-1-0-15, B803021. Roderick MacKenzie. "An Account of the Athabasca Indians by A Partner of the North West Company."

F471-1-0-16, B803021. George Keith. "An Account of MacKenzie's River Department."

F471-1-0-17 B803021. John McDonnell. "North West Company's Western Posts."

MU 2200. Edward Umfreville. "Journal of a Passage in a Canoe from Pais Plat in Lake Superior, to Portage de l'Isle in Riviere Ouinipique."

MU 2200. Roderick Mackenzie. "An Account of the Athabasca Indians by a Partner of the North West Company."

Thomas Fisher Rare Book Library

77 box 2. Manuscript Collection. "Northwest Company Papers: Indian Ledgers, Etc. [Typescript.]."

Toronto Metropolitan Reference Library Baldwin Reading Room

S13. George Nelson Collection. Journals, 1802–1839. Journal. "No. 1" 27 April 1802–April 1803. Journal. "No. 5" June 1807–Oct. 1809. Journal. "B" 1 May–June 8, 1819. Journal. 1 Sep. 1808–31 Mar 1810. Journal. 1 April 1810–1 May 1811.

Miscellaneous. "Volume 1: Miscellaneous recipies, vocabularies, etc."

OTTAWA
Library and Archives Canada

MG19 A2. Edward Ermatinger. "1821/1822 Memorandum Book."

MG19 A2. Edward Ermatinger. "Memoranda 1826."

MG19 A2. Edward Ermatinger. "Memorandums for 1823."

MG19 A2. Edward Ermatinger. "Old memo book and journal of Edward Ermatinger 1823–1830." MG19 A17 to A20. "Autobiographical Notes of John McDonald of Garth a Partner in the North West Company 1791–1816."

MONTREAL
McCord Museum

M15467. W. Gray. "The Beaver Club, Rules and Regulations of the Beaver Club."

QUEBEC

Archives de folklore et d'ethnologie

BM 537. Collection E.M. Massicotte.

Bobine 2, enregistrement 100. Collection Huguette Théberge. Enreg no. 16.

Collection Anne-Marie Doyon.

MN 275. Collection of C.M. Barbeau.

MN 3023. Collection E.Z. Massicotte.

MS no 1. Collection of Luc Lacourcière.

MS no 167. Collection of C.M. Barbeau.

MS no 591. Collection J.T. LeBlanc.

Personal Correspondence

Alan Corbiere. E-mail correspondence. 2 April 2019.

Peter Ittinuar. E-mail correspondence. 27 March 2019.

Secondary Sources

Agnew, Vanessa. "A 'Scots Orpheus' in the South Seas, Or, the Use of Music on Cook's Second Voyage." *Journal for Maritime Research* 3, no. 1 (2001): 1–27.

– *Enlightenment Orpheus: the Power of Music in Other Worlds*. New York: Oxford University Press, 2008.

Allen, Robert S. *His Majesty's Indian Allies: British Indian Policy in The Defence of Canada, 1774–1815*. Toronto & Oxford: Dundurn Press, 1992.

Amtmann, Willy. *Music in Canada 1600–1800*. Cambridge: Habitex Books, 1975.

Anderson, Fred. *Crucible of War: The Seven Years' War and the Fate of Empire in British North America, 1754–1766*. New York: Alfred A. Knopf, 2000.

Angel, Michael. *Historical Perspectives on the Ojibwa Midewiwin: Preserving the Sacred*. Winnipeg: The University of Manitoba Press, 2002.

Arthur, Eric, Howard Chapman, and Hart Massey, eds. *Moose Factory 1673 to 1947*. Toronto: University of Toronto Press, 1949.

Asch, Michael. *Kinship and the Drum Dance in a Northern Dene Community*. Edmonton: Boreal Institute for Northern Studies, 1988.

Askin, John. "Fur-Trade on the Upper Lakes 1778–1815." In *Collections of the State Historical Society of Wisconsin*. Edited by Reuben Gold Thwaites. Madison: Published by the Society, 1910.

– *The John Askin Papers*, edited by Milo M. Quaife. Volume 1: 1747–1795. Detroit: Detroit Library Commission, 1928.

Aubert, Pierre. *Missions de La Congrégation Des Missionnaires Oblats de Marie Immaculée*. Paris: Typographie Hennuyer et Fils, Rue du Boulevard, 7.

Axtell, James. "Babel of Tongues: Communicating with the Indians in Eastern North America." In *The Language Encounter in the Americas*. Edited by Edward G. Gray and Norman Fiering. New York: Berghahn Books, 2000.

Back, Captain George. *Narrative of the Arctic Land Expedition to the Mouth of the Great Fish River, and Along the Shores of the Arctic Ocean, In the Years 1833, 1834, 1835*. Edmonton: M.G. Hurtig LTD. Booksellers & Publishers, n.d.

Baker, Theodore. *On the Music of North American Indians (1882)*, reprinted. New York: Da Capo Press, 1977.

Baldwin, Betsey. "200 Years of Treaty Annuities." *Active History*, 19 December 2018. http://activehistory.ca/2018/12/200-years-of-treaty-annuities/.

Ballantyne, Robert M. *Hudson's Bay or Every-Day Life in the Wilds of North America: During Six Years' Residence in the Territories of the Honourable Hudson's Bay Company* (1848), reprinted. Edmonton: Hurtig Publishers, 1972.

Ballantyne, Tony, and Antoinette Burton, eds. *Bodies in Contact: Rethinking Colonial Encounters in World History*. Durham, NC: Duke University Press, 2005.

Barbeau, Marius. *Canadian Folklore: The French Folklore Bulletin*. New York: The French Folklore Society, 1946.

– *En Roulant Ma Boule, Répertoire de la chanson folklorique française au Canada*. Part 2. Ottawa: Musée National du Canada, 1982.

– *Folk-Songs of Old Quebec*. Song translations by Regina Lenore Shoolman. National Museum of Canada, 1934.

– *Huron and Wyandot mythology: with an appendix containing earlier published records*. Ottawa: Government Printing Bureau, 1915.

– *Jongleur Songs of Old Quebec*. Interpreted into English by Sir Harold Boulton and Sir Ernest MacMillan. Toronto: The Ryerson Press, 1962.

– "La complainte de Cadieux, coureur de bois (ca. 1709)." *The Journal of American Folklore* 67 no. 264 (April-June 1954): 163–83.

– *Le Rossignol Y Chante, Répertoire de la chanson folklorique française au Canada*. Part 1. Duhamel: 1962.

– *Répertoire de la chanson folklorique française au Canada*. 3 vols. Ottawa: Musée National du Canada, 1982.

– "The Ermatinger Collection of Voyageur Songs (ca. 1830)." *Journal of American Folklore* 67 (April–June 1954): 147–61.

– *Trois Beaux Canards (92 versions canadiennes)*. Montreal: Éditions Fides, 1947.

– "Voyageur Songs of the Missouri." *Bulletin of The Missouri Historical Society* 10, no. 3 (April 1954): 336–50.

Barbeau, Marius, and Edward Sapir. *Folk Songs of French Canada*. New Haven, 1925.

Barman, Jean. *Iroquois in the West*. Montreal/Kingston: McGill-Queen's University Press, 2019.

Barnes, Robert M. *A History of the Regiments & Uniforms of the British Army*. London: Seeley Service & Co. Limited, 1950.

– *The Uniforms & History of the Scottish Regiments: Britain-Canada-Australia-New Zealand-South Africa: 1625 to the Present Day*. London: Seeley Service & Co. Limited, 1956.

Bassett, Harvey. "Christmas in the Fur Trade." *The Beaver*, outfit 272 (December 1941): 18–23.

Basso, Keith. *Wisdom Sits in Places: Landscape and Language Among the Western Apache*. Albuquerque: University of New Mexico Press, 1996.

Beardy, Flora, and Robert Coutts, eds. *Voices from Hudson Bay: Cree Stories from York Factory*. Montreal/Kingston: McGill-Queen's University Press, 1996.

Beattie, Judith Hudson. "'My Best Friend:' Evidence of the Fur Trade Libraries Located in the Hudson's Bay Company Archives." *Épilogue* 8, nos. 1 and 2 (1993): 1–31.

Beaudoin, Thérèse. *L'Été Dans la Culture Québécoise XVII-XIX siècles*. Québec: Institut Québécois de Recherche sur la Culture, 1987.

Beaugrand, Honoré. *La Chasse Galerie, and Other Canadian Stories*. Montreal: 1900.

Béland, Madeleine. *Chansons de voyageurs, coureurs de bois et forestiers*. Quebec: Presses de l'Université Laval, 1982.

Benn, Carl. *Native Memoirs from the War of 1812: Black Hawk and William Apess*. Baltimore: Johns Hopkins University Press, 2014.

Benton-Banai, Edward. *The Mishomis Book: The Voice of the Ojibway*. Red School House, 1988.

Bell, Catherine. *Ritual Theory, Ritual Practice*. Oxford: Oxford University Press, 1992.

Bigsby, John J. *The Shoe and Canoe: Or Pictures of Travel in The Canadas: Illustrative of Their Scenery and of Colonial Life; With Facts and Opinions on Emigration, State Policy, and Other Points of Public Interest* (1850), reprinted. New York: Paladin Press, 1969.

Binnema, Theodore, and Gerhard J. Ens, eds. *Edmonton House Journals, Correspondence, and Reports 1806–1821*. Calgary: Historical Society of Alberta, 2012.

Binnema, Theodore, Gerhard J. Ens, and R.C. Macleod. *From Rupert's Land to Canada*. Edmonton: University of Alberta Press, 2001.

Bird, Louis. *The Spirit Lives in the Mind: Omushkego Stories, Lives, and Dreams*. Edited by Susan Elaine Gray. Montreal/Kingston: McGill-Queen's University Press, 2007.

Blacking, John. *How Musical Is Man?* Seattle: University of Washington Press, 1973.

Blakeslee, D.J. "The origin and spread of the calumet ceremony." *American Antiquity* 46 (1981): 759–68.

Blessing, Fred K. "The Ojibway Indians Observed." *Occasional Publications in Minnesota Anthropology*. St Paul: Minnesota Archaeological Society, 1977.

Bloechl, Olivia A. *Native American Song at the Frontiers of Early Modern Music*. Cambridge: Cambridge University Press, 2008.

Boas, Franz. Introduction and afterword by Herbert S. Lewis. *Anthropology & Modern Life* (1928), reprinted. New Brunswick, NJ: Transaction Publishers, 2004.

Boatner, Mark M. *Military Customs and Traditions* (1956), reprinted. Westport Connecticut: Greenwood Press, 1976.

Bock, Philip K. *Modern Cultural Anthropology: An Introduction by Philip K. Bock.* Edited by Anthony F.C. Wallace. New York: Knopf, 1969.

Bohr, Roland. *Gifts from the Thunder Beings: Indigenous Archery and European Firearms in the Northern Plains and the Central Subarctic, 1670–1870.* Lincoln and London: University of Nebraska Press, 2014.

Borrows, John, and Michael Coyle. *The Right Relationship: Reimagining the Implementation of Historical Treaties.* Toronto: University of Toronto Press, 2017.

Bourdieu, Pierre. *Outline of a Theory of Practice.* Translated by Richard Nice. Cambridge: Cambridge University Press, 1977.

Brackenridge, Henry Marie. *Views of Louisiana: By Henry Marie Brackenridge* (1814), reprinted. Ann Arbor: University Microfilms, Inc., 1966.

Bradbury, John. *Travels in the Interior of America, in the Years 1809, 1810, and 1811; Including a Description of Upper Louisiana, Together with The States of Ohio, Kentucky, Indiana, and Tennessee, With the Illinois and Western Territories, And Containing Remarks and Observations Useful to Persons Emigrating to Those Countries.* Ann Arbor: University Microfilms, Inc., 1966.

Brannan, John, ed. *Official Letters of the Military and Naval Officers of the United States, During the War with Great Britain in the Years 1812, 13, 14, & 15: with some additional letters and documents elucidating the history of that period.* Washington City: Way & Gideon, 1823.

Brown, Jennifer S.H. "Duncan, Cameron." *Dictionary of Canadian Biography Online.* Revised 1988. http://www.biographi.ca/009004- 119.01-e.php?&id_nbr=3288.

– *An Ethnohistorian in Rupert's Land: Unfinished Conversations.* Edmonton: Athabasca University Press, 2017.

– *Strangers in Blood: Fur Trade Company Families in Indian Country.* Vancouver: University of British Columbia, 1980.

Browner, Tara. *Heartbeat of the People: Music and Dance of the Northern Pow-Wow.* Chicago: University of Illinois Press, 2004.

– *Music of the First Nations: Tradition and Innovation in Native North America.* Chicago: University of Illinois Press, 2009.

Bruchac, Margaret M., Siobhan M. Hart, and H. Martin Wobst, eds. *Indigenous Archaeologies: A Reader in Decolonization.* Walnut Creek, CA: Left Coast Press, 2010.

Brumwell, Stephen. *The British Soldier and War in the Americas, 1755–1763.* Cambridge: Cambridge University Press, 2002.

Bryce, George. *The Remarkable History of the Hudson's Bay Company: Including that of The French Traders of North-Western Canada and of the North-West, XY, and Astor Fur Companies.* Third Edition. Toronto: William Briggs, 1910.

Byrd, Jodi. *The Transit of Empire: Indigenous Critiques of Colonialism*. Minneapolis: University of Minnesota Press, 2011.

Byrnside, Ronald L. *Music: Sound and Sense*. Dubuque: W.C. Brown, 1985.

Bücher, Karl. *Arbeit und Rhythmus*. Leipzig: B.G. Teubner, 1896.

Burley, Edith I. *Servants of the Honourable Company: Work Discipline, and Conflict in the Hudson's Bay Company, 1770–1879*. Toronto: Oxford University Press, 1997.

Burns, Richard Allen. "Where Is Jody Now? Reconsidering Military Marching Chants." In *Warrior Ways: Explorations in Modern Military Folklore*. Edited by Eric A. Eliason and Tad Tuleja. Boulder: University Press of Colorado, 2012.

Calloway, Colin G. *White People, Indians, and Highlanders: Tribal People and Colonial Encounters in Scotland and America*. Oxford: Oxford University Press, 2008.

Cameron, Duncan. In *Les Bourgeois De La Compagnie Du Nord-Ouest, Original Journals Narratives Letters, Etc. Relating to the Northwest Company. Récits De Voyages Lettres Et Rapports Inédits Relatifs Au Nord-Ouest Canadien*. Edited by L.R. Masson. Vol. 2 (1899–1890), reprinted. New York: Antiquarian Press LTD, 1960.

Cameron, Michaela. "Singing with Strangers in Early Seventeenth-Century New France." In *Empire of the Senses: Sensory Practices of Colonialism in Early America*, edited by Daniela Hacke and Paul Musselwhite, 88–112. Leiden: Brill, 2018.

Carpenter, Edmund, and Marshall McLuhan, eds. *Explorations in Communication: An Anthology*. Boston: Beacon Press, 1960.

Carver, Jonathan. "Captain Jonathan Carver's Journal." In *The Northwest*, edited by Payette, B.C. Astoria, Oregon: Columbia River Maritime Museum: Printed Privately for Payette Radio Limited, 730 St James St W. Montreal, Canada., 1964.

– *Travels through the Interior Parts of North America, in the Years 1766, 1767, and 1768, 3rd Ed*. London, England: C. Dilly; H. Payne; J. Phillips, 1781.

Chamberlin, J. Edward. *If This Is Your Land, Where Are Your Stories? Reimagining Home and Sacred Space*. Cleveland: Pilgrim Press, 2003.

Champlain, Samuel De. *The Works of Samuel de Champlain in Six Volumes*. Translated by H.H. Langton 1615–1618. Vol. 3. Toronto: The Champlain Society, 1929.

Chappell, Lieut. Edward, R.N. *Narrative of a Voyage to Hudson's Bay in His Majesty's Ship Rosamond: Containing Some Account of the North-Eastern Coast of America and of the Tribes Inhabiting That Remote Region*. London: J. Mawman Ludgate Street, 1817.

Chartier, Roger. "Text, Symbols, and Frenchness." *Journal of Modern History* 57 (1985): 682–95.

Chartrand, Paul L.A.H. *Pierriche Falcon: The Michif Rhymester: Our Métis National Anthem: The Michif Version: A commentary on Falcon's Song, Michif language and nationalism, with Michif translations of Falcon's other songs*. Saskatoon: Gabriel Dumont Institute, 2009.

Cheechoo, James. *Shay Chee Man*. Compact disc and cassette. Moose Factory: Kwiskhegun Productions, 1998.

Child, Brenda J. *Holding Our World Together: Ojibwe Women and the Survival of Community*. Introduction by Colin Calloway. New York: Viking, 2012.

Choquette, Leslie. "Center and Periphery in French North America." In *Negotiated Empires: Centers and Peripheries in the Americas, 1500–1820*, edited by Christine Daniels and Michael V. Kennedy. Introduction by Jack P. Greene and Amy Turner Bushnell. New York & London: Routledge, 2002.

Classen, Constance. *The Deepest Sense: A Cultural History of Touch*. Urbana and Chicago: University of Illinois Press, 2012.

Clendinnen, Inga. *Dancing with Strangers: Europeans and Australians at First Contact*. Cambridge: Cambridge University Press, 2005.

Cocking, Matthew et al. "Journal of Occurrences and Transactions at Cumberland House by Mr. Matthew Cocking and Others, Commencing the 4th July 1776 and Ending the 4th July 1777 By William Walker." In *Cumberland and Hudson House Journals 1775–82: The Publications of the Hudson's Bay Record Society*, edited by E.E. Rich. London: The Hudson's Bay Record Society, 1951.

Coirault, Patrice, ed. *Répertoire des Chansons Françaises de tradition orale. Ouvrage révisé et complété par Georges Delarue, Yvette Fédoroff et Simone Wallon. Tome II. La vie sociale et militaire*. Paris: Bibliothèque nationale de France, 2000.

Colden, Cadwallader. *The History of the Five Indian Nations of Canada, Which Are Dependent on the Province of New-York in America, and Are the Barrier between the English and French in That Part of the World: With Accounts of Their Religion, Manners, Customs, Laws and Forms of Government*. 2nd ed. London: T. Osborne, 1747.

Colpitts, George. *Pemmican Empire: Food, Trade, and the Last Bison Hunts in the North American Plains, 1780–1882*. Cambridge: Cambridge University Press, 2014.

Conant, Francis P. "Rocks that ring: their ritual setting in northern Nigeria." *Transaction of the New York Academy of Sciences* 23, no. 2 (1961): 155–62.

Connor, Thomas. In *Five Fur Traders of the Northwest: Being the Narrative of Peter Pond and the Diaries of John MacDonell, Archibald N. McLeod, Hugh Faires, and Thomas Connor*, edited by Charles M. Gates. Introduction by Grace Lee Nute. St Paul: The University of Minnesota Press, 1933.

Cooper, T.H. *A Practical Guide for the Light Infantry Officer: Comprising Valuable Extracts from All the Most Popular Works on the Subject; with Further Original Information: And Illustrated by A Set of Plates, on an Entire New and Intelligible Plan; Which Simplify Every Movement and Manoeuvre of Light Infantry* (1806), reprinted. London: Redwood Press, 1970.

Corbiere, Alan, and Ruth Phillips. "A Dehe-igan (Drum) from Manitoulin Island." *Native Drums*. http://www.native-drums.ca/index.php/Scholars/Deheigan?tp=a&bg=1&ln=e. Retrieved 13 May 2019.

Corbin, Allain. *Village Bells: Sound and Meaning in the 19th-Century French Countryside*. New York: Columbia University Press, 1998.

Corrigan, Samuel W., ed. *Readings in Aboriginal Studies*. Brandon: Bearpaw Publishing, 1995.

Cox, Ross. *The Columbia River: Or Scenes and Adventures during a Residence of Six Years on the Western Side of the Rocky Mountains among Various Tribes of Indians Hitherto Unknown; Together with "A Journey across the American Continent."* Edited and with an Introduction by Edgar I. Stewart and Jane R. Stewart. Norman: University of Oklahoma Press, 1957.

Creighton, Donald. *The Commercial Empire of the St. Lawrence: 1760–1850*. Toronto: Ryerson Press, 1937.

Crowley, John E. "'Taken on the Spot': The Visual Appropriation of New France for the Global British Landscape." *Canadian Historical Review* 86, no. 1 (2005): 1–28.

Cunningham, Hugh. *Leisure in the Industrial Revolution, 1780–1880*. London: Croom Helm, 1980.

Darnell, Regna. *And Along Came Boas: Continuity and Revolution in Americanist Anthropology*. Philadelphia: J. Benjamins, 1998.

Darnton, Robert. "History and Anthropology." In *The Kiss of Lamourette*. New York: Norton, 1990.

– *The Great Cat Massacre: And Other Episodes in French Cultural History, Peasants tell tales: The Meaning of Mother Goose*. New York: Basic Books, 1984.

Dechêne, Louise, and Hélène Paré. *Le Peuple, L'État et la Guerre Au Canada Sous le Régime Français*. Quebec: Boréal (Editions du), 2008.

Deloria, Vine Jr. *The World We Used to Live In: Remembering the Powers of the Medicine Men*. Golden, Co: Fulcrum Publishing, 2006.

Den Otter, A.A. *Civilizing the Wilderness: Culture and Nature in Pre-Confederation Canada and Rupert's Land*. Edmonton: The University of Alberta Press, 2012.

Densmore, Frances. *Cheyenne and Arapaho Music*. Southwest Museum, 1936.

– *Chippewa Music* (1910–1913), reprinted. 2 Vols. New York: Da Capo Press, 1972.

– *Menominee Music*. Indiana University, 1932.

– *Music of Acoma, Isleta, Cochiti, and Zuñi Pueblos*. Washington: US Government Printing Office, 1957.

– *Music of the Indians of British Columbia* (1943), reprinted. New York: Da Capo Press, 1972.

– *Northern Ute Music*. Washington: US Government Printing Office, 1922.

– *Pawnee Music*. Washington: US Government Printing Office, 1929.

– *Teton Sioux Music*. Washington: US Government Printing Office, 1918.

– *The American Indian and Their Music* (1926), reprinted. New York: Johnson Reprint Corporation, 1970.

– "The Study of Indian Music in the Nineteenth Century." *American Anthropologist* 29, no. 1 (January–March 1927): 77–86.

– *Yuman and Yaqui Music*. Washington: US Government Printing Office, 1932.

Devine, Heather. *The People Who Own Themselves: Aboriginal Ethnogenesis in a Canadian Family, 1660–1900*. Calgary: University of Calgary Press, 2004.

Dewdney, Selwyn. *The Sacred Scrolls of the Southern Ojibway*. Toronto: University of Toronto Press, 1975.

Di, Hu. "Approaches to the Archaology of Ethnogenesis: Past and Emergent Perspectives." *Journal of Archaeological Research* 21, no. 4 (2013): 371–402.

Diamond, Beverley. *Native American Music in Eastern North America: Experiencing Music, Expressing Culture*. New York, Oxford: Oxford University Press, 2008.

Diamond, Beverley, M. Sam Cronk, and Franziska Von Rosen. *Visions of Sound: Musical Instruments of First Nations Communities in Northeastern America*. Chicago: University of Chicago Press, 1994.

Dowd, Gregory Evans. *War Under Heaven: Pontiac, the Indian Nations, & the British Empire*. Baltimore & London: John Hopkins University Press, 2002.

Drake, Samuel G., ed. *Indian Captivities: Or, Life in the Wigwam; Being True Narratives of Captives Who Have Been Carried Away by the Indians, from the Frontier Settlements of the United States, from the Earliest Period to the Present Time*. Buffalo: Derby, Orton & Mulligan, 1853.

Driver, Harold E. *Indians of North America*. Chicago: University of Chicago Press, 1961.

Duckworth, Harry W., ed. *The English River Book: A North West Company Journal and Account Book of 1786*. Montreal/Kingston: McGill-Queen's University Press, 1990.

Dueck, Byron. *Musical Intimacies and Indigenous Imaginaries: Aboriginal Music and Dance in Public Performance*. New York: Oxford University Press, 2013.

Duffy, Christopher. *The Military Experience in the Age of Reason*. London and New York: Routledge & Kegan Paul, 1987.

Dunn, John. *History of the Oregon Territory and British North America Fur Trade: With an Account of the Habits and Customs of the Principal Native Tribes on the Northern Continent*. London: Edwards and Hughes, 1844.

Eccles, W.J. "The Social, Economic, and Political Significance of the Military Establishment in New France." *The Canadian Historical Review* 52, no. 1 (1971): 1–22.

Edwards, Sophie A. "La Cloche: Passage and Place." Master's thesis. Laurentian University. 2008.

Ens, Gerhard J. *Homeland to Hinterland: The Changing Worlds of the Red River Metis in the Nineteenth Century*. Toronto: University of Toronto Press, 1996.

– "The Battle of Seven Oaks and the Articulation of a Metis National Tradition, 1811–1849." In *Contours of a People: Metis Family, Mobility, and History*, edited by Nicole St-Onge, Carolyn Podruchny, and Brenda Macdougall. Norman: University of Oklahoma Press, 2012.

Ens, Gerhard J., and Joe Sawchuk. *From New Peoples to New Nations: Aspects of Metis History And Identity from the Eighteenth to the Twenty-First Centuries*. Toronto: University of Toronto Press, 2016.

Epstein, Dena J. "Slave Music in the United States before 1860: A Survey of Sources (Part I&2)." Music Library Association, *Notes* 20 (Spring 1963): 195–212; (Summer 1963): 377–90.

Erasmus, Peter. *Buffalo Days and Nights: As Told to Henry Thompson.* Calgary: Glenbow-Alberta Institute, 1976.

Ermatinger, Edward. *Edward Ermatinger's York Factory Express Journal being a record of journeys made between Fort Vancouver and Hudson Bay in the years 1827–1828.* Introduction by C.O. Ermatinger. Ottawa: Royal Society of Canada, 1912.

Ewers, John C. *Indian Life on the Upper Missouri.* Norman: University of Oklahoma Press, 1968.

Exercise for the Foot: With the Differences to Be Observed in the Dragoon Exercise 1757: By Order of H.R.H. Prince William Augustus Duke of Cumberland, Etc., Etc. Ad Illustrations from A Plan of Discipline Compiled for the Use of The Militia of The County of Norfolk (1759), reprinted. Bloomfield & Alexandria Bay: Museum Restoration Service, 2004.

Fagg, Bernard. *The Rock Gong Complex Today and in Prehistoric Times.* Nigeria: Ibadan University Press, 1956.

Fenton, William N., and Gertrude Prokosch Kurath. *The Iroquois Eagle Dance: An Offshoot of the Calumet Dance.* Washington, DC: United States Government Printing Office, 1953.

Ferland, Marcien. *Chansons à répondre du Manitoba.* Éditions du Blé, 1979.

Fischer, David Hackett. *Champlain's Dream: The European Founding of North America.* New York: Simon & Schuster, 2008.

Fletcher, Alice C. *A Study of Omaha Indian Music.* Lincoln and London: University of Nebraska Press, 1994.

– *The Hako: A Pawnee Ceremony.* 1900th–1901st ed. Twenty-Second Annual Report of the Bureau of American Ethnology to the Secretary of the Smithsonian Institution. Washington: Government Printing Office, 1904.

Fornasiero, Jean, and John West-Sooby. "Cross-Cultural Inquiry in 1802: Musical Performance on the Baudin Expedition to Australia." In *Conciliation on Colonial Frontiers Conflict, Performance and Commemoration in Australia and the Pacific Rim,* edited by Kate Darian-Smith and Penelope Edmonds. New York and London: Routledge, 2015.

Foucault, Michel. *Discipline & Punish: The Birth of the Prison.* Translated by Alan Sheridan. New York: Vintage Books, 1979.

Fraser, Simon. *The Letters and Journals of Simon Fraser 1806–8.* Edited by W. Kaye Lamb. Toronto: The MacMillan Company of Canada Limited, 1960.

Frobisher, Martin. *A True Discourse of the Late Voyages of Discouerie, for the Finding of a Passage to Cathaya, by the Northvveast, Vnder the Conduct of Martin Frobisher Generall Deuided into Three Bookes. In the First Wherof Is Shewed, His First Voyage ... Also, There Are Annexed Certayne Reasons, to Proue All Partes of the Worlde Habitable, with a Generall Mappe Adioyned. In the Second, Is Set Out His*

Second Voyage … In the Thirde, Is Declared the Strange Fortunes Which Hapned in the Third Voyage … VVith a Particular Card Therevnto Adioyned of Meta Incognita. London: George Best, 1584.

Gallat-Morin, Élisabeth, and Jean-Pierre Pinson, eds. *La Vie Musicale en Nouvelle-France*. Québec: Septentrion, 2003.

Garry, Nicholas. *The Diary of Nicholas Garry Deputy-Governor of the Hudson's Bay Company: A Detailed Narrative of His Travels in the Northwest Territories of British North American in 1821*. Edited by W.J. Noxon and Mr. Francis N.A. Garry. Ottawa: Transactions of the Royal Society of Canada, 1900.

Gates, Charles M. *Five Fur Traders of the Northwest: Being the Narrative of Peter Pond and the Diaries of John MacDonell, Archibald N. McLeod, Hugh Faires, and Thomas Connor*. Introduction by Grace Lee Nute. St Paul: The University of Minnesota Press, 1933.

Gennep, Arnold van. *The Rites of Passage*. Translated by Monika B. Vizedom and Gabrielle L. Caffee. London: Routledge & Kegan Paul, 1960.

Gibbons, Roy W. *Folk Fiddling in Canada: A Sampling*. Ottawa: University of Ottawa Press, 1981.

Gibson, James R. *Otter Skins, Boston Ships and China Goods: The Maritime Fur Trade of the Northwest Coast, 1785–1841*. Montreal/Kingston: McGill Queen's University Press, 1992.

Gioia, Ted. *Healing Songs*. Durham: Duke University Press, 2006.

– *Work Songs*. Durham and London: Duke University Press, 2006.

Gist, Christopher. *Christopher Gist's Journals: With Historical, Geographical and Ethnological Notes and Biographies of His Contemporaries*. Edited by William M. Darlington. Pittsburgh: J.R. Weldin, 1893.

Given, Brian. *A Most Pernicious Thing: Gun Trading and Native Warfare in the Early Contact Period*. Ottawa: Carleton University Press, 1994.

Glover, Richard. "York Boats." *The Beaver* (March 1949): 19–23.

Gluckman, Max, and Victor Turner. *Essays on the Rituals of Social Relations: By Daryll Forde, Meyer Fortes, Max Gluckman, Victor W. Turner*. Manchester: Manchester University Press, 1962.

Goodman, Glenda. "Sounds Heard, Meaning Deferred: Music Transcription as Imperial Technology." *Eighteenth Century Studies* 52, no. 1 (Fall 2018): 39–45

Gordon, Tom. "Found in Translation: The Inuit Voice in Moravian Music." *Newfoundland and Labrador Studies* 22, no. 1(2007): 287–314.

Grabowski, Jan, and Nicole St-Onge. "Montreal Iroquois *engagés* in the Western Fur Trade, 1800–1821." In *From Rupert's Land to Canada*, edited by Binnema, Ens, and Macleod. Edmonton: University of Alberta Press, 2001.

Gramsci, Antonio. *Prison Notebooks*. Edited with Introduction by Joseph A. Buttigieg. Vol. 1. New York: Columbia University Press, 1992.

Grant, Johnny. *A Son of the Fur Trade*. Edited by Gerhard J. Ens. Edmonton: The University of Alberta, 2008.

Grant, Peter. "The Sauteux Indians." In *Les Bourgeois de La Compagnie Du Nord-Ouest. Original Journals Narratives Letters, Etc. Relating to the Northwest Company. Récits de Voyages Lettres et Rapports Inédits Relatifs Au Nord-Ouest Canadien.* Edited by L.R. Masson. Vol. 2. (1889–90), reprinted. New York: Antiquarian Press, 1960.

Greenblatt, Stephen, ed. *Cultural Mobility: A Manifesto.* New York: Cambridge University Press, 2010.

Greene, Roland, Stephen Cushman, Clare Cavanagh, Jahan Ramazani, Paul F. Rouzer, Harris Feinsod, David Marno, and Alexandra Slessarev, eds. *The Princeton Encyclopedia of Poetry and Poetics.* Princeton, NJ: Princeton University Press, 2012.

Greenman, Emerson Frank. *Old Birch Island Cemetery and the Early Historic Trade Route, Georgian Bay, Ontario.* Ann Arbor: University of Michigan Press, 1951.

Greer, Allan. *Peasant, Lord, and Merchant: Rural Society in Three Quebec Parishes, 1740–1840.* Toronto: University of Toronto Press, 1985.

– *The People of New France.* Toronto: The University of Toronto Press, 1997.

Grisé, Yolande. "La Présence De Thomas Moore, Auteur De A Canadian Boat Song, Dans La 'Poésie Canadienne-française, Au XIX Siècle." *Journal of Canadian Studies* 33, no. 1 (1997–98): 48–71.

Gutsche, Andrea, Barbara Chrisholm, and Russell Floren. *The North Channel and St. Mary's River: A Guide to the History.* Toronto: Lynx Images Incorporated, 1997.

Gwyn, Julian. "Johnson, Sir William." *Dictionary of Canadian Biography Online*, 1979. http://www.biographi.ca/en/bio/johnson_william_4E.html.

Haines, John. "Marius Barbeau et le Moyen-Âge." In *Around and About Marius Barbeau: Modelling Twentieth-Century Culture*, edited by Lynda Jessup, Andrew Nurse, and Gordon E. Smith. Ottawa: Canadian Museum of Civilization, 2008.

Hall, R.L. "The evolution of the calumet-pipe." In *Prairie Archaeology: Papers in Honor of David A. Maerris*, edited by G.E. Gibbon. University of Minnesota Publications in Anthropology 3 (1983): 37–52.

Hansom, Joseph. "A Journal of the Most Remarkable Transactions and Occurrences at Cumberland House from 2d July 1778 to 8th June 1779 by Joseph Hansom." In *Cumberland and Hudson House Journals 1775–82: The Publications of the Hudson's Bay Record Society.* Edited by E.E. Rich. London: The Hudson's Bay Record Society, 1951.

Hargrave, James. *Letters from Rupert's Land, 1826–1840: James Hargrave of the Hudson's Bay Company.* Edited with Introduction by Helen E. Ross. Montreal/Kingston: McGill-Queen's University Press, 2009.

Harmon, Daniel Williams. *A Journal of Voyages and Travels in the Interior of North America: Between the 47th and 58th Degrees of N. Lat., Extending from Montreal Nearly to the Pacific, a Distance of about 5,000 Miles: Including an Account of the Principal Occurrences During a Residence of Nineteen Years in Different Parts of the Country.* Toronto: George N. Morang & Company, 1904.

Harris, Cole. "Arthur J. Ray and the Empirical Opportunity." In *New Histories for Old: Changing Perspectives on Canada's Changing Pasts*, edited by Ted Binnema and Susan Neylan. Vancouver: UBC Press, 2007.

Harris, Marvin. *The Rise of Anthropological Theory*. New York: Crowell, 1968.

Havard, Gilles. *The Great Peace of Montreal of 1701: French-Native Diplomacy in the Seventeenth Century*. Translated by Phyllis Aronoff and Howard Scott. Montreal/Kingston: McGill-Queen's University Press, 2001.

Harvey, Douglas S. *The Theatre of Empire: Frontier Performances in America, 1750–1860*. London: Pickering & Chatto, 2010.

Hawks, John. *Orderly Book and Journal of Major John Hawks: On the Ticonderoga-Crown Point Campaign, under General Jeffrey Amherst 1759–1760*. New York: The Society of Colonial Wars in the State of New York, 1911.

Head, George. *Forest Scenes and Incidents, in The Wilds of North America; Being A Diary of A Winter's Route From Halifax to the Canadas, and During Four Months' Residence in the Woods on the Borders of Lakes Huron and Simcoe* (1829), reprinted. Toronto: Coles Publishing Company, 1970.

Healy, W.J., ed. *Women of Red River: Being a Book Written from the Recollections of Women Surviving from the Red River Era* (1923), reprinted. Winnipeg: Peguis Publishers, 1967.

Hearne, Samuel. *A Journey from Prince of Wales's Fort in Hudson's Bay to the Northern Ocean in the Years 1769, 1770, 1771 and 1772*. Edited by J.B. Tyrrell. Toronto: The Champlain Society, 1911.

Hébert, Raymond M. "Identity, Cultural Production and the Vitality of Francophone Communities Outside Québec." In *Images of Canadianness: Visions on Canada's Politics, Culture, Economics*. Edited by Leen d'Haenens. Ottawa: University of Ottawa Press, 1998.

Hemphill, C. Dallett. *Bowing to Necessities: A History of Manners in America 1620–1860*. New York: Oxford University Press, 1999.

Henry, Alexander. *Travels & Adventures In Canada and the Indian Territories: Between the Years 1760 and 1776: By Alexander Henry Fur Trader*. Edited with Notes by James Bain. New Ed. Toronto: George N. Morang & Company, LTD, 1901.

Henry, Alexander the Younger. *New Light on the Early History of the Greater Northwest: The Manuscript Journals of Alexander Henry*. Edited by Elliott Coues. Vol 1. Minneapolis: Ross & Haines; New York: F. Harper, 1897.

– *The Journal of Alexander Henry the Younger 1799–1814: "Red River and the Journey to the Missouri."* Edited with Introduction by Barry M. Gough. 2 vols. Toronto: The Champlain Society, 1988.

Herbert, Trevor, and Helen Barlow. *Music & the British Military in the Long Nineteenth Century*. Oxford University Press, 2013.

Heriot, George. *Travels through the Canadas, Containing a Description of the Picturesque Scenery on Some of the Rivers and Lakes; with an Account of the*

Productions, Commerce, and Inhabitants of Those Provinces. To Which Is Subjoined a Comparative View of the Manners and Customs of Several of the Indian Nations of North and South America (1807), reprinted. Edmonton: M.G. Hurtig, 1971.

Herzog, George. "Musical Styles in North America." *Proceedings of the 23rd International Congress of Americanists* (New York, 1930).

– "Plains Ghost Dance and Great Basin Music." *American Anthropologist* 37 (1935): 403–19.

– "Special Song Types in North American Indian Music." *Zeitschrift für vergleichende Musikwissenschaft* 3/1-2 (1935): 1–11.

Hickerson, Harold. "Notes on the Post-Contact Origin of the Midewiwin." *Ethnohistory* 9, no. 4 (Autumn 1962): 404–23.

Hindley, Alan, and Brian J. Levy. *The Old French Epic: An Introduction*. Louvain, Belgium: Peeters, 1983.

"History of Fort la Cloche." *Hudson's Bay Company Archives*. http://www.willisville.ca/History%20of%20Fort%20La%20Cloche.htm. Retrieved 2 December 2019.

Hoefnagels, Anna, and Beverley Diamond. *Aboriginal Music in Contemporary Canada: Echoes and Exchanges*. Montreal/Kingston: McGill-Queen's University Press, 2012.

Hoffer, Peter Charles. *Sensory Worlds in Early America*. Baltimore & London: The Johns Hopkins University Press, 2003.

Hoffman, Walter J. "Medewiwin of the Ojibwa," *Seventh Annual Report, Bureau of Ethnology, 1885–1886*. Washington, DC: Government Printing Office, 1891.

Hofmann, Charles. "Frances Densmore and the Music of the American Indian." *Journal of American Folklore* 59 no. 231 (January–March 1946): 45–50.

Horbostel, Erich M. von. "Melodie und Skala." *Jahrbuch der Musikbibliothek Peters* 20 (1912): 11–23.

Hornbostel, Erich M. von, and Curt Sachs. "Classification of Musical Instruments." Translated by A. Baines and Klaus P. Wachsmann. *The Galpin Society Journal*. 14 (1961): 3–29.

Howay, Frederick W., ed. *Voyages of the Columbia to the Northwest Coast, 1787–1790 and 1790–1793*. Boston, MA: Not indicated, 1941.

Howes, David, ed. *The Varieties of Sensory Experience: A Sourcebook in the Anthropology of the Senses*. Toronto: University of Toronto Press, 1991.

Howison, John. *Sketches of Upper Canada, Domestic, Local, and Characteristic: To Which Are Added, Practical Details for the Information of Emigrants of Every Class; And Some Recollections of The United States of America* (1821), reprinted. Toronto: Coles Publishing Company, 1970.

Hugill, Stan, ed. *Shanties from the Seven Seas: Shipboard Work-Songs and Songs Used as Work- Songs from the Great Days of Sail*. Routledge & Kegan Paul, 1979.

Hutchinson, Gerald M. "Evans, James." *Dictionary of Canadian Biography*, 1988. http://www.biographi.ca/en/bio/evans_james_7E.html.

Iacovetta, Franca, Frances Gwyripa, and Marlene Epp, eds. *Sisters or Strangers: Immigrant, Ethnic and Racialized Women in Canadian History*. Toronto: The University of Toronto Press, 2004.

Indian Treaties and Surrenders. From 1680 to 1890 – In Two Volumes. Ottawa: Queen's Printer, 1891.

Innis, Harold. *Peter Pond: Fur Trader and Adventurer*. Toronto: Irwin & Gordon, LTD., 1930.

– *The Fur Trade in Canada: An Introduction to Canadian Economic History*. Toronto: University of Toronto Press, 1999.

Isham, James. *James Isham's Observations on Hudsons Bay, 1743:and Notes and Observations on a Book Entitled "A Voyage to Hudsons Bay in the Dobbs Galley," 1749*. Edited with Introduction by E.E. Rich. London: The Champlain Society for the Hudson's Bay Record Society, 1949.

Jackson, Michael D. "Political Paradox: The Lieutenant Governor in Saskatchewan." *Saskatchewan Politics: Into the Twenty-first Century*. Regina: Canadian Plains Research Center, University of Regina, 2001.

Jaenen, Cornelius. "Amerindian Views of French Culture in the Seventeenth Century." *Canadian Historical Review* 55 (1974): 261–91.

– *Friend and Foe: Aspects of French-Amerindian Cultural Contact in the Sixteenth and Seventeenth Centuries*. New York: Columbia University Press, 1976.

Jaenen, Cornelius and Cecilia Morgan, eds. *Material Memory: Documents in Pre-Confederation History*. Don Mills, ON: Addison Wesley, 1998.

Jameson, Anna. *Winter Studies and Summer Rambles in Canada*. Toronto: McClelland & Stewart, 1923.

Jennings, Francis, William Fenton, Mary A. Druke, and David R. Miller, eds. *The History and Culture of Iroquois Diplomacy: An Interdisciplinary Guide to the Treaties of the Six Nations and Their League*. Syracuse: Syracuse University Press, 1985.

Jessup, Lynda, Andrew Nurse, and Gordon E. Smith, eds. *Around and About Marius Barbeau: Modelling Twentieth-Century Culture*. Ottawa: Canadian Museum of Civilization, 2008.

Jobson, Christopher. *Looking Forward, Looking Back: Customs and Traditions of the Australian Army*. Wavell Heights: Big Sky Publishing Pty Ltd., 2009.

Johnson, Sherry, Beverley Diamond, and C.K. Szego, eds. *Bellows & Bows: Historic Recordings of Traditional Fiddle & Accordion Music from Across Canada*. St John's: Research Centre for the Study of Music, Media & Place, 2012.

Johnson, Warren. "Warren Johnson's Journal 1760–1761." In *The Papers of Sir William Johnson*. Volume XIII. Albany: The University of the State of New York, 1962.

Johnson, William. *The Papers of Sir William Johnson*. 13 Vols. Albany: University of the State of New York, 1921–65.

Johnson, Basil. *Manitous: The Spiritual World of the Ojibway*. St Paul: Minnesota Historical Society Press, 2001.

– *Ojibway Heritage*. Lincoln: University of Nebraska, 1990.

Jones, James. "Commonplace and Memorization in the Oral Tradition of the English and Scottish Popular Ballads." *The Journal of American Folklore* 74 no. 292 (April–June 1961): 97–112.

Kallmann, Helmut. *A History of Music in Canada 1534–1914*. Toronto: University of Toronto Press, 1960.

Kallmann, Helmut, Gilles Potvin, and Kenneth Winters. *Encyclopedia of Music in Canada*. Toronto: University of Toronto Press, 1981.

Kane, Paul. *Wanderings of an Artist Among the Indians of North America: From Canada to Vancouver's Island and Oregon Through the Hudson's Bay Company's Territory and Back Again*. Toronto: The Radisson Society of Canada Limited, 1925.

Keesing, Roger, and Andrew Strathern. *Cultural Anthropology: A Contemporary Perspective*, 3rd ed. New York: Harcourt Brace College Publishers, 1998.

Keillor, Elaine. *Music in Canada: Capturing Landscape and Diversity*. Montreal/Kingston: McGill-Queen's University Press, 2006.

Keillor, Elaine, Timothy Archambault, and John Kelly, eds. *Encyclopedia of Native American Music of North America*. Santa Barbara: Greenwood, 2013.

Keith, George. *Récits De Voyages Lettres Et Rapports Inédits Relatifs Au Nord-Ouest Canadien*. Edited by L.R. Masson. Vol. 2 (1889–1890), reprinted. New York: Antiquarian Press LTD, 1960.

Kennicott, Robert. "Robert Kennicott." *Transactions of the Chicago Academy of Sciences*. 1 (1867): 133–226.

Kohl, J.G. *Kitchi Gami: Wanderings Round Lake Superior*. Minneapolis: Ross and Hanes, 1956.

Koskoff, Ellen. *The Concise Garland Encyclopedia of World Music: Africa; South America, Mexico, Central America, and the Caribbean; The United States and Canada; Europe; Oceania*. Routledge, 2008.

Kroeber, Alfred L. *Cultural and Natural Areas of Native North America*. Berkeley: University of California Press, 1947.

Kunst, Jaap. *Musicologica: A Study of the Nature of Ethno-musicology, Its Problems, Methods and Representative Personalities*. Amsterdam: Indisch Instituut, 1950.

Lacourcière, Luc. "The Present State of French-Canadian Folklore studies." *Journal of American Folklore* LXXIV no. 294 (1961): 373–82.

Lacroix, Benoît, et Conrad Laforte. "Religion traditionnelle et les chansons des coureurs de bois." *Revue de l'Université Laurentienne*, Sudbury 12, no.1 (November 1979): 11–42

Laforte, Conrad. "Le Répertoire Authentique des Chansons D'aviron de nos Anciens Canotiers (Voyageurs, Engagés, Coureurs de Bois)." *Présentations à la Société royale du Canada*. 38. Ottawa: La Société, 1982–83.

– *Survivances Médiévales dans la chanson folklorique: Poétique de la chanson en laisse.* Québec: Les Presses de L'iniversité, 1981.

Lambert, John. *Travels through Canada, and the United States of North America, in the Years 1806, 1807, & 1808. to Which Are Added, Biographical Notices and Anecdotes of Some of the Leading Characters in the United States.* Vol. 1. London: C. Cradock and W. Joy, 1813.

Landes, Ruth. *Ojibwa Religion and the Midéwiwin.* Madison: The University of Wisconsin Press, 1968.

Lane, Belden C. *Landscapes of the Sacred: Geography and Narrative in American Spirituality*, 2nd ed. Baltimore: Johns Hopkins University Press, 2001.

– *The Solace of Fierce Landscape: Exploring Desert and Mountain Spirituality.* Oxford: Oxford University Press, 1998.

Lanman, James. "The American Fur Trade." *Hunt's Merchants' Magazine* 3, no. 189 (September, 1840).

Langley, Thomas. *The Eighteen Manoeuvres for His Majesty's Infantry.* (1794), reprinted. Hemel Hempstead: Bill Leeson with permission of the British Library, 1988.

La Rochefoucauld – Liancourt, Duc de. *La Rochefoucault-Liancourt's Travels in Canada 1795: With Annotations and Strictures by Sir David William Smith, Bart., Sometime Deputy Surveyor-General, Etc., of Upper Canada: Edited with Notes by William Renwick Riddell, LL.D., F.R. Hist. Socy. Etc, Justice of the Supreme Court of Ontario.* Toronto: Printed and Published by A.T. Wilgress, Printer to the King's Most Excellent Majesty, 1917.

La Rue, Hubert. "Les chansons populaires et historiques du Canada." *Le Foyer canadien / Recueil littéraire et historique.* Quebec. Tom I. (1863): 321–84.

– "Les chansons populaires et historiques du Canada," *Le Foyer canadien, / Recueil littéraire et historique.* Quebec. Tom III. (1865): 5–72.

Laut, Agnes C. *The Adventurers of England on Hudson Bay: A Chronicle of the Fur Trade in the North.* Toronto: Glasgow, 1914.

Laxer, Daniel Robert. "A Reservoir of Voices: Franco-Ontarien Folksongs." *Ontario History* CI, no. 1 (2009): 46–63.

– "'Row, Brothers, Row': Canadian Boat Songs, Imperial Glee, and National Identity, 1805–1867." *Journal of Canadian Studies* 50, no. 1 (Winter 2016): 70–99.

Leary, James. *Medicine Fiddle: A Humanities Discussion Guide, a Film by Michael Loukinen.* Marquette: Northern Michigan University, 1992.

Lederman, Anne. "Aboriginal Fiddling: The Scottish Connection." In *Irish and Scottish Encounters with Indigenous peoples: Canada, the United States, New Zealand, and Australia*, edited by Graeme Morton, and David A. Wilson. Montreal/Kingston: McGill-Queen's University Press, 2013.

– "Old Indian and Métis Fiddling in Manitoba: Origins, Structure and the Question of Syncretism." *The Canadian Journal of Native Studies*. 8/2 (1988): 205–30.

– "Old Native and Metis Fiddling in Two Manitoba Communities: Camperville and Ebb and Flow." *Master's Thesis*. York University. (1986).

Lefroy, John Henry. *In Search of the Magnetic North: A Soldier-Surveyor's Letters from the North-West 1843–1844*. Edited by George F.G. Stanley. Toronto: The MacMillan Company of Canada LTD, 1955.

Les Soirées Canadiennes [3e Année], 6e Livr. (juin [1863])]. Québec: Brousseau Frères, 1863.

Levitin, Daniel. *The World in Six Songs: How the Musical Brain Created Human Nature*. London: Aurum Press, 2009.

– *This Is Your Brain on Music: The Science of a Human Obsession*. New York: Penguin, 2007. Liberty, Margot. "The Sun Dance." *Readings in Aboriginal Studies*, edited by Samuel W. Corrigan. Brandon: Bearpaw Publishing, 1995.

Long, John B. *Early Western Travels, Vol. 2: John Long's Journal, 1768–1782*. Edited by Thwaites, Reuben Gold. Cleveland, OH: Arthur H. Clark Co., 1904.

– *Readings in Canadian History: Original Sources from Canada's Living Past*. Edited by George W. Brown. Toronto: J.M. Dent & Sons Limited, 1940.

Longmoor, Robert. "Journal of the Most Remarkable Transactions and Occurrences Inland from 27th September 1778 to 12th May 1779 by Robert Longmoor." In *Cumberland and Hudson House Journals 1775–82: The Publications of the Hudson's Bay Record Society*, edited by E.E. Rich. London: The Hudson's Bay Record Society, 1951.

Lutz, John Sutton. *Makúk: A New History of Aboriginal-White Relations*. Vancouver: UBC Press, 2008.

– *Myth and Memory: Stories of Indigenous-European Contact*. Vancouver: UBC Press, 2011.

M'Gillivray, Duncan. *The Journal of Duncan M'Gillivray of the North West Company at Fort George on the Saskatchewan, 1794–5*. Introduction, Notes and Appendix by Arthur S. Morton. Toronto: The MacMillan Company of Canada Limited, 1929.

Macdonell, John. In *Five Fur Traders of the Northwest: Being the Narrative of Peter Pond and the Diaries of John MacDonell, Archibald N. McLeod, Hugh Faires, and Thomas Connor*. St Paul: The University of Minnesota Press, 1933.

Macdougall, Brenda. *One of the Family: Metis Culture in Nineteenth-Century Northwestern Saskatchewan*. Vancouver: UBC Press, 2011.

Macdougall, Brenda, Nichole St-Onge, and Carolyn Podruchny, eds. *Contours of a People: Metis Family, Mobility, and History*. University of Oklahoma Press, 2012.

MacGregor, J.G. *Peter Fidler: Canada's Forgotten Surveyor: 1769–1822*. Toronto: McClelland and Stewart Limited, 1966.

Mackenzie, Alexander. *The Journals and Letters of Sir Alexander Mackenzie*. Edited by W. Kaye Lamb. Toronto: MacMillan of Canada, 1970.

– *Voyages from Montreal Through the Continent of North America to the Frozen and Pacific Oceans in 1789 and 1793 with an Account of the Rise and State of the Fur Trade*. 2 vols. Toronto: George N. Morang & Company, 1903.

Mackerness, Eric David. *A Social History of English Music*. Routledge, 2013.

MacLeod, Margaret. *Songs of Old Manitoba: With Airs, French and English Words, and Introductions*. Toronto: The Ryerson Press, 1960.

MacTaggart, John, 1791–1830. *Three Years in Canada: An Account of the Actual State of the Country in 1826–7–8, Comprehending Its Resources, Productions, Improvements and Capabilities, and Including Sketches of the State of Society, Advice to Emigrants, &c*. 2 vols. London: H. Colburn, 1928.

Malhiot, François Victor. "A Wisconsin Fur-Trader's Journal, 1804–05." In *Collections of the State Historical Society of Wisconsin*. Edited by Reuben Gold Thwaites. Madison: Published by the Society, 1910.

Malloy, John S. *The Plains Cree: Trade, Diplomacy, and War, 1790 to 1870*. Winnipeg: University of Manitoba Press, 1990.

Manitowabi, Darrel. "Sinmedwe'ek: The other-than-human grandfathers of North-central Ontario." In *Papers of the 39th Algonquian Conference*. London: The University of Western Ontario, 2008.

"March." *Grove Music Online*, 20 January 2001. https://www.oxfordmusiconline.com/grovemusic/view/10.1093/gmo/9781561592630.001.0001/omo-9781561592630-e-0000040080.

"March." *The Harvard Dictionary of Music*. Edited by Don Michael Randel. Harvard University Press, 2003.

Marquette, Jacques, and Louis Jolliet. *Early Narratives of the Northwest*. Edited by Louise Phelps Kellogg. New York: Charles Scribner's Sons, 1917.

Martin, Calvin. *Keepers of the Game: Indian-Animal Relationships and the Fur Trade*. Berkeley: University of California Press, 1978.

Masson, L.R. *Les Bourgeois de La Compagnie Du Nord-Ouest: Récits de Voyages, Lettres et Rapports Inédits Relatifs Au Nord-Ouest Canadien: Publiés Avec Une Esquisse Historique et Des Annotations Par L.R. Masson* (1899–1890), reprinted. 2 vols. New York: Antiquarian Press LTD, 1960.

Matthews, Maureen. *Naamiwan's Drum: The Story of a Contested Repatriation of Anishinaabe Artefacts*. Toronto: University of Toronto Press, 2016.

Matthews, Maureen, and Roger Roulette. "Fair Wind's Dream: *Naamiwan Obowaajigewin*." In *Reading Beyond Worlds: Contexts for Native History*. Edited by Jennifer S.H. Brown and Elizabeth Vibert. 2nd ed. Peterborough: Broadview Press, 2003.

McCormack, Patricia A. "Transatlantic Rhythms: To the Far Nor'Wast and Back Again." In *Irish and Scottish Encounters with Indigenous Peoples: Canada, the United States, New Zealand, and Australia*. Edited by Graeme Morton and David A. Wilson. Montreal/Kingston: McGill-Queen's University Press, 2013.

McDonald, Archibald. *Peace River: A Canoe Voyage from Hudson's Bay to Pacific by Sir George Simpson in 1828: Journal Of the Lat Chief Factory, Archibald McDonald (Hon. Hudson's Bay Company), Who Accompanied Him*. Edited with notes by Malcolm McLeod. Edmonton: M.G. Hurtig, 1971.

McDonald, John. "John McDonald of Garth Autobiographical Notes 1791–1816." In *Les Bourgeois de La Compagnie Du Nord- Ouest. Original Journals Narratives Letters, Etc. Relating to the Northwest Company. Récits de Voyages Lettres et Rapports Inédits Relatifs Au Nord-Ouest Canadien*. Vol. 2. Quebec: A. Coté, 1890

McDonell, John. "Mr. John McDonnell: Some Account of the Red River (About 1797) With Extracts from His Journal 1793–1795." In *Les Bourgeois De La Compagnie Du Nord-Ouest: Récits De Voyages, Lettres Et Rapports Inédits Relatifs Au Nord-Ouest Canadien: Publiés Avec Une Esquisse Historique Et Des Annotations Par L.R. Masson* (1889–1890), reprinted. New York: Antiquarian Press LTD, 1960.

– "The Diary of John Macdonell." In Gates, *Give Fur Traders of the North-west*, 63–119.

McKay, Ian. *Quest of the Folk: Antimodernism and Cultural Selection in Twentieth-Century Nova Scotia*. Kingston/Montreal: McGill-Queen's University Press, 1994.

McKenzie, James. "The King's Posts and Journal of a Canoe Jaunt Through the King's Domains, 1808. The Saguenay and the Labrador Coast." In *Les Bourgeois de La Compagnie Du Nord- Ouest. Original Journals Narratives Letters, Etc. Relating to the Northwest Company. Récits de Voyages Lettres et Rapports Inédits Relatifs Au Nord-Ouest Canadien*. Vol. 2. Quebec: A. Coté, 1890.

McLeod, Archibald Norman. In *Five Fur Traders of the Northwest: Being the Narrative of Peter Pond and the Diaries of John MacDonell, Archibald N. McLeod, Hugh Faires, and Thomas Connor*. Edited by Charles M. Gates with an introduction by Grace Lee Nute. St Paul: The University of Minnesota Press, 1933.

McGee, Timothy J. *The Music of Canada*. New York: W.W. Norton & Company, 1985.

McGillivray, Simon. *The North West Company in Rebellion: Simon McGillivray's Fort William Notebook, 1815*. Edited and introduction by Jean Morrison. Thunder Bay Historical Museum Society, 1988.

McGreggor, Arthur J. *Wiigwaaskingaa: Land of Birch Trees*. Maniwaki: Anishinabe Printing, 1999.

McLean, John. *Notes of a Twenty-Five Year's Service in the Hudson's Bay Territories*. Toronto: Champlain Society, 1932.

McLeod, Norma. "Ethnomusicological Research and Anthropology." *Annual Review of Anthropology* 3 (1974): 99–115.

McNally, Michael D. *Ojibwe Singers: Hymns, Grief, and a Native American Culture in Motion*.New York: Oxford University Press, 2000.

Merriam, Alan P. *Ethnomusicology of the Flathead Indians*. Chicago: Aldine Publishing Company, 1967.

– *The Anthropology of Music*. Evanston, IL: Northwestern University Press, 1964.

Merritt, Richard D. *On Common Ground: The Ongoing Story of the Commons in Niagara-on-the-Lake*. Toronto: Dundurn, 2012.

Middleton, Richard. *Pontiac's War: Its Causes, Course and Consequences*. New York: Routledge, 2007.

Miller, Jay. *Lushootseed Culture and the Shamanic Odyssey: An Anchored Radiance*. Lincoln: University of Nebraska Press, 1999.

Miller, Jim R. "Compact, Contract, Covenant: The Evolution of Indian Treaty-Making." *New Histories for Old: Changing Perspectives on Canada's Native Pasts*. Edited by Theodore Binnema and Susan Neylan. Vancouver: UBC Press, 2011.

Mishler, Craig. *The Crooked Stovepipe: Athapaskan Fiddle Music and Square Dancing in Northeast Alaska and Northwest Canada*. Urbana and Chicago: University of Illinois Press, 1993.

Momryk, M. "Ermatinger, Lawrence." In *Dictionary of Canadian Biography*, 1979. http://www.biographi.ca/en/bio/ermatinger_lawrence_4E.html.

Montgommery, Louis de. *La Milice française*. Paris: 1636.

Moogk, Peter. "The Liturgy of Humiliation, Pain, and Death: The Execution of Criminals in New France." 88, no.1 (March 2007): 89–112.

Moore, Thomas. *A Canadian boat song. Arranged for three voices by Thos. Moore*. London: James Carpenter, 1805.

– *Odes, Epistles and Other Poems*. Vol 2. 2nd ed. London: James Carpenter, 1807.

Morrison, Jean. "Grant, Peter." *Dictionary of Canadian Bibliography*, 1988. http://www.biographi.ca/en/bio/grant_peter_7E.html.

Morrison, Jean, ed. *The North West Company in Rebellion: Simon McGillivray's Fort William Notebook, 1815*. Thunder Bay: Thunder Bay Historical Museum Society, 1988.

Morton, Graeme and David A. Wilson, eds. *Irish and Scottish Encounters with Indigenous Peoples: Canada, the United States, New Zealand, and Australia*. Montreal/Kingston: McGill-Queen's University Press, 2013.

Muckle, Robert James. *The First Nations of British Columbia: An Anthropological Survey*, 2nd ed. Vancouver: UBC Press, 2007.

Muir, Edward. *Ritual in Early Modern Europe*. 2nd ed. Cambridge: Cambridge University Press, 2005.

Nassaney, Michael S. *The Archaeology of the North American Fur Trade*. Gainesville: University of Florida Press, 2015.

Nelson, George. *My First Years in the Fur Trade: The Journals of 1802–1804*. Edited by Laura Peers and Theresa Schenck. St Paul: Minnesota Historical Society Press, 2002.

Nettl, Bruno. *Blackfoot Musical Thought: Comparative Perspectives*. Kent, OH: The Kent State University Press, 1989.

– *Excursions in World Music*, 2nd ed. Prentice Hall, 1997.

– *Folk and Traditional Music of the Western Continents*. 2nd ed. New Jersey: Prentice-Hall, Inc., 1973.

– *Music in Primitive Culture*. Cambridge: Harvard University Press, 1956.

– "Musical Areas Reconsidered," in *Essays in Musicology in Honor of Dragan Plamenac*. Pittsburg: University of Pittsburgh Press, 1969.

– *The Study of Ethnomusicology: Twenty-Nine Issues and Concepts*. Urbana and Chicago: University of Illinois Press, 1983.

– *The Study of Ethnomusicology: Thirty-one Issues and Concepts*, New Ed. Urbana and Chicago: University of Illinois Press, 2005.

Nettl, Bruno, Elaine Keillor, and Victoria Levine. "Amerindian Music." *Grove Music Online*, 20 January 2001. https://www.oxfordmusiconline.com/grovemusic/view/10.1093/gmo/9781561592630.001.0001/omo-9781561592630-e-0000045405.

Newman, Peter C. *Company of Adventurers: How the Hudson's Bay Empire Determined the Destiny of a Continent*. Toronto: Penguin Canada, 2005.

Neylan, Susan, and Theodore Binnema, eds. *New Histories for Old: Changing Perspectives on Canada's Native Pasts*. Vancouver, UBC Press, 2011.

Norris, John. *Marching to the Drums: A History of Military Drums and Drummers*. Gloucestershire: The History Press, 2012.

Nute, Grace Lee. *The Voyageur* (1931), reprinted. St Paul: Minnesota Historical Society Press, 1955.

O'Brian, John, and Peter White, eds. *Beyond Wilderness: The Group of Seven, Canadian Identity, and Contemporary Art*. Montreal/Kingston: McGill-Queen's University Press, 2007.

O'Keeffe, Eamonn. "Musical Warriors: Military Music and Musicians in the Napoleonic British Army." Undergraduate thesis, Oxford University, 2017.

O'Toole, Darren. "From Entity to Identity to Nation: The Ethnogenesis of the Wiisakodewininiwag (Bois-Brûlé) Reconsidered." In *Métis in Canada: History, Identity, Law & Politics*. Edited by Christopher Adams, Gregg Dahl, and Ian Peach. Edmonton: University of Alberta Press, 2013.

O'Toole, Fintan. *White Savage: William Johnson and the Invention of America*. Albany: State University of New York Press, 2009.

Ong, Walter. *Orality and Literacy: The Technologizing of the Word*. London: Routledge, 1982.

Orden, Kate van. *Music, Discipline, and Arms in Early Modern France*. Chicago: University of Chicago Press, 2005.

Owings, Alison. *Indian Voices: Listening to Native Americans*. New Brunswick, NJ: Rutgers University Press, 2011.

Pagden, Anthony. *The Fall of Natural Man: The American Indian and the Origins of Comparative Ethnology*. Cambridge: Cambridge University Press, 1982.

Paper, Jordan. "Cosmological implications of pan-Indian Sacred Pipe Ritual," in
    Samuel W. Corrigan, ed. *Readings in Aboriginal Studies*. Brandon: Bearpaw
    Publishing, 1995.
– *Offering Smoke: The Sacred Pipe and the Native American Religion*. University of
    Idaho Press, 1988.
Paquet, Gilles, and Jean-Pierre Wallot. "'Nouvelle-France/Quebec/Canada: A World
    of Limited Identities.'" In *Colonial Identity in the Atlantic World, 1500–1800*.
    Edited by Nicholas Canny. Princeton: Princeton University Press, 1987.
Park, Willard Z. *Shamanism in Western North America*. Evanston and Chicago:
    Northwestern University Studies in Social Science, 1938.
Parkman, Francis. *History of the Conspiracy of Pontiac: and the war of the North
    American tribes against the English colonies: after the conquest of Canada*. Boston:
    C.C. Little and J. Brown, 1851.
– *Montcalm and Wolfe*. Vol. 1. Boston: Little, Brown, and Company, 1891.
– *Pioneers of France in the New World: Champlain and his Associates*. Little, Brown,
    1899.
Parmenter, John. "After the Mourning Wars: The Iroquois as Allies in Colonial
    North American Campaigns." *William and Mary Quarterly* 64, no. 1 (2007):
    39–76.
Parr, Joy. "Notes for a More Sensuous History of Twentieth-Century Canada: The
    Timely, the Tacit, and the Material Body." *Canadian Historical Review* 82, no. 4
    (2001): 720–45.
– *Sensing Changes: Technologies, Environments, and the Everyday, 1953–2003*.
    Vancouver: UBC Press, 2010.
Pearen, Shelley. *Exploring Manitoulin*. Revised Edition. Toronto: University of
    Toronto Press, 1996.
Peers, Laura. *The Ojibwa of Western Canada, 1780 to 1870*. Winnipeg:
    The University of Manitoba Press, 1994.
Perea, John Carlos. *Intertribal Native American Music in the United States*. New York
    & Oxford: Oxford University Press, 2014.
Perrault, Jean-Baptiste. *Jean-Baptiste Perrault Marchand Voyageur Parti de Montréal
    Le 28e de Mai 1783*. Edited with introduction by Louis P. Cormier. Montreal:
    Boréal Express, 1978.
Perry, Adele. *On the Edge of Empire: Gender, Race, and the Making of British
    Columbia, 1849–1871*. Toronto: University of Toronto Press, 2001.
Peterson, Jacqueline, and Jennifer Brown, eds. *The New Peoples: Being and Becoming
    Métis in North America*. St Paul: Minnesota Historical Society Press, 1985.
Pisani, Michael V. *Imagining Native America in Music*. New Haven & London:
    Yale University Press, 2005.
Podruchny, Carolyn. "Baptizing Novices: Ritual Moments among French Canadian
    Voyageurs in the Montreal Fur Trade, 1780–1821." *Canadian Historical
    Review* 83, no. 2 (June 2002): 165–95.

‑ "Festivities, Fortitude, and Fraternalism: Fur Trade Masculinity and the Beaver Club, 1785–1827." In *Race and Gender in the Northern Colonies*. Edited by Jan Noel. Toronto: Canadian Scholars' Press Inc., 2000.

‑ *Making the Voyageur World: Travelers and Traders in the North American Fur Trade*. Toronto: University of Toronto Press, 2006.

Podruchny, Carolyn, and Laura Peers, eds. *Gathering Places: Aboriginal and Fur Trade Histories*. Vancouver: UBC Press, 2010.

Polanyi, Karl, Conrad M. Arensberg, and Harry W. Pearson, eds. *Trade and Market in the Early Empires*. Washington: Henry Regnery Company, 1971.

Pomedli, Michael. *Living with Animals: Ojibwe Spirit Powers*. University of Toronto Press, 2014.

Pond, Peter. In *Five Fur Traders of the Northwest: Being the Narrative of Peter Pond and the Diaries of John MacDonell, Archibald N. McLeod, Hugh Faires, and Thomas Connor*. Edited by Charles M. Gates with an introduction by Grace Lee Nute. St Paul: The University of Minnesota Press, 1933.

Porter, James. "James Porter's Slave Lake Journal of 1800–1." In *North of Athabasca: Slave Lake and Mackenzie River Documents of the North West Company, 1800–1821*. Montreal/Kingston: McGill-Queen's University Press, 2001.

Potherie, La. "Adventures of Nicolas Perrot, by la Potherie, 1665–1670." In *Early Narratives of the Northwest*, edited by Louise Phelps Kellogg. New York: Charles Scribner's Sons, 1917.

Pratt, Mary Louise. *Imperial Eyes: Travel Writing and Transculturation*. 2nd edition. London: Routledge, 2008.

Pritzker, Barry M. *A Native American Encyclopedia: History, Culture, and Peoples*. New York: Oxford University Press, 2000.

Pulsipher, Jenny Hale. "Gaining the Diplomatic Edge: Kinship, Trade, Ritual, and Religion in Amerindian Alliances in Early North America." In *Empires and Indigenes: Intercultural Alliance, Imperial Expansion, and Warfare in the Early Modern World*, edited by Wayne E. Lee. New York: New York University Press, 2011.

Raffan, James. *Emperor of the North: Sir George Simpson and the Remarkable Story of the Hudson's Bay Company*. Toronto: HarperCollins, 2007.

Raibmon, Paige. *Authentic Indians: Episodes of Encounter from the Late-Nineteenth-Century Northwest Coast*. Durham: Duke University Press, 2005.

Randall, Walter H. "Genthon the Fiddler." *The Beaver*. (December 1942): 15–17.

Rath, Richard Cullen. *How Early America Sounded*. Ithaca and London: Cornell University Press, 2003.

Ray, Arthur. *Indians in the Fur Trade: Their Role as Hunters, Trappers and Middlemen in the Lands Southwest of Hudson Bay, 1660–1870*. Toronto: University of Toronto Press, 1974.

Ray, Arthur, and Donald. B. Freeman. *"Give Us Good Measure": An Economic Analysis of Relations between the Indians and the Hudson's Bay Company before 1763*. Toronto: University of Toronto Press, 1978.

Reed, Charles Bert. *Masters of the Wilderness*. Chicago: University of Chicago Press, 1914.

Rich, E.E. *The Fur Trade and the Northwest to 1857*. Toronto: McClelland and Stewart, 1976.

– *History of the Hudsons Bay Company in three volumes*. 3 vols. Toronto: McClelland and Stewart, 1960.

– *Montreal and the Fur Trade*. Montreal: McGill University Press, 1966.

Richards, Jeffrey. *Imperialism and Music: Britain 1876–1953*. Manchester: Manchester University Press, 2001.

Richter, Daniel K. *The Ordeal of the Longhouse: The Peoples of the Iroquois League in the Era of European Colonization*. Chapel Hill, 1992.

– *Trade, Land, Power: The Struggle for Eastern North America*. Philadelphia: University of Pennsylvania Press, 2013.

– "War and Culture: The Iroquois Experience," *The William and Mary Quarterly*, Third Series 40, no. 4 (Oct. 1983): 528–59.

Richter, Daniel K., and James. H. Herrell, eds. *Beyond the Covenant Chain: The Iroquois and Their Neighbors in Indian North America, 1600–1800*. Syracuse: Syracuse University Press, 1987.

Roberts, Helen H. *Musical Areas in Aboriginal North America*. New Haven: Yale University Publications in Anthropology, 1936.

Robertson, Colin. *Colin Robertson's Correspondence Book*. Edited with Introduction by E.E. Rich. Toronto: Champlain Society, 1939.

Robinson, Henry M. *The Great Fur Land, or, Sketches of Life in the Hudson's Bay Territory*. New York: G.P. Putnam's Sons, 1879.

Rodgers, Bob. *The Fiddlers of James Bay*. Montreal: National Film Board of Canada, 1980.

Rogers, Robert. *A Concise Account of North America: Containing a Description of the Several British Colonies on That Continent, Including the Islands of Newfoundland, Cape Breton, &c. as to Their Situation &c*. London: The Author, J. Millan, 1765.

Ross, Alexander. *The Fur Hunters of the Far West*. Edited by Quaife, Milo Milton. Chicago: R.R. Donnelley & Sons Co., 1924.

Ross, Eric. *Beyond the River and the Bay: Some Observations on the State of the Canadian Northwest in 1811 with a View to Providing the Intending Settler with an Intimate Knowledge of That Country*. Toronto: University of Toronto Press, 1970.

Rotstein, Abraham. "Innis: The Alchemy of Fur and Wheat." *Journal of Canadian Studies* 12 (Winter 1977): 6–31.

– "Trade and Politics: An Institutional Approach." *Western Canadian Journal of Anthropology* 3 (1972): 1–28.

Rust, Frances. *Dance in Society: An Analysis of the Relationship Btween the Social Dance and Society in England from the Middle Ages to the Present Day*. London: Routledge & Kegan Paul, 1969.

Sacchetti, Jane D. "Rock gongs, bell rocks, ringing rocks, tocsin rocks – unknown in North America? Pity!" *Arch Notes*. Ontario Archaeological Society 4, no. 5 (September/October 1999): 8–14.

Saler, Bethel, and Carolyn Poduchny. "Glass Curtains and Storied Landscapes: The Fur Trade, National Boundaries and Historians." *Bridging National Borders in North America: Transnational and Comparative Histories*. Durham, NC: Duke University Press, 2010.

Salisbury, Neal. "The Indians' Old World: Native Americans and the Coming of Europeans." *The William and Mary Quarterly* 53, no. 3 (July 1996): 435–58.

"Salish Myth Narratives." In *Music of the First Nations: Tradition and Innovation in Native North America*. Edited by Tara Browner. Urbana and Chicago: University of Illinois Press, 2009.

Sandlos, John. *Hunters at the Margin: Native People and Wildlife Conservation in the Northwest Territories*. Vancouver: UBC Press, 2007.

Sawatzky, Roland. "From Trade Routes to Rural Farm: The Biography of the Pierre Bruce Fiddle." *Agricultural History 92, no. 2* (Spring 2018): 244–60.

Schafer, R Murray. *The Soundscape: Our Sonic Environment and the Tuning of the World* (1977), reprinted. Rochester, Vermont: Destiny Books, 1994.

– *The Tuning of the World*. Toronto: McClelland and Stewart Limited, 1977.

Schlereth, Thomas J., ed. *Cultural History and Material Culture: Everyday Life, Landscapes, Museums* Charlottesville: University of Virginia, 1992.

– *Material Culture Studies in America*. Rowman Altamira, 1982.

Schmidt, Wilhelm. *The Culture Historical Method of Ethnology*. New York: Fortuny's, 1939.

Sercombe, Laurel. "The Story of Dirty Face: Power and Song in Western Washington Coast Salish Myth Narratives." In *Music of the First Nations: Tradition and Innovation in Native North America*. Edited by Tara Browner. Champaign: University of Illinois Press, 2009.

Shoemaker, Nancy. "Categories." In *Clearing a Path: Theorizing the Past in Native American Studies*. Edited by Nancy Shoemaker. New York: Routledge, 2002.

Simpson, George. *Fur Trade and Empire: George Simpson's Journal Entitled Remarks Connected with the Fur Trade in the Course of a Voyage from York Factory to Fort George and Back to York Factory 1824–25*. Edited with Intro by Frederick Merk. Cambridge, MA: The Belknap Press of Harvard University Press, 1968.

– *Journal of Occurrences in the Athabasca Department, by George Simpson, 1820 and 1821, and Repor*. Edited by E.E. Rich with a foreword by Lord Tweedsmuir and an introd. by Chester Martin. Toronto: The Champlain Society, 1938.

– *Part of Dispatch from George Simpson Esqr, Governor of Ruperts Land to the Governor & Committee of the Hudson's Bay Company, London, March 1, 1829: Continued and Completed March 24 and June 5, 1829*. Edited by E.E. Rich. Introduction by W.S. Wallace. Toronto: Champlain Society, 1947.

– *The Publications of the Hudson's Bay Record Society Simpson's Athabasca Journal: Journal of Occurrences in the Athabasca Department by George Simpson, 1820 and 1821, and Report.* Edited by E.E. Rich. London: The Champlain Society for the Hudson's Bay Record Society, 1938.

Skaggs, David, and Larry Nelson, eds. *Sixty Years' War for the Great Lakes, 1754– 1814.* East Lansing: Michigan State University Press, 2010.

Slover, John, and Dr Knight. "Indian Atrocities: Narratives of the Perils and Sufferings of Dr. Knight and John Slover, Among the Indians, During the Revolutionary War, with Short Memoirs of Col. Crawford and John Slover." In *Captivity Tales* (1867), reprinted. New York: The Arno Press, A New York Times Company, 1974.

Small, Christopher. *Musicking: The Meanings of Performing and Listening.* Wesleyan University Press, 1998.

Smith, Gordon E. "Ethnomusicological Modelling and Marius Barbeau's 1927 Nass River Field Trip." In *Around and About Marius Barbeau: Modelling Twentieth-Century Culture.* Edited by Lynda Jessup, Andrew Nurse, and Gordon E. Smith. Ottawa: Canadian Museum of Civilization, 2008.

Smith, James. "Of the Remarkable Occurrences in the Life and Travels of Colonel James Smith, (Late a Citizen of Bourbon County, Kentucky,) During His Captivity with the Indians." In *Indian Captivities: Or, Life in the Wigwam; Being True Narratives of Captives Who Have Been Carried Away by the Indians, from the Frontier Settlements of the United States, from the Earliest Period to the Present Time.* Edited by Samuel G. Drake, Buffalo: Derby, Orton & Mulligan, 1853.

Smith, Mark M. *Listening to Nineteenth-Century America.* University of North Carolina Press, 2001.

– "Still Coming to 'Our' Senses: An Introduction." *The Journal of American History* (September 2008): 378–80.

Smith, Theresa. *The Island of the Anishinaabeg: Thunderers and Water Monsters in the Traditional Ojibwe Life-World.* Lincoln and London: University of Nebraska Press, 1995.

Speck, Frank G. *Naskapi: The Savage Hunters of the Labrador Peninsula* (1935), reprinted. Norman: University of Oklahoma Press, 1977.

Stephen, Scott P. *Masters and Servants: The Hudson's Bay Company and Its North American Workforce, 1668–1786.* Edmonton: Univrsity of Alberta Press, 2019.

Stevenson, Winona. "The Red River Indian Mission School and John West's 'Little Charges,' 1820–1833." *Native Studies Review* 4, nos. 1 and 2 (1988): 129–65.

Steward, Julian H. *Some Western Shoshoni Myths.* Bureau of American Ethnology Bulletin 136. Washington, DC: Government Printing Office, 1943.

Sturgis, William. *The Journal of William Sturgis.* Edited by and introduction by S.W. Jackman. Victoria: Sono Nis Press, 1978.

"Summary of Excavation Block 00–07." Royal Alberta Museum. Borden: F; Pi-63. Catalogue #2127.

Taché, Joseph-Charles. *Forestiers et Voyageurs* (1863), reprinted. Montreal: Fides, 1946.

Tanner, John. *A Narrative of the Captivity and Adventures of John Tanner (US Interpreter at the Saut de Ste. Marie) During Thirty Years Residence Among the Indians in the Interior of North America.* Edited by prepared for the press by Edwin James, M.D. Minneapolis: Ross & Haines, 1956.

Taylor, Alan. *The Civil War of 1812: American Citizens, British Subjects, Irish Rebels, & Indian Allies.* New York: Knopf Doubleday Publishing Group, 2010.

– *The Divided Ground: Indians, Settlers, and the Northern Borderland of the American Revolution.* New York: Vintage Books, 2006.

Teit, James Alexander. *Traditions of the Thompson River Indians of British Columbia: Collected and Annotated by James Teit.* Introduction by Franz Boas (1898), reprinted. Boston: Houghton, Mifflin, 1969.

Teskey, Nancy, and Gordon Brock. "Elements of Continuity in Kwakiutl Traditions." *American Music Research Center Journal* 5 (1995): 37–55.

"The Hopkins Book of Canoe Songs." *The Beaver* (Autumn, 1971): 54–7.

"The Middle Ground Revisited." *William and Mary Quarterly* 63 (January 2006).

Thistle, Paul C. *Indian-European Trade Relations in the Lower Saskatchewan River Region to 1840.* Winnipeg: The University of Manitoba Press, 1986.

Thomas, L.G. "Ermatinger, Edward." In *Dictionary of Canadian Biography*, 1972. http://www.biographi.ca/en/bio/ermatinger_edward_10E.html.

Thompson, David. *Columbia Journals.* Edited by Barbara Belyea. Seattle: University of Washington Press; Montreal/Kingston: McGill-Queen's University Press, 2007.

– *The Writings of David Thompson: The Travels, 1850.* Edited with an introduction by William E. Moreau. Montreal/Kingston: McGill-Queen's University Press, 2009.

Thompson, Edward P. *The Making of the English Working Class.* London: Victor Gollancz Ltd., 1965.

Thompson, James. *A Bard of Wolfe's Army: James Thompson, Gentleman Volunteer, 1733–1830.* Edited by Earl John Chapman and Ian Macpherson McCulloch. Montreal: Robin Brass Studio, 2010.

Thrush, Coll. "Vancouver the Cannibal: Cuisine, Encounter, and the Dilemma of Difference on the Northwest Coast, 1774–1808." *Ethnohistory* 58, no. 1 (21 December 2011): 1–35.

Thwaites, Reuben Gold, ed. *The Jesuit Relations and Allied Documents: Travels and Explorations of the Jesuit Missionaries in New France, 1610–1791.* Vol. 27 & Vol. 50. Cleveland: The Burrows Brothers. http://puffin.creighton.edu/jesuit/relations/relations_27.html. Retrieved 15 March 2013.

Tilley, Christopher Y. *A Phenomenology of Landscape: Places, Paths, and Monuments.* Oxford: Berg, 1994.

Timberlake, Henry. *The Memoirs of Lt. Henry Timberlake: The Story of a Soldier, Adventurer, and Emissary to the Cherokees, 1756–1765.* Edited by King, Duane H. Cherokee. NC: Museum of the Cherokee Indian Press, 2007.

Tomlinson, Gary. *Singing in the New World*. Cambridge: Cambridge University Press, 2007.

Trenk, Marin. "Religious Uses of Alcohol among the Woodland Indians of North America." *Anthropos* 96, no. 1 (2001): 73–86.

Trigger, Bruce. *Children of Aataentsic: A History of the Huron People to 1660*. Kingston/Montreal: McGill-Queen's University Press, 1987.

– *Natives and Newcomers: Canada's "Heroic Age" Reconsidered*. Montreal/Kingston: McGill-Queen's University Press, 1985.

Troman, Derek. *Rowley and the Jews Harp* (1953). http://rowleyvillage.webs.com/ rowleyandthejewsharp.htm. Retrieved 8 July 2013.

Thistle, Paul C. *Indian-European Trade Relations in the Lower Saskatchewan River Region to 1840*. Winnipeg: The University of Manitoba Press, 1986.

Turgeon, Laurier. "The Tale of the Kettle: Odyssey of an Intercultural Object." *Ethnohistory* 44, no. 1 (winter 1997): 1–29.

Turkel, William J. *The Archive of Place: Unearthing the Pasts of the Chilcotin Plateau*. Vancouver: UBC Press, 2007.

Turnbaugh, W.A. "Calumet ceremonialism as a nativistic response." *American Antiquity*. 44 (1979): 685–91.

Turner, Victor. *Dramas, Fields, and Metaphors: Symbolic Action in Human Society*. Ithaca: Cornell University, 1975.

– *The Ritual Process: Structure and Anti-Structure*. Chicago: Aldine Publishing Company, 1969.

Waldman, Carl. *Encyclopedia of Native American Tribes*, 3rd ed. New York: Checkmark, 2006.

Walhausen, Johann J. *L'Art militaire pour l'infanterie*. Frankfurt: 1615.

Warkentin, Germaine. "Introduction." Pierre-Esprit Radisson. *The Voyages*. Vol. 1. Montreal/Kingston: McGill-Queen's University Press, 2012.

Washburn, Wilcomb E. "Symbol, Utility, and Aesthetics in the Indian Fur Trade." In *Aspects of the Fur Trade: Selected Papers of the 1965 North American Fur Trade Conference*. St Paul: Minnesota Historical Society, 1967.

Weld, Isaac. *Travels through the States of North America, and the Provinces of Upper and Lower Canada, During the Years 1795, 1796, and 1797*. 2 vols. London: Printed for John Stockdale, Piccadilly, 1807.

Wentzel, Willard-Ferdinand. In *Les Bourgeois de La Compagnie Du Nord-Ouest. Original Journals Narratives Letters, Etc. Relating to the Northwest Company*. Edited by L.R. Masson, first edition. Volume 1 (1889–90), reprinted. New York: Antiquarian Press LTD, 1960.

– "W.F. Wentzel's Journals of 1804–7." In *North of Athabasca: Slave Lake and Mackenzie River Documents of the North West Company, 1800–1821*. Montreal/ Kingston: McGill-Queen's University Press, 2001.

Wellesz, Egon, ed. *Ancient and Oriental Music*. London: Oxford University Press, 1957.

Whidden, Lynn. *Essential Song: Three Decades of Northern Cree Music*. Waterloo: Wilfred Laurier University Press, 2007.

– "Métis Music." Edited by Lawrence Barkwell, Leah Dorion and Darren R. Préfontaine. *Metis Legacy: A Metis Historiography and Annotated Bibliography*. Winnipeg: Pemmican Publications, 2001.

– "The Songs of Their Fathers." *Ethnologies* 25, no. 2 (2003): 107–30.

Whidden, Lynn, ed. *Métis Songs: Visiting was the Métis Way*. Regina: Gabriel Dumont Institute, 2004.

White, Bruce. "Encounters with Spirits: Ojibwa and Dakota Theories About the French and their Merchandise." *Ethnohistory* 41, no. 3 (1994): 369–405.

– "'Give Us a Little Milk': The Social and Cultural Significance of Gift Giving in the Lake Superior Fur Trade." In *Rendezvous: Selected Papers of the 4th North American Fur Trade Conference*, edited by T.C. Buckley. St Paul: North American Fur Trade Conference, 1981.

White, Richard. *The Middle Ground: Indians, Empires, and Republics in the Great Lakes Region, 1650–1815*. New York: Cambridge University Press, 1991.

Widder, Keith R. *Beyond Pontiac's shadow: Michilimackinac and the Anglo-Indian War of 1763*. East Lansing: Michigan State University Press, 2013.

Wilcocke, Samuel H. *Récits de Voyages Lettres et Rapports Inédits Relatifs Au Nord-Ouest Canadien*. Vol 2. (1889–90), reprinted. New York: Antiquarian Press LTD, 1960.

Wilkins, Frances. "The Fiddlers of James Bay: Transatlantic Flows and Musical Indigenization among the James Bay Cree." *MUSICultures* 40, no. 1 (2013): 57–99.

Williamson, Peter. "A Faithful Narrative of the Sufferings of Peter Williamson, Who Settled near the Forks of the Delaware in Pennsylvania Having Been Taken by the Indians in His Own House, October 2d, 1754." In *Indian Captivities: Or, Life in the Wigwam; Being True Narratives of Captives Who Have Been Carried Away by the Indians, from the Frontier Settlements of the United States, from the Earliest Period to the Present Time*, edited by Samuel G. Drake. Buffalo: Derby, Orton & Mulligan, 1853.

Willmott, Cory. "Shape, Rattle and Roll: Forms and Functions of Metal in Anishnaabe Aesthetic Traditions." *Center for Rupert's Land Studies Colloquium*, May 20–22, 2010.

Willmott, Cory, and Kevin Brownlee. "Dressing for the Homeward Journey: Western Anishinaabe Leadership Roles Viewed through Two Nineteenth-Century Burials." In *Gathering Places: Aboriginal and Fur Trade Histories*, edited by Carolyn Podruchny and Laura Peers. Vancouver: UBC Press, 2010.

Wissler, Clark. *North American Indians of the Plains*. New York: American Museum of Natural History, 1927.

Wissler, Clark. *The American Indian*. New York: McMurtrie, 1917.

Witcomb, Henry, and Edmond Tiret. *Dictionary of Nautical Terms*. Challamel, 1883.

Witgen, Michael. *An Infinity of Nations: How the Native New World Shaped Early North America*. Philadelphia: University of Pennsylvania Press, 2011.

Wolfenden, Madge. "Tod, John." *Dictionary of Canadian Biography Online*, 1982. http://www.biographi.ca/009004-119.01- e.php?BioId=39994.

Woodfield, Ian. *English Musicians in the Age of Exploration, Sociology of Music*. Stuyvesant, NY: Pendragon Press, 1995.

Van Kirk, Sylvia. *"Many Tender Ties," Women in Fur-Trade Society in Western Canada, 1670–1870*. Winnipeg: Watson & Dwyer Publishing Ltd., 1980.

Vander, Judith. *Shoshone Ghost Dance Religion: Poetry Songs and Great Basin Context*. Urbana and Chicago: University of Illinois Press, 1997.

Vaughan, James H. *Rock paintings and rock gongs among the Marghi of Nigeria*. London: W. Clowes and Sons, 1962.

Vecsey, Christopher. *Traditional Ojibwa Religion and Its Historical Changes*. Philadelphia: American Philosophical Society, 1983.

Vennum, Thomas. *The Ojibwa Dance Drum: Its History and Construction*. St Paul: Minnesota Historical Society Press, 2009.

Verchères, Thomas de Boucherville. *War on the Detroit: The Chronicles of Thomas Verchères De Boucherville and the Capitulation by an Ohio Volunteer*. Edited by Milo Milton Quaife. Translated by Mrs. L. Oughtred Woltz & M.M. Quaife. Chicago: The Lake Side Press R.R. Donnelley & Sons Co., 1940.

Vibert, Elizabeth. *Traders' Tales: Narratives of Cultural Encounters in the Columbia Plateau, 1807–1846*. Norman and London: University of Oklahoma Press, 1997.

Index

alcohol, 7–8, 13, 18, 20, 46–7, 149, 166, 179, 200–1, 217–18
All Saints Day, 200
Animikeeg. *See* thunderbird
Anishinaabe, 6, 10, 12, 16, 29–30, 38, 43, 94, 126, 128, 232–4; birch bark scrolls, 157–8; drums, 70, 80; healing songs, 182–9; hunting songs, 161–6; Midéwiwin, 166–70, 180; musical influence, 226; pipe ceremony, 92; pipe dance, 96–9; spirit lodge, 171–5; Wabanowiwin, 175–82; war dance, 99, 104
Anishinaabemowin, 125, 152–3, 174–5
Assiniboine, 35, 38, 100, 159, 179; song, 51–2; war dance, 103

bagpipes, 62–3, 72, 232; on arrival, 77–80; in dances, 75–6, 197; as recreation, 76–7; in warfare, 74–5
band (musical), 19, 64–5, 67, 69–70, 72–3, 78
baptisms, travelling ritual, 45–7, 109, 123–4, 200
Barbeau, Marius, 118, 120–1, 135, 137, 143, 146, 150, 152
Bayley, Charles, 192
birch bark scrolls. *See* Wiigwaasabak
Bird, Louis, 22, 24, 28–9

bombardes, 207
Brown, Jennifer, 12
Buckingham House, 44
bugle, 62–3, 72–4, 76–9

Cadieux, Jean, 115–23
calumet. *See* ceremonial pipe
cannon, 19, 25, 27–8, 30, 37–43, 49, 75, 111, 197, 231
Carlton House, 202
celebrations, arrivals, 200; holidays, 48, 196–202; weddings, 105, 200, 225
ceremonial pipe, 11, 82–106
Champlain, Samuel de, 26, 133
chanson à repondre, 202
chanson en laisse, 130, 132, 136–46, 153, 234
Cheechoo, James, 72, 226
chorus, voyageur, 130, 132, 136, 138–41, 143, 149–55; Indigenous, 177, 179, 187
Christmas, 48, 196, 201, 212, 224–5, 227–8
complaintes, 115–25, 137
conjuring, 160–3, 171–4, 184–5
Cox, Ross, 133, 148, 187, 205–6, 213
Cree, 12, 29, 38, 51, 56, 79, 108, 131, 231; ceremonial pipe, 99–100;

conjuring songs, 172–5; drums, 72–3, 160; fiddle, 212, 225–6, 229; healing songs, 184; hunting songs, 159–61; war dance, 96–7, 103
Cumberland House, 7, 221

dances. *See* by type
Densmore, Francis, 158, 253n12
Douglas, Harvey, 13
Douglas, James, 41
drums, 3, 17–19, 52, 55, 62–73, 80, 83, 85, 90, 98, 104, 159–70, 173, 177–80, 186–9, 191, 197, 212, 231–3

Easter Sunday, 199
Erasmus, Peter, 18, 22, 223–4
Ermatinger, Edward, 20, 73–4, 130–2, 137–41, 165, 202, 210–15, 218, 235
Ermatinger, Francis, 42,
Ermatinger, Lawrence, 34, 138, 215
ethnogenesis, 17, 235–6

Falcon, Pierre, 9, 20, 153, 156, 215
feu de joie, 19, 36–43
fiddle, 11, 13, 17, 19, 23, 72–3, 191, 193–8, 204–7, 210–13, 215, 219, 220, 222–9; book, 211
fife, 67, 73–4, 197
firearms, 24–49, 63, 131, 201, 230
flute, 67, 76, 191, 194, 197, 200, 207, 210, 211, 213–14, 218–19
Fort Albany, 27
Fort Alexander, 209
Fort Alexandria, 103–4, 201–2
Fort Carillon, 74, 91
Fort Chipewyan, 8, 40, 52, 76, 216
Fort Connelly, 211
Fort Dauphin, 38, 100
Fort des Prairies, 202
Fort Detroit, 10
Fort Dunvegan, 79, 200

Fort Edmonton, 207–8, 224
Fort Garry, 222
Fort George (on the North Saskatchewan), 39, 44
Fort La Cloche, 127
Fort Madison, 68
Fort Michilimackinac, 68
Fort Niagara, 74, 171
Fort Pitt, 6, 10
Fort Simpson, 220
Fort St James, 78
Fort Vancouver, 42, 105, 210
Fort Wedderburn, 76, 216–17
Fort White Earth, 208
Fort William, 107, 196–7, 203–5, 208, 210, 219, 227
Fort William Henry, 91
Fort Yukon, 227–8
Fraser, Simon, 55–6
French River, 21, 108, 123, 125, 127

Gagnon, Ernest, 134, 136–7, 143, 146, 150
Garry, Nicholas, 42, 45, 117, 124, 140, 148–9
Gist, Christopher, 94
Grand Portage, 7, 21, 34, 51, 75, 124, 131, 138, 196–8
Grant, Cuthbert, 9
Grant, Peter, 98, 153, 168
Great Bear Lake, 186, 206
gunpowder, 12–13, 16, 19, 22, 25–6, 29–34, 37, 39–40, 45, 48–9, 171, 231
guns. *See* firearms

Harmon, Daniel, 75, 103–4, 113, 123, 197–201
Haudenosaunee (Iroquois), 10–11, 26–7, 89–91, 105–6, 111, 122, 208, 232
healing ceremony, 180–90

Hearne, Samuel, 7, 184–5
Henley House, 7
Henry, Alexander (the elder), 7–8,
    50–2, 63, 67, 92, 99, 113, 123, 125–7,
    153, 171, 182
Henry, Alexander (the younger), 47,
    73, 124, 167, 179
Hogmanay, 217
holidays, 17, 45, 48, 135, 191, 198, 200,
    219, 224, 228, 234, 236. *See also*
    specific holidays by name
hornpipes, 204
Hudson Bay, 3, 5–7, 9, 22, 25–8, 31,
    35–6, 40, 46, 50, 72, 76, 130, 191–4;
    fur trade, 5, 42, 46, 176, 193, 236
Hudson's Bay Company, 3–10, 14, 19,
    22, 25, 27–8, 31–2, 35, 37, 41–2, 44,
    48, 56–7, 72– 3, 75, 80, 82, 101, 105,
    114, 117, 138, 151, 153, 172–3, 176,
    182, 187, 191–200, 203, 208, 212–18,
    221–2, 224, 226–8, 231, 233–4

Île-à-la-Crosse, 44
Innis, Harold, 12, 159, 236
Inuit, 3–4, 54, 72, 153,

jaw harps, 207–10, 229
jigging, 191, 216, 227, 236
jigs, 191, 204
Joliet, 855, 88

Kahnawake, 122, 151
Kahnesatake, 151

Lac La Pluie, 168, 205
La Cloche, 125–9
Lake Huron, 126–7
Lake of Two Mountains, 71, 208, 210
Lake Ontario, 207
Lake Superior, 75, 94, 97, 124, 148,
    163, 175, 197, 205

Mackenzie, Alexander, 8, 35, 40–1, 44,
    47, 50, 52, 61, 100, 115, 124, 186
marches, 19–20, 65, 69, 70, 72, 77,
    130, 132, 136, 139–40, 156, 214–15
Marquette, 85, 88
marriages, 11–12, 16, 93, 104–5, 200,
    226
McDonnell, John, 140, 17
McGillivray, William, 154
medicine man, 162, 183–8
Métis, 9, 17–18, 21, 105, 151, 153, 156,
    191, 193, 215–16, 221, 223–5, 227–9,
    234–6
Midéwiwin, 22, 29, 158, 166–71,
    176–7, 179–81, 188, 234
missionaries, 15, 21, 88, 189, 192–3,
    222–4
mobility, 107–8, 113
Moose Factory, 19, 27, 72, 193, 231
music, definition, 14
musical instruments, 51–3, 57, 61–80,
    171, 173, 191–229
muskets. *See* firearms

Nanabozho and Na-na-bush, 164–5
Nelson, George, 38, 104, 110, 115, 157,
    161, 168, 174–5, 188, 200–2
New Year's Day, 46–8, 194, 196,
    201–2, 217–18
North Saskatchewan River, 44, 51, 99
North West Company, 7–9, 22, 32, 35,
    37, 39–41, 44–8, 52, 57, 71, 76, 80,
    96, 98, 103–4, 127, 131, 139, 151, 153,
    155, 168, 174, 176, 187, 191–2, 197,
    199–209
North West gun, 32–4
Norway House, 9, 77, 79, 150, 219

Omushkego, 24–5, 28, 191, 212, 231
Oswego, 91–2
Oxford House, 219

peace-pipe. *See* ceremonial pipe
Perrot, Nicholas, 82–3
Pond, Peter, 6–7, 37, 63–4, 196
portages, 21, 32, 64, 77, 94, 108, 124, 207; *portage de sept chutes*, 115–23
Prince of Wales's Fort, 184–5

Ray, Arthur, 13, 15, 31, 159
Red River, 8–9, 38, 47, 98, 151, 153, 164, 167–8, 170, 173, 179, 191
Red River Jig, 227–8, 231, 235
reels, 191, 203–5, 210–12, 217, 219, 220, 222, 226–7, 230, 235
retrenchment, 221–2
Rich, E.E., 12

salutes (firearm), 17, 19, 36–42, 48, 85, 114, 217, 230
Sault Ste Marie, 127, 156, 168, 171, 179, 184, 188, 218, 226
Schafer, R. Murray, 108
serpents, 29, 34
set dance, 226
shaking tent. *See* spirit lodge
sheet music, 212–15
Shell River Fort, 17, 199
signals, 17, 19, 25, 29, 31, 37, 40–5, 49, 67–8, 74, 77, 80, 118
Simpson, George, 9, 19, 42, 48, 63, 76, 137, 139, 192, 216, 221, 233
Slave Lake, 39, 206
songbooks, 212–15
soundmark, 108, 125, 127–8
soundscape, 5, 18–19, 25, 30, 32, 35, 37, 43, 49, 68–9, 108, 110–11, 126, 197, 223–4, 231–2
soundways, 9–11, 14, 16, 19, 21–2, 42, 45–6, 107–29, 230–3
spirit lodge, 22, 167, 171–5
spoons, 203

St Andrew's Day, 200
step dancing, 11, 13, 191, 212, 225–7, 231, 235
St Lawrence, 25–7, 40, 67, 74, 81, 88, 110, 122, 134, 138, 143, 151, 192, 197, 204, 212; fur trade, 22, 36, 42, 45–6, 50, 63, 92, 107–8, 127, 133, 152, 176, 193–4, 232
strathspey, 204
Swan River, 202

Tanner, John, 29, 38, 43, 164, 180
Tête-au-Brochet, 168
Thompson, David, 51, 56, 60–1, 96, 148, 160, 172, 176, 186
thunderbirds, 28–30, 34, 70
Tod, John, 73–4, 211, 213, 215, 218, 219
trading posts. *See specific posts by name*
Troupes de la Marine, 75, 147

Van Kirk, Sylvia, 12, 16, 55
verse, 129, 132, 136, 138–43, 149
vocables, 23, 150–1
vocal music, paddling songs, 130–56; at trading post, 202–3
voyageur songs: *chansons d'aviron*, 130–56; *complaintes*, 115–25

Wabanowiwin, 234, 175–81
waltz, 205, 211, 214
war dances, 81–2, 90–106, 232
Wentzel, Willard-Ferdinand, 18, 47, 137
Wiigwaasabak, 157–8
windigo, 186

XY Company, 8, 44, 97, 199

York Factory, 39, 42, 73, 130–1, 146, 150, 193–4, 212–14